Mind, Self and Person

ROYAL INSTITUTE OF PHILOSOPHY SUPPLEMENT: 76

EDITED BY

Anthony O'Hear

CAMBRIDGE
UNIVERSITY PRESS

CAMBRIDGE
UNIVERSITY PRESS

University Printing House, Cambridge CB2 8BS, United Kingdom

One Liberty Plaza, 20th Floor, New York, NY 10006, USA

477 Williamstown Road, Port Melbourne, VIC 3207, Australia

314-321, 3rd Floor, Plot 3, Splendor Forum, Jasola District Centre, New Delhi - 110025, India

79 Anson Road, #06-04/06, Singapore 079906

Cambridge University Press is part of the University of Cambridge.

It furthers the University's mission by disseminating knowledge in the pursuit of education, learning and research at the highest international levels of excellence.

www.cambridge.org
Information on this title: www.cambridge.org/9781107545663

A catalogue record for this publication is available from the British Library

ISBN 978-1-107-54566-3 Paperback

Cambridge University Press has no responsibility for the persistence or accuracy of URLs for external or third-party internet websites referred to in this publication, and does not guarantee that any content on such websites is, or will remain, accurate or appropriate.

Contents

List of Contributors

Mark Sprevak – University of Edinburgh

Paul Snowdon – University College, London

Eric Olson – University of Sheffield

Lucy O'Brien – University College, London

Rory Madden – University College London

Patricia Churchland – University of California, San Diego

Galen Strawson – The University of Texas at Austin

Lynne Rudder Baker – University of Massachusetts Amherst

Barry Dainton – University of Liverpool

P.M.S. Hacker – St John's College, Oxford

Thomas Pink – Kings College, London

Tim Crane – Peterhouse, Cambridge

Ted Honderich – University College, London

David Bakhurst – Queen's University

Preface

This volume contains papers based on the lectures given in the Royal Institute of Philosophy's London Lectures series for 2013–14. The topic the lecturers were asked to speak and write on, Mind, Self and Persons, has been in the forefront of philosophical enquiry throughout the history of the subject, and, as will be evident from this volume, is as lively and contested an area of investigation in 2014, as it was in the days of the ancient Greeks.

The topic is not only lively: as the papers collected here amply demonstrate it covers a wide range of issues: consciousness itself, the mind and its relation to the body, the self, the nature of the human person, personal identity, the relation of the mind to morality, the existence of group minds and the implications of what we think about the mind for education. These and other topics are vigorously investigated by a distinguished group of leading figures in current philosophy of mind.

The Royal Institute of Philosophy is deeply grateful to the contributors both for their lectures and for the papers presented here: and I would also like to thank Adam Ferner for his editorial work on the book, and for the index.

Finally, readers might be interested to know that podcasts of the lectures as originally delivered are available on the Royal Institute of Philosophy's website (http://royalinstitutephilosophy.org/publications/video/mind-self-and-person/).

doi:10.1017/S1358246115000016   © The Royal Institute of Philosophy and the contributors 2015
Royal Institute of Philosophy Supplement **76** 2015   1

Group Minds and Explanatory Simplicity

MARK SPREVAK AND DAVID STATHAM

Abstract

This paper explores the claim that explanation of a group's behaviour in term of individual mental states is, in principle, superior to explanation of that behaviour in terms of group mental states. We focus on the supposition that individual-level explanation is superior because it is simpler than group-level explanation. In this paper, we consider three different simplicity metrics. We argue that on none of those metrics does individual-level explanation achieve greater simplicity than a group-level alternative. We conclude that an argument against group minds should not lay weight on concerns of explanatory simplicity.

Introduction

In three papers, Robert Rupert presents arguments against group minds.[1] These criticisms motivate the conclusion that although the discovery of group minds is an open empirical possibility, there are strong reasons for thinking that no group minds exist. One of Rupert's principal arguments against group minds is an argument from *explanatory simplicity*. His claim is that, for any explanation of intelligent behaviour that appeals to group minds, there exists an alternative explanation couched solely in terms of the minds of individuals. According to Rupert, an *individual-level explanation*, which makes no reference to group minds will be simpler than its *group-level* alternative, which does make reference to group minds. Simpler explanations are, everything else being equal, better explanations. Therefore, individual-level explanations are, everything else being equal, preferable to their more complex group-level alternatives.

---

[1] R. D. Rupert, 'Minding One's Cognitive Systems: When Does a Group of Minds Constitute a Single Cognitive Unit', *Episteme* **1** (2005), 177–88; R. D. Rupert, 'Empirical Arguments for Group Minds: A Critical Appraisal', *Philosophy Compass* **6** (2011): 630–39; R. D. Rupert, 'Against Group Cognitive States' in *From Individual to Collective Intentionality: New Essays*, edited by S. Chant, F. Hindriks, and G. Preyer (Oxford University Press, 2014).

doi:10.1017/S1358246115000132

Mark Sprevak and David Statham

In his invocation of the principle of explanatory simplicity, Rupert overlooks a great deal of this notion's complexity. We aim to explicate this notion and its various dimensions and, in doing so, to assess the relevance of each dimension to the issue of group-level explanation. We conclude that, whichever way explanatory simplicity is analysed, there is no warrant for thinking that individual-level explanations are simpler than group-level alternatives. Hence, this particular route to argue against the existence of group minds is blocked.

A Tale of Two Types of Agent

Rupert claims that no matter the intelligent behaviour a group displays, an explanatory story involving only cognitive properties of *individuals* is always available:

> In all of the cases that involve the relevant explananda, there seem to be available complete causal explanations couched in terms of the cognitive states of individuals (together with causal contributions of noncognitive, physical structures).[2]

Rupert claims that these individual-level explanations are preferable to group-level explanations. According to Rupert, this is because individual-level explanations are more simple. This consideration is the opening move in Rupert's inference to the best explanation against the existence of group minds.

Let us see an example of Rupert's argument in action.

An impressive display of intelligent behaviour by a group occurs when Microsoft develops a new operating system (OS). How does a group (Microsoft) produce this behaviour? Two types of story could be told. One is formulated exclusively at the level of individual agents: it refers to the cognitive properties of individual employees, to the interactions between employees, and to the organisational structure of the corporation that governs these interactions. The other introduces group agents as protagonists: it ascribes cognitive properties (such as beliefs, desires, and intentions), not only to individual employees, but also to groups of individuals, such as teams within Microsoft or the corporation as a whole.

What do these two stories look like?

An individual-level explanation of Microsoft's production of a new OS might begin by referring to the cognitive states of the individuals comprising the corporation's executive: their *beliefs* that a new OS is

---

2   Rupert, 'Empirical Arguments for Group Minds', 635.

4

required; their *desires* to produce this new OS within the next three years; and their *intentions* to undertake the necessary activity to ensure that these desires are fulfilled. The goal of producing a new OS can be broken down into several sub-goals: the production of its graphical content, its software compatibility, its compatibility with a range of hardware, and so on. Groups of programmers would be tasked with producing the code required to achieve each of these sub-goals and each programmer would adjust their cognitive states accordingly.

Each programmer would be ascribed a set of beliefs about the activities they would need to perform to achieve the sub-goal with which they have been tasked: the belief that producing a satisfactory user interface will require two years of work; the belief that a particular programming language would be most appropriate to this task; and the belief that weekly consultations with the corporation's executive will be necessary, and so on. Each programmer would have a set of relevant desires, intentions, and other cognitive states: she might, for example, have the desire to achieve her sub-goal within a particular time frame, to do so to the best of her ability, to exploit her newly gained competence with a particular programming language, and so on.

That an individual employee can be attributed cognitive states requires that the individual instantiate a *cognitive architecture*. This is to say that the individual is structured in such a way as to comprise a set of mechanisms whose tightly integrated activity contributes causally to that individual's intelligent behaviour. The *cognitive states* attributed to the individual are realised by the integrated activity of the mechanisms which comprise that individual's cognitive architecture. These states enter into causal series in which each state is caused by, and subsequently causes or modifies, other cognitive states. These causally connected series of cognitive states constitute *cognitive processes*. And it is in virtue of the realisation of these cognitive processes that the individual comes to behave intelligently and produce a wide range of cognitive phenomena (from choosing a suitable route to work in the morning to successfully coding a graphical user interface).

Thus, to treat an individual employee as genuinely *cognitive* is to attribute to that individual a related set of *cognitive properties*. The individual instantiates a cognitive architecture: a set of integrated cognitive mechanisms (such as working memory, a language processor, and visual object-recognition mechanisms). The integrated activity of these mechanisms realises cognitive states (beliefs, desires, and memories; representations of words, tasks, and problems; and so on). These states are connected in causal series to constitute cognitive processes (decision-making, problem-solving, and so on). And in virtue of the individual's instantiation of these various cognitive properties, that individual is able to produce a variety of cognitive phenomena.

Each individual employee is attributed in the individual-level explanation a set of related cognitive properties. Crucially, of course, it is only *individual* employees who are attributed cognitive properties, not any extra-individual entity or collection of entities.

An individual-level explanation of Microsoft's behaviour would of course need to appeal to more than this. It would need to refer to the various processes by which individual employees communicate the content of their cognitive states, and the results of their cognitive processes, to other employees. These communicative processes would include face-to-face linguistic interactions, the production of written memos, email, video-conferencing, record-keeping, and so on. An individual-level explanation would also need to refer to the non-cognitive physical structures used to facilitate individual cognitive processes and inter-individual communicative processes. A corporation like Microsoft makes use of all sorts of digital computers, hard drives and other storage devices, telecommunications devices, and old-fashioned pen and paper, amongst other things. Finally, of crucial importance would be a description of the corporation's organisational structure and the procedures and rules which determine how the activity of its numerous individual employees is coordinated and channelled towards the production of a new OS. This would include reference to sets of implicit and explicit rules, the hierarchical organisation of employees, the corporation's departmental structure, the procedural standards for communication between departments, and so on.

An individual-level causal explanation of Microsoft's production of a new OS would clearly be a complex and multifaceted explanation that would make reference to an enormous number of individual cognitive properties, interactive and communicative processes, rules and organisational structures, and various non-cognitive structures and processes.

What about the group-level story? A group-level explanation would ascribe cognitive properties, not only to individual employees, but also to groups of individuals. The relevant groups may be of various sizes and their membership could overlap. The groups may include small teams of programmers, larger engineering teams, entire software divisions, or the corporation as a whole. Just as individual employees are attributed a set of related cognitive properties, so a group would be treated as a cognitive system that instantiates a cognitive architecture and realises cognitive states that combine in causal series to constitute cognitive processes.

For example, Microsoft's organisational structure, which plays the crucial role of integrating and coordinating the activity of individual employees in the individual-level explanation, may be equated with a cognitive architecture. This architecture is comprised of a large set of mechanisms whose activation may realise cognitive states. But whereas the cognitive mechanisms comprising an individual employee's cognitive architecture consist of various neural systems in the employee's brain, the cognitive mechanisms that comprise Microsoft's cognitive architecture consist of groups of individual employees and their supporting physical apparatus. The group-level cognitive states are realised by individual employees in interaction with each other and with their supporting physical apparatus. The group-level cognitive processes are the causal series in which each of these cognitive states is caused by, and causes or modifies, the others.

This presentation of the group-level explanation suggests that it is a rival to the individual-level explanation in the sense that it might eliminate the need for individual-level talk: individual-level cognitive properties, inter-individual interaction, and non-cognitive physical structures would be discarded in favour of group cognitive properties. But it need not be so. We will suppose in what follows that the group-level explanation retains reference to the various individual-level cognitive properties and non-cognitive physical structures described in the individual-level explanation.

It is conceivable that the similarity between a particular group and a cognitive agent is too superficial, or in other ways insufficient, to justify attribution of cognitive properties to that group. Both advocates and critics of group cognition agree that some level of functional similarity – the correct level of which is disputed – between a group and an individual cognitive agent is required in order for the attribution of mental properties to a group to be warranted at all. Nevertheless, in order to facilitate a discussion of explanatory simplicity, these considerations will be temporarily set aside. The claim at issue is not that Microsoft's production of a new OS genuinely constitutes a real-world example of group cognition. The claim is that, *if* a case such as the Microsoft example did warrant both an individual-level and a group-level explanation, and *if* two such complete causal explanations *could indeed be given*, the individual-level explanation would be superior in terms of explanatory simplicity.

Granted our task is to assess explanatory simplicity (and not some other dimension of adequacy of group-level explanation), it is important to tally up, as Rupert does, the nature and quantity of additional postulates made by group-level explanation. The additional postulates of group-level explanation consist of an additional set of

Mark Sprevak and David Statham

cognitive properties: the instantiation, in virtue of the corporation's organisational structure, of a cognitive architecture; the realisation, in virtue of this architecture, of cognitive states over and above those realised by individual employees; and the realisation via the causal series of these cognitive states, of cognitive processes over and above those realised by individual employees.

Assuming, as per the above concession, that the group-level explanation retains reference to all individual-level cognitive properties and non-cognitive physical structures, the two explanations appear to sit roughly in a relation of containment. The group-level explanation posits all that the individual-level explanation posits, plus an additional set of properties, the group-level cognitive properties. Therefore it seems reasonable to conclude, as Rupert does, that individual-level explanation must be the simpler hypothesis. If one can explain the group's behaviour without introducing additional cognitive properties possessed by groups, why, everything else being equal, introduce those group-level cognitive properties?

The aim of this paper is to show that this conclusion is unwarranted. Individual-level explanation is not simpler than, and hence (all else being equal) preferable to, group-level explanation. Our strategy in this paper is to examine how simplicity should be measured. We consider three approaches: qualitative parsimony, qualitative parsimony, and theoretical elegance. We argue that on none of these measures does individual-level explanation count as more simple than group-level explanation. We conclude that concerns about simplicity cannot be straightforwardly used, as Rupert wants, to argue against the existence of group minds.

Qualitative Parsimony

One dimension of simplicity is parsimony. Parsimony concerns the number of entities posited by an explanation. How does one go about counting these entities? There seem to be two possibilities: count the *kinds* of entity postulated or count the *number of entities* postulated and subsumed under each kind. Counting the number of kinds gives a measure of *qualitative* parsimony; counting the number of entities subsumed under each kind gives a measure of *quantitative* parsimony.[3] Qualitative parsimony is the focus of this section; quantitative parsimony is the focus of the next.

---

[3]   D. K. Lewis, *Counterfactuals* (Oxford: Blackwell, 1973).

Group Minds and Explanatory Simplicity

How do considerations of qualitative parsimony apply in the Microsoft case? On the assumption that both the individual-level and group-level explanations are otherwise adequate, the individual-level explanation might appear more qualitatively parsimonious for the simple fact that it includes only those kinds that are already in use throughout standard cognitive science. In other words, the individual-level explanation helps itself only to the cognitive kinds of architecture, state, and process that are already attributed to individual humans in cognitive scientific explanations. In contrast, the group-level explanation of the Microsoft's production of a new OS makes additional postulates: it attributes cognitive properties to Microsoft at the group-level.

It is of crucial importance, however, to the group-level explanation that the additional postulates involve attribution of *the same kind* of properties to Microsoft as are attributed to its individual employees. The architecture that the group-level explanation takes Microsoft to instantiate is, *ex hypothesi*, of the same cognitive kind as the architecture instantiated by individuals. And the states and processes that Microsoft is attributed in virtue of its instantiating this cognitive architecture are again, *ex hypothesi*, cognitive states and processes of the same kind as are attributed to its individual humans.

The cognitive states attributed to Microsoft are *additional instances* of individual-level cognitive states: beliefs, desires, intentions, and so on. The group-level states are individually distinct from any of the individual-level cognitive states attributed to particular employees. But the group-level states are individually distinct in the sense that they constitute new instances of the same cognitive kind as are attributed to individual employees. The claim – the innovation – that makes the group-level explanation of Microsoft's production of a new OS interesting is that Microsoft instantiates additional instances of the same kind of cognitive properties as are attributed to individual humans. The same is true of any group-level cognitive explanation. These explanations are interesting precisely because of the similarity they posit between individual-level properties and group-level properties. A group-level explanation that attributed utterly alien cognitive properties – so different as to fail to fall under any same-kind relation to those of individual humans – would not count as a group *mind* hypothesis at all.

Understood correctly, group-level explanations do not postulate additional cognitive kinds, only additional instances of existing kinds. Therefore, an appeal to qualitative parsimony as a strategy to argue against group-level explanations would miss the mark. There are no extraneous kinds to 'shave off' by dispensing with group-level explanation, only attribution of existing kinds to new particulars.

9

Mark Sprevak and David Statham

Quantitative Parsimony

Might group-level explanations be less simple than individual-level alternatives because group-level explanations postulate extra instances of cognitive kinds? Does a group-level explanation of, say, Microsoft's behaviour introduce unnecessary instances of cognitive architecture, states and processes? In this section, we argue that concerns about quantitative parsimony do not tell against group-level explanation.[4]

Nolan provides an instructive case study on the value of quantitative parsimony.[5] Nolan's study concerns the postulation of the neutrino in the explanation of beta decay. In attempting to explain a puzzling drop in the energy of nuclei during beta decay, Wolfgang Pauli postulated the existence of a new kind of subatomic particle, the neutrino. When developing the neutrino-based explanation, there was no available means of determining how many of the new subatomic particles were released during beta decay. The total mass-energy to be accounted was known, but whether this mass-energy was best accounted by one, two, or a million neutrinos was an open question. Once the release of a single neutrino has been postulated, why not postulate the release of two neutrinos each with half the mass-energy of one neutrino? Or a million neutrinos with a millionth of the mass-energy? At the time, the one-neutrino and the million-neutrino explanations could both have accommodated the empirical data. Nolan argues that it was nevertheless rational, in light of consideration of quantitative parsimony, for Pauli to favour the one-neutrino explanation. Nolan defends this in two ways.

First, one may make a brute appeal to intuition. That the one-neutrino explanation is superior to the million-neutrino explanation (or any other such explanation) is an intuition that many otherwise rational enquirers share. It may seem reasonable to endorse this, at least pending countervailing evidence, even if it does not admit of explicit justification. Second, one may appeal to the successful track

[4] Appeal to quantitative parsimony is far from uncontroversial as a means of selecting between rival explanations. Lewis, *Counterfactuals*, says, 'I subscribe to the general view that qualitative parsimony is good in a philosophical or empirical hypothesis; but I recognise no presumption whatever in favour of quantitative parsimony' (87). Alex Oliver argues that, despite our undeniable bias towards explanations with quantitative parsimony, we should not trust this as a guide to the truth ('The Metaphysics of Properties', *Mind* **105** (1996), 1–80).

[5] D. Nolan, 'Quantitive Parsimony', *The British Journal for the Philosophy of Science* **48** (1997), 329–343.

record of quantitatively parsimonious explanations. Quantitative parsimony has led to the selection of explanations that have gone on to prove their worth in other ways. A case in point is the one-neutrino explanation. Pauli's explanation was subsequently vindicated. Even if the reasons for the success of quantitative parsimony remain obscure, its success alone appears to lend some justification to the principle's continued application.

The cases in which quantitative parsimony play a part might seem trivial when the number of entities postulated (for example, atoms or subatomic particles) is compared with the potentially infinite number of other entities in the universe. This seems to pose a problem if one endorses an 'infinite ontology' view of the universe. One could argue that against this infinite background, a numerical increase in entities of one particular kind is trivial or negligible. Why should it matter that an explanation adds a few more entities to our scientific ontology when this ontology already includes the infinity of other kinds of entities which occupy an infinite universe?

Against this thought, Nolan contends that, irrespective of the potential infinity of entities subsumed under all extant kinds, it is nevertheless important to minimise the number of entities subsumed by any one particular kind. Thus, for example, even against the background of infinite mathematical entities to which the mathematical Platonist is committed, the addition of 'seventeen million little neutral particles being produced in every case of Beta-decay', as opposed to the addition of just one such particle, still makes a significant difference.[6]

We will follow Nolan in his understanding quantitative parsimony. Recall that the group-level explanation claims that Microsoft, as a group, instantiates a cognitive architecture with instances of cognitive states over and above those of its individual employees. Is an individual-level explanation more quantitatively parsimonious than this group-level account (assuming, as above, that both explanations can be given)?

At first glance, the answer appears to be a clear 'yes'. At the end of the previous section we said that the group-level explanation posits extra *instances* of cognitive architectures, states, and processes, although it does not posit new kinds. Granted this, the group-level explanation appears to do worse in terms of quantitative parsimony: it posits more instances of cognitive properties than individual-level explanation. On closer examination, however, the case against group-level explanation is not so clear.

---

[6] Nolan, 'Quantitative Parsimony', 340.

Mark Sprevak and David Statham

An initial objection that might be levelled by an advocate of individual-level explanation is that the group-level explanation attributes to the Microsoft corporation a *cognitive architecture*, whilst at the same time appealing to the cognitive architectures of the individual employees. If this attribution involves the postulation of an additional entity, then it seems to fall foul of considerations of quantitative parsimony when compared to individual-level alternatives.

Understood correctly, however, the group-level explanation does not postulate the instantiation of a cognitive architecture as an *additional* entity over and above those postulated in the individual-level explanation. Rather, it *identifies* the organisational structure of the corporation, as described in the individual-level explanation, with a genuinely cognitive architecture. The individual-level explanation must already include this organisational structure in order to explain the interactions that take place between the corporation's individual employees. It is committed to there being an executive, external information stores, a variety of sub-components in the form of teams of individual employees, and various other non-cognitive physical structures. In order to make sense of the interactions between these features and to explain how they are coordinated in the production of a new OS, the individual-level explanation cannot merely postulate their existence. It must also give an account of the rules and procedures governing their interaction.

In attributing to the corporation a cognitive architecture, the group-level explanation does not postulate an extra structure over and above the structure already described at the individual-level. It claims that, properly understood, this structure *is* an instance of a cognitive architecture.

What about the additional cognitive states and processes? It seems that they must violate the principle of quantitative parsimony. Even if Microsoft as a corporation instantiates a cognitive architecture, an advocate of quantitative parsimony could say that the cognitive states attributed to the corporation in the group-level explanation constitute extraneous additions to number of instances of cognitive states postulated in the individual-level explanation. The individual-level explanation makes reference to the cognitive states of individual employees. The group-level explanation makes reference to these cognitive states plus an extra set of cognitive states at group level. The group-level explanation therefore seems inferior in terms of quantitative parsimony.

Let us pause and consider this more carefully. First, we need to ask how the instances of cognitive states postulated by each explanation are counted. Consider the cognitive state of *intending to develop a new OS*. Let us suppose that the individual-level explanation attributes this state to the corporation's CEO, amongst other individual employees. The group-level explanation retains these attributions and, additionally, attributes the state of *intending to develop a new OS* to the corporation as a whole.

Here is one method by which we could go about counting cognitive states. Beginning with the CEO, we say that his state of intending to develop a new OS is one cognitive state to which the individual-level explanation is committed. On top of this, let us suppose that he simultaneously *believes* that the development of a new OS is a financial necessity. This gives us two cognitive states. Simultaneously, he *desires* to make as much money as possible for the corporation during his time as CEO, giving us a total of three cognitive states. Assuming, for the sake of brevity, that the CEO's cognitive states are limited to only these three, we could go on to count the cognitive states of all the other individual employees in a similar manner. At the end of this process, we add up the cognitive states that have been attributed to each individual employee, and this gives us the total number of cognitive states to which the individual-level explanation is committed.

Suppose, for the sake of argument, that the group-level explanation is committed to those individual-level cognitive states too. But it goes further and attributes cognitive states at the group-level. We count these group-level cognitive states, add them to the total number of individual-level cognitive states, and this gives us the number of cognitive states to which the group-level explanation is committed. Patently, using this method of counting cognitive states, the group-level explanation is committed to a greater number of cognitive states than the individual-level explanation.

This method of counting cognitive states gives us the total number of *occurrent* cognitive states attributed by the explanations. The method might seem appealing. However, it relies on an implausibly atomistic view of the nature of cognitive states.

Cognitive states ought not to be treated as entities in the same way as material objects whose existence can be treated independently of the existence of all other such objects. If we are counting the number of chairs in a room, then counting only the 'occurrent' chairs – those that are present in the room at one particular point in time – is unproblematic. The existence of each of these chairs, and the location of each chair, stands largely independent of the existence or location of any other chair. The existence of any single chair, and the location of the chair, entails almost nothing about the existence or location of any other chair. Cognitive states are different, or so the objection goes. The fact that a cognitive architecture instantiates a particular cognitive state at a given moment in time *does* entail further facts about other cognitive states. The existence of a particular cognitive state cannot be treated in isolation from other cognitive states.

This approach to cognitive states falls under the broad heading of *dispositionalism*. The core of dispositionalist theories – the idea that is of the greatest significance for the discussion of group-level cognitive states – can be illustrated by some simple examples. We will give these to demonstrate the strength of the view as a broadly correct characterisation of cognitive states, and superior to the occurrent characterisation above.

Consider that *I believe that my house contains six rooms*. At a given point in time I am laying down plans for my latest DIY project and this has given me cause to think about the total number of rooms in my house. I say to myself 'there are six rooms in my house'. It seems entirely reasonable that at this given point in time, we should attribute to me the occurrent belief *that my house has six rooms*. It seems uncontroversial that I have at least this one belief at this point in time.

What about the belief *that my house contains more than three rooms?* I might never have cause during the course of my DIY project to entertain this as a proposition, and it might plausibly be the case that at no point in my life does the belief *that my house contains more than three rooms* ever become occurrent. Does this mean that I do not believe that my house contains more than three rooms? Maintaining that I do not seems to neglect a crucial feature of beliefs. I am *disposed* to assent to statements or answer questions in accordance with the non-occurrent belief.

It is the important sense in which I believe *that my house contains more than three rooms*, regardless of the actual occurrence of this belief, which is captured by the dispositionalist claim we are interested in here. The claim is that, in virtue of the structure possessed by my cognitive architecture, I am disposed to respond in a particular way to a whole set of possible stimuli and other dispositional mental states – to assent to a whole set of possible statements, to answer questions in a particular way, and so on.

Returning to Microsoft example, the CEO was attributed three cognitive states, one of which was the intention to develop a new OS. Construed in dispositional terms, however, his single state of intending entails many others. If the CEO intends to develop a new OS, he presumably also intends to develop a new OS which can be made available for the use of Microsoft's customers. He intends that this

OS will run successfully on existing hardware, that it will enable the use of more than one piece of software, and so on. And these entailments are not limited to intentions. If the CEO intends to develop a new OS he presumably also *believes* that the development of a new OS is possible, and he believes that it is within the capability of the corporation to develop a new OS. Presumably he also has beliefs about what an OS is, what a corporation is, and his position within the corporation such that he can intend to develop a new OS in the first place, and so on.

To say that the CEO instantiates the cognitive state of intending to develop a new OS but none of the other inferentially-related cognitive states seems to neglect an essential feature of what it is to instantiate a cognitive state. We want to suggest, then, that cognitive states are not best characterised as solely occurrent states. Rather, in virtue of having a cognitive architecture and instantiating cognitive states, the CEO possesses a whole set of related dispositional mental states.

If we treat cognitive states in dispositional terms, how do we count them?

There are presumably limits in principle to the number of occurrent states that a single cognitive architecture can instantiate at any given point in time, even if those limits are difficult to discern. Limited neural resources and limited number of cognitive mechanisms that comprise the cognitive architecture of an individual of finite size mean that the number of occurrent cognitive states instantiated at any given moment is finite.

In contrast, the number of dispositions that an individual has, in virtue of their instantiating a cognitive architecture is, in principle, unlimited. If I believe *that my house contains six rooms*, and I also believe *that my house contains more than three rooms*, presumably I also believe *that my house contains fewer than seven rooms*. I am disposed to assent to the statement that my house contains fewer than seven rooms. Surely, then, I also believe *that my house contains fewer than eight rooms*, and fewer than nine rooms, and ten rooms, and so on *ad infinitum*. Construed dispositionally, there is no point in this sequence at which it makes sense to terminate. There is no principled limit on the number of rooms to which I would be disposed to respond *that my house contains fewer*.

In the Microsoft case, there is likewise no principled limit to the number of cognitive states we should attribute to its CEO once it has been accepted that he intends to develop a new OS. The simplest example of this fact could be given just by considering that, if the CEO intends to develop *one* new OS, he also intends to develop *less than two* new OSs, and *less than three* new OS, and so on. It is not just that the limits to the number of these cognitive states are difficult to discern. Rather, there are no such limits. There seems, then, to be the very real possibility that, construed in dispositional terms, the number of instances of cognitive states falling under each kind in individual-level explanation of Microsoft's behaviour is *unlimited*.

If individual-level explanation is committed to an unlimited number of instances of cognitive states (beliefs, intentions, desires, etc.), then the addition of further instances of these kinds attributed to groups would offer no overall increase in number. Even if the number of group-level cognitive instances were similarly unlimited, there would still be no overall increase. This is bad news for anyone wishing to use quantitative parsimony to argue in favour of individual-level explanation. Our first intuition that the number of individual cognitive states plus the number of group cognitive states must be greater than the number of individual cognitive states breaks down once we introduce an unlimited number of dispositional cognitive states.

Despite its initial intuitive plausibility, quantitative parsimony does not lend credence to individual-level explanation being more simple than group-level explanation. Insofar as cognitive property instances can be counted at all, adding further instances via group-level explanation does not increase our total commitments.

Theoretical elegance

The final measure of explanatory simplicity we consider is *theoretical elegance*. Theoretical elegance concerns the structure and length of the explanation, rather than the entities or kinds to which it is committed.[7]

Two ways of understanding theoretical elegance are considered below: explanations that minimise the number of primitive predicates employed, and explanations that minimise the length of the explanation. We argue that neither provides the grounds for thinking that individual-level explanations are more simple than group-level alternatives.

Explanations employ primitive and non-primitive predicates. Both kinds of predicate are used to express the ideas that a theory contains. The primitive predicates are those which are undefined: they receive

---

[7] A. Baker, 'Simplicity' in *The Stanford Encyclopedia of Philosophy*, edited by E. N. Zalta, Fall 2013, http://plato.stanford.edu/archives/fall2013/entries/simplicity/.

no definition or analysis within the explanation. The non-primitive predicates are defined: they receive a definition in terms of the predicates included elsewhere within the explanation.

In the Microsoft example, the primitive predicates might include *has the belief that a new OS is required, has the desire to produce the new OS within the next three years*, and so on. Additionally, many predicates related to the non-cognitive properties of physical structures and the predicates needed to explain the organisation of the corporation are likely to be primitive.

According to our assumption in Section 2, the group-level explanation will include all the primitive predicates of the individual-level explanation. The additional postulates in the group-level explanation are the group-level cognitive properties, and therefore the only additional predicates in the group-level explanation could be those predicates relating specifically to the instantiation of cognitive properties at the group-level: those needed to explain why and how a group-level architecture is a *group-level* architecture; why and how the additional states being postulated are *group-level* states, and so on.

These group-level predicates are the subject matter of group-level explanations and will therefore need to be explained and defined within the group-level explanation. These group-level predicates will *not* remain undefined because it is the concern of such an explanation to explain why and how cognitive properties are instantiated at the group level, and what it means to have the group-level properties in the sense intended by the explanation. Therefore, the (additional) group-level predicates will not be primitive.

This means that the group-level explanation will not include any more primitive predicates than the individual-level explanation. So, with regard to elegance *qua* minimum number of primitive predicates, group-level explanations are no worse off than individual-level explanations.

If the Microsoft group-level explanation replaces reference to individual-level cognitive properties and the various non-cognitive physical structures mentioned in the individual-level explanation with reference to only a single cognitive system and its properties, group-level explanation could be shorter. Even if group-level explanation retains reference to all the properties and structures of individual-level explanation, there will nevertheless be aspects of the group's activity whose lengthy individual-level explanations can be replaced with shorter group-level explanations.

For example, consider retrieval of information from a non-cognitive information store, such as a hard drive. For an individual-level explanation, this would need to be explained with description of an

Mark Sprevak and David Statham

individual employee's processes of interaction with the hard drive and how information on the hard drive influences that individual's cognitive states and processes. This would involve, for example, facts about the physical encoding of the information on the hard drive, the content of the information, the employee's sensory interaction with the hard drive, their conceptualisation of the information, and their endorsement of the information. The explanation may plausibly draw on other elements too, such as translation between natural languages in order for the employee to capable of conceptualising the information in the first place. The explanation also needs to explain how, once the information has affected the cognitive states of an individual, this then affects the behaviour of the corporation as a whole.

In a group-level explanation, this set of processes by which the information contained on a hard drive comes to influence an individual's cognitive states and processes, and by which these states and processes are communicated to and influence other individual employees, could be given a much shorter explanation in terms of *the corporation*'s group-level cognitive states being influenced by states of *the corporation*'s long-term memory. Thus, even if group-level explanation elsewhere retains reference to the same individual-level cognitive properties and non-cognitive structures as individual-level explanation, there will be cases where group-level explanation can compress non-trivial sets of statements made by the individual-level explanation of certain processes.

This mirrors a discussion by Clark and Chalmers of the appeal of the extended mind hypothesis.[8] Clark and Chalmers argue that when explaining Otto's behaviour, certain stages in the explanation become unnecessary once one switches to an explanation couched in terms of a single extended cognitive system.[9] The description of Otto's transit to The Museum of Modern Art need not, they argue, make reference to Otto's belief that The Museum of Modern Art's location is recorded in his notebook, or to the fine-grained details of Otto's sensorimotor interaction with his notebook. In the extended-mind version of the explanation, this whole process is glossed simply as the retrieval of information from Otto's long-term extended memory in the service of fulfilling his desires. The non-extended alternative involving a detour through Otto's beliefs about his notebook takes 'one step too many' and is 'pointlessly complex'.

[8] A. Clark and D. J. Chalmers, 'The Extended Mind', *Analysis* **58** (1998), 7–19
[9] Clark and Chalmers, 'The Extended Mind', 13.

Group Minds and Explanatory Simplicity

Likewise, if a group-level explanation of Microsoft's production of a new OS is available, many stages of the individual-level explanation seem pointlessly complex. Ensembles of processes can be glossed as the execution of a single group-level cognitive process, such as retrieval of information from long-term memory. The set of statements describing this will be significantly shorter than the statements required to explain the same process in purely individual-level terms. As a result, even if the group-level explanation retains reference to individual-level cognitive properties and non-cognitive structures, there will be opportunities to substantially reduce the number of statements used in the explanation and there is a possibility that the group-level explanation will be shorter and more elegant.[10]

Conclusion

Individual-level explanations of intelligent behaviour are not always simpler than group-level explanations. This is not to say that particular individual-level explanations are not superior to group-level explanations. Nor is it to rule out an argument that individual-level explanation is better based on another, non-simplicity-based, metric. Nor is it to rule out a general non-explanatory-value-based argument against group minds. Our aim has only been to show that appeal to explanatory simplicity is not enough to show that group-level explanation is inferior to individual-level explanation.

University of Edinburgh
Mark Sprevak (mark.sprevak@ed.ac.uk)
David Statham (d.statham@ed.ac.uk)

[10] The authors are listed here in alphabetical order; both authors have contributed equally to this work. We would like to thank Anthony O'Hear for inviting us to present this paper at the Royal Institute of Philosophy, and the audience for their useful questions and suggestions. We would like to thank Robert Rupert for helpful comments on an earlier draft of this paper.

19

Philosophy and the Mind/Body Problem

PAUL F. SNOWDON

Abstract
The thesis of the paper is that it is an illusion to think that the mind/body problem is one that philosophy can expect to solve. The basic reason is that the problem is one of determining the real nature of conscious states, and philosophy lacks the tools to work this out. It is argued that anti-materialist arguments in philosophy tend to rely on modal intuitions which lack any support. It is then argued that pro-materialist arguments, such as those of Smart and of Papineau, are dubious because they either yield a conclusion that is too conditional on what other types of research might discover, or rely on premises that anyone who is not already a materialist can simply query. Even if these points are correct the main thesis remains fairly speculative, but at least some support for it is presented.

In this paper I wish to propose, and try to provide support for, a con-jecture about the mind/body problem. The conjecture has two sides. (1) Despite the mind/body problem having been a focus of massive attention in post-war philosophy, indeed, having received as much attention as any problem has, no good grounds of a philosophical kind have been adduced or discovered for favouring a particular answer to the problem. We might call this the 'No Progress Report'. (2) The basic explanation for this failure is that the problem, when correctly conceived, is a scientific one, an empirical one, rather than a philosophical one. Philosophers do not have the right tools to settle that sort of question.

This conjecture reflects the opinion that the basic choice in the mind/body problem is between affirming a materialist (or physical-ist) view, and affirming a denial of that view. This has not always been regarded as the fundamental question, but in what I am calling the 'conjecture' the claim is that there have been no good reasons for pre-ferring one of these options to the other. Thus, the first part of the overall conjecture can itself be regarded as a conjunction of two claims; (A) there are no good reasons of a philosophical kind to say that materialism is false and (B) there are no good reasons of a philo-sophical kind to say that materialism is true.

My view is that conjecture (A) is somewhat easier to support than conjecture (B). The reason is that objections to materialism frequent-ly have the following structure. The first premise in the argument

doi:10.1017/S1358246115000120   ©The Royal Institute of Philosophy and the contributors 2015
Royal Institute of Philosophy Supplement **76** 2015

Paul F. Snowdon

claims that something or other, which I shall call, C is an implication of materialism. The second premise in the argument claims that C is false; i.e. not C. Taken together the falsity of materialism follows. But as I hope to make a case for saying, philosophers have tended to locate a value for C in this recurring pattern that might be called 'modal'; they tend to claim that if materialism is true then so and so must at least be *possible*, or, perhaps, *impossible*, and then the suggestion is that the modal implication is false. The suspicion that the conjecture reflects is that the final affirmative modal premises in these types of anti-materialist arguments are not properly supported. The attitude is that even in the absence of a theory about the epistemology of modality it is reasonable to be suspicious of such modal claims.

By contrast the arguments in support of materialism do not have a recurring structure or content; they can be any assemblage of premises that together imply materialism is true. There is no limitation in advance to their content. At this point I retreat somewhat to the following claim; the actual arguments that in fact have been presented are not sound, with no good reason being contained in them for supposing that materialism must be true. However, I do have one reason of a general sort to defend this speculation. The fundamental question that is being asked in the mind/body problem is – what is the *real nature* of mental processes? Principally, do such processes or states have a real nature that is exhausted by elements or features that count as physical? A good analogous question is; what is the real nature of *water*? If that comparison is correct then surely it seems likely that the only route to an answer is via the hard work of analysing as far as one can what is really, actually, present when such processes or features are present. This seems to be an empirical or more generally a scientific question. If that progression of thoughts looks cogent then there is a general reason to be suspicious of philosophy as the discipline that can reveal the truth about this issue.

In fact, the two conjectures that I have separated can be regarded as flowing from the same basic idea; the idea that we want to know what the *real* nature of mental states and processes is. The modal based criticism of materialism fail because the basis for the modal judgements is too flimsy to reveal anything about the real nature of things; and the failure of philosophy to support materialism reflects the fact that philosophy has no proper method for revealing truths about real natures of spatio-temporal processes.

Such a conjecture is, actually, one that many people would accept; it is accepted, for example, by lots of scientists, who are sceptical of the pretensions of philosophy in this area. The weakness in their dismissal of philosophy is that they tend not to know what kinds of considerations philosophers have actually adduced, since they do not read much, if any, philosophy. This ignorance of philosophy means that they make their criticisms from a position of weakness. I am trying to support the same claim on the basis of a more informed consideration of what philosophers do actually say.

I need to stress that I do not think that I can prove or strongly substantiate the conjecture here. I want, rather, to propose it and to assemble some considerations in its favour.

1. The Mind/Body Problem and the Self/Body Problem

It is helpful, I think, to begin by making a comparison between two problems. The first is what I am calling the mind/body problem; the second is what I like to call the self/body problem. These are not the same problem, but they are linked, and comparing the styles of argument that philosophers have employed to settle them will, I hope, turn out to be valuable.

The mind/body problem asks what the relation is between what the word 'mind' stands for here and what the word 'body' stands for here. The word 'mind' stands for certain aspects or features of the world, what we might label the 'mental features'. No definition of that label needs to be given; we give examples of what the label covers and people catch on to what is meant; examples of mental features are the occurrence of experiences, such as having a pain or seeing a table, and the presence of psychological features such as having a belief or a desire or an intention. These are not the only examples that are normally used – but for present purposes they are enough. The word 'body' here stands for physical occurrences and aspects of the world – again, the label is anchored by examples. Examples would be neurons firing in a certain region of the brain, or weighing a certain amount, and so on. What we want to know is; what is the relation between the former features and the latter sort of features?

Now, I want to stress that this question is about what we can call the REAL nature of these mental features. It is obvious to us that the physical is widespread in the world and that physical things can be and are present in the absence of any mental features; the focus of the question is – what is the nature of the mental features, in particular, do they have a real nature that involves in their being present nothing more than a conglomeration of physical features, or does their presence require or involve more than that?

Paul F. Snowdon

It is quite natural to reach for explications of the problem along lines such as; are mental features anything over and above physical features; are they nothing but physical features? Do they come down to physical features? Or, perhaps, is their presence constituted by the presence of physical features? These all seem natural, suggestive and non-technical forms of words for fixing the kind of relation that we want to inquire about. Philosophers have also introduced technical or semi-technical expressions for the relevant relation. They talk about the mental being supervenient on the physical, and of the mental being reducible to the physical.

I want to note that materialism in the philosophy of mind is not the thesis that everything is physical – we should not link materialism with such issues as whether God exists and is not physical – nor is it a question about whether it is possible for there to be non-physical mental states, nor whether perhaps there are some non-physical mental states somewhere – it is a question about the real nature of the mental states that we have and are familiar with.

These remarks have been by way of an introduction to the mind/body problem. I want, though, to compare that problem with what I am calling the self/body problem. What problem is that?

In the self/body problem, if posed about me, the relata are myself, that is whatever object the word 'I' picks out when used by me, and that object we call 'my body'. What is the relation between those things? This is of course the central question that Descartes asks about himself. Now, the simplest candidate relation is that of identity. Descartes in fact wishes to claim something much stronger than the thesis that I and my body are not identical, but he certainly needs to claim at least that. So we can ask; how well does he support this weaker non-identity claim? He argues for the non-identity by selecting supposed property differences between myself and my body. In his famous argument in Meditation VI one supposed difference is that my body is essentially extended but that I am not. Another supposed difference is that I am essentially a thinking thing, but my body is not. Now, what surely strikes us, as we stare at these contrasting claims, is that the modal claims Descartes implies (or makes) about me have no obvious justification. Why is Descartes entitled to say that I am not essentially extended? Descartes' reason to think he is not essentially extended is that when he thinks about himself he cannot there and then discern a reason for thinking that he must be extended. The reply to this, more or less immediately provided by Arnauld in his masterly Fourth Set of Objections, was, in nuce, that this failure to find a reason cannot be transformed into a positive reason to deny that he is essentially extended. It is quite simply and

24

solely the absence of a positive reason. Why does Descartes affirm that he is essentially thinking? That rests on a confusion of an epistemic claim that he (obviously) must be thinking (since he is considering a problem) with the metaphysical thesis that must think at all times he exists. Once that confusion is set aside we simply need to accumulate evidence as to whether we do always think, and as Locke pointed out we do not seem to! He noticed that we fall asleep! Neither modal claim is secure enough to play the role of premises in an argument determining our nature.

Consideration of Descartes' treatment of the Self/Body problem suggests two morals. The first is that we should be very careful about assenting to modal judgements which are supposed to lead to substantial metaphysical conclusions. Second, when assessing such modal claims we have no vantage point to determine their truth prior to investigating in some more ordinary way the actual nature of the things we are dealing with. These are morals which I hope to apply, in the next section, to some standard anti-materialist arguments.

2. Anti-Materialist Arguments

As well as providing us with some morals that I hope will guide our engagement with some anti-materialist arguments , the brief analysis above of Descartes' famous arguments, supposedly supporting his conclusion that we are distinct from our bodies , and that, therefore, our mental processes involve non-bodily elements, has also turned those anti-materialist arguments aside. There are, of course, other famous anti-materialist arguments (or lines of thought) associated with, for example, Sellars, Nagel, and Jackson (to name but a few) but I want in this present paper to focus on a style of argument that originates with Kripke,[1] and which in a modified form is also central to David Chalmer's approach. I think that it is this style of argument that has had most influence recently, leading to a popularity for anti-materialism. I propose however to formulate what I see as the central inference in my own terms, and to discuss it without looking in detail at the text of these formidable writers. I am doing that because it seems to me that the grounds for suspicion about them can be brought out in a fairly direct way. Anyway, that is what I shall try to do here.

[1]   In Kripke, S, *Naming and Necessity* (Cambridge Mass., Harvard University Press, 1982)

Paul F. Snowdon

The background to the sort of argument I am considering is the idea, shared by philosophers responsible for the revival of materialism in the 1950's, is that the materialist identities are contingently true. It was assumed this followed from the idea that claims in favour of these identities will be empirically supported. They held too that the identities that science had already endorsed – say that heat is molecular motion – are contingent, and such identities provided the model for what materialists took themselves to be postulating. For many people this shared conception was overturned by Kripke who persuaded many of us that identity judgements, flanked by rigid designators, are not contingent, but are, rather, if true necessarily true, and if false necessarily false. Armed with this logical result linking identity and necessity Kripke devised a type of objection to the identities central to materialism.

If, say, it is proposed that pain (or having a pain) is identical to C-fibre firing, then, given the character of the designator involved, it is a claim that implies that necessarily pain is C-fibre stimulation. But it seems that it is possible for there to be C-fibre firings without pain being felt. Why is that? The possibility claim is based, at root, on our capacity to imagine or conceive of it happening – an exercise of imagination that seems quite simple and easy. All I need to do is to imagine a subject with firing C-fibres but feeling no pain. It could be myself or another.

This all seems very simple, but anyone attempting to refute the suggested materialist identity in this way seems to have armed themselves with a pattern of argument with which they can give philosophical refutations of current chemistry and physics. If water is H2O then necessarily water is H2O, but it seems as easy to imagine that there is water without H2O, as it is to imagine C-fibre firings without pain. In the blink of an eyelid a massive chemical insight has been achieved, and the nature of water has been rendered totally mysterious.

Sadly, no-one would take such philosophical chemistry seriously. On one interpretation of his view Kripke's highly ingenious response to what is in effect this problem is to attempt to draw a contrast between the water/H2O case and the pain/C-fibre firing case. He proposed that what we are counting as imagining water without H2O is really not that at all. We are, rather, imagining a substance which is phenomenally like water, which appears like water, without H2O, and of course that is a possibility, whereas when we imagine C-fibre firing without pain that is precisely what we are doing. In this way the objection to the materialist identity survives, without current chemistry being cast into the flames. This, however, does not quite have the ring of truth. For one thing, it seems that if I were to imagine water in my basement I would generate precisely the same imagery that I do when I apparently imagine water without H2O. How can that be imagining water in one case but not the other? But further, what, we might ask, are we doing when we imagine C-fibre firing without pain? The answer is we simply imagine no pain, painlessness, and, as it were, imaginatively say to, or represent to, ourselves – (and) the body's C-fibres are not firing. If that is an accurate account of what such imagining is one has to ask how being able to do that can ground a rejection of a substantial proposal about the nature of pain and its physical basis.

What I want to suggest here is that we should conclude that there cannot really be any legitimate basis for affirming a real possibility for either water or for pain in the imaginative capacities we have in relation to the phenomena involved. With both water and pain the order of investigation has to be to discern the nature of the thing in question, thereby grounding, if possible, identities and necessities, and on the basis of that assign reality to any suggested possibilities. We have no route to determining the possibilities by any exercise of armchair conceivings thereby settling claims about the real nature of anything. Such imaginings are amongst the easiest things we can do, and they cannot ground any insights into reality. These are simply the morals we learnt from Descartes' arguments.

The same pattern of argument is possessed by an objection to materialism that has gripped people recently. The argument is that materialism entails that zombies are impossible, but, obviously, they are possible, so materialism is false. David Chalmers has presented this case very powerfully, though he embeds it within a somewhat more complex framework than the one I am employing.[2] Now, a zombie is a creature that is physically exactly like one of us but which lacks conscious experience. It seems to me quite reasonable to say that if materialism gives a correct account of the real nature of conscious states then zombies are impossible. Since the physical states that zombies possess are the states which according to the theory are conscious states they cannot have the physical states without having the mental states.

Again, though, the question this argument faces is why in advance of considering the tenability of the theoretical proposal we are entitled to affirm that zombies are possible. The answer is that we can imagine that they are, or that we cannot rule them out from out

[2]   See Chalmers, D., *The Conscious Mind* (Oxford University Press, 1996), ch. 3.

Paul F. Snowdon

armchairs in any way. But imagining a zombie is child's play; we simply imagine a body being physically identical to say my body now, and that is to do nothing more than visualising a body and, so to speak, saying to oneself its exactly like mine now, and imagine it insensate. That is easy, but it is surely obvious that such a simple exercise cannot yield any insight into the nature of the phenomenon in question. And an inability to locate an impossibility in the idea of a zombie by simply thinking about it with great intensity for any length of time cannot be turned into a demonstration of possibility. That confusion is the one exposed by Arnauld in relation to Descartes.[3]

My suggestion is that this style of argument is transparently weak. But in effect if philosophers are to argue against materialism arguments of this general style are what they most (and must) usually offer. It is plain though that there is no lever here to oppose a serious theory of the nature of conscious states. It is time for philosophers to acknowledge that they cannot offer any serious reasons to acknowledge the falsity of materialism.[4]

3. Pro-materialist Arguments

Making a case for thinking that there are no good pro-materialist arguments is, for a reason given earlier, not easy. But in an abbreviated form the way I want to propose to think about them is that either the premises are too far away from the core of the issue to give significant weight to favour materialism, or they are too near to materialism itself and are such that no one who is not already a materialist should believe them.

In the space available here I shall restrict myself to two arguments, one of both sorts, or so I shall argue.[5]

The first one comes from Smart's justly famous early paper 'Sensations and Brain Processes' published in 1959.[6] Smart's paper

---

[3]   My argument is, in a compressed form, in agreement with the sort of verdict that Robert Kirk ultimately proposes about this sort of case, which in fact he invented and analysed thoroughly.

[4]   Another confusion in some philosophical opposition to materialism is that of confusing providing a metaphysically coherent alternative to materialism with actually assembling evidence that their alternative is true and materialism is false.

[5]   I may of course be wrong in how I classify the two pro-materialist arguments I consider, but that would not be a fatal error.

[6]   Smart, J.J.C. 'Sensations and Brain Processes' in the *Philosophical Review* **68** (1959), 141–56

is one of a number that appeared about the same time and which succeeded in revising the way people thought about the mind/body problem. Prior to the movement which brought the psycho-physical identity theory to prominence amongst philosophers it had been assumed, first, that the basic choice in the philosophy of mind was between Cartesian dualism and its denial, and, second, that conceptual and a priori considerations of some sort could be adduced to reject dualism. This was the attitude of Ryle, Strawson, and, perhaps, something like if fits what Wittgenstein supposed.[7] The movement that Smart belonged to had the effect of persuading people that the basic choice is between physicalism and its denial, and that that choice is not decidable on a priori grounds. I am in agreement with those two claims, and I hold that Smart is one of the people who should be credited with persuading people that they are true.

However, in his famous paper Smart presents a general argument in favour of accepting the physicalist view. The overall argument is, as I read it, based on an appeal to Ockham's 'razor', which we can count as saying that other things being equal we should accept simpler theories. The main aim of the Smart's paper is to show that other things are equal, and that materialism is the simpler theory. It is hard not to agree with Smart that materialism is simpler than its denial; in effect materialism reduces mental features to physical ones, whereas its denial involves saying there are physical features and also distinct mental ones. It is also hard not to agree with Ockham's principle. The basic problem with Smart's argument lies in the claim that we are in a position to affirm that other things *are* equal. Smart's strategy to show that other things are equal is to take what he considers to be the difficulties with materialism and to provide answers to them. His actual discussion, I want to suggest, suffers from two deficiencies. The first is that he does not select all the difficulties, and so whatever the accuracy of what he does say about the ones he confronts, he is not in a position to say that other things are equal. The second is that he obviously does not reply adequately to some of the difficulties he does discuss. So, again, we

---

[7] There is an interesting historical issue here; the description I have given of the background approach to the issue applies to the period around the Second World War and after it. It is not at all clear that the same assumptions applied to the treatment of the mind/body problem before that. If they did not it is interesting to ask what the earlier assumptions were, and why different ones came to dominate philosophical practice at about the time of the Second World War.

Paul F. Snowdon

cannot derive from his paper the conclusion that 'other things are equal'.[8] There is though a further and serious issue which Smart's method raises. Smart's approach assumes that the context of discussion he is in will acquaint him with the difficulties that need answering. That, however, represents a massive assumption, which has no obvious justification. Smart is assuming that materialism is a philosophical proposal, and so the context of discussion is philosophy. It seems closer to the truth to say it is a highly general empirical theory, and so Smart is simply not in a position to feel confident as to what the difficulties are. He is in no position to feel he can say with confidence that other things really are equal. We can say that Smart is too far away from the sort of issue that it is to be able to say anything that leaves us confident as to what is actually true.

The second pro-materialist argument I wish to focus on is one that Professor Papineau calls the 'Causal Argument'. He has expounded this argument on numerous occasions but I wish to concentrate on the account he presents in his book *Thinking About Consciousness*.[9] In that book he describes the argument as the 'one definitive argument for materialism'.[10] This sounds as if he thinks that the argument is unanswerable, but he does say later that 'the argument may not be conclusive', so it is probably accurate to summarise his attitude as thinking that it is, at least, a very strong argument.[11] The argument rests on three premises, which I shall initially formulate in Papineau's words.

---

[8]   I do not here have the space to support this verdict on Smart's discussion, but I assume that most people would agree with what I say. But one example where his discussion is on the wrong tracks would be the topic-neutral analyses he proposed for psychological reports, which should strike anyone as unacceptable.

[9]   Papineau, D. *Thinking about Consciousness* (Oxford, Clarendon Press, 2002). My reason for choosing Papineau's version for discussion is not that the line of thought embodied in the argument is his sole invention, but, rather, that he provides an especially clear and thoroughly considered version of the argument. The advantage of focussing on Papineau is the thoroughness with which he presents the argument. There is, though, one disadvantage. Others expound arguments of more or less the same structure but they do not necessarily build in all the assumptions that Papineau does, some of which I shall base criticisms on, so there is a degree of loss of generality in the present discussion.

[10]   Papineau, *Thinking about Consciousness*, 15.

[11]   Ibid., 16.

Philosophy and the Mind/Body Problem

(1)   Conscious mental occurrences have physical effects.
(2)   All physical effects are fully caused by purely physical prior histories.
(3)   The physical effects of conscious causes aren't always overdetermined by distinct causes.

The conclusion of the argument is that materialism is true, which Papineau explains as meaning that 'the conscious occurrences mentioned in (1) must be identical with some part of the physical causes mentioned in (2)'.[12]

Filling the premises out a little bit will help to convey the force of the argument, though I am aware that many reading this will be able to do this filling out for themselves. Claim (1) rests on such standard examples as someone's feeling thirsty, which is a conscious mental occurrence, leading to, or bringing it about that, he or she moves towards the fridge to get a beer. That movement is a physical effect of a conscious mental occurrence. It is obviously reasonable to think of this claim as being what we would call 'common sense'. Premise (2) is Papineau's formulation of what he calls the 'Completeness of Physics'. This represents, according to him, a finding of current physical science. It has therefore the status of a claim that philosophers must simply accept and cannot challenge. (2) then adds a scientific finding to the common sense of (1). What (3) adds is an apparently reasonable claim about causation. Papineau's view is that there can be overdetermination of effects by causes, but that it can hardly be true that whenever a conscious mental event causes a physical movement there is an over-determined effect – brought about by the physical causal chain but also by another causal chain initiated by the conscious mental occurrence. Again, there is a strong inclination to agree with that.

Before I start analysing this line of thought I want to cast some gentle aspersions on one feature of Papineau's general understanding of the issue that emerges in his discussion before he sets out the causal argument.[13] The feature is that Papineau says that what makes

---

[12]   These quotations come from Papineau, *Thinking about Consciousness*, 17–18.
[13]   Another feature of his discussion that I shall consider only in a footnote is that Papineau envisages a critic of materialism saying that it is evidence that the popularity of the position is, in some sense, merely a matter of fashion, that is has become popular only in the second half of the twentieth century. Papineau's response to this worry is to say that this fact has an historical explanation, which is that the position rests on the scientific principles of the completeness of physics, which is a scientific finding that has only emerged in that period. I am inclined to respond to this by remarking 1] that

consciousness so 'philosophically interesting' is that 'having a conscious experience is like something'.[14] This is an insight that he credits to Nagel, and one remarkable feature of current philosophical discussion of the mind/body problem is how many philosophers share this view. I am sceptical about two components of this remark. The first thing that strikes me as odd here is that if it is true that talking about 'being like something' captures a very important feature of consciousness, (which is the so-called Nagelian insight), why describe that as something that makes consciousness *'philosophically interesting'*? If it is the crucial property of consciousness then it is presumably a feature that anyone theorising about it – whether a philosopher or not – needs to take note of. To think that this important feature makes the phenomenon 'philosophically' interesting is, in effect, to think that the question as to its status is a philosophical question, an attitude that this essay is dedicated to undermining. The second reservation that I wish to advance is that it seems to me not at all likely that the Nagelian slogan does highlight the most important feature of consciousness. All I can do here is to make a start at generating a doubt. One question is; what does the slogan actually mean? One use of 'like' is to record similarities or resemblances – as in, 'She is like her elder sister'. But it cannot be a deep point about consciousness that it resembles something, since everything resembles something, or if there can be things which do not resemble anything, then there can be experiences which do not resemble anything. Another use of 'like' is simply to report the way something is. Thus when we ask 'What is her boyfriend like?' all we are requesting is to be told how the boyfriend is – is he, say, kind or witty, or handsome? We are not asking to be told that he resembles someone. Relative to this use to be told that consciousness is like something is to be told that it is some way – say painful – and, of course, conscious experiences have to be some way. Again, however, everything is some way! There is, therefore, the suspicion that the slogan really picks out nothing of special interest about consciousness at all.[15]

---

the fact that a view becomes popular rather late in our intellectual history is in itself no evidence at all that its acceptance is merely a matter of fashion, and so that is not a charge that needs answering, and 2] that it probably is not true that what leads philosophers to accept materialism is anything quite so general as the 'completeness of physics'.

[14]   Papineau, *Thinking about Consciousness*, 13.

[15]   I try to substantiate this scepticism in Snowdon 'On the What-it-is-like-ness of Experience' in *The Southern Journal of Philosophy* Vol **48** No. 1 (2010), 8–27

Philosophy and the Mind/Body Problem

I want now to engage with the causal argument itself. Before doing so, I need to stress that I do not think that the points I shall make amount to the last words about it. There are evidently responses to the points that I have not anticipated, and there are aspects to the argument I have not properly understood yet. However, the first point that I wish to make is that it is not clear that the argument as presented leads to the materialist conclusion. What is that conclusion? As Papineau puts it at one point it is the claim that 'conscious states must be ...identical to brain states, or something similar'.[16] Clearly by this Papineau means at least that *all* human conscious states must be physical states of the sort he picks out. Does the argument get to that conclusion? There are two problems. Are we in a position to affirm premise (1)? Many of us would be inclined to assent to the (type of) example that Papineau gives, but are we in a position to say that every conscious state causes a physical state? It would not be unreasonable to suppose that we do not know that that is true. But that immediately means that any consequence derived by this argument will only apply to conscious states that fall under (1), and we cannot confidently affirm that is all conscious states. There is a second restriction. The argument works by deriving a consequence from a problem with a certain sort of over-determination – expressed in premise (3). However, when Papineau expresses the denial of over-determination he merely says that 'the physical effects of conscious causes aren't always over-determined by distinct causes'. This means that the consequences of the need to rule out over-determination only applies to some cases. We have no idea how many is 'some'. If, therefore, the materialist conclusion does follow for some of the cases the general conclusion is more or less this – of those conscious states in us which have physical effects, (which we may not be able to say is even most of the) at least some of them are identical to physical states. As it stands this conclusion is not materialism.

Is there a reply to this problem? It seems to me that if there are no other problems with the argument then it can be said that it gives the conclusion that some conscious states are physical states. But is there a way to get from that to the general conclusion that materialism is true? One suggestion would be that it would simply be reasonable to generalise to such a conclusion. If some conscious mental states are physical states then all are. Now, that is certainly a proposal that has something to be said for it, but assessing it raises issues not often faced up to. Are we entitled or obliged to hold in advance that

[16]   Papineau, *Thinking about Consciousness*, 14.

33

Paul F. Snowdon

conscious experiences have basically a uniform nature? It is an assumption of philosophical debate about the mind/body problem that a uniform universal account will be true, but once that assumption has been queried it does not seem to be unquestionable.

A supplementary response though that could be made is that if the argument shows that some conscious mental states are physical states then it also shows that there are no sound arguments showing that that conscious states cannot be physical states. That would mean that anti-materialists have no arguments and so there cannot be any block to generalising to materialism. It would be a matter of some significance to have discredited standard anti-materialist arguments, but this response simply assumes that any problems for materialism must consist in highly general philosophical arguments, that if sound, apply to every case. That assumption is not legitimate once the assumption is no longer being made that the appropriate method here is simply philosophical argumentation. My feeling then is that there is a not obviously repairable gap in the argument, even if each premise is accepted.

I want next to suggest that a second problem (or gap) arises even if we accept all the main premises. The reason to adopt the property identification that is central to physicalism (for the purposes of engaging with the present argument) is that it is the way to avoid over-determination. The conscious mental property doing the work is the physical property doing the work; so the work is not being done twice over. But the movement of reasoning here is not obviously correct. The assumption is that only identity between properties avoids the threat of over-determination. How, though, have we been persuaded to think that there are no other possible relations between properties which can also avoid the over-determination threat? Thus, in the domain of objects, it is quite popular to think that there can be constitution relations between non-identicals – say the lump of clay and the statue – without that generating problems of causality. Maybe the same is possible for properties. I do not here want to develop such an account, nor am I affirming some such alternative is actually possible. The point is simply that the transition to identity is not obviously correct.

I want to suggest, though, that there are other problematic aspects to the argument. I want to engage next with premise (3) – the over-determination premise. Papineau's view is that over-determination is possible, but, he says that not every case where a conscious mental state causes a physical effect can be a case of over-determination. Now, it is not doubt true that as we approach this argument we would tend to be sceptical that causation by mental states could always be cases of over-determination. In fact, many of us would be rather amazed if it could ever be a case of over-determination. However, Papineau's own position is more problematic. He allows that there is nothing problematic in a general way about over-determination, and so for him the problem resides in the idea that it could always be over-determination. This, though, faces the following question; if most of the cases could be cases of over-determination, why could not all cases be so? One might add; what investigations should convince us that not all cases are cases of over-determination? It cannot, surely, be correct to simply base the central argument for materialism on a conviction which is based on no investigation or special argument.

Now, I want to make a general remark about premise (2) – the completeness of physics. Many important questions could be raised here, some suggested by what can be described as a bravura study that Papineau presents of the emergence of this idea, in the Appendix to his book. A viewpoint which seems reasonable to me, in the light of that Appendix, (though I may have missed part of its point), is that if anyone is seriously of a mind to think that conscious mental states are causally efficacious in the physical world without there being over-determination, he or she would simply not accept the claim which is what is understood as the completeness of physics. They would resist it by thinking that the empirical research which leads people to hold the view has overlooked something. It is not clear quite how specific one would have to be to react in this way. This sort of possible response is what leads me to say that this premise is one that one would be likely to endorse only if one is more or less already a physicalist.[17]

Finally, I want finally to pick out and express some scepticism about what seems to be Papineau's attitude towards the argument under investigation in two respects. First, Papineau points out, quite correctly, that the abstract claim which is the conclusion of the causal argument does not say what physical property any given conscious mental property is identical with. Science on the other hand can, by correlational research, 'establish specific pairings' but cannot, by itself, establish that the paired properties are actually identical. So, according to him, the abstract conclusion of the causal argument is 'needed' to 'licence the move from the' correlations to the 'identifications'.[18] Two things seem questionable about this attitude.

---

[17] Perhaps I should say – only if one is already not any sort of dualist. Clearly eliminativists, who are not physicalists in the sense meant here, can endorse this premise.

[18] All quotes here are from Papineau, *Thinking about Consciousness*, 21.

Paul F. Snowdon

First, an established correlation between mental state (type) M1 and physical state (type) P1 in itself does not yield an identity. Maybe they are simply instantiated together without being identical. No philosophical argument or principle can validate the inference to identity from correlation since such an inference is not safe. More significantly, though, the attitude seems to be that empirical research, which is to say science, needs an abstract philosophical argument to support claims about specific property identities. This seems highly unlikely. Surely scientific research can accumulate evidence of property identities given its own resources. It is not necessary to explain here how that is possible. All that is required is to acknowledge it obviously is possible. Further, unless this were possible it is hard to see how the general philosophical argument itself could work, since it depends on the general claim that physics is complete, which presumably rests on property identifications prior to the general philosophical argument. Second, Papineau says (on page 23) that 'there remains the possibility that the anti-materialist arguments to be examined later will show that conscious mind and brain cannot be identical. If this is so, then one of the premises of the causal argument must be false, And in that case premise 1 seems a likely a candidate as any.' This however seems to pitch us back to a point made above about Smart. First, Papineau evidently assumes that should any difficulty emerge it will be from philosophical arguments of the kind he is about to consider. But that is unjustified, unless we suppose that the problem is a philosophical issue. Second, it confers upon the argument a character rather different to how it seems to be presented. Initially it seemed to be an argument that should convince us that there are no difficulties with materialism, since it shows us that it is true. Now it becomes an argument that subsequent investigation – of whatever sort – might undermine. It becomes like Smart's argument a ceteris paribus argument, and the idea that it is a definitive argument has been adandoned.

I have tried to generate a sense that both the arguments of Smart and of Papineau are not as powerful as their proponents think, and thereby to at least raise the question whether philosophers have convincingly supported materialism.

4. Conclusion

In a short paper like this it is impossible to present a strong case in favour of the major cultural shift that is needed if its central claim about the limitations of philosophy are correct. Its assessment of

Philosophy and the Mind/Body Problem

each argument it deals with will no doubt be met by the counter-claim that these assessments are defective and overlook something. Or the overall argument will be met by the claim that there is a power-ful but overlooked argument for or against materialism. This is inev-itable. On the other side we can say a few things. 1] If the central idea in this paper is worth some time of day its defence has to start some-where, with all these inevitable limitations. 2] I hope that the negative evaluation of the typical arguments offered by both sides is not obvi-ously flawed, and if that is granted my general claim receives some support. 3] There is, it seems to me, the strong general point that the debate about the nature of conscious mental states is a debate about the real nature of processes that we undergo, and are familiar with in their relatively superficial aspects, and investigations into such matters seems, in a broad sense, scientific and empirical. I hope these considerations make the proposal worth thinking about. I do not propose though to try to think through here what the cultural consequences of acceptance of this idea would be, beyond remarking that the consequences would relate both to the conduct by philoso-phers of the mind/body debate, but also to the way philosophers discuss serious ontological questions generally.[19]

University College London
p.snowdon@ucl.ac.uk

[19] I am very grateful to Anthony O'Hear for the invitation to take part in the lecture series out of which this volume grew, and also to Adam Ferner for help both with the actual talk and with the paper. I also wish to thank Lucy O'Brien, Rory Madden, Penelope Rowlatt, and others who took part in a seminar at UCL at which the paper was read, and to a number of people in the audience at the talk in Royal Institute. Many thanks too to Joel Yurdin and the seniors at Haverford College for discussion of the issues raised here.

On Parfit's View That We Are Not Human Beings

ERIC T. OLSON

Abstract

Derek Parfit claims that we are not human beings. Rather, each of us is the part of a human being that thinks in the strictest sense. This is said to solve a number of difficult metaphysical problems. I argue that the view has metaphysical problems of its own, and is inconsistent with any psychological-continuity account of personal identity over time, including Parfit's own.

1. The Narrow Criterion

Derek Parfit endorses a view of personal identity over time that he puts like this:

> If some future person would be uniquely psychologically continuous with me as I am now, and this continuity would have its normal cause, enough of the same brain, this person would be me. If some future person would neither be uniquely psychologically continuous with me as I am now, nor have enough of the same brain, this person would *not* be me. In all other cases, there would be no answer to the question whether some future person would be me.[1]

He calls this a 'narrow, brain-based psychological criterion'. It is 'psychological' by saying that someone can be me only if he is then psychologically continuous with me as I am now – or rather uniquely so, to rule out branching. 'Narrow' views say that our persistence requires psychological continuity with some physical qualification, for instance that one's basic mental capacities be 'continuously physically realized'.[2] 'Broad' psychological-continuity views, by contrast, say that anyone uniquely psychologically continuous with me, no matter how he got to be that way, is me. Suppose I underwent what Shoemaker calls a 'brain-state transfer': my brain is erased and its contents copied to your brain, resulting in someone

---

[1]   'We are Not Human Beings', *Philosophy* **87** (2012), 5–28.
[2]   Peter Unger, *Identity, Consciousness, and Value* (New York: Oxford University Press, 1990), 109.

doi:10.1017/S13582461115000107   © The Royal Institute of Philosophy and the contributors 2015
Royal Institute of Philosophy Supplement **76** 2015

psychologically like me but otherwise like you. This person would be me on a broad view but not on a narrow one, since my mental capacities would not be continuously realized: the machine simply destroys them and creates new capacities just like them in your brain.[3] Parfit's version says that psychological continuity has to be caused by the continued existence of my brain or a sizeable part of it, making it 'brain-based'.

In fact Parfit doesn't say that the brain-state-transfer recipient would not be me, but that there is no answer to the question of whether he would be.[4] For someone *not* to be me, Parfit says, he must be neither uniquely psychologically continuous with me nor have enough of my brain. Thus, because the transfer recipient would be uniquely psychologically continuous with me but would have none of my brain, he would be neither me nor not me. The same goes for the being left behind with my original brain, now erased: he could not be me because he would not be psychologically continuous with me, and could not be distinct from me because he would have my brain.

The narrow criterion is an answer to the question of what it takes for us to persist through time. Parfit has recently argued from this and other considerations to an answer to another question: what are we? His proposal here that we are not human beings. Rather, each of us is the thinking part of the human being: something like the brain. It is this second view that I will be mainly concerned with. But the narrow criterion is interesting in itself, and I will start with it.

2. Peculiarities of the Narrow Criterion

Recall Shoemaker's brain-state transfer, where my brain is erased and its contents copied to another brain, resulting in someone uniquely

---

[3]   My mental capacities don't exist in electronic form within the machinery, though the information represented in my mental contents does. For a good definition of psychological continuity, see Sydney Shoemaker, 'Personal Identity: A Materialist's Account', in Shoemaker and Richard Swinburne (eds), *Personal Identity* (Oxford: Blackwell, 1984), 89–91. The transfer story is from page 108.

[4]   When Parfit says that the question of whether someone would be me has no answer, I take him to mean no straight, yes-or-no answer. Rather, the person would be neither definitely me nor definitely not me, much as the answer to the question of whether it's raining may be that it's neither definitely raining nor definitely not raining. If this is right, then the question *has* got an answer – a unique correct answer, in fact – and Parfit's formulation is misleading. But I don't know what else he could mean.

On Parfit's View That We Are Not Human Beings

psychologically continuous with me but with none of my brain. According to the narrow criterion, this person would be neither me nor not me. But if my brain states were copied to *two* beings, both recipients would definitely not be me. (None would be either uniquely psychologically continuous with me nor have enough of my brain.) Why should there be a definite fact about my survival in a double transfer but not in a single transfer? The reason is not that branching is always fatal: if each half of my brain were transplanted into another head, the narrow view implies that each resulting person would be neither me nor not me, since each would have enough of my brain. So I definitely don't survive in the double transfer, but there is no answer as to whether I survive in the single transfer or in the double brain transplant. Why this combination of verdicts?

Parfit's thinking may be that our persistence through time consists of two factors: unique psychological continuity and the persistence of enough of the same brain. If both are present, you survive. If both are absent, you perish. If just one is present, you neither survive nor perish. The first factor is present in the single but not in the double transfer; the second is absent in both. So you perish in the double transfer but your fate is indeterminate in the single transfer. In the double transplant, the second factor – having enough of the same brain – is present, but not the first; so again it is indeterminate what happens to you. If this is right, we can put the narrow criterion more clearly like this (call it View 1):

A future person is me if he is uniquely psychologically continuous, then, with me as I am now, and he then has enough of my brain. A future person is not me if he is then neither uniquely psychologically continuous with me nor has enough of my brain. Otherwise there is no answer to the question of whether a future person would be me.

But whatever its attractions, View 1 appears to be inconsistent. Imagine a 'half-successful double-brain transplant'. Each of my cerebral hemispheres is transplanted into a different head. One recipient ends up psychologically continuous with me, but the second hemisphere is erased so that the one who gets it is not psychologically continuous with me. View 1 implies that the first recipient is definitely me, since he is uniquely psychologically continuous with me by having enough of my brain.[5] And the two recipients are definitely

---

[5] One cerebral hemisphere is clearly enough. No psychological-continuity theorist that I know of would deny that one could survive a hemispherectomy – a real though rare operation. And Parfit himself says that

Eric T. Olson

distinct from each other. It follows that the second recipient, the one with the 'erased' hemisphere, is definitely not me. (If $x = y$ and $y \neq z$, then $x \neq z$.) Yet View 1 implies there is no answer to the question of whether the second recipient is me, since he has enough of my brain but is not psychologically continuous with me. (The narrow criterion as stated has the same implication.)

Parfit's formulation suggests a way of avoiding this problem. Maybe someone's having enough of my brain, by itself, does nothing to enable me to survive, but is relevant only if it supports psychological continuity. This gives the two factors, unique psychological continuity and having enough of the same brain, an unequal status: though survival requires both, the second makes a difference only when it accompanies and causes the first. That would give us something like this (View 2):

> A future person is me if he is uniquely psychologically continuous, then, with me as I am now, and this is caused by his then having enough of my brain. A future person is not me if he is not then psychologically continuous with me. Otherwise there is no answer to the question of whether a future person would be me.

This avoids inconsistency by implying that someone who had enough of my brain but was not psychologically continuous with me would definitely not be me. But it isn't going to make anyone happy. Imagine a variant of the brain-state transfer that copies my states to another brain without erasing them from mine. View 2 implies that both resulting people would be neither me nor not me, since each would be psychologically continuous with me but not uniquely so. (View 1 and the original narrow criterion have the same implication.) Yet the procedure does me no more harm than an MRI scan. Surely I could survive it if I could survive anything.

We could block this implication by amending the first clause (View 3):

> A future person is me if he is psychologically continuous, then, with me as I am now, this is caused by his then having enough of my brain, and no one else relates in these ways to me then. A future person is not me if he is not then psychologically continuous with me. Otherwise there is no answer to the question of whether a future person would be me.

---

someone who was psychologically continuous with me by getting half my transplanted brain would be me if the other half were destroyed: see *Reasons and Persons* (Oxford: Clarendon Press, 1984), 254.

On this view the person who had my brain at the end of the variant transfer would be me because he alone, after the transfer, would be both psychologically continuous with me and such that this was caused by his having enough of my brain. But this is again inconsistent. It implies that the recipient of the transfer (who would have none of my brain) would be neither me nor not me, since he would satisfy neither the first nor the second clause. Yet if I am definitely the one who has my brain after the transfer, and the one with my brain is definitely not the transfer recipient, then I am definitely not the recipient.

We could make View 3 consistent by changing its second clause (View 4):

> A future person is me if he is psychologically continuous, then, with me as I am now, this is caused by his then having enough of my brain, and no one else relates in these ways to me then. A future person is not me if he is either not then psychologically continuous with me or hasn't got enough of my brain. Otherwise there is no answer to the question of whether a future person would be me.

In this case the variant-transfer recipient would satisfy the second clause, and thus would definitely not be me. View 4 has the important consequence that there can be indeterminacy only where two or more beings are at once psychologically continuous with me and have enough of my brain (or perhaps where psychological continuity or the like holds to an intermediate degree). Yet Parfit clearly wants to say that there is indeterminacy in a far wider range of cases – any where no amount of reflection yields any strong conviction about who would be who.

What should Parfit say here? View 4 has no apparent advantage over the usual, industry-standard narrow psychological-continuity view:

> A future person is me *iff* he is then psychologically continuous with me as I am now, this continuity is continuously physically realized, and at no time between now and that future date do two people relate in this way to me as I am now.

This differs from View 4 by not requiring you to have the same brain to survive, and by implying that you definitely don't survive in the double brain-transplant case. More generally, it rules out any indeterminacy except in cases where the individual conditions hold to an intermediate degree. Whether that makes it more or less attractive than View 4 depends on why anyone might be drawn to Parfit's narrow criterion in the first place. That, unfortunately, is a question he never answers.

3. Why Parfit Thinks We're Not Human Beings

I turn now to Parfit's view that we are not human beings. Why does he say this? And why does he suppose instead that we are parts of human beings?

We *appear* to be human beings – that is, human organisms. I see a human being in the mirror. Isn't it *me* I see?

There is also a powerful argument for this view. Normal human beings can think. In fact they seem to have the same psychological properties that we have. But if they do, yet we are not human beings, it follows that there are two thinking beings wherever we thought there was just one. Human beings will also satisfy ordinary definitions of 'person', such as Locke's: the human being I see in the mirror is 'a thinking intelligent being, that has reason and reflection, and can consider itself as itself, the same thinking thing, in different times and places'.[6] So there are two different people thinking these thoughts. How could I ever know which one I am – the animal person or the nonanimal person? If I think I'm the nonanimal person, the animal person will be equally convinced, on the same grounds, that *he* is the nonanimal. No possible evidence, it seems, could favour one alternative over the other. Even if I were not a human being, it's hard to see how I could ever know it. The obvious solution to this problem of 'too many thinkers' is to say that we are human beings.

Most of those who deny that we are human beings try to avoid the problem by saying that human beings are not psychologically just like we are: despite appearances, they don't think, or satisfy Lockean definitions of personhood. But that is hard to defend. What could prevent a normal human being from using its brain to think? If human beings don't think, that can only be because it is metaphysically impossible for a living organism to have any mental property at all. The property of being alive – alive in the sense that organisms are alive – must be incompatible with the property of having beliefs or being conscious. What appears to be a living, conscious being would have to be a compound of a living but unconscious being and a conscious but nonliving being. This is a sort of substance

---

[6] John Locke, *An Essay Concerning Human Understanding*, ed. P. Nidditch (Oxford: Clarendon Press, 1975), 335.

dualism – not Descartes' dualism of mind and matter, but a monstrous dualism of mind and life.

Parfit denies that we are human beings for three reasons. The first is familiar: our being human beings – 'animalism' – has counterintuitive consequences about our persistence – consequences inconsistent not just with the narrow criterion but with any psychological-continuity account of personal identity over time.[7] Suppose your brain were put into my head. The resulting person would remember your life, and not mine. He would have your beliefs, preferences, plans, and other mental properties, for the most part at least. Who would he be? Animalism implies that he would be me with a new brain. The operation simply moves an organ from one animal to another, like a liver transplant.[8] There are two human beings in the story; one of them loses its brain and becomes an empty-headed vegetable or corpse, and the other has its brain removed and replaced with yours. According to animalism, you are the donor organism and I am the recipient. You get an empty head; I get your brain. I should wake up mistakenly convinced that I was you.

Most people find it more plausible to suppose that the one who got your transplanted brain would be you. But no human being would go with its transplanted brain. It would follow that even though you are never actually going to have a brain transplant, you have a property that no human being has, that of *possibly* going with your transplanted brain. And in that case you are not a human being. This is the *transplant problem*.

Parfit's second objection to our being human beings is subtly different.[9] Suppose your brain is removed from your head as before, only this time it's kept alive in a vat rather than transplanted. It may be possible for your brain in this condition to think more or less normally. (This is contentious, though many philosophical thought experiments assume it. I won't dispute it here.) That would make it a

---

[7]   'We are Not Human Beings', 9–11

[8]   If an entire detached brain *would* be an organism (see Peter van Inwagen, *Material Beings* (Ithaca: Cornell University Press, 1990), 169–181, let only the cerebrum be transplanted. This applies also to the remnant-person problem described below.

[9]   Mark Johnston, '"Human Beings" Revisited: My Body is Not an Animal', in Dean Zimmerman, ed., *Oxford Studies in Metaphysics* **3** (Oxford: Oxford University Press, 2007), 33–74; Parfit, 'We Are Not Human Beings', 11–12; Eric Olson, 'The Remnant-Person Problem', in Stephan Blatti and Paul Snowdon, eds., *Essays on Animalism* (Oxford: Oxford University Press, forthcoming).

person. This 'remnant person' would not be a human being – that is, an organism. It would be alive only in the way that a kidney awaiting transplant is alive–in that its individual cells are kept alive. Nor was it previously a human being: there was only one human being there before your brain was removed, and the operation merely gave it an empty head.

That some people are not organisms is perfectly compatible with *our* being organisms. It could be that we are human beings and God is an immaterial person. But if some *human* people were not organisms, we ought to wonder why there isn't such a person associated with every human being. If an inorganic human person could live in a vat, why not in a head? And if there were such a person in my head, he would either be a second person in addition to me, which would be absurd, or he would be me, in which case I should not be a human being.

Animalists will also find it hard to say where the remnant person could have come from. If she existed (and was a person) before the operation, they will have to say that there were then two people within your skin: the human being who got an empty head and the remnant person who went into the vat. Presumably there would again be two people wherever we thought there was just one. If the remnant person did not exist before the operation, on the other hand, then the operation must have brought her into being. But how can you create a new person just by cutting away sustaining tissues?

It's hard to find a plausible account of the nature of remnant people and of what happens to them in this case that is compatible with animalism, or with any other view according to which we are the size of human beings. This is the *remnant-person problem*.

Finally, Parfit says, animalism faces its own problem of too many thinkers: the *thinking-parts problem*.[10] Isn't your *brain* conscious and intelligent? It would be (we have supposed) if it were kept alive in a vat. But that could hardly *make* your brain conscious and intelligent: it couldn't be that the surrounding tissues prevent the brain in your head from thinking or being conscious, and removing it from its natural habitat would suddenly give it those capacities. If so, then your brain must be conscious and intelligent even now. It must be a person by any ordinary definition. Yet if you are a human being, your brain isn't you. Animalism appears to imply that you have a smaller person within you. How, then, could you ever know

[10]   'We Are Not Human Beings', 13f.; see also Eric Olson, *What Are We?* (New York: Oxford University Press, 2007), 215–219.

whether you are the animal person or the brain person? This looks no less worrying than the original thinking-animal problem.

4. The Embodied-part View

Parfit says there is 'an obvious solution' to all four problems: the thinking-animal problem, the transplant problem, the remnant-person problem, and the thinking-parts problem. It is that we are not human beings, but parts of them. Specifically, each of us is the part that thinks our thoughts in the strictest sense: we are 'the conscious, thinking, and controlling parts of human beings'.[11] Parfit assumes that an organism thinks by having a smaller part that thinks – the brain or some part of the brain – much as a locomotive is powerful by having a powerful engine as a part. (I take 'thinking' to include all mental activites and properties.) The organism has its mental properties derivatively. But not every part of a thing can think only derivatively: it can't be that an organism thinks by having a smaller part that thinks, and that smaller part thinks by having an even smaller thinking part, and so on forever. At some point there must be something that thinks in its own right. That thing is the person.

So the proposal makes three claims: (1) for every thinking organism, there is just one nonderivative thinker, which (2) is a part of the organism and (3) is the person. Parfit calls this the *embodied-part view*. (The name, I presume, alludes to the fact that in normal cases we are 'attached' parts of human beings rather than detached or 'disembodied' ones kept in a vat or the like. 'Thinking-part view' would be a more perspicuous name, as it would tell us what part of the human being each of us is. But I will adopt Parfit's terminology in order to avoid confusion with the thinking-parts problem.)

This would solve the thinking-animal problem by implying that human organisms don't really think. (I will discuss why not in the next section.) In a way, perhaps, the animal is a thinker in addition to me. But it thinks only insofar I am a part of it, whereas I think independently of my parthood relations to other thinkers. There is only one true, nonderivative thinker of my thoughts. I can know that I am not the human being because I know that I am the true thinker of my thoughts – arguably it belongs to the content of first-person thoughts that they refer to the being who thinks them nonderivatively.

11 'We Are Not Human Beings', 14.

It would solve the transplant problem by implying that you would go with your transplanted brain. You are the brain (or some part of it) all along. The operation does not change your size, but literally moves you from one head to another, like repotting a plant.

It would solve the remnant-person problem by saying that the remnant person is you. Again, the operation simply moves you from your head to the vat.

And it would solve the thinking-parts problem by saying that there is only one part of a human being that thinks nonderivatively: me. I have no thinking parts.

The proposal has a further advantage over animalism that Parfit doesn't mention. Some say that in special cases of conjoined twinning, a single human being has two brains that function as independently as yours and mine.[12] In such cases, they argue, there are two different people. So at least one of those people, and probably both, must be something other than a human being. But if a two-headed human being would 'contain' two people who were not animals, we should expect each ordinary human being to contain one nonanimal person – someone of the same metaphysical nature as the 'twin people'. So animalism implies that there are two people wherever we thought there was just one, an animal person and a non-animal person. The embodied-part view solves the problem by saying that the number of people in both twinning cases and ordinary ones is the number of brains.[13]

Solving these five hard problems is a great merit, and the embodied-part view deserves a hearing. Its implication that we are just a few inches tall, or that few of us have ever really seen ourselves or anyone else, would be a small price to pay. I think the view faces far more serious metaphysical objections. It also looks incompatible with anything like Parfit's narrow criterion. Alterations to make it compatible create further problems, as well as diminishing its problem-solving virtues.

---

[12]   Tim Campbell and Jeff McMahan, 'Animalism and the Varieties of Conjoined Twinning', *Theoretical Medicine and Bioethics* **31** (2010), 285–301.
[13]   Animalists have their own responses to these problems. On the transplant objection, see Olson, *The Human Animal* (New York: Oxford University Press, 1997), 42–69; on the remnant-person problem, see Olson, 'The Remnant-Person Problem'; on the thinking-parts problem, see van Inwagen, *Material Beings*, 81–97, Olson, *What Are We?*, 215–219; on the twinning problem, see van Inwagen, *Material Beings*, 188–212, Olson 'The Metaphysical Implications of Conjoined Twinning', *Southern Journal of Philosophy* **52** (2014), 24–40.

On Parfit's View That We Are Not Human Beings

5. Thinking-subject Minimalism

Which part of the organism is the nonderivative thinker, the 'thinking part'? Perhaps we can assume that it would have to include at least some of the brain. It couldn't be a hand or a finger. But that is consistent with its being the animal's upper half, or the head, or the entire brain, or this or that part of the brain. Which is it? For that matter, why not the entire organism? Why must an organism have a smaller part that thinks nonderivatively? Why, in other words, should it be impossible for an organism think in its own right?

The embodied-part view implies that this question must have an answer. If there were no saying what part of the organism was the thinking part, there would be no saying what we are – whether heads or brains or even whole organisms. That would be incompatible with the claim that we are not human beings.

Parfit says little about this. He suggests that the thinking part is no larger than a brain, but never says why. I suppose the answer must be something like this: a true thinker has to be made up of all and only the objects directly involved in its thinking. Human beings cannot think because they have superfluous parts – feet, for instance – that have no direct involvement in their mental activities (or rather, those going on within them). Having feet as parts is metaphysically incompatible with thinking. So my feet cannot be parts of me. Call this principle *thinking-subject minimalism*.[14] Without it or something similar, it would be entirely arbitrary to say that I am a brain rather than some other part of an animal, or indeed a whole animal.

I think minimalism is trouble. As far as I know, the only argument for it is that it would help solve the five problems (if that counts). It certainly gets no support from Parfit's narrow criterion, or from his view that we are essentially thinking beings. In fact on closer examination it looks incompatible with them.

Consider first how it could be generalized. Minimalism can hardly be just a principle about thinking. If an animal cannot think because it has parts not directly involved in its thinking, something analogous ought to hold for other activities. Because an animal has parts not directly involved in its walking, for instance, it must walk only in a derivative sense. There must to be a unique part of the animal that walks strictly speaking: its walking part. It will presumably be different from the part that talks, the part that eats, and the part that sleeps, since the things directly involved in an animal's walking will not be those directly involved in its talking, eating, or sleeping. And these

---

[14]   Olson, *What Are We?*, 87–90.

Eric T. Olson

other parts will be different from each other. What we think of as a single being that does many things must really be an assemblage of many beings that each do only one thing. I, the thinking part, never do anything but think. It would be impossible for me to walk or talk or eat, except in the loose and derivative sense of being a part of an animal that has walking, talking, and eating parts. I only give orders; other beings, which are not even parts of me, carry them out. In this respect minimalism resembles the Cartesian view that I am an immaterial substance.

If that isn't worrying enough, it will be hard to say what parts of an organism are directly involved in thinking or any other activity, as opposed to only indirectly involved or not involved at all. Since I couldn't think unless my brain had a supply of oxygenated blood, my heart and lungs are involved in my thinking. But if the thinking part of the animal is no bigger than the brain, they're not directly involved. (Neither, presumably, are those parts of the brain that deliver the blood.) Why not? What is it for something to be directly involved in someone's mental activities?

Walking is easier to visualize. Which part of an animal is the walking part? When I swing my arms as I walk, are they *directly* involved in my walking, as my feet are, or only indirectly involved? What could settle this question? And even my feet have parts that make no evident contribution to my walking – toenails, for instance. At most only certain parts of my feet seem directly involved. But which ones? Suppose I have excess water in my feet owing to poor circulation, hindering my walking. In that case it seems that not all the water molecules in my feet would be directly involved in my walking, though some must be. Yet it's not as if some of these molecules are the excess ones. What hinders my walking is not the presence of particular molecules in addition those that 'belong there', but simply that there is too much water.

I doubt whether there is any principled way of saying which molecules are directly involved in my walking, which are only indirectly involved, and which are not involved at all. The point is not merely epistemic. Not even complete knowledge of the microphysical details would tell us which are which. Nor is it merely that some molecules are neither definitely directly involved in my walking nor definitely not directly involved. If we are material things of any sort, we're bound to have fuzzy edges. The problem is that there is no principled way of drawing even a vague boundary around the walking part of me. And thinking is unlikely to differ in this respect from walking. Minimalism appears to imply that there is no saying which things are parts of me, and thus no saying which thing I am.

50

But there is trouble for minimalism even if there really is an absolute distinction between the things directly involved in thinking and those not directly involved. If some things are directly involved in my thinking generally, some will be directly involved in specific mental activities. Some neurones will be directly involved when I imagine people's faces; others – different ones – will be directly involved when I try to remember their names. And any reason to suppose that a true thinker must be composed of just those things directly involved in its thinking looks like an even better reason to suppose that a true imaginer or rememberer must be composed of just those objects directly involved in its imagining or remembering, respectively. The thing that imagines faces will be either too big to remember names, by having parts not directly involved in that remembering, or too small, by not including such parts – or both, of course. More generally, if it makes sense to speak of a neurone's being directly involved in thinking, then every mental activity will involve different neurones, and must therefore be performed by a different part of the organism. These parts may overlap. There may even be a part they all share (the reticular activating system, perhaps). But they are nevertheless different objects.

It follows that a human being hasn't got one nonderivative 'general' thinker within it, but rather a crowd of narrow specialists: one that only imagines, another that only remembers, a third that does nothing but think about metaphysics, and so on. What we take to be a person able to perform all sorts of mental operations is really many beings, each able to perform only one. If, as Locke said, a person is by definition both intelligent and self-conscious, then there are no people, and we do not exist. That is incompatible not only with Parfit's embodied-part view, but with any familiar account of what we are.

6. The Embodied-part View and Identity Over Time

But set aside worries about thinking-subject minimalism. Suppose each human being really has got a unique thinking part. For the sake of simplicity, let it be the brain, though the point is the same whatever part of the organism it might be.

Physiologists tell us that my brain came into being early in gestation, long before it could support any mental activity. If I am my brain, as the embodied-part view appears to imply, then I must have persisted then without any psychological continuity. That is incompatible with any view on which psychological continuity is necessary for me to persist, including Parfit's narrow criterion.

Or imagine that when I die my brain is fixed in formaldehyde and kept in a jar. It looks as if my brain would still exist then (and the same would go for any other part of the organism that I might be). That is, the brain in the jar is the brain that was once in my head. But if my brain could be pickled, and I am my brain, then I could be pickled. Again, I could persist without being psychologically continuous with anything.

Someone might argue that the pickled brain was never in my head, but is a brand-new object created by the fixing process, and that the embryonic, precognitive brain does not survive to maturity, but ceases to exist when it begins to produce thought and is replaced by a new brain. But that would make our beliefs about the persistence of brains badly unreliable, casting doubt on the assumption that my brain could continue existing when transplanted or kept alive in a vat. If we are brains, that would undermine all claims about our persistence through time.

Now the narrow criterion as Parfit states it speaks only of what it takes for a future person to be me. It says nothing about future *non*-people, never mind past ones. It tells us what it takes for someone to persist *as a person*, but not what it takes for someone to persist in general. If my pickled brain would not count as a person (it certainly wouldn't then satisfy anything like Locke's definition), that might seem to make the narrow criterion compatible with my existing in the jar.

I think Parfit stated his view as he did because he assumed, like other psychological-continuity theorists, that a person is a person essentially, and none of us could exist as a nonperson. On that assumption it would make no difference if we replaced 'future person' in his account with 'future being': the two formulations would be logically equivalent. If Parfit really did mean to tell us only what it takes for someone to persist as a person, his narrow criterion would be radically incomplete. It would tell us nothing about what would happen to us in a wide range of cases. It would allow me to become a lifeless corpse, or even a laurel tree or a pillar of salt. It would be compatible with any claim at all about what sort of thing I could come to be, as long as I was not then a person. Nor would it tell us when we came into being: whether at the earliest point when there was the right sort of psychological continuity, at fertilization, or even earlier. I doubt whether that was Parfit's intention. It certainly isn't that of other psychological-continuity theorists.

7. Functioning Brains

Everything Parfit has ever said about personal identity rules out my existing in formaldehyde. If my brain could exist in formaldehyde, then I am not my brain. What am I, then? Parfit doesn't say. He makes only the suggestive remark that people stand to their brains as animals stand to their bodies.[15] The thought seems to be that the atoms making up an organism – a fish, say – also compose a second material thing that is not a fish, but rather the fish's body. This object is empirically indistinguishable from the fish for as long as the two coexist. They have the same shape, size, mass, chemical composition, anatomical and cellular structure, and so on. Yet they are different. One difference is that when the fish dies, it ceases to exist, while its body carries on in a nonliving state.

So an organism shares its matter with another object, its body, having different persistence conditions. And so does a human brain (supposing that that is the right organ): it shares its matter with the conscious, thinking, controlling part of a human being. When the brain loses the capacity to support thought, it simply ceases to function and carries on in a nonfunctioning state (like the fish's body); but the other thing (like the fish) vanishes. We might call this other thing the *functioning brain*. Since we are functioning brains and not brains, we cannot not exist in formaldehyde. Nor did we exist in an unconscious embryonic state.

I am sceptical about Parfit's metaphysics of organisms and their bodies.[16] I am even more sceptical about functioning brains. Why suppose that a brain shares its matter with an object physically identical to it but with different modal properties? Consider the claim that there is such a thing as my *waking brain*: a thing just like my brain except that it can exist only as long as it is awake. When I fall asleep, my waking brain instantly vanishes (replaced, perhaps, by a 'sleeping brain' that is essentially asleep). It returns to being when I wake up again. I can see no reason to believe in the existence of functioning brains that is not equally a reason to believe in the existence of waking brains. And if there are waking brains, there are probably also

---

[15] 'We Are Not Human Beings', 15. He does contrast our being brains with our being 'embodied minds' or 'embodied persons', saying that he prefers the last (15–17). But what these proposals amount to and how they differ is never explained.

[16] I discuss some better alternatives in 'The Person and the Corpse', in Ben Bradley *et al.*, eds., *The Oxford Handbook of Philosophy of Death* (New York: Oxford University Press, 2013), 80–96.

things just like brains except that they are essentially thinking about philosophy, essentially sober, or essentially north of the equator, and likewise for every combination of such properties. Where is this going to end? Is there, for *every* property my brain currently has, a thing just like it but having that property essentially?

That would be an extraordinary metaphysical claim, and we ought to accept it only on the basis of an extraordinary argument. Parfit gives no argument at all. In any event, the claim raises a problem of too many thinkers infinitely worse than those the embodied-part view was supposed to avoid. If there is any interesting connection between the mental and the physical, we should expect physically identical objects in physically identical surroundings to have the same mental properties.[17] So my waking brain, my sober brain, and all the other objects of their ilk ought to be psychologically identical to my functioning brain. If my functioning brain is a person in Locke's sense, then my waking brain and my sober brain will be too. There will be a vast number of people – probably an uncountable infinity – wherever we thought there was just one. How could I know which person I was? For all I could ever find out, it seems, I might be one who can exist only as long he continues writing this sentence. In that case I could never know anything about what it takes for me to persist through time.

Maybe there are functioning brains but no essentially waking brains and the like. But even if this mysterious claim were true, there would still be my brain itself (or some part of it): a thing physically and mentally identical to me, yet not me. It would be a second person within my skin. How could I know whether I was the brain person who could be pickled or the functioning-brain person who couldn't be? This is a version of the thinking-parts problem that Parfit thought he had solved. For that matter, our brains would be human people able to persist without psychological continuity, contradicting Parfit's narrow criterion.

Parfit will need to say that the functioning brain is the only thinking part of the organism, and that the brain itself thinks only in the loose and derivative sense of relating in some way to the functioning brain. Each normal human being contains only one person. But how could there be two physically identical objects, in identical surroundings, only one of which can think? The embodied-part view says that human beings cannot think because they have parts not directly

[17] Or at least the same intrinsic mental properties: my doppelganger in another galaxy may think about a city physically identical to Vienna, but he cannot think about Vienna.

involved in thinking. But this does nothing to explain why my brain can't think: it has exactly the same parts as my functioning brain, which by hypothesis are just those parts of the organism directly involved in my thinking.

So Parfit cannot solve the new thinking-parts problem in the way that he would solve the thinking-animal problem, by saying that my brain doesn't think because it has parts not directly involved in thinking. Nor can he solve it in the way that he would solve the original thinking-parts problem, by saying that I *am* my brain, as that is incompatible with the narrow criterion.

8. Alternatives

The best way of salvaging Parfit's views may be to say that my functioning brain is a *temporal* part of my brain (or of the relevant spatial part of my brain). The assumption here is that for every matter-filled region of space-time, there is a concrete material thing – just one – occupying precisely that region. This implies that every part of my brain's career is the career of a temporal part of my brain. This part, for as as long as it exists, is physically just like my brain. My functioning brain would then be the mereological sum of those temporal parts of my brain that function in the appropriate sense – or, better, the largest sum of its temporal parts, each of which is psychologically continuous with every other. It would have come into being several months after my brain did, when, in the course of my foetal or infant development, the right sort of psychological continuity first began. If my brain is fixed in formaldehyde, its preserved temporal parts will not be parts of my functioning brain either. And Parfit might take thinking-subject minimalism to apply to temporal as well as spatial parts, so that every temporal part of a thinker must be directly involved in its thinking. That would enable him to say that my brain cannot think for much the same reason that a human being cannot: because it has parts not directly involved in thinking (its foetal and pickled temporal parts). This would solve the thinking-parts problem – though it would retain the troubling commitment to thinking-subject minimalism. It is the view defended in Hud Hudson's fine book *A Materialist Metaphysics of the Human Person*.[18]

Parfit often argues in a way that seems to presuppose an ontology of temporal parts. For instance, he says that if there are such things as people, there must also be such things as 'day-people', who are just

[18]   Ithaca: Cornell University Press, 2001.

Eric T. Olson

like people except that they must have an uninterrupted stream of consciousness.[19] There is a day-person now writing these words, who will cease to exist when I next fall asleep. If you and I were composed of arbitrary temporal parts, some of them really would be day-people, and their existence would follow from our own. Otherwise their existence looks eminently doubtful. But over the course of his career Parfit has declined every opportunity to endorse an ontology of temporal parts.

Alternatively, he could give up the narrow criterion and say that we are brains in the ordinary sense. That would avoid both the thinking-parts problem and the mysterious ontology of functioning brains. It would imply, of course, that our persistence consists in some sort of brute-physical continuity. I really could be pickled. I would go with my brain if it were transplanted, but not because that organ secures psychological continuity. If you don't like that, Parfit could point out that *all* views of personal identity over time have unattractive consequences, and remind us that numerical identity is unimportant: whether a past or future being is me or someone else is not itself something that I have any reason to care about. What matters practically is some sort of psychological continuity.

Yet another possibility would be to say that we are immaterial, and solve the too-many-thinkers problems by saying that no material thing could ever think or be conscious. That would mean giving up both the narrow criterion and the embodied-part view, though it would have the considerable advantage of not requiring thinking-subject minimalism or any controversial claims about the ontology of material things.

Or he could concede that we are human beings after all. I cannot see that he has any better options than these.[20]

University of Sheffield
e.olson@sheffield.ac.uk

---

[19]   *Reasons and Persons*, 292.
[20]   For comments on ancestors of this paper I thank Radim Belohrad, Stephan Blatti, Galen Strawson, and Alex Moran. I am also grateful to Derek Parfit for discussions of these and related matters.

Ambulo Ergo Sum[1]

LUCY O'BRIEN

Abstract
It is an extraordinary thing that Descartes' famous *Cogito* argument is still being puzzled over; this paper is another fragment in an untiring tradition of puzzlement. The paper will argue that, if I were to ask the question 'do I have a grounds for thinking that I exist?' the *Cogito* could provide for a positive answer. In particular, my aim in this is to argue, in opposition to recent discussion by John Campbell, that there is a way of construing conscious thinking on which the *Cogito* can be seen to provide a non-question begging argument for one's own existence.

1. Do I Exist?

It is an extraordinary thing that Descartes' famous *Cogito* argument is still being puzzled over. For over three hundred years philosophers have argued about how long the *Cogito* argument is, about how many parts it has, about what it aims to do, and about whether it works. This paper is another fragment in that untiring tradition of puzzlement.

Let us assume that the *Cogito* seeks to answer the question 'do I exist?' If I were, for any reason, looking for re-assurance about my own existence and were thereby led to ask the question 'do I have a grounds for thinking I exist?' would the *Cogito* furnish me with a positive answer? I am going to argue that the *Cogito* can be construed in such a way that it does provide for a positive answer to that question. In the *Second Meditation*, Descartes engages in thought, judges 'I am thinking' (*cogito*), and from that, rightly in my view, infers 'I exist' (*sum*). We can do the same. On my understanding of it, the *Cogito* is an argument type that enables each of us to establish our own existence simply on the basis of our own conscious acts of thinking. A subject who engages in conscious thought, judges (on that basis) that they are thinking, may rightly infer on that basis that they exist.

[1] I am grateful for comments from audiences at the Royal Institute of Philosophy, at research seminars in Southampton and Dublin, and at the Oxford Graduate Conference and conference on 'Self and Agency' in Liege. Particular thanks for written comments to Daniel Whiting, and to Sarah Patterson and Rory Madden for helpful discussion.

doi:10.1017/S1358246115000090 ©The Royal Institute of Philosophy and the contributors 2015
Royal Institute of Philosophy Supplement **76** 2015

Lucy O'Brien

John Campbell in his 'Lichtenberg and the *Cogito*' argues in favour of *Cogito*-scepticism. Campbell claims that the *Cogito* is either too weak to provide us with an existential conclusion, or it is question begging.[2] Either way, the grounds of the *Cogito* do not, on his view, provide a subject with a reason to judge she exists.

My aim in this is to argue, against the *Cogito*-sceptic, that there is a way of construing conscious thinking on which the *Cogito* can be seen to provide a non-question begging argument for one's own existence.

2. Campbell's Objection to the *Cogito*

To start let us set out the target argument in the way that Campbell does, and state his objection. The target argument runs as follows:

Engagement in (1) A particular act of conscious thinking;
Judgment: (2) I am thinking;
Judgment, by inference: (3) I exist.[3]

So understood, the Cogito argument has three parts. The first part is not a premise or a judgment: it is an *occurrence*. In particular, it is an engagement in a particular act of conscious thinking. The second part of the argument is a judgment: the judgment 'I am thinking'. This judgment is supposed to be grounded in, but not inferred from, the first part – the engagement in a particular act of conscious thinking. The third part of the argument is the conclusion we are aiming at: the judgment 'I exist'. The judgment 'I exist' follows by inference from the judgment 'I am thinking'.

The target argument according to Campbell faces a dilemma: *either* we get to the conclusion by begging the question, *or* we do not get to conclusion.

[2]   John Campbell, 'Lichtenberg and the Cogito', *Proceedings of the Aristotelian Society*, **122** (2012), 361–378.
[3]   This way of setting out the argument is due to Peacocke's 'Descartes' Defended', *Aristotelian Society Supplementary Volume*, **86** (1), 109–125 to which Campbell's paper is a reply. Peacocke argues there, as I do here, that the *Cogito* is successful. And we are to a large extent in agreement as to why. Peacocke's defence rests on metaphysical and conceptual points: on the dependence of conscious events on subjects, and on what is required for mastery of the first person. My concern here is particularly to explore the implications of a thesis about *how* our thoughts depend on us as subjects, for a thesis of direct awareness of ourselves, and look at how that impacts on the success, or otherwise, of the *Cogito*.

Let us consider the *'either'* fork first. The claim, in essence, is that (3) needs to be assumed to get from (1) to (2): you need to have knowledge of your own existence i.e. knowledge of the conclusion 'I exist' in order to be able to move from engagement in the particular act of conscious thinking to the judgement that 'I am thinking'. The grounds for the claim that engagement in conscious acts of thinking are insufficient to ground judgements about thinkers are to a large extent the traditional Lichtenbergian grounds: '"Thinking is going on" is what one should say, just as one says "Lightning is occurring". Saying *"Cogito"* is too much, as soon as one translates it as "I am thinking"'[4]

How do I know *merely* from a particular act of conscious thinking that *I* am thinking? Maybe all I can know is that there is thinking going on? In order for me to know that the thinking occurrences are being had me, do I not already need to have some reason, either independent of the fact that I am thinking, or invoked by it, for believing that I exist? And if I need already to have these reasons, then I can get my transition between (1) and (2), but I have begged the question because I am using independent grounds for (3) to make the transition. Thus, the argument needs to assume what it seeks to establish to get from the first step – the act of conscious thinking – to the second. If the use of 'I' in (2) implies that a self exists, then you need to know you exist before you are entitled to use it to report your conscious thinking and so, as Campbell explains it:

> The transition from (1) to (2) therefore cannot be thought of as grounding or explaining one's knowledge of one's own existence.

(1) a particular conscious thought

Knowledge of my own existence

(2) I am thinking

(3) I exist

The downward arrows indicate transitions from one state to another. (This way of using arrows was suggested to me by

---

[4] George Lichtenberg, *Schriften und Briefe, Vol. II.* (Munich: Carl Hanser Verlag), §76, 412. (transl. Tyler Burge, 'Reason and the first Person' C. Wright, B. Smith & C. Macdonald (eds), *Knowing Our Own Minds*, (Oxford University Press, 2000).

Lucy O'Brien

Pryor 2012; see also Wright 2008.) The horizontal arrow indicates that my knowledge of my own existence is required for the transition from state (1) to state (2) to be capable of generating knowledge that I am thinking. In this situation, we cannot regard the transitions (1)–(3) as explaining how it is that I know of my own existence. Rather, my knowledge of my own existence has to come from somewhere else, somewhere quite outside the range of *Cogito*-style reasoning.[5]

Now let us turn to the '*or*' fork. The claim on this fork of the dilemma is that while there may be a way to get from (1) to (2), without assuming (3), it is a way that then does not allow us to get to (3).

Suppose we claim that we can ground the judgment 'I am thinking' in an engagement in a conscious act of thinking without already assuming that 'I exist' because uses of 'I' need not carry referential import. Rather in judging that 'I am thinking' I am operating with a use of 'I' that has merely perspectival import. To illustrate the possibility of a notion having perspectival, but not referential import, Campbell looks to the case of temporal notions. I may not realize that there are time zones when I identify the current time as '5 o'clock', but I am doing so relative to the time zone I occupy. It does not follow, he argues, that in holding that it is '5 o'clock' I am referring to that time zone.[6] The suggestion is that we may use 'I' in a way that is relative to the person I am but does not refer to the person I am. The thought seems to be that I may use 'I' in a way that is relative to the subject I am, even when I do not realize I am a one subject rather than another. And if that is so then we can get from (1) to (2) without assuming (3). However, we then face a problem with the move from (2) to (3). If we construe the 'I am thinking' non-referentially we are not then entitled to move from 'I am thinking' to 'I exist'. Using the arrow diagram used by Campbell we can represent the situation as follows:

(1) a particular conscious thinking

No assumption that I exist

(2) I am thinking

?

(3) I exist

---

[5] Campbell, 'Lichtenberg and the *Cogito*', 365.
[6] Ibid., 369.

3. Can We Avoid Begging the Question?

I think it is clear that if we withdraw to a use of 'I' which is non-referential, then there is no getting from (2) the judgment 'I am thinking to (3) the judgment 'I exist', unless we have a similarly 'non-existential' notion of existence – and what could that be? So, our only hope if we want maintain the claims of the *Cogito* to provide us with a way of gaining knowledge of our existence is to challenge the question-begging charge. In particular we need a way to challenge the claim that an engagement in a conscious act of thinking is not sufficient to warrant a subject in moving to the judgment 'I am thinking', unless she independently assumes her own existence.

Campbell compares the *Cogito* to Moore's famous 'Proof the External World' and draws out interesting parallels between the two.[7] Campbell construes Moore's argument as follows:

Engagement in (1b) a visual perception of your hands
Judgment: (2b) this is one hand, and this is another hand;
Judgment: (3b) external objects exist.[8]

Both arguments seem to have three components, the first of which is a psychological conscious occurrence, the second of which is an indexical or demonstrative judgment, and third of which is an existential judgment. In Moore's argument we have a conscious visual perception that grounds without inference the indexical judgment 'this is one hand, and this is another hand', from which we can infer the existential judgment that 'external objects exist'. In the *Cogito* argument we have a conscious act of thinking that grounds the indexical judgment 'I am thinking', from which we can infer the existential judgment that 'I exist'.

It is commonly objected that Moore's argument fails because we need to assume knowledge of the existence of external objects in order to be warranted in moving from (1b) to (2b). Now Moore's argument was famously thought to involve a problem of a similar kind to the Lichtenbergian problem that Campbell puts to the *Cogito* argument, namely that it is acceptable to move from (1b) to (2b), only when we have assumed or independently establish (3b) – which was supposed to be our conclusion. So again we're faced with the dilemma that, either we get to the conclusion by begging the question, or we don't get to the conclusion.

[7] G. E. Moore, 'Proof of an External World', *Proceedings of the British Academy*, **25** (1939), 273–300.
[8] Campbell, 'Lichtenberg and the *Cogito*', 376.

Lucy O'Brien

The familiar complaint against Moore's argument is usually fleshed out *via* an argument from illusion. Suppose I have a visual perception of my hands, and I judge on that basis that 'this is one hand, and this is the other hand', it may be objected that you cannot justifiably move to the conclusion that 'external objects exist', unless you assume that your visual experience was caused by your hands. After all, it is objected, if you had been hallucinating, or be subject to an illusion, you could have had the same visual experience and it *not* be caused by your hands. If that is true then it looks as though you are going to have to assume existence of external objects, alongside with your visual perception, in order to move to your conclusion that external objects exist – and that is begging the question. If instead we try to row back from the assumption that external objects exist, and construe the judgment 'this is one hand, and this is another hand' in such a way that can be grounded on the visual perception alone, we will not, the argument goes, have sufficient resources to reach an existential conclusion. When I judge that 'this is one hand, and this is another hand' I am not thereby referring to any external object. My uses of 'this' are used with perspectival, but non-referential, import and used properly across veridical and illusory cases.

So, we see a parallel objection to both the *Cogito* and to Moore's argument. In relation to both we can object that a conscious experience is not itself able to deliver up knowledge of the existence of objects: selves or hands. To draw our conclusions we need already to know that there is some object or self *beyond* the experience; we need to know that it is not a *mere experience* of nothing, had by nothing. But to rely on such knowledge would be to beg the question.

Despite so elegantly bringing out the parallels between the two arguments Campbell's central concern is in fact to claim a contrast between them. Campbell rehearses an increasingly popular defence of Moore's argument, but claims that a parallel response is not available to the defender of the *Cogito*. It is that claim I want to examine.

What is the popular defence of Moore's argument against the charge of question begging? It is to point out that while it is true that on certain ways of construing the nature of visual perception one would need to add a further assumption (that, say, an external object is the causal source, or the represented object, of the perceptual experience) in order to justifiably draw the conclusion that external objects exist, such a construal is not compulsory. There are other ways to construe the nature of visual experiences on which such an added assumption would not be required. Suppose, we take a relationalist, or direct realist view of visual experiences. On such a view to have a visual perception of a hand is to have an experience in virtue of standing in a direct relation to a hand. If there were no hand, there would be no such visual experience. Therefore, if we are actually seeing one hand and then another hand, that visual experience *can by itself* function as grounds for the judgment 'this is one hand, this is another hand' without any independent premise being required. So if, as Campbell puts it, it is possible to argue that the external object is not in fact 'beyond' or 'external to' the visual perception, but rather the visual experience 'encompass[es] the external object', then the visual experience will be 'enough on its own to generate knowledge of the existence of external objects'.[9]

Having rehearsed the resources of a relationalist response to the question-begging challenge facing Moore's argument, Campbell makes this intriguing remark: 'in contrast, in case of the *Cogito* there seems no possibility of a disjunctive or relational understanding of your relation with your thought on which your encounter with the thought encompasses not just the thought but the thinker'.[10]

For the remainder of this paper I want explore whether we should accept that there is no such possibility. Could we not construe what it is to be engaged in a conscious act of thinking in such a way that it 'encompass[es] me' and is 'enough on its own to generate knowledge' that I exist?

4. Solvitur Ambulando?

I want to suggest that the prospects for the view that in being engaged in a conscious act of thinking a subject has a direct experience of herself of a kind sufficient in itself to ground the judgment 'I am thinking' might be made more evident if we think about our experience of acts and activities other than thinking.

Let us, for example, think about the conscious activities of walking or jumping. Walking and jumping are things that I do. They are also things I am aware of doing as I do them.

The first question to ask about our awareness of such activities is whether we have any reason to be more skeptical of having a direct awareness of them, than that we have direct awareness of our hands or coffee cups. When I am conscious of my walking or my jumping, my walking and my jumping seems to be as immediate and directly accessible to me as anything given in perception. And when I am conscious of your walking or jumping, your walking

---

[9] Campbell, 'Lichtenberg and the *Cogito*', 377.
[10] Ibid.

and jumping seems to be as immediate and directly accessible to me as anything else given in perception.

The second question to ask is how we should understand the relation that holds between our awareness of the actions and activities, and our awareness of the agents that carry them out. Let us suppose you have an awareness of my walking. You see me walk across the room, for example. We would think it very odd if you were to claim that while you saw my walk you could not, or did not, see me. Rather, when you see me walking what you see *is me doing something*: you see me in a certain mode, carrying out a certain set of bodily movements that are my walking.

The thought is that if you put the answers to the two questions just asked together, then there is scope to claim that we can be directly aware of agents in being directly aware of their actions. If we are aware of activities or actions by being aware of an agent doing something, and we are directly aware of those actions then the agent would seem to be a candidate for being 'encompassed' within the experience of the activity.

If it turns out that there is no insurmountable impediment to my understanding my awareness of my action (walking or jumping) as a direct relation to these activities, and that the relationship between actions and activities and the agents that carry them out is such that if you are aware of the action or activity you are aware of a mode of an agent, then we begin to have the resources to mount a response, of a kind the relationalist about visual perception mounts against the charge that Moore's argument begs the question, to the charge that the *Cogito* begs the question.

There are three claims made by the view being mooted. The third is supposed to follow from a proper understanding of the first two. The three claims are:

1. *A direct awareness of action thesis*: when we consciously act we are directly aware of the activity/action. When we are conscious of others acting we are directly aware of the activity/action.
2. *An activities and actions as modes of an agent thesis*: activities or actions are dependent on agents, in virtue of being *modes* of agents – they are ways an agent is being, or has been.
3. *A direct awareness of agent thesis*: to be directly conscious of an activity/action is to be directly conscious of a way an agent is, and so directly conscious of an agent. (For example, to be directly conscious of a jumping is to be conscious of the jumper jumping, to be directly conscious of a walking is to be conscious of the walker walking.)

Let us suppose that claims 1–3 are true of our awareness of walking. If they are then we have reason to think we have available to us an argument that is capable of being used to establish our own existence that does not fall foul of either the insufficiency charge, or the charge of question begging. We can call the argument the *Ambulo* argument. Its structure is similar to that of the *Cogito,* and of Moore's argument, and comes in three parts: A psychological occurrence, an indexical judgment, and an existential claim:

Engagement in (1) A particular conscious walking;
Judgment: (2) I am walking
Judgment, by inference: (3) I exist.

The *Ambulo* – assuming theses 1–3 are true of a subject engaged in consciously walking – is successful in grounding in a non-question begging way the judgment 'I am walking'.

It is able to do so in the same way that Moore's argument is able to ground the judgment that external objects exist in our direct awareness of them. We have construed the experience of acting is such a way that the acting, and so the actor, is not beyond or external to the conscious experience, but is 'encompassed' in it. In consciously walking I'm directly aware of the walking and thereby of the walker, and can on that basis infer that I exist. And of course if the *Ambulo* works as a proof of my existence then there is shed more where that came from. For example:

Engagement in (1) A particular conscious jumping;
Judgment: (2) I am jumping;
Judgment, by inference (3) I exist.

Let us then turn back to the intricacies of the *Cogito.* If they can be made to work with the right assumptions about the nature of our experience of activities and their relations to agents, and if thinking is rightly understood as an activity of a subject – along the lines that walking and jumping are – might we in fact have a non-question begging *Cogito* argument. Suppose, as well 1–3, we also claim:

4. *Thinking is an activity of an agent thesis*: thinking is an activity of an agent in the same way that walking, jumping, and so on, are activities of an agent.

When we then go back to the *Cogito* we are able to see a form of argument which would, if what seems to be true for walking is true of thinking, provide us with conception of conscious activity that is able to give us direct awareness of ourselves if we are engaged in such an activity – and in doing so can ground the judgment, I am thinking, and in term the judgement 'I exist':

Engagement (1) A conscious act/activity of thinking
Judgement: (2) I am thinking
Judgment, by inference: (3) I exist

5. Gassendi's *Ambulo*

The idea that we should look to the *Ambulo* argument alongside the *Cogito* argument to throw light on the latter is not a new one. It is already there in Gassendi's objections to Descartes. Gassendi points out that there is nothing very special in the form of argument provided by the *Cogito* and claims that Descartes 'could have made the same inference from any one of [his] actions, since it is known by the natural light that *whatever acts exists*'.[11]

Descartes' replies to Gassendi as follows:

You say that I could have made the same inference from any one of my other actions, but that is far from the truth. Because my thought is the only one of my actions of which I am completely certain...For example, I can't say 'I am walking, therefore I exist', except by adding to my walking my awareness of walking, which is a thought. The inference is certain only if the premise concerns this awareness and not the movement of my body; because it can happen e.g. in dreams that I see to myself to be walking but am really not doing so. And so from the fact that I think I am walking I can very well infer the existence of a mind that thinks but not the existence of a body that walks. The same holds for all the other cases.[12]

For our purposes there are three things to note about this exchange. First, Descartes' objection parallels the standard objection to Moore's argument. He points out that we cannot know for certain that we are walking because we have erroneously had the experience

[11] J. Bennett (ed.), *Objections to the Mediations and Descartes' Replies*, 'Fifth Objections (Gassendi) and Descartes' replies: Objections to Second Meditation; Objection 1'. www.earlymoderntexts.com/pdfs/descartes1642/pdf, page 86.
[12] J. Bennett (ed.), *Objections to the Mediations and Descartes' Replies*, 'Fifth Objections (Gassendi) and Descartes' replies: Objections to Second Meditation; Reply to Objection 1', www.earlymoderntexts.com/pdfs/descartes1642/pdf, page 87.

of walking even when we are not – for example, when we are dreaming. This fact is supposed to undermine the possibility of the *Ambulo* giving us knowledge that we exist. Descartes assumes that our experience of walking is not to be construed as essentially involving walking. But if we were to adopt relationalism about our experience of walking we could deny this. Second, Descartes does *not* deny that 'it is known by the natural light that whatever acts exists' and does not dispute the idea that if you know the act you know that the actor exists. The third thing to note about Descartes' response to the argument is that his concern is to emphasize that in the case of walking, in contrast to thinking, you don't know the act with certainty. You might think you are walking – as in a dream – but you might be wrong. So, what thinking is supposed to give us is certainty. The point here is that if walking is activity of mine, then nothing has been said to block a non-question begging argument for my existence. The conditional nature of that claim should be noted here. If walking is *not* an activity of mine that picks out a way I am, then being aware of walking will not be a way of being aware of myself. And Descartes might indeed be skeptic about walking as an action of the subject. It is a delicate question whether Descartes takes the subject of my bodily activities to be me – if the subject of those activities is a conjoined mind and body. If, instead, only acts of the mind are properly acts of the subject, then walking might be some act of mind that is mine, plus a caused or conjoined bodily activity which is the act of some other thing. If that were the case, and I were directly aware of both the act of mind and the bodily activity I would be aware of two things only one of which is me. If I were directly aware only of the act of mind then I would be directly aware only of me – but I would not be aware of my walking.

However, *if* walking is a proper activity of the subject, and the subject is directly aware of it, this suggests that a possible, if anachronistic, reply is available to Gassendi. It may be, he could reply, that we cannot know with certainty that I am walking on the basis of my conscious activity of walking. But if you grant that my experience incorporates my walking, and by so doing incorporates me as that of which it is a mode, I can know, non-infallibly, on that basis that I exist.

We need, in other words, to separate out the question of whether experience can provide non-question begging grounds for existence claims, from the question of whether it delivers certainty in the face of the sceptic. If we are interested just in the first question, about whether or not the *Ambulo* argument gives us non-question begging grounds for our existence, then Descartes' response does not close off a positive answer. We have got a reason, through our experience of walking, to believe that we exist. Certainty is another issue. It is true that we may be wrong about whether we are actually walking – we could be dreaming – but in that case we have not, on the account of engaging in conscious acting being considered, got a conscious experience of walking. All we have is an illusion of walking, and that was never claimed to offer us grounds for a proof of our existence. And note that certainty over our acts and activities does not get much easier if we limit ourselves to activities that do not involve movements of the body – which we might think are not primary activities of the self for Descartes. Consider covert activities such as guessing or supposing. Whether or not a subject is supposing, or guessing, or even judging, might seem to imply certain dispositional features: whether they are prepared to discharge the supposition, whether they lack knowledge on the matter they are guessing about, whether they are prepared to use their judgement as a reason in a argument. Given this it seems clear that one can make sense of someone taking themselves to be supposing, guessing, judging when those features do not obtain and so, when they are in fact not supposing, guessing or judging. They only have the illusion of doing so. It is no surprise that certainty is hard to come by, but it is worth noting that it is hard to come by both in relation to covert psychological acts/activities such as supposings and guessings, and overt psychological activities such as walkings and jumpings.

We will come back to whether the activity of thinking has a special capacity to secure certainty in a way that the other activities don't. But for the moment let me sum up where we have got to. I have claimed that if in engaging in a conscious action we have a direct experience of our actions which is to understood in the way that the relationalist Moorean thinks that I have direct experience of my hand, then we have available to us a form of *Cogito* argument that can, in a non-question-begging way, provide grounds for knowledge of our own existence.

I have not provided arguments, and am not going to, for the claim that we do indeed have direct experience of our actions, and of us acting. I think the view that in acting we have an experience of our actions which encompasses those actions, and their agents is right – and indeed may be more plausible than the parallel view in relation to visual perception. However, my interest in this paper is only to identify the space for it, and establish the conditional conclusion that if the view were right, and if thinking is the activity of an agent, then there is a non-question begging version of the *Cogito*.

However, before turning to objections, there is scope to emphasise an advantage that would flow from such a view of our experience of our actions – other than providing a working version of the *Ambulo*, and in turn the *Cogito,* on the assumption that thinking is a form of acting. The view has much the same advantage that tends to advertised by the relationalist about perception in general: that it concords with our sense of being in direct contact with that which we are aware of. If we did not have direct experiences of our walkings, jumpings and so on, we would face the prospect of residing in a phenomenological bubble of action awareness with the actions themselves always something that's beyond our experience of them. It is often claimed by relationists about perception that non-relationalism leaves a subject alienated from the world by 'a veil of perception'. If there is such an alienation, then the extent of it is hugely magnified if the separation is not just between me and the external world, but between me and every one of my activities – both covert and overt. Every action I carry out – my walking, jumping, supposing and guessing – would be somehow distinct from and beyond my experience of it. That kind of picture would be decisively set aside if one accepted the relationalist view.

6. Limits and Obstacles

(i) *The nature of thinking.* One thing one might say in response to the above discussion is: look, I accept the *Ambulo* argument. I am convinced that, if we take walking to be a genuine mode or way a subject might be behaving, then in being directly aware of the walking I am directly aware of the subject walking. And if we do that, then the *Ambulo* is an argument I can use to prove my own existence. Suppose I am lying in a floatation tank and start to have doubts about whether I exist – perhaps I start to worry that I am merely some kind of cognitive ether and have no real existence. All I need to do is to get out and walk. If I engage in the conscious activity of walking I will have all the grounds I need to prove that I exist.

But that, the objection runs, is not going to resurrect the *Cogito*. It is not going to resurrect the *Cogito* because we've got no reason to think that *thinking* is an activity of a subject, awareness of which provides awareness of the subject. If I am a human being and my walking is way a human being is behaving then it is plausible to think one's consciousness of my walking is consciousness of me. But, it might be urged, thinking is something quite different. Thinking is not a way a whole human being behaves in the way that walking is – and

when I am aware of my thinking I am not aware of the human being –
I am aware only of the thinking disconnected from it being my thinking. It is further step, requiring rational support to take awareness of
my thinking an evidence of my existence.

I have said that I am not going to argue for the view that thinking
is an activity of a subject and has *no reality without being a mode of the
subject*. And I am not. Nor am I going to argue that we should think of
ourselves as human beings for whom thinking and walking are active
modes in similar ways. My argument is conditional – if that is the
right view of thinking and walking then the argument works.

However, I do want to urge in reply to the objection presented, that
on the most common sense picture of what we in fact are, the natural
thing to think about thinking is that, just like walking, and jumping,
it is an activity of a human being. If we ask the question 'What do
human beings do?' we might very well answer along the following
lines: 'Well, we walk, jump, dance, talk, think, question, argue,
skip and a whole lot of other things'. Thinking, questioning, doubting, all fall very naturally into a set of activities that are given as an
answer to the question 'What do we human beings do?'

That this is a natural and common sense thing to say about thinking – that is just another on of the many kinds of activities that human
being get up to – can be brought out if we look at how we qualify attributions of thinking to people. We use much the same adverbs to
qualify ongoing cognitive activities as ongoing overt physical ones.
We think slowly, we can get interrupted thinking, we can think fre-
netically and anxiously. That there is such a continuity between the
overt physical activities of a subject and thinking is brought out by
the fact that one of the ways you can think, is by talking. Talking is
very often a way of thinking. Sometimes we think by talking to
others: we often do not think the thought and then work out how
to communicate it. We just talk. Sometimes we think by talking
out loud to ourselves, and sometimes by talking to ourselves in
what Ryle called 'silent soliloquy'. Similarly, we can think by
writing – to ourselves or to others. Of course, sometimes we think
without talking or writing at all – even to ourselves. We have,
however, no reason to hold that in such thinking a subject is operating
in a fundamentally different mode from when she is talking or
writing. Obviously, if you think out loud you need to move your
mouth, or if you are working out your thoughts on paper you have
to move your hands, whereas if you are engaged in silent soliloquy,
or thinking without talking or writing at all, you need only engage
a more restricted part of your body. It would only be if our awareness
of our talking and writing amounted only to our awareness of the

movement of our arms and lips that this would give us a reason to hold that there is a radical asymmetry between being aware of ourselves engaged in talking and writing, and awareness of ourselves in covert thinking. Our awareness of our talking and writing does not amount only to our awareness of the movement of our arms and lips – if it involves it at all.

We have no obvious reason to hold that there is an asymmetry between our awareness of different kinds of thinking such that when we are consciously engaged in talking out loud we are aware of ourselves in virtue of consciously engaging in such talking, but when we are engaged in covert thinking we are not.

The other thing to wonder when one worries about whether thinking is really an activity of a subject is to ask 'what *is* the alternative picture?' There is a way of talking about conscious thought that makes it sound like a kind of phenomenological glitter. On this picture there could be phenomenological stuff going on in all sorts of unlikely places – conscious ripples disturbing murky puddles on Alpha Centuri. Or perhaps the idea is that that there could be brain fragments that could carry on the activity of thinking without there being any subject doing the thinking? But that is a very peculiar view – maybe I can survive if enough of my brain does – but if all we are left with is fragments we have little reason to suppose we are left with any thinking either. Ryle talks about the 'elastictities of uses of "I" and "me"'. He asks us to:

> consider some contexts in which 'I' and 'me' can certainly not be replaced by 'my body' or 'my leg'. If I say 'I am annoyed that I was cut in the collision, while I might accept the substitution of 'my leg was cut' for 'I was cut', I should not allow 'I am annoyed' to be reconstructed in such a way. It would be simply absurd to speak of 'my head remembering', 'my brain doing long division'.[13]

I agree with Ryle: the whole of me does these things, not bits of me – even if the whole of me can shrink to something quite small. Further, and similarly, it seems to me confusing to talk of 'my legs walking' or 'my lips talking'. Of course, these issues will not be settled until we settle what thinking is, and settle how we can coherently talk about thinking. It may be that the conditions on thinking can be met other than by whole subjects in certain conditions. But I think it very likely that they will not be.

[13]   G. Ryle, *The Concept of Mind*, 180–81.

Lucy O'Brien

(ii) *Knowing a thinker exists vs knowing I exist.*[14] There is a second objection that might be raised even if it is agreed that there way of construing the relation between awareness of activities, and their agents, that means that the standard Lichtenbergian objection would not get any traction. The fact that you will not get 'thinking going on' unless you have a subject thinking – along with the fact that this is known 'by the natural light' – will get you knowledge that the subject exists. Still, the objection runs, you will not get anything as strong as the conclusion that 'I exist' – the most you will get is the conclusion 'Someone exists'. The fact that the subject that exists is *me* is additional to knowing that a subject exist.

This suggests the possibility of a non first-personal, existential version of the *Ambulo*:

Engagement in (1) A conscious walking
Judge: (2) Someone is walking
Infer the judgment: (3) Therefore, Someone exists

My response to this objection is threefold.

First, even if this objection is right about the inaccessibility of the first person judgement it is wrong to think that we can get only an existential conclusion. We can also reach a demonstrative conclusion – 'this subject' who walking I am aware of exists; 'this subject' whose thinking I am aware of exists:

Engagement in (1) A conscious walking
Judge: (2) This subject is walking
Infer the judgment: (3) Therefore, This subject exists

Second, the fact that we have identified an existential and demonstrative version of the *Ambulo* is itself of note. If it is granted that awareness of an activity of a self is sufficient to ground awareness of a subject and warranted judgements about that subject – whether or not I know it that that self is me – we have re-positioned the gap that was supposed to be surpassed. It is no longer a gap between an act of thinking and its subject, but between a thinking subject and identifying who that subject is.

Three, we do have forms of direct awareness of activities of subject that themselves may warrant only the demonstrative and existential conclusions – such as when we see someone walk – whether we see another, or see ourselves reflected in a mirror. However, when we ourselves engage in the conscious activities of walking or thinking, when we are the walker and the thinker, our

---

[14]   Thanks to Daniel Whiting for raising this issue.

72

awareness of what we are is through a distinct form of awareness – an awareness we have through being the agent of the activity. If that is right then, without positive reasons to think that I cannot be walking or thinking – or that I am subject to an illusion of agents awareness, my conscious walking or thinking will always provide a warrant for judging 'I am walking' or 'I am thinking'.

(iii) *Hume's Intuition:* Something that might still worry us about the above way of trying to secure the epistemological respectability of the *Cogito* is the thought 'what happened to Hume's intuition?' Wasn't Hume right to observe that when we introspect we find ourselves *missing* in some way? As Hume famously put it says:

> For my part, when I enter most intimately into what I call myself, I always stumble on some particular perception or other, of heat or cold, light or shade, love or hatred, pain or pleasure. I never can catch myself at any time without a perception, and never can observe any thing but the perception.

We have, I think, all been a bit mesmerized by this quotation. There are two things peculiar about it. One, is the idea in order to catch myself I *need* to catch myself without my perceptions, and need to observe anything other than the perceptions. If I manifested myself to introspection in perceptions, then the way to catch myself is to catch the perceptions. Imagine Hume had been worrying about whether external objects show up in vision. Are they not somehow missing? After all, he might have argued:

> For my part, when I perceive an object, I always stumble on some particular quality or other, of square or spherical, light or heavy, blue or green. I never can catch the object at any time without a quality, and never can observe any thing but the quality.

Now it maybe that Hume himself would in fact say that – but this way of seeing things does not capture a common sense way to report our phenomenology of the world and our capacities to be acquainted with ordinary objects. And I don't think his quotation about the self should be reported, as it so often is, as the natural and common sense way to report our phenomenology of the self.

The second peculiar thing to note is the list of things Hume thinks we should pay attention to in our efforts to try to find ourselves in introspection. Suppose he had instead 'entered most intimately into himself' and stumbled across his thinking, his looking, his seeing, his calculating, his talking, his walking, his dancing and jumping, but declared that he never caught himself without any of these things, then I think we would want to reply: 'Well, you've been there all the time; you have already stumbled across yourself.' What Hume seems to be asking for is observation of the self bare of all it's activities; we should no more think we can experience a self bare of its activities than we should think we can experience an object bare of its qualities. If activities are ways I may be, nothing justifies the expectation that to be aware of myself I need stumble on my 'self' on its own, bare and stripped of its activities? Whatever the self *is* we are aware of it in its activities.

(iv) *Certainty.* It seems to me that we have, given certain assumptions about the nature of activities and what we experience when we experience them, good reason to take ourselves to have available a working version of the *Ambulo* and the *Cogito*. I will end by asking whether we have a reason, as Descartes thought, to prefer the latter to the former because it gives us certainty. Do we get more with the *Cogito* than the *Ambulo*? The *Ambulo* gives us warrant for existence of subjects, but will not survive doubt about whether I am really walking or just suffering an illusion to that effect. Might the *Cogito* do better, and so doing give us not only warrant for our own existence but certainty about our own existence?

Well that depends on whether, on the picture being presented, I could coherently be wrong about, or doubt, whether I am thinking? Suppose it seems to me that I am thinking – could I be wrong? Well, if its seeming to me that I am thinking involves my thinking 'I am thinking', then I cannot be wrong – I am thinking 'I am thinking' and so what I am thinking is self-verifying. However, perhaps there is another way to understand what would have to be going on for it to seem to me that I am thinking. Perhaps all that need be involved is an occurrence that has a *feel* just like *this*, this thinking now going on, but which is an occurrence that is not a thinking: it is an occurrence which fails a condition on thinking for one reason or another. If it is possible for there to be an occurrence that has a feel just like the feel of running through the *Cogito* argument, but it is not a running of the Cogito argument because it does not involve thinking at all, then a thinking subject running through the *Cogito* may coherently wonder whether something like is going on rather than that she is thinking through the *Cogito*. However, if she does so she can comfort herself with the thought that were that to be the case she is not wondering anything – wondering takes thinking; and she is not running through the *Cogito* – running through the *Cogito* takes thinking. She cannot in fact have even have engaged in the first step of the *Cogito*; she cannot have engaged in an act of conscious thinking. If all that is going on is a conscious non-thinking occurrence that feels like this, then she will not get her conclusion, but she will not her premises or her argument either. She will have done nothing. However, I have argued that, as long as she started with *a conscious thinking* – although doing so might come with meeting significant conditions – she *may* be able to get her conclusion without begging the question.

University College London
l.obrien@ucl.ac.uk

The Place of The Self in Contemporary Metaphysics[1]

RORY MADDEN

Abstract
I explain why the compositionalist conception of ordinary objects prevalent in contemporary metaphysics places the manifest image of the human self in a precarious position: the two theoretically simplest views of the existence of composites each jeopardize some central element of the manifest image. I present an alternative, *nomological* conception of ordinary objects, which secures the manifest image of the human self without the arbitrariness that afflicts compositionalist attempts to do the same. I close by sketching the consequences of the recommended position for the traditional personal identity debate about the nature and persistence of human selves.

1. Introduction

What is the place of the self in contemporary metaphysics?

In one respect the self has been dethroned from the elevated position it occupied in earlier, especially Kantian and post-Kantian, philosophy. The prevailing outlook of metaphysics as it is practiced in departments of analytic philosophy today is an unabashedly realist one. An idealist view of the self as in some sense the metaphysical ground of the empirical world – an Archimedean point upon which the objects of enquiry depend for their existence or nature – is these days not so much argued against as completely ignored. The typical presupposition of recent work is that we human selves are relatively small, transient, physical objects in a larger world of physical objects quite independent of us. To take one very recent example: a disagreement between two august contributors to the debate about personal identity turns on the question of whether we are whole animals, or smaller parts of animals.[2] At no point is the possibility entertained that we might be entities transcending

---

[1] Thanks to the audience at the Royal Institute of Philosophy for their comments and questions, and to Nicholas K. Jones for discussion.
[2] Derek Parfit, 'We Are Not Human Beings', *Philosophy* **87** (2012), 5–28. Eric Olson, 'Parfit on Human Beings', in *Mind, Self and Person* edited by Anthony O'Hear (Cambridge University Press, forthcoming)

doi:10.1017/S1358246115000089

Rory Madden

the world of ordinary physical objects altogether. To do so nowadays would seem eccentric. The majority position in contemporary metaphysics is that we human selves are items of the same broad category as other individual macroscopic physical occupants of the mind independent empirical world. We human selves are *ordinary objects*.

Is there anything general to be said about the nature of this broad category? It is fair to say that the orthodox view today is that ordinary objects of different kinds – cats, mountains, tables, and so on – are one and all *composites*. The orthodox view is not merely that there is some sense or other in which ordinary objects may be viewed as variously having components, divisions, organs, bits, sections. The orthodoxy is that this viewpoint on ordinary objects is the metaphysically perspicuous one: in explaining how an ordinary object is built up in a certain way from its parts one reveals what the thing most basically or fundamentally *is*. Call this orthodox view of the nature of ordinary objects *compositionalism*: it is the view that the metaphysically basic or fundamental characterization of an ordinary object specifies the way in which the thing is built up from its parts.[3]

A natural extension of compositionalism is the view that differences of kind within the broad category of ordinary objects are to be explained in terms of differences in the composition of things from parts, either differences in the parts themselves or differences in the ways in which things are built up from given parts. In particular, the existence of something of the kind *human* will consist in something being generated from certain parts in a characteristic way. Schematically, let us say that on the compositionalist view the nature of a human self is fundamentally explained in terms of *some things being arranged human-wise*.[4]

---

[3]   Representatives of this tradition include many of the biggest names in contemporary metaphysics: David Lewis, *The Plurality of Worlds* (Blackwell, 1986), Peter van Inwagen, *Material Beings* (Cornell University Press, 1990), Kit Fine, 'Things and Their Parts', *Midwest Studies in Philosophy* **XXIII** (1999), Ted Sider, *Four-Dimensionalism* (Oxford University Press, 2001), Kathrin Koslicki, *The Structure of Objects* (Oxford University Press, 2008).

[4]   The terminology 'arranged *K*-wise' is van Inwagen's (*Material Beings*, 109), picking out a potentially complex relational condition distinctive of the parts of *K*s, a condition which may be met by pluralities of different cardinalities (as pluralities of different cardinalities may each be arranged in a circle). But it should be noted that compositionalism is not as such committed to the position that the nature of an ordinary thing is fundamentally to be explained in terms of a *relation* among parts. An alternative is to think of an ordinary thing as generated by a certain function or *operation*

78

The Place of The Self in Contemporary Metaphysics

Now in point of historical fact it seems unlikely that the predominance in metaphysics of a compositionalist view of the nature of ordinary objects in general, and of human selves in particular, can be traced to the persuasive power of any particular published philosophical arguments. Its appeal to recent generations of tyro philosophers is more plausibly explained by other factors, including the ease of pictorial grasp of the view, the opportunities it offers for rigorous refinement by means of the ready analytic tools of mereology, and the absence of any salient alternative. An especially powerful factor us surely compositionalism's perceived affinity with what Wilfrid Sellars called 'the scientific image'.[5] The findings of theoretical physics in particular, having application to every system in the natural world, rightly earn the attention of metaphysicians interested in the basic nature of things. What does theoretical physics say about ordinary objects such as humans? As Sellars himself puts it 'man as he appears to the theoretical physicist [is] a swirl of physical particles, forces, and fields'.[6] Like other large scale objects, man as he appears to the theoretical physicist a complex dynamic arrangement of more basic physical elements or stuff. The metaphysician's compositionalist view of man can thus claim inspiration from the theoretical physicist's image of man.

Sellars famously contrasted the scientific image with what he called the *manifest image*, which he described as 'the framework in terms of which man came to be aware of himself as man-in-the-world'.[7] While Sellars' own characterization of the manifest image has some additional details, we can understand the content of the manifest image to consist in those propositions that would result from a pre-theoretical articulation of how things appear to us, unprejudiced by opinion about the unobservable posits of science. Thus according the

---

upon given things, in the way one could think of a *set* as generated by the application of the operation of 'set-building' to some given elements. There need be no metaphysically illuminating relation among the elements of a set so generated (see Kit Fine, 'Towards a Theory of Part', *Journal of Philosophy* **107** (2010), 559–589). In what follows 'things arranged K-wise' will be used loosely, to cover both things being related in a certain way distinctive of the parts of Ks, and things being input to a generative operation in a way distinctive of Ks.

[5] Wilfrid Sellars, 'Philosophy and the Scientific Image of Man', in Wilfrid Sellars, *Empiricism and the Philosophy of Mind* (London: Routledge & Kegan Paul Ltd, 1963), 1–40
[6] Sellars, 'Philosophy and the Scientific Image of Man', 20
[7] Ibid., 6

Rory Madden

manifest image we humans find ourselves in a colourful, solid world, our actions imbued with meaning and value.

As Sellars sees philosophy one of its central tasks is to develop a 'comprehensive synoptic vision'[8] of how the scientific image and the manifest image hang together, and indeed it has been a preoccupation of philosophy since the early modern era to understand how, if at all, such manifest phenomena as colour, or value, might fit with a modern scientific worldview. In this paper I want to make a contribution to this general philosophical task for the special case of the human self.

First I shall explain how the vaguely science-inspired compositionalist view of ordinary objects prevailing in contemporary metaphysics places the manifest image of the human self in a precarious position: the two theoretically simplest views of the existence of composites each jeopardize a central element of the manifest image of the human self. I shall then present an alternative, non-compositionalist, or *nomological* conception of the nature of ordinary objects. This view not only immunizes these elements of the manifest image against the dual threats posed by composition, it has a better claim than compositionalism to properly respect the scientific image. I close by sketching how the proposed nomological conception of ordinary objects promises to shed light on the traditional personal identity debate about our nature and persistence.

2. The Manifest Image of the Human Self

In order to explain the threat compositionalism in contemporary metaphysics poses to the manifest image of the human self we need first to say something about which aspects of the manifest image concern the human self.

Recall that the content of the manifest image consists in those propositions that would result from a pre-theoretical articulation of how things appear to us, unprejudiced by opinion about unobservable posits. The question now is which such propositions concern the human self. A sceptic might reply that no such propositions concern the human self: the so-called self is an obscure theoretical posit of metaphysics, any conception of which must be deeply historically conditioned by theology, politics, and other sociological forces. Even if there is such a thing as the self, its existence and character can hardly be read off from theoretically unprejudiced reflection on how

---

[8] Sellars, 'Philosophy and the Scientific Image of Man', 19

things immediately appear to us, as one might describe the apparent colour of surfaces in one's immediate environment.

This scepticism deserves more attention that I can give it here but I believe it can be sidelined for present purposes by appeal to a thin, or *minimal* conception of the human self. In deference to the reflexive etymology of the word, let us use 'self' simply to pick out a potential reference of a use of the first person pronoun or other device of reflexive reference, abstracting away from the word's richer connotations of autonomy, ultimate value, immateriality, integrity, and so on.

Now on this minimal understanding there could be many as many kinds of selves as there are kinds of potential referents of the first person: there could be Martian, angelic, or robotic selves if such things could reflexively refer. So let us say that a more specifically *human* self is a potential referent of first person reference that is, as it were, local to us. A human self is a referent of 'I' related in some close way to a human body. Given that uses of 'I' are referentially co-ordinated with uses of 'you' and 'he' – my use of 'I' co-referring with your use of 'you' in conversation with me, and with an onlooker's use of 'he' – on the minimal conception of the self the content of the manifest image of the human self will simply consist in the propositions we would articulate, through theoretically unprejudiced reflection on appearances, by means of personal pronouns such as these.

It remains a difficult task to specify this class of propositions in any less general terms. As the lively debate about the richness of the content of experience attests, it is not always obvious what is obvious. Still, our readiness to use personal pronouns in response to experience of each other and ourselves strongly suggests at least a couple of basic elements of the manifest image of the human self. Where 'here' refers to the place I now seem to be occupying (a small desk chair as it happens):

Existence: there is at least one human self here

Sparseness: there is no more than one human self here

These are not theory-laden attributions of controversial properties like freedom, or ultimate value. These simply concern the number or distribution of things we talk about with the ordinary use of personal vocabulary. These two claims plausibly articulate something central and obvious about our first-person perspective on ourselves – and also about our second- or third-personal perspectives on one another. Not only does it seem to me that there is just one human self in this chair, it would also seem to you that there is one human self in this chair.

3. The Threats of Compositionalism

On a compositionalist view of ordinary objects the metaphysically basic characterization of an ordinary object specifies the manner in which it is built up from its parts. Applied to human selves, the view is that a human self is something built up from things in a certain way, from things arranged human-wise. How does this metaphysics of the human self jeopardize the manifest image of the human self?

The threat to the manifest image of the human self arises from reflection on the conditions under which things are generated or built up from parts. Consider by analogy the case of sets. Suppose that we have three given objects: an apple, a banana, and a cherry. Let us ask, which sets may be formed with only these pieces of fruit as members? As a heuristic we can identify these sets in turn by means of imagined acts of 'collecting' or 'gathering'. First one can gather up each piece of fruit singly – so there are the three singleton sets {a}, {b}, {c} – and one can gather them up in pairs – so we get three doubleton sets {a, b}, {a, c}, {b, c} – and finally we can gather all three together to make the three membered set {a, b, c}. So there are seven sets with only these pieces of fruit as members.

But now suppose an interlocutor takes the following contrary view. There are in fact only *six* sets with only the given fruit as members. While one can gather things up in every other way, one cannot gather up the banana and cherry to make the doubleton set {b, c}.

In response to this odd proposal one will request some explanation for the otherwise arbitrary sounding restriction on set formation. Suppose the request is answered with the assertion that set formation is restricted in this way because banana and cherry make a uniquely repulsive flavour combination (at least when unmitigated by the addition of further flavours).

This explanation seems implausible. Why? It seems implausible because the relation of co-palatability is intuitively irrelevant to whether the operation of set-formation has application to certain things. There is nothing in the nature of the operation that makes sense of this putative restriction in its application. A lack co-palatability among things does not seem to be the right sort of factor to 'block' the act of gathering them up into a set.

A conventional view is more plausible: if we are going to accept the existence of any entities corresponding to these notional acts of gathering then we should accept the existence of every logically possible result of such acts of gathering. That is to say, the only restrictions on set formation should relate to the avoidance of contradiction.

Now what about ordinary objects? Of course the usual compositionalist view is not that ordinary objects are *sets*. They have parts
rather than members in the set-theoretic sense, and there is no
'empty' ordinary object, as there might be an empty set corresponding to the act of gathering up nothing at all. A more detailed theory
could identify ordinary objects with the results of classical mereological summing, or yet some other composition operation on given
things.[9] Still, on any such view we can ask under which conditions
such things are formed, under which conditions the relevant composition operation has application.

Once again, a theoretically non-arbitrary view seems to be this: if
we accept the existence of any entities corresponding to the composition operation then we should accept the existence of every logically
possible application of the operation. This means that ordinary
objects belong to a category that is extremely *abundant* in its instances. To use Lewis's notorious example, there is a composite resulting from the summing of an undetached front half of a trout in
one location, and the undetached back half of a turkey in some
distant location. Unlike cats or trees for example, these *trout-
turkeys* do not normally attract our attention. But it would be arbitrary to deny that such composites are formed.[10]

In pursuit of a more sparse conception of the category to which
ordinary objects belong, various more restrictive views of composition have been proposed.[11] Although this is not the place to
defend the point fully it seems to me that any such proposal must
share the basic defect of the co-palatability restriction on set-
formation: it is always going to be difficult to see why the proposed
restriction should have any relevance to the *existence* of composites
(as opposed to aspects of their individual character, like salience, or
integrity): it is mysterious why a composition operation on things
should be sensitive to whether the putative inputs to the operation

[9]   See Fine, 'Things and Their Parts', for the view that ordinary material
things are 'rigid embodiments' or 'variable embodiments', composites in
some respects more set-like in their character than classical mereological
sums.
[10]   For expressions of the view that it would be arbitrary to deny that
ordinary objects form a vanishingly small subset of a massively plenitudinous class, see Stephen Yablo, 'Identity, Essence and Indiscernibility',
Journal of Philosophy **84** (1987), 293–314, Fine, 'Things and Their Parts',
John Hawthorne, *Metaphysical Essays* (Oxford University Press, 2006)
[11]   For examples of restrictive theories of composition see Van Inwagen,
Material Beings, and Gary Hoffman and Joshua Rosenkrantz, *Substance: its
Nature and Existence* (Routledge, 1996)

Rory Madden

are fastened together like the parts of a material unity, or caught up in the life like the parts of a living organism. There is nothing in the nature of a composition operation as such to make sense of any such non-logical restriction, or block. To speak metaphorically, how could the operation know in advance to proceed in its application to some things only if the further thing it would go on to generate has the sort of individual character stereotypical of the objects we commonsensically recognize?

The abundant view is theoretically simple, then, but it arguably threatens our manifest image of the world in more than one way. First, we are surely ordinarily inclined to reject the claim that there are, overlapping with me in my chair right now, a massive number of kinds of macroscopic physical object of the same general category as the objects we ordinarily recognize. Second, the abundant view also jeopardizes, for any given ordinary kind of object, the claim that there are only so many instances of the kind to a region. Why? Here is a pertinent example: observe that there are millions of massively overlapping pluralities of atoms in my chair right now, differing by just a single atom. Millions of these pluralities are as properly 'arranged human-wise' as any other. But if the operation of composition is not restricted then it should have application respectively to each of these pluralities, generating a human self for each plurality. Thus the theoretically non-arbitrary abundant view of composition not only generates many more kinds of object than we would ordinarily countenance, it also generates a vast multiplicity of human selves in my chair right now.[12] This is the first threat to the manifest image of the human self: a theoretically non-arbitrary view of composition threatens Sparseness.

Abundance is not the only view of composition that refuses to draw an arbitrary theoretical line. One might agree that *if* there are any entities corresponding to a composition operation then there are entities corresponding to every logically possible application of the operation. But, in the spirit of nominalism about abstract objects, one could deny the antecedent: one could take the view that the most economical view of reality should dispense with the entire shadowy host of massively overlapping entities putatively existing in addition to the given, non-composite, fundamental building blocks of reality.[13] This *eliminativist* view of composites is as

---

[12]   This is an instance of the so-called Problem of the Many. See Peter Unger 'The Problem of the Many', *Midwest Studies in Philosophy* **V** (1980), 411–467
[13]   For this eliminativist view see Cian Dorr and Gideon Rosen, 'Composition as Fiction', in *The Blackwell Guide to Metaphysics* edited by

theoretically elegant as abundance but it appears to be equally incompatible with an element of the manifest image of the human self. It threatens Existence, the claim that there is at least one human self in this chair. If human selves are ordinary objects if they are anything at all, ordinary objects are composites if they are anything at all, but there are no composites, then there is not even one human self in this chair.

So the two theoretically non-arbitrary views of composition, abundance and eliminativism, jeopardize Sparseness and Existence respectively. What are the options for those inclined to defend the manifest image of the human self?

One option would be to make a special exception for human selves. It might be claimed that the human self is not, like a cat, table, or tree, an ordinary material object. It is a more exotic kind of object, perhaps an immaterial soul as traditionally conceived.[14] I shall not pursue this option here, for two reasons. First, the option ignites a range of traditional worries about dualism, for example about psychophysical interaction. The second reason is this. Although there is perhaps a special Cartesian introspective appeal to the two claims about the existence and sparseness of human selves, the immaterialist option leaves untouched the compositionalist threat to parallel, but also compelling, claims about the existence and sparseness of ordinary objects, like cats, tables and trees. The idea that there are billions of cats, or tables, or trees where there seems to be just one present – or no cats, tables or trees at all – is not much less offensive to the manifest image of things than eliminativism or abundance about human selves. A more general response would be preferable.

Another response of course is to concoct a restricted view of composition, on which composites are generated under conditions corresponding roughly to the manifest image of the population of ordinary objects. It might be insisted that the fact that this position is arbitrary

Richard Gale (Blackwell, 2002), and Ted Sider 'Against Parthood' in *Oxford Studies in Metaphysics Volume 8*, edited by Karen Bennett and Dean Zimmerman (Oxford University Press, 2013), 237–93

[14] Zimmerman and Unger have each in effect suggest that immaterialism is required in order to save the manifest image of the human self from the overpopulation worries that beset materialist views. See Dean Zimmerman, 'Material People', in *The Oxford Handbook of Metaphysics*, edited by Michael Loux and Dean Zimmerman (Oxford University Press, 2003), and Peter Unger, 'The Mental Problem of the Many', in *Oxford Studies in Metaphysics volume 1*, edited by Dean Zimmerman (Oxford University Press, 2004), 195–222

from the point of view of theoretical reflection on the nature of composition is just too bad. Manifest appearances defeat theoretical virtue.

However, this position is precarious because it is not clear that manifest appearances should be treated at unshakeable bedrock in this way. Of course they are our starting point, but when theoretically highly elegant views of composition have come into consideration it is not clear that the evidential force of appearances is not thereby rebutted or undercut.[15]

It is a difficult question when, if at all, the theoretical virtues of a metaphysical theory defeat apparent counterevidence, and it is a large question beyond the scope of this paper. But whichever way we go on the question, a compositionalist view of ordinary objects will be stuck with an intellectual tension: we seem not to be able to find a position that simultaneously respects manifest appearances and theoretical non-arbitrariness.

4. The Nomological Conception of Ordinary Objects

I want to suggest a way forward. We can save manifest appearances, without denying that the human self is an ordinary object, and without denying either of the two theoretically non-arbitrary views of composition. The trick is to deny the presupposition that ordinary objects are composites, that ordinary objects are things fundamentally characterized in terns of their generation from parts.

We may begin by noting that it has become commonplace in recent metaphysics to draw a certain distinction among the truths about a given kind of thing. One can distinguish between those truths that reveal what things of the kind fundamentally are, and those truths that are, as it were, incidentally true – even necessarily true – of things of the kind. For example it is necessarily true that water is H_2O, and it is also necessarily true that water is such that $2 + 2 = 4$. But intuitively only the former necessary truth tells us what water *is*.[16]

Now it is true, perhaps necessarily true, that macroscopic objects of ordinary human experience have parts in various senses: trees have trunks, cats have claws, whiskers, front halves and back halves;

---

[15]   Sider, 'Against Parthood', mounts a tenacious defence of the position that the ideological economy of eliminativism about composites defeats ordinary appearances to the contrary.

[16]   See Kit Fine 'Essence and Modality', *Philosophical Perspectives* **8** (1994), 1–16

inspect the paths they occupy more closely and one will find trajectories of cells, molecules, atoms, and even smaller constituents. But it is optional to regard these truths as the metaphysically basic truths about these kinds of objects. It is optional to explain what ordinary objects fundamentally *are* in terms of their composition from parts.

What is the alternative? To begin to see the alternative we should ask why it is that things like cats, trees, and humans attract our attention and interest. One could easily get the impression from reading contemporary metaphysics that we humans have simply found ourselves implanted with a random set of 'intellectual intuitions' about the existence of a certain restricted menu of kinds. But in fact the ordinary objects that we latch onto in perception and thought have a distinctive character: they are robust, stable, invariants, which enable prediction, manipulation, explanation, and counterfactual-supporting generalization at higher scales than fundamental physics. In other words, corresponding to the ordinary kinds that we recognize are an indefinite range of true lawlike generalizations, of biology, mechanics, folk-psychology, geology, and other special sciences. These true lawlike generalizations mention the individual activity and properties of the objects in question, rather than their composition from parts.

The proposal I am recommending is to treat *these* truths, lawlike truths to the effect that Ks ϕ in conditions C ... rather than compositional truths to the effect that Ks have such and such parts structured in such and such ways... as the truths which reveal what Ks most fundamentally are. The metaphysically basic characterization of an ordinary kind of object states the lawlike activity of things of that kind. Call this the *nomological conception* of ordinary objects.

I am contrasting the nomological conception of an ordinary object as fundamentally a subject of high-level lawlike activity characteristic of its kind, with the compositionalist view that an ordinary object is fundamentally the result of the kind-characteristic application of a composition operation to some things. Why prefer the nomological conception?

One appealing, though not decisive, feature of the view is its harmonization of the metaphysics and epistemology of the macroscopic world. We do not in fact discover the existence of high-level kinds by asking under what conditions smaller things generate larger things; rather we discover them figuring in their own right in strong, simple, counterfactual supporting generalizations at larger scales than physics. On the metaphysical view that these objects just *are* subjects of characteristic lawlike activity, this epistemology makes perfect sense.

Rory Madden

Another advantage of the view is its capacity to sideline spurious puzzles that arise on a compositionalist view of ordinary objects. Take the so-called 'grounding problem' about coinciding objects like the statue and the lump of clay.[17] How, it is wondered, could two objects composed of the same physical parts structured in the same way at a time nevertheless differ in their counterfactual propensities and other properties? Indeed, on the view that an object just *is* something structured from parts in a certain way it can start to seem mysterious how there could be room here for two objects at all. On the nomological view that an ordinary object just *is* a locus of lawlike activity, we count two objects by counting two distinct paths of lawlike activity. There is one thing that would persist and continue to transmit momentum and so on through a flattening process, and one thing that would not. Conversely the latter individual would continue to transmit certain aesthetic and cultural effects through certain changes in material, where the former would not. There is nothing especially puzzling about the fact that two such paths could pass through a single plurality of low-level physical elements at a single time. The nomological generalizations definitive of the kinds in question feature in sciences at a higher level than fundamental physics. Indeed the possibility of coincident objects is arguably the flipside to multiple-realizability, another phenomenon that supports the irreducibility or 'autonomy' of high-level special science kinds.[18] Multiple-realizability: the possibility that Ks could be realized microphysically in different ways shows that to be a K is not just to be arranged microphysically in a certain way. Coincidence: the possibility that a K and an incompatible K^* could both be microphysically arranged in the same way also shows that to be a K is not just to be arranged microphysically in a certain way.[19]

[17] See Karen Bennett, 'Spatio-Temporal Coincidence and The Grounding Problem', *Philosophical Studies* **118** (2004), 339–371

[18] On multiple realizability and the autonomy of the special sciences see Jerry Fodor, 'Special Sciences (Or: The Disunity of Science as a Working Hypothesis)', *Synthese* **28** (1974), 97–115

[19] I do not mean to suggest that there are no broadly compositionalist approaches to the grounding problem on the market. On the 'four-dimensionalist' view that ordinary objects have *temporal* parts as well as spatial parts, a difference in parts can be found between (temporarily) coinciding objects (See Lewis, *The Plurality of Worlds*, and Sider, *Four-Dimensionalism*). The 'hylomorphic' view that ordinary objects have *formal* parts as well as material parts also permits a difference in parts between coinciding objects (See Koslicki, *The Structure of Objects*, and Kit Fine, 'Coincidence and Form', *Proceedings of the Aristotelian Society*

The Place of The Self in Contemporary Metaphysics

For the rest of this section however I want to focus on the way in which the nomological conception of ordinary objects resolves the intellectual tension with which I closed the previous section. The puzzle of finding a view of composition that is both theoretically non-arbitrary and also consistent with the manifest image of a fairly sparse population of ordinary objects presupposes the usual compositionalist view that the ordinary objects that feature in the manifest image just are composites. If instead we suppose that these ordinary objects are fundamentally characterized not in terms of their generation from parts but instead in terms of their characteristic high-level lawlike activity then both eliminativist and abundant views of the population of composites are perfectly *compatible* with the manifest image of a fairly sparse population of ordinary objects. After all it is not obvious that the manifest image has anything whatsoever to say about the population of mereological sums, impure sets, Finean rigid embodiments and variable embodiments, or any other kind of thing defined in terms of composition broadly speaking. One might rather regard composites as quasi-abstract objects, plenitudinous or non-existent according to one's taste. What would be offensive to appearances is the view that there are billions of things of the *same general category* as cats, trees, and humans, overlapping me in my chair right now – or else that there are no members of the category at all. If the non-compositional, nomological, conception of ordinary objects is correct then the theoretically elegant views of composition do not have these consequences: a relatively sparse population of ordinary objects is compatible with the existence of billions or none of the objects of the distinct category of composite.

We can further illustrate the compatibilist nature of the nomological conception by reconsidering the 'problem of the many', which, recall, was generated by an abundant view of composition in combination with compositionalism about ordinary objects. On the view that a cat, say, just is the result of composition applied to a plurality of parts arranged cat-wise, we arrive at the bizarre conclusion that there are as many cats as there are pluralities of tiny parts arranged cat-wise i.e. very many cats indeed. What does the contrasting nomological view that an ordinary object is a locus of high-level lawlike

---

Supplementary Volume **LXXXII** (2008), 101–118). But I believe that in the light of the availability of a non-compositionalist picture of ordinary objects, the appeal to differences in (intuitively unfamiliar) parts starts to look like a theory-driven, Procrustean attempt to force the facts into a compositionalist mould.

activity say about this situation? On this view we are freed up to say there is a single object present whose nomological nature enables manipulation, prediction, explanation at a higher scale. As Dennett puts a similar idea, each of the slightly different pluralities of tiny parts is a fuzzy or 'noisy' presentation of numerically one and the same high-level predictive 'real pattern'.[20]

There is a *prima facie* difficulty here. Let it be granted that a single high-level pattern is presented by each of the slightly different pluralities of tiny parts. It might be objected that a pattern is something universal, or type-like. But in that case one and the same high-level object would be present *wherever* tiny parts are arranged cat-wise. This would amount to a problem of too *few* cats: after all we ordinarily take it that cat-wise arranged pluralities of tiny parts sometimes *do* correspond to numerically distinct cats, viz. when they are in quite widely separated locations. A cat is not multiply located like a universal. On the other hand if we try to particularize the pattern by reference to particular pluralities of parts, counting token patterns by counting token pluralities of tiny parts presenting the universal pattern-type, then we are back to the problem of the many, for there are many such pluralities.

The nomological conception of an ordinary object as a *locus* or *path* of high-level nomological activity suggests a solution to this difficulty. Corresponding to each of the massively overlapping pluralities is exactly the *same* set of predictions and causal consequences for the instantiation of high-level special science properties along a spatiotemporal trajectory. Corresponding to each of the massively overlapping pluralities is the same raised chance, for a given subsequent region of time and space, that something will be breathing, purring, pouncing, mouse-killing, at that region. This contrasts with the case of two cat-wise arranged pluralities presenting spatially widely separated cats: we will find that corresponding to these pluralities are *distinct* predictive and causal consequences for characteristic high-level activity going on at given subsequent regions of time and space. While this is not the place for a more detailed development of the picture, the basic proposal is to count token 'real patterns' by distinct spatiotemporal paths of high-level lawlike activity. On the nomological view, then, multiple overlapping pluralities can correspond to a single ordinary object, in line with the manifest image.[21]

[20] Daniel Dennett, 'Real Patterns', *Journal of Philosophy* **88** (1991), 27–51

[21] See Nicholas K. Jones, 'Multiple Constitution', *Oxford Studies in Metaphysics volume 9*, edited by Karen Bennett and Dean Zimmerman

The Place of The Self in Contemporary Metaphysics

We are free to hold in addition that the many overlapping cat-wise arranged pluralities correspond to many composites – many things, which, like sets, or mereological sums, are fundamentally characterized by applications of some compositional operation to the respective pluralities. But on the nomological view none of these things is a cat. So there is no clash with the manifest image of a relatively sparse population of cats.

That is a major advantage of the nomological view. But isn't compositionalism about ordinary objects the metaphysical view properly respectful of the scientific image? Isn't Sellars obviously right to say that 'man as he appears to the theoretical physicist [is] a swirl of physical particles, forces, and fields'? In fact what Sellars says here is quite dubious. Man arguably does not appear to the theoretical physicist at all. The terms of theoretical physics denote the large-scale structure of the cosmos and the finest structure of matter. Man does not get a mention. It is philosophy, not physics, which makes the metaphysical claim that man just is a composite generated from the subject matter of physics. The sciences that do directly concern the ordinary objects of human experience are not fundamental physics but the high-level special sciences: biology, folk-psychology, anthropology, and so on. The nomological conception of ordinary objects as loci of activity governed by the laws of these high-level special sciences, and not compositionalism, is the metaphysical view most naturally suggested by the scientific image of such objects.

What about the arbitrariness worry for conveniently sparse ontologies of the macroscopic world? Recall the general worry about restricted views of composition: it seems theoretically arbitrary to suppose that the generation of composites should be restricted in a way that corresponds to the manifest image. Does a similar worry afflict the nomological conception of ordinary objects? No. If an ordinary object just *is* a locus of high-level nomological activity then there is nothing arbitrary about the view that the population of this category is relatively sparse. It is an empirically discoverable fact that there is a relatively sparse set of kinds that feature in the explanatory lawlike generalizations of the special sciences. Things like trout-turkeys with a bizarre scattered gerrymandered nature do

---

(Oxford University Press, forthcoming) for a detailed presentation of an 'Aristotelian' solution to the Problem Of The Many in roughly this spirit. The view that ordinary objects are individuated by nomological activity along a spatio-temporal path is developed extensively in David Wiggins, *Sameness and Substance Renewed* (Cambridge University Press, 2001)

not figure in the simple, strong, explanatory generalizations of the high-level special sciences.

Perhaps from the point of the view of the philosopher's armchair there remains something puzzling here. After all there seems to be no *a priori* scrutable reason for reality to have the sparse high-level nomological structure that it does (or indeed for reality to have any high-level nomological structure at all: as Fodor puts it bluntly – not himself expecting an answer any time soon – 'why is there anything except physics?'[22]) But this species of 'arbitrariness' is just an aspect of the contingency of the empirically given structure of the universe. The claim that there are in fact certain high-level laws rather than other conceivable such laws seems no more theoretically objectionable than the claim that the universe in fact has certain laws of physics, or the claim that the universe in fact had certain initial conditions. That's just the way of the empirical world.

5. The Personal Identity Debate

Let us review the situation. We identified two elements of the manifest image of the human self, Existence and Sparseness. Given a theoretically non-arbitrary view of composition – abundance or eliminativism – it is hard to hold onto these elements of the manifest image on the supposition that the human self is a composite. The proposed way forward is not to adopt the view that the human self is some extraordinary object, but instead to deny the general conception of ordinary objects as composites. The recommended alternative is to view ordinary objects as subjects of characteristic high-level lawlike activity. This position is compatible with either non-arbitrary view of the existence of composites.

So far, however, the discussion has proceeded at a general level, without close attention to the application of the nomological conception of ordinary objects to the case of human selves in particular. A convenient way to fill in the picture of the human self is to ask the questions characteristic of the traditional personal identity debate. This will occupy the remainder of the paper.

The personal identity debate is centrally concerned with two questions. First: what are we? Second: under what conditions do we persist? These questions can be understood as asking, in the material mode, about the nature and persistence conditions of whatever things

[22]   Jerry Fodor, 'Special Sciences: Still Autonomous After All These Years', *Philosophical Perspectives* **11** (1997), 149–163

we refer to using our personal pronouns. That is to say, they ask about the nature and persistence conditions of human selves.

First consider the nature of human selves. On the nomological conception of ordinary objects, human selves are fundamentally subjects of lawlike activity characteristic of their kind. The question now is which are the special sciences of human selves? Where are the relevant lawlike generalizations about the activity of human selves to be found?

In its way the position in the personal identity debate known as *animalism* suggests an answer to this question.[23] On the animalist view that we are fundamentally biological organisms of a certain kind, the lawlike generalizations of *biology* might be thought to be those definitive of our nature. We human selves are fundamentally subjects of activity distinctively governed by the lawlike generalizations of biology: we are things that grow, metabolize, reproduce, and so on.

An opposing neo-Lockean psychological view of our nature can be seen as instead emphasizing folk psychology, or the disciplines of cognitive science.[24] We human selves are fundamentally subjects of activity governed by the lawlike generalizations of these special sciences in particular.

However there is no evident rationale for singling out any one of these special sciences as especially definitive of human selves. I would recommend instead what might neutrally be called a *naturalist* position in the personal identity debate. According to this view, human selves, like many other ordinary objects, are fundamentally subjects of characteristic activity governed by laws from a whole *range* of the special sciences. The imagery of the university campus of separate buildings each housing a department with its own proprietary objects of study can obscure the fact that a single object may fall under the laws of multiple special sciences. For example artifacts like statues or tools are at once fruitful objects of study of material science, art history, perceptual psychology, and ethology. Likewise the human self is at once the fruitful object of study of biology, ecology, psychology, anthropology, sociology, history, and so on. This inclusive naturalism about the nature of human selves is the least arbitrary way of applying the general nomological conception of ordinary objects to the case of human selves.

---

[23]   Van Inwagen, *Material Beings*, Paul Snowdon, 'Persons, Animals, and Ourselves' in *The Person and the Human Mind* (Clarendon, 1990), Eric Olson, *The Human Animal* (Oxford University Press, 1997)

[24]   For a classic statement of a neo-Lockean view, see Sydney Shoemaker, 'Personal Identity: A Materialist's Account', in Sydney Shoemaker and Richard Swinburne, *Personal Identity* (Blackwell, 1984)

However, recent contributors to the personal identity debate have tended to insist upon an exclusive decision between biological and psychological conceptions of our nature. Why? The answer probably has something to do with the seminal influence of the second question, the question about our persistence. Consider the following plausible claim about our persistence: each one of us was once a mindless fetus. It follows, observes the animalist against the neo-Lockean, that psychological continuity cannot be necessary for our persistence. On other hand it is plausible that each one of us could be whittled down to a thinking cerebrum in a vat, without the usual continuity of biological capacities for breathing, metabolism, etc. So, observes the neo-Lockean against the animalist in turn, biological continuity cannot be necessary for our persistence. One gets the impression, then, that intuitive verdicts about persistence force an awkward choice between a psychological and biological theory of our nature. One must take a side.

What does naturalism about human selves say about our persistence? If we think that a human self is fundamentally a subject of activity governed by the lawlike generalizations of a range of special sciences then it seem to me that a *cluster theory* is the obvious companion view about our persistence. On this view we associate with human selves a range, or cluster, of activities over time, a range of ways of transmitting high-level causal influence along a path, corresponding to the range of lawlike generalizations of the special sciences with application to human selves. This range will include, as subset, both psychological continuities and metabolic biological continuities. But there is no theoretical point in claiming, as the animalist and neo-Lockean both do, that one of these subsets is individually *necessary* for human persistence. Instead we can say that a human self persists just in case there is a sufficient continuity of characteristic activity along a path, without prejudice as to whether it is comes from the psychological or narrowly biological elements of the cluster. So this view is in fact compatible with *both* of the plausible verdicts about persistence just mentioned: we can take the view that in both the fetus and the cerebrum in a vat cases, enough of the cluster of lawlike activity definitive of human selves is preserved for these to count as cases of human persistence. In this respect naturalism is more attractive than both animalist and neo-Lockean views of our persistence.[25]

---

[25] It is an interesting question, to be left for another occasion, what the naturalist should say about a 'fission'-type case, in which a human is not

The Place of The Self in Contemporary Metaphysics

This is no more than a sketch of the naturalist view of the nature and persistence of human selves. But I hope to have said enough to indicate why its prospects are bright. The view promises to sidestep a debate between two dominant but problematically narrow positions in the debate about our nature and persistence. The view flows naturally from a general conception of ordinary objects. This general conception, as we have seen, preserves the manifest image without the arbitrariness that afflicts compositionalist attempts to do the same. It is in this theoretical framework that we should hope find a satisfying place for the self in metaphysics.

University College London
r.madden@ucl.ac.uk

---

whittled down to a cerebrum but is instead divided into cerebrum and otherwise intact cerebrum-complement.

The Neurobiological Platform for Moral Values

PATRICIA S. CHURCHLAND

Abstract

What we humans call *ethics* or *morality* depends on four interlocking brain processes: (1) *caring* (supported by the neuroendocrine system, and emerging in the young as a function of parental care). (2) *Learning local social practices and the ways of others* – by positive and negative reinforcement, by imitation, by trial and error, by various kinds of conditioning, and by analogy. (3) *Recognition of others' psychological states (goals, feelings etc.)*. (4) *Problem-solving in a social context.* These four broad capacities are not unique to humans, but are probably uniquely developed in human brains by virtue of the expansion of the prefrontal cortex.[1]

1. Where Do Values Come From?[2]

Values are not in the world in the way that seasons or the tides are in the world. This has sometimes provoked the idea that moral values come from the supernatural world. A more appealing hypothesis is that moral values are not other-worldly; rather they are social-worldly. They reflect facts about how we feel and think about certain kinds of social behavior. Those processes are drivers of behavior.

The values of self-survival and self-maintenance are not in the world either. But we are not surprised that they shape the behavior of every animal. No one suggests self-survival values are other-worldly. Instead, it is easy to see how the biological world came to be organized around such values. Unless the genes build a brain that is organized to avoid danger, and seek food and water, the animal will not long survive nor likely reproduce. By contrast, an animal that is wired to care about its own self-maintenance has a better shot at having offspring. So certain self-oriented values are favored by natural selection.

---

[1]   This formulation is based on Chapter 1 of my book, *Braintrust: What Neuroscience Tells us About Morality* (Princeton University Press, 2011).

[2]   The text that follows is adapted from Chapter 4, 'The Brains Behind Morality'; *Touching a Nerve*, (New York: Norton, 2013).

doi:10.1017/S1358246115000041   ©The Royal Institute of Philosophy and the contributors 2015

Royal Institute of Philosophy Supplement **76** 2015   97

Patricia S. Churchland

The hallmark of moral values is that they involve self-cost in the care of others. Self-care seems to be in conflict with other-care. How can the neuronal organization to support such values be selected for?

2. The Hungry Brains of Homeotherms

The evolution of the mammalian brain marks the emergence of social values of the kind we associate with morality. (This story is probably true of birds too, but for simplicity I shall leaves birds aside for now, regrettably.) Sociality appears to have evolved many times, but the flexibility associated with mammalian sociality is strikingly different from the sociality of insects. The evolution of the mammalian brain saw the emergence of a brand new strategy for having babies: the young grow inside the warm, nourishing womb of the female. When mammalian offspring are born, they depend for survival on the mother. So the mammalian brain has to be organized to do something completely new: take care of others in much the way she take cares of herself. So just as I keep myself warm, fed and safe, I keep my babies warm, fed and safe.

Bit by evolutionary bit, over some 70 million years, the self-care system was modified so that care was extended to babies. Now, genes built brains that felt pain when the babies fell out of the nest. Also new, when the babies felt pain owing to cold or separation or hunger, they vocalized. This too caused the mother pain and made her respond to diminish the pain. These new mammalian brains felt pleasure when they were together with their babies, and the babies felt pleasure when they were cuddled up with their mother. They liked being together; they disliked being separated. The ancient pleasure and pain systems were extended to respond to social stimuli.

What was so advantageous about the way early mammal-like reptiles made a living that set the stage for this whole new way of having babies and extending care? The answer is energy sources.

The first reptiles that happened to be *homeotherms* had a terrific advantage – they could hunt at night when the cold-blooded competition was sluggish. Pre-mammals probably feasted on sluggish reptiles lying around waiting for the sun to come up, or at least they could forage without fear of reptilian predators. Homeotherms also managed well in colder climates, thus opening new feeding and breeding ranges.

Homeothermy requires a lot of energy, so warm-blooded animals have to eat about ten times as much as comparably sized poikilotherms.[3] If you have to take in a lot of calories to survive, it may help to have a brain that can adapt to new conditions by being smart and flexible. Biologically speaking, it is vastly faster to build brains that can learn prodigiously than to rig a genome that builds brains with reflexes for every contingency that might crop up. To accommodate learning, the genome has to have genes that get expressed to make new protein to add wiring to embody new information. That is much less complex than altering a genome so that it builds a brain that can know at birth how to react in many different circumstances.[4] Notice that using a learning strategy to tune up the brain for strategic survival also means that at birth the offspring have only basic reflexes. Mammalian babies are dependent.

Learning requires circuitry that can respond to experience in an adaptive manner yet also work hand in hand with the old motivational, pain and drive systems long in place. Laminar cortex is a remarkable computational solution to the Big Learning problem. It can provide the kind of power and flexibility needed for learning, and also for advantageous planning, and efficient impulse control. Gene duplication allows for the smooth addition of cortical subfields, since the basic recipe for a patch of six-laminar organization of cortex appears to be easily repeatable. Hence size of cortex is expandable in response to ecological pressures.

Exactly how the six-layer cortex emerged from the loosely organized one-to-two layer of reptilian dorsal cortex is largely lost in our ancient past. Nevertheless, comparisons of the brains of different existing species as well as studies of brain development from birth to maturity can tell us a lot.[5] It is known that cortical fields supporting sensory functions vary in size, complexity, and in the connectivity portfolio as a function of a particular mammal's lifestyle and ecological niche. For example, flying squirrels have a very large visual cortical field, whereas the platypus cortex has a tiny visual field but large somatosensory fields. The ghost bat, a noctural mammal that relies on precise echo-location to hunt, has a relatively huge auditory field, a

[3]   Lane, Nick. Chapter 8, 'Hot Blood', in *Life Ascending: The Ten Great Inventions of Evolution* (New York: W. W. Norton, 2009).
[4]   Quartz, S.R. and Sejnowski T.J. 'The Constructivist Brain', *Trends in Cognitive Sciences* 3 (1999), 48–57; Quartz, S.R. and Sejnowski T.J. *Liars, Lovers and Heroes* (NY: William Morrow, 2003).
[5]   Krubitzer, L. (2007) 'The magnificent compromise: cortical field evolution in mammals', *Neuron* 2 (2007), 201–08; Krubitzer, L. and Kaas J. 'The evolution of the neocortex in mammals: how is phenotypic diversity generated?', *Current Opinion in Neurobiology* 15 (2005), 444–53.

Patricia S. Churchland

small visual field, and a somatosensory field much smaller than that of the platypus.[6] Among rodents there are very different styles of moving – flying squirrels, swimming beavers, tree-climbing squirrels, for example. This means that there will also be organizational differences in the parts of the brain that are associated with skilled movement, including motor cortex. In all mammals, frontal cortex is concerned with motor function. In front of the motor regions is prefrontal cortex – areas concerned with control, sociality, and decision-making. All of these cortical fields have rich pathways to and from the whole range of subcortical regions.

Brains are energy hogs, and the calorie intake of homeotherms is high not just to keep body temperature constant, but also to keep their big brains in business. Moreover, because young mammalian brains are so immature at birth, their calorie intake is especially high. Because mammals eat so much more than reptiles, a given range supports fewer of them. Dozens of lizards can feed quite well on a small patch but a patch that size will support fewer squirrels and even fewer bobcats. The implication for litter size is that the more successful strategy may to produce fewer rather than many offspring, and to invest heavily in their welfare to independence and reproductive maturation.

3. Social Bonding

Why do mammalian mothers typically go to great lengths to feed and care for their babies? After all, such care can be demanding, it interferes with feeding, and it can be dangerous. Two central characters in the neurobiological explanation of mammalian other-care are the simple nonapeptides, *oxytocin* and *vasopressin*. The hypothalamus regulates many basic life-functions, including feeding, drinking, and sexual behavior. In mammals, the hypothalamus secretes oxytocin, which triggers a cascade of events with the end result that the mother is powerfully attached to her offspring; she wants to have the offspring close and warm and fed. The hypothalamus also secretes vasopressin, which triggers a different cascade of events so that the mother protects offspring, defending them against predators, for example.[7]

[6] Krubitzer L, Campi KL, Cooke DF. 'All rodents are not the same: A modern synthesis of cortical organization', *Brain, Behavior and Evolution,* **78** (2011), 1, 51–93.
[7] Porges, S.W. and Carter, C.S. 'Neurobiology and evolution: Mechanisms, mediators, and adaptive consequences of caregiving', in *Self*

The Neurobiological Platform for Moral Values

The lineage of oxytocin and vasopressin goes back about 500 million-years, long before mammals began to appear. In reptiles these nonapeptides play various roles in fluid regulation and in reproductive processes such as egg-laying, sperm ejection, and spawning stimulation. In mammalian males, oxytocin is still secreted in the testes, and still aids sperm ejaculation. In females it is secreted in the ovaries and plays a role in the release of eggs. In mammals, the roles of oxytocin and vasopressin in both the body and the brain were expanded and modified, along with circuitry changes in the hypothalamus to implement post-natal maternal behavior, including suckling and care.[8]

During pregnancy, genes in the fetus and in the placenta make hormones that are released into the mother's blood; (e.g. progesterone, prolactin, and estrogen.) This leads to a sequestering of oxytocin in neurons in the mother's hypothalamus. Just prior to parturition, progesterone levels drop sharply, the density of oxytocin receptors in the hypothalamus increases, and a flood of oxytocin is released from the hypothalamus.

The brain is not the only target of oxytocin, however. It is released also in the body during birth, facilitating the uterine contractions. During lactation, oxytocin is needed for milk ejection, but is also released in the brain of both mother and infant with a calming influence. Assuming the typical background neural circuitry and assuming the typical suite of other resident neurochemicals, oxytocin facilitates attachment of mother to baby. *And* of baby to mother.[9]

Interest and Beyond: Toward a New Understanding of Human Caregiving, (ed.) S.L. Brown, R.M. Brown, and L.A. Penner (Oxford: Oxford University Press, 2007); Keverne E.B. 'Genomic Imprinting and the Evolution of Sex Differences in Mammalian Reproductive Strategies', *Advances in Genetics* **59** (2007): 217–43; Cheng Y, Chen C, Lin C-P, Chou K-H, Decety J. 'Love hurts: An fMRI study', *NeuroImage* **51** (2010), 9.

[8] Carter, C.S., Grippo, A.J., Pournajafi-Nazarloo, H. Ruscio, M., and Porges, S.W. 'Oxytocin, vasopressin, and sociality' in *Progress in Brain Research* **170** (eds) Inga D. Neumann and Rainer Landgraf (Mew York: Elsevier, 2008), 331–6; Young, L. and Alexander, B. *The Chemistry Between Us: Love, Sex and the Science of Attraction* (New York: Penguin, 2012).

[9] Broad K.D, Curley J.P, and Keverne E.B, 'Mother–Infant Bonding and the Evolution of Mammalian Social Relationships', *Philosophical Transactions of the Royal Society B: Biological Sciences* **361**:1476 (2006),

Patricia S. Churchland

Physical pain is a 'protect myself' signal, and these signals lead to corrective behavior organized by self-preservation circuitry. In mammals, the pain system is expanded and modified; protect myself and *protect my babies*. In addition to a pathway that identifies the kind of pain and locates the site of a painful stimulus, there are pathways responsible for emotional pain, prominently associated with the cingulate cortex, but also subcortical structures such as the amygdala. So when the infant cries in distress, the mother's emotional pain system responds and she takes corrective action. Another cortical area, the insula, monitors the physiological state of the entire body. When you are gently and lovingly stroked, this area sends out 'emotionally-safe' signals (*doing-very-well-now*). The same emotionally-safe signal emerges when the baby is safe and content. And of course the infant responds likewise to gentle and loving touches: *ahhhhh, all is well, I am safe, I am fed*. Safety signals down-regulate vigilance signals such as cortisol. When anxiety and fear are down-regulated, contentment and peacefulness can take their place.

The expression of maternal behavior also depends on the endogenous opiods. This means that during suckling and other kinds of infant care, the opiods down-regulate anxiety, allowing for peaceful responses. If opiod receptors are experimentally blocked, maternal behavior is blocked. This has been observed, for example, in rats, sheep, and rhesus monkeys.[10] A reasonable speculation is that the endogenous cannabinoids also play an important role, but much about the extensive cannabinoid system remains unknown.

Although some mammals, such as marmosets and titi monkeys are biparental, in many species, the father takes no interest in parenting and shows none of the mother's attachment to the infant. There are many variations on the basic circuitry regulating parental behavior, depending on a species' ecological niche and how it makes its living. For example, sheep refuse to suckle any lamb that is not

---

2199–214; Keverne E.B. and Curley J.P. 'Vasopressin, oxytocin and social behaviour', *Current Opinion in Neurobiology* **14** (2004), 777–783.
[10]   Martel F.L., Nevison C.M., Rayment F.D., Simpson M.J., and Keverne E.B., *Psychoneuroendocrinology* **18** (1993), 307–321; Keverne, E.B. 'Understanding well-being in the evolutionary context of brain development', *Philosophical Transactions of the Royal Society of London B* **359**:1449 (2004), 1349–58; Broad K.D, Curley J.P, and Keverne E.B, 'Mother–Infant Bonding and the Evolution of Mammalian Social Relationships', *Philosophical Transactions of the Royal Society B: Biological Sciences* **361**:1476 (2004), 2199–214.

their own, whereas pigs and dogs will often suckle nonkin, and even infants of other species.

Studies on rodents of the effect of separation of a pup from the mother (3 hours a day for the first two weeks of life) reveal experience-dependent changes in oxytocin and vasopressin synthesis, as well as changes in brain-specific regions of receptors for oxytocin and vasopressin. Behaviorally, the pups that were separated from their mothers showed heightened aggression and anxiety. In some way that is not yet entirely understood, the rats' brains and behavior were altered in a deprived social environment.[11] In a set of important finding on the relationship between stress regulation, genes expression and social behavior, Michael Meany and colleagues have shown in rodents that during infancy, licking and loving stimulates gene expression that affects the density of receptors for oxytocin in the hypothalamus. More generally, parental tending, or lack thereof, regulates neuroendocrine responses to stress.[12] They also showed that variations in maternal care of female infants is associated with subsequent variations in maternal care displayed by those same females to the next generation of infants. This is a remarkable epigenetic effect. It suggests that neglect or abuse adversely affects the capacity for normal caring, and hence for normal socialization. Further research will explore this matter.

Here is where we are in the values story: that anything has value *at all* and is motivating *at all* ultimately depends on the very ancient neural organization serving survival and well-being. With the evolution of mammals, the rudimentary 'self-caring organization' is modified to extend the basic values of being alive and well to selected others – to *Me and Mine*. Depending on the evolutionary pressures to which a species is subject, caring may extend to mates, kin, and to friends. Social mammals do tend to show attachment and caring behavior to others besides their own offspring. Exactly which others come within the ambit of caring depends, as always, on the species, how it makes its living, and whether it is thriving. The pain of another's distress and the motivation to care seems to fall off with social distance. By and large, motivation to care seems to

[11]   Veenema, A. 'Toward understanding how early-life social experiences alter oxytocin- and vasopressin-regulated social behaviors', *Hormones and Behavior* **61**:3 (2012), 304–312.

[12]   Meany, M.J. 'Maternal care, gene expression, and the transmission of individual differences in stress reactivity across generations', *Annual Review of Neuroscience* **24** (2001), 1161–92.

be stronger for offspring than for affiliates, for friends than for strangers, for mates than for friends, and so on.

If the maternalization of the brain means that care extends to offspring via mechanisms in the hypothalamus, are those same mechanisms modified to extend care to mates and others? The answer is not entirely clear at this point. Nevertheless, prairie voles (*Microtus ochrogaster*), who tend to bond for life, have provided an important avenue of research on this question. In this context, *bonding* means that mates prefer the company of each other to that of any other vole. Bonded mates like to be together, the male guards the nest, and they show stress when separated. Male prairie voles also participate in rearing the pups. In prairie voles, permanent bonding typically occurs after the first mating. Bonding does not imply sexual exclusivity, but regardless of other mating interactions, the pair remains as mates that spend a lot of time together and share parenting.

Montane voles, by contrast, do not exhibit comparable social behavior, nor does the male have any role in guarding the nest or rearing the pups. They are not social, and do not like to huddle or hang out with each other.

Because these two species are so very similar, save for their social behavior, the intriguing question is this: what are the relevant differences between the brains of prairie voles and montane voles? It turned out that the differences were not macrostructural. Rather, one major difference is microstructural, pertaining mainly to oxytocin, vasopressin, and differences in the density of receptors that can bind those hormones.

In one region of the reward system (the *nucleus accumbens*), the prairie voles contrast with the montane voles in having a higher density of receptors for *oxytocin*. In another region of the reward system (*ventral pallidum*) prairie voles have a higher density of receptors for *vasopressin*. It should also be noted that both males and females have oxytocin and vasopressin, along with their cognate receptors.

The differences in receptor density are one circuit-level difference that help explain long-term attachment of mates after the first mating, but there are other factors involved as well. For example, after mating, the mates need to be able to recognize one another as individuals. Recognition requires learning, which is mediated by the neurotransmitter, dopamine. So if you block the receptors for dopamine, the vole cannot remember whom it was she mated with, and so bonding with a particular mate does not occur. It should also be noted that the receptor density portfolio seen in prairie voles may not extend to all pair-bonders. For example, in mice, the density of vasopressin receptors in the ventral pallidum does not distinguish monogamous from promiscuous species of mice.[13] For technical and ethical reasons, essentially nothing is known about human non-apeptide receptor densities.

Though very common among birds, strong mate preference is somewhat uncommon in mammals. Only about three percent of mammals, including prairie voles, pine voles, California deer mice, beavers, titi monkeys and marmosets show mate attachment.

How exactly do oxytocin and vasopressin regulate other-care? A proper answer would involve the details of all the relevant circuitry and how the neurons in the circuits behave. Unfortunately, these details are not yet known.[14] What is known is that in rodents oxytocin down-regulates the activity of neurons in the amygdala, a structure mediating fear responses and avoidance learning, among other things.[15] When animals are in high alert against danger, when they are preparing to fight or flee, stress hormones are high and oxytocin levels are low. When the threat has passed and the animals is among friends, hugging and chatting, stress hormones back off and oxytocin levels surge. So not only are the amygdala-dependent fear responses down-regulated, but the brainstem switches from fight-and-flight preparation to rest-and-digest mode.

Is oxytocin the *love molecule* or the *cuddle molecule*, as has sometimes been suggested? No. The serious research on oxytocin reveals how very complicated is its action, and how complicated is the circuitry underlying social attachment.[16] Some remarkable claims about correlations between strength of love and blood levels of oxytocin are so astonishing as to raise a flag regarding experimental procedures.[17] Caution is in order.

[13] Goodson, J.L. 'Deconstructing sociality, social evolution and relevant nonapeptide functions', *Psychoneuroendocrinology* (http://dx.doi.org/10.1016/j.psyneuen.2012.12.005).
[14] Ibid.
[15] Panksepp, J. 'Feeling the Pain of Social Loss', *Science* **302**: 5643 (2003), 237–9; Panksepp J. and Biven L. *The Archaeology of Mind: Neuroevolutionary Origins of Human Emotions* (New York: Norton, 2012).
[16] Churchland, P.S. and Winkielman, P. 'Modulating social behavior with oxytocin: How does it work? What does it do?', *Hormones and Behavior* **61** (2012), 392–399.
[17] McCullough, M.E., Churchland, P.S., Mendez, A.J. 'Problems with measuring peripheral oxytocin: Can data on oxytocin and human behavior be trusted?', *Neuroscience and Behavioral Reviews* (2013), http://dx.doi.org/doi:10.1016/j.neubiorev.2013.04.018.

Patricia S. Churchland

Lest it be thought that if something is good, more of it will be better, here is a cautionary note. If extra oxytocin is injected into the brain of a happily mated female prairie vole, her degree of mate attachment actually wanes, not rises, and she may become promiscuous.

4. Morality in Humans

The foregoing constitutes a very brief overview of what is known about how oxytocin and vasopressin operate in the brain to create a platform for sociality, and hence for morality. But how do we get from a general disposition to care about others, to specific moral actions, such as telling the truth, respecting the goods of others, and keeping promises? How to we get from familial caring to broader community-wide values such as honesty, loyalty and courage? The answer has two intertwined parts: *learning by the young*, and *problem-solving by everyone*.

In group-living species such as humans, lemurs and baboons, learning the local conventions and the personality traits of individuals, knowing who is related to whom, and avoiding blackening one's own reputation become increasingly important. Learning, especially by imitation, is the mammalian trick that gets us both flexibility and well-grooved skills. Problem-solving, in the context of learning by trial and error, is the complementary trick that leads to stable social practices for avoiding such problems as conflict.

Children observe, sometimes quite automatically and implicitly, sometimes explicitly and with reflection, the advantages of cooperation. Two children rowing a boat gets them across the lake much faster; two turning the long skipping rope allows doubles skipping, turn-taking means everyone gets a chance so the games do not break down. Men working together can raise a barn in one day. Women working together feed all the men and the children. Singing in a group with parts makes beautiful music. Pitching a tent is easier with two people, and hiking together provides safety. A child quickly comes to recognize the value of cooperation.[18]

This does not mean that there is a gene 'for cooperation'. If you are sociable, and you want to achieve some goal, then a cooperative tactic can seem a fairly obvious solution to a practical problem. As

---

[18]   On the formation of group identity in children, see Killen, M. and Rutland, A. *Children and Social Exclusion: Morality, Prejudice and Group Identity* (Oxford: Wiley-Blackwell, 2013).

philosopher David Hume observed, a crucial part of your socialization as a child is that you come to recognize the value of social
practices such as cooperation and keeping promises. This means
you are then willing to sacrifice something when it is necessary to
keep those practices stable in the long run. You may not actually
articulate the value of such social practices. Your knowledge of
their value may even be largely unconscious, but the value shapes
your behavior nonetheless. Primatologist Sarah Brosnan suggests
this is true also of nonhuman primates.[19]

In this context it is important to remember that although all
mammals are born immature and learn a great deal during development, the period of human immaturity is especially long and the
amount of learning is prodigious. For example, about 50% of a
human brain's connections emerge after birth, and the human
adult brain weighs about five times that of the infant brain.[20]

Moreover, in the period leading up to puberty the human brain
undergoes substantial pruning and therewith a decrease in connectivity, whereas rodent brains and monkey brains do not show the same
degree of pre-pubertal pruning. Jean-Pierre Changeux has argued
that these particular epigenetic features of human brain development
– extended immaturity and pre-pubertal pruning – enable learning of
complex social and cultural organization.[21] More succinctly,
Changeux proposes that the unique developmental profile is what
has made human culture, including its moral institutions, possible.
Interestingly, this unusually long period of immaturity may
depend only a few regulatory genes that extend the period of epigenetic responsivity to the social and physical environments.[22]

What I call *problem-solving* is part of a general capacity to do smart
things, and to respond flexibly and productively to new circumstances. Social problem-solving is directed toward finding suitable
ways to cope with challenges such as instability, conflict, cheating,
catastrophe and resource scarcity. It is probably an extension to the

[19] Brosnan S.F. 'A hypothesis of the co-evolution between cooperation
and response inequity', *Frontiers in Decision Neuroscience* (2011), doi:
10.3389/fnins.2011.00043.
[20] Huttenlocher P.R. and Dabholkar A. S. 'Regional differences in synaptogenesis in human cerebral cortex', *Journal of Comparative Neurology*
387 (1997), 167–178; Bourgeois, J.P. 'Synaptogenesis, heterochrony and
epigenesis in mammalian neocortex', *Acta Pediatrica Supplement* **422**
(1997), 27–33.
[21] Changeux, J.-P. *Neuronal Man* (Neew York: Pantheon Books, 1985).
[22] Keverne, E.B. and Curley J.P. 'Epigenetics, brain evolution and
behavior', *Frontiers in Neuroendocrinology* **29** (2008), 398–412.

Patricia S. Churchland

social domain of a broader capacity for problem solving in the physical world. Depending on what you pay most attention to, you may be more skilled in the social domain or in the nonsocial domain, or vice versa. From this perspective, moral problem-solving is, in its turn, a special instance of social problem-solving more broadly.[23]

Although evaluating how to proceed with a particular case is frequently the most pressing concern, the more fundamental problem concerns general principles and institutional structures that undergird well-being and stability. The development of certain practices as normative – as the right way to handle *this* problem – is critical in a group's cultural evolution.[24] These norms are established principles enjoining group members against such behavior as embezzlement and other specific forms of cheating. Motivated to belong, and recognizing the benefits of belonging, humans and other highly social animals find ways to get along, despite tension, irritation, and annoyance. Social practices may differ from one group to another, especially when ecological conditions are different. The Inuit of the Arctic will have solved some social problems differently from the Pirahã of the Amazonian basin in Brazil, if only because social problems are not isolated from the physical constraints such as climate and food resources.[25]

Similarities in social practices are not uncommon, as different cultures hit upon similar solutions to particular problems. Subtle and not so subtle differences may also obtain. This is akin to common themes in other practices, such as boat-building or animal husbandry. Particular cultures developed skills for building particular styles of boats – dugout canoes, birch bark canoes, skin-backed kayaks, rafts with sails, junks for fishing on the rivers, and so forth. After many generations, the boats made by separate groups are exquisitely suited to the particular nature of the waters to be traveled on and the materials available. Notice too that many different cultures learned to use the stars for navigation. Some picked up the trick from travelers, others figured it out independently, just as conventions for private property occurred in different groups as their size

[23] Peterson, Dale. *The Moral Lives of Animals* (NY: Bloomsbury Press, 2011).
[24] Kitcher, P.S. *The Ethical Project* (Cambridge, MA: Harvard University Press, 2012).
[25] Hoebel, E.A. *The Law of Primitive Man* (Cambridge MA: Harvard University Press, 1954), Chapter 5; Everett D. *Don't Sleep, There are Snakes: Life and Language in the Amazonian Jungle* (New York: Pantheon Books, 2009).

expanded as agricultural practices became widespread. I am reasonably confident that there is no gene for navigating by the stars.

Though expressions of moral values can vary across cultures, they are not arbitrary, in the way that the conventions for funerals or weddings tend to be. Matters of etiquette, though important for smoothing social interactions, are not serious and momentous as moral values are. Truth-telling and promise-keeping are socially desirable in all cultures, and hence exhibit less dramatic variability than customs at weddings. Is there a gene for these behaviors? Though that hypothesis cannot be ruled out, there is so far no evidence for a truth-telling or a promise-keeping gene. More likely, practices for truth-telling and promise-keeping developed in much the same way as practices for boat building. They reflected the local ecology and are a fairly obvious solution to a common social problem.[26]

Being reminded of the variability in what counts as morally acceptable helps us acknowledge that standards of morality are not universal. More generally, it reminds us that moral truths and laws do not reside in Plato's heaven to be accessed by pure reason. It reminds us that perorations about morality are often mixed with a whole range of emotions, including fear, resentment, empathy and compassion.[27]

5. Tensions, Conventions and Balance

The mammalian brain is organized both for self-care and to develop care for others, but on many occasions, the two conflict. Social life brings benefits, but it also brings tensions. We compete with siblings and friends for resources and status; we also need to cooperate with them. Some individuals are temperamentally more problematic than others. Sometimes you have to tolerate others who are irritating or noisy or smelly.

Social life can often be very subtle, calling for judgment, not strict adherence to rules. As Aristotle and the Chinese philosopher, Mencius, well realized, you cannot prepare for every contingency or for every situation that may crop up in life. Judgment is essential. Sometimes telling a lie *is* the right thing to do – if it saves the group from a madman threatening to blow up a bomb, for example.

[26]   Hoebel, E.A. *The Law of Primitive Man* (Cambridge MA: Harvard University Press, 1954), Chapter 5.
[27]   Decety, J. 'The neuroevolution of empathy', *Annals of the New York Academy of Sciences.* **1231** (2011), 35–45.

Patricia S. Churchland

Sometimes breaking a promise *is* the right thing to do – if it prevents a truly terrible catastrophe, such as the meltdown of a nuclear reactor. There are no rules for determining when something is a legitimate exception to prohibitions such as *don't lie, don't break a promise,* and *don't steal.* Children quickly learn about prototypical exceptions, and apply fuzzy-bounded categories rather than hide-bound rules.[28] Balance, as all wise moral philosophers have emphasized, may not be precisely definable, but it is needed to lead a good social and moral life. Not every beggar can be brought home and fed, not all your kidneys can be donated, not every disappointment can be remedied.[29]

6. Concluding Remarks

The capacity for moral behavior is rooted in the neurobiology of sociality, and in mammals depends on nonapeptides oxytocin and vasopressin, as well as on elaborated cortical structures that interface with the more ancient structures mediating motivation, reward, and emotion. The neural mechanisms supporting social behavior are tuned up epigenetically by social interactions and by learning the social practices of the group, and by figuring out how to best deal with new social problems. Emerging after the advent of agriculture and the growth of large groups, organized religions would have built upon existing social practices, perhaps augmenting them in ways relevant to new social demands. Although it is known that oxytocin and vasopressin are critical in social behavior, much about their roles as well as the circuitry with which they interact remains unknown.

University of California, San Diego
pschurchland@ucsd.edu

---

[28] Killen, M. and Smetana, J.G. (eds), *Handbook of Moral Development* (Mahwah N.J.: Lawrence Erlbaum Associates, 2006); Park, Y. and Killen, M. 'When is peer rejection justifiable? Children's understanding across two cultures', *Cognitive Development* **25** (2010): 290–31.
[29] Schwartz, B. and Sharpe, K. *Practical Wisdom: The Right Way to do the Right Thing* (NY: Riverhead Books, 2010).

'The Secrets of All Hearts': Locke on Personal Identity[1]

GALEN STRAWSON

Abstract

Many think John Locke's account of personal identity is inconsistent and circular. It's neither of these things. The root causes of the misreading are [i] the mistake of thinking that Locke uses 'consciousness' to mean memory, [ii] failure to appreciate the importance of the 'concernment' that always accompanies 'consciousness', on Locke's view, [iii] a tendency to take the term *person*, in Locke's text, as if it were (only) some kind of fundamental sortal term like 'human being' or 'thinking thing', and to fail to take proper account of Locke's use of it as a 'forensic' term (§26). It's well known that Locke uses *person* as a forensic term, but the consequences of this have still not been fully worked out.

1. Introduction

Many people think that John Locke's account of personal identity is inconsistent and circular. In fact it's neither of these things – Locke has been massively misunderstood. The blame for the misunderstanding falls principally on two otherwise admirable bishops – Berkeley and Butler – and an otherwise admirable doctor of divinity

---

[1] This paper summarizes one of the central lines of argument in my book *Locke on Personal Identity: Consciousness and Concernment* (Princeton, NJ: Princeton University Press, 2011, revised edition, 2014). On many points I am in agreement with Udo Thiel (see e.g. Thiel 'Personal Identity', in *The Cambridge History of Seventeenth-Century Philosophy*. Vol 1. (ed.) M. R. Ayers and D. Garber (Cambridge: Cambridge University Press,1998), and Thiel, *The Early Modern Subject: Self-consciousness and Personal Identity from Descartes to Hume* (Oxford: Oxford University Press, 2011)). When I cite a work I give the first publication date or estimated date of composition while the page reference is to the edition listed in the bibliography. When quoting Locke I use the fourth (1700) or fifth (1706) edition (*An Essay concerning Human Understanding* (ed.) P. Nidditch. Oxford: Clarendon Press, 1689–1700, 1975). I refer to the paragraphs of Locke's chapter on 'Identity and diversity' simply by their numbers (e.g. §9). In quotations I mark my emphases in italics and the author's in bold (only some of Locke's own italics indicate emphasis).

doi:10.1017/S1358246115000144   ©The Royal Institute of Philosophy and the contributors 2015

Royal Institute of Philosophy Supplement **76** 2015   111

Galen Strawson

– Thomas Reid.[2] Their influence has been such that almost no one since their time has had a chance to read what Locke wrote without prejudice. Another bishop – Bishop Law – put things right in 1769, when he was Master of Peterhouse, Cambridge, and Knightbridge Professor of Philosophy, in his *Defence of Mr. Locke's Opinion Concerning Personal Identity*. But no one paid any lasting attention.

The root cause of the misunderstanding, perhaps, has been the tendency to read the term 'person' in Locke's *Essay* as if it were simply a sortal term like 'human being' or 'thinking thing', a term for a standard temporal continuant. This approach is bound to lead to error because it fails to take proper account of Locke's use of 'person' as what he calls a 'forensic' term (§26).

Many have acknowledged the importance of the forensic use, but they've continued to suppose that Locke's principal aim is to provide criteria of diachronic identity for persons considered simply as persisting subjects of experience, and so considered independently of forensic matters. They have thought that Locke is trying to answer the following canonical question about personal identity: [i] consider a subject of experience at time t_1 (2000, say) who is a person as we ordinarily understand this term – call this person 'P_1'. [ii] Consider a subject of experience at a later time t_2 (2015, say) who is a person as we ordinarily understand this term – call this person 'P_2'. Question: What has to be the case for it to be true that P_1 at (time) t_1 is the same as person P_2 at (time) t_2, the same persisting subject of experience?

Locke isn't interested in this question – not as it is ordinarily understood. He takes the notion of a persisting subject of experience or locus of consciousness for granted in his discussion of personal identity, and answers four other questions:

---

[2]   The most well known formulations of the inconsistency objection are found in Berkeley's *Alciphron: or the Minute Philosopher* (in *Philosophical Writings,* (ed.) D. Clarke (Cambridge: Cambridge University Press, 1732/ 2008) and Reid's *Essays on the Intellectual Powers of Man* (ed.) D. Brookes (Edinburgh: Edinburgh University Press, 1785/2002). The circularity objection is standardly attributed to Butler (in the First Appendix (*First Dissertation*), in *The Analogy of Religion* (2nd ed., London: Knapton, 1736). It was, however, stated by Sergeant in 1697, and Sergeant adapted it from a debate between South and Sherlock that was well known in Butler's time, in which South (1693) made it validly against Sherlock (1690). See Thiel 'Personal Identity' (1998), 875–7, 898. Garrett also argues that both objections fail ('Locke on Personal Identity, Consciousness, and "Fatal Errors"', *Philosophical Topics* **31** (2003), 95–125).

[A]   what does a subject of experience that qualifies as a person consist of, ontologically speaking, considered at any given time?
[B]   what mental capacities must a subject of experience have in order to qualify as a person?
[C]   what sorts of changes of substantial composition can a subject of experience that qualifies as a person undergo while continuing to exist?
[D]   which actions is a subject of experience who qualifies as a person responsible for at any given time?

These are the questions he sets himself to answer and does answer – as I will now try to show. (For **[A]** see in particular section 9, for **[B]** section 10, for **[C]** and **[D]** section 12.)

2. 'Subject of experience'

Let me establish an uncommitted term that allows one to refer neutrally to *the kind of thing that Locke is concerned with when he raises the question of its personal identity* (the aim is to avoid begging or obscuring any relevant questions and triggering irrelevant questions). The term must be neither *soul* nor *man* nor *person*, all of which Locke famously distinguishes from each other (§7). Nor can it be any of the terms he uses interchangeably with *soul*, i.e. *immaterial substance* (§14), (*immaterial*) *spirit* (§14, 15), *immaterial being* (§14), *individual immaterial substance* (§23), *immaterial thinking thing* (§23); nor any of the terms he uses interchangeably with *man*, i.e. *rational animal* (§8, parrots being *sub judice*) and (*human*) *animal* (§§6, 8). Nor can it be any of the terms Locke uses when he wishes to put aside the question of whether 'that which is conscious in us' (§25) is material or immaterial – terms like *intellectual substance* (§13) and *thinking substance* (§13, §23). These terms also fail to be neutral in the required way, if only because they introduce the notion of substance, for one of the things that Locke aims to question is precisely whether a person is or must be supposed to be a substance.

The same goes for *conscious thinking thing* (§17), 'that *thinking thing* that is in us' (§27), *thinking being* (§25), *intelligent being* (§25), and other such terms. For *thing* and *being*, here, are essentially the same as *substance*. Nor is *self* a sufficiently neutral choice, for Locke treats *self* as synonymous with *person*.[3] There are, among all his

---

[3]   Thiel uses *self* as the uncommitted term, in effect, and successfully makes the key points about Locke in this way, but the term is not ideal given that Locke uses it interchangeably with *person* in 2.27.

Galen Strawson

unhelpfully numerous terms, some that could perhaps serve as the uncommitted term. One possibility is *intelligent agent* (§26), or *individual agent* (§13), but at certain points problems arise even with *agent*.[4] Locke's use of 'consciousness' as a count noun in §23 – 'could we suppose two distinct incommunicable consciousnesses acting the same body, the one constantly by day, the other by night' – might serve the purpose. It is, in a sense, exactly what we want, and it's Locke's own use. It would, however, be confusing to use 'consciousness' in this way in this paper, in addition to using it in the more standard way as a non-count noun.

I propose therefore to introduce my own term: *subject of experience*. The entity that Locke is concerned with, when he raises the question of what its personal identity consists in, is a subject of experience. Not any kind of subject of experience, such as an elephant or a dog or a fox (2.1.19, 2.11.7), but a subject of experience whose mental capacities are such that it qualifies as a person (§§9, 26). Subjects of experience of any species can be persons, so long as they possess the requisite capacities, but Locke's principal concern is unsurprisingly with ourselves, human persons, human subjects of experience considered either at a particular time in life or on the Day of Judgement. This is where he starts from – the given fact of complex, self-conscious, diachronically persisting personalitied subjects of experience like ourselves who are born, live, and die (but who may, he crucially argues, conceivably survive switches of body and soul), who act, who are capable of pleasure and pain, happiness and misery, and who are on Locke's view eventually resurrected. In asking about the *personal identity* of such subjects of experience, Locke's focus is always on the forensic issue of what they're (morally and legally) responsible for. His question is about their personal identity in the sense of their moral or legal identity, their overall standing when it comes to the question of moral and legal responsibility.

3. 'Person'

The word 'person' has a double use and has perhaps always done so. In its most common use, today as in the seventeenth century, it denotes a human being considered as a whole: a *person₁* as I will say. But a less common use, henceforth *person₂*, is no less available

---

[4]   '*The mind*' is another candidate term, given Locke's use of it (see e.g. §§13, 23), but this choice would cause other unclarities. As for *rational being*, it is identified with person in §9 and with thinking being in §8.

to us, no less natural and no less readily understood. This is the use that allows one to say of a human being 'She isn't the same person any more' or 'He's become a completely different person'. When Henry James writes of one of his early novels 'I think of... the masterpiece in question ... as the work of quite another person than myself ... a rich ... relation, say, who ... suffers me still to claim a shy fourth cousinship' (1915, 562–3) he knows perfectly well that he's the same human being (person₁) as the author of that book. It's just that he doesn't feel he's the same person₂ as the author of that book and we all know what he means – even though the notion of a person₂ is somewhat vague. Here James is using the word 'person' in the familiar way that allows one to distinguish the person or self that one is from the human being that one is considered as a whole.

The person₂ use of 'person' is plainly connected to the notion of personality, and we ordinarily think of personality as a property of a creature, not as a thing of any sort; and yet when we use 'person' to mean a person₂ we do still think of it as denoting a thing or entity of some sort – a subject of experience, a 'self'. We don't think that we're using the word just as a way of talking about personality, where personality is a mere property of a person₁. Much of the difficulty of exposition of Locke's view lies in a similar fact about his use of 'person'.

A Lockean person – a *Person*, as I'll say, using an initial capital letter to mark Locke's special use of the term (except when quoting Locke or others) – is certainly not a person₁, i.e. (or e.g.) a human being. A (Lockean) Person isn't a person₂ either as ordinarily conceived (i.e. an instance of the kind of thing that Henry James takes himself to be in 1915 when he says that he's a different person from the person who wrote his early novel). Locke's use of 'person' does share certain features with the person₂ use. It shares [i] the person₂ use's fundamental connection with the property-denoting notion of personality (or rather, in Locke's case, the property-denoting notion of one's overall moral personality or standing). But it also shares with the person₂ use [ii] the person₂ use's property of being naturally taken to denote a thing of some sort, i.e. not merely a property, but rather something that is naturally thought of as a temporal continuant, however vague its temporal boundaries. And the trouble is that [i] and [ii] pull in different directions. Lockean Personal identity is not simply a matter of the diachronic identity of a temporal continuant, in spite of the [ii]-affinity. To take proper account of the [i]-affinity is to see that there's a key sense in which one's overall moral personality or being changes all the time, on Locke's view, simply insofar as one engages in new actions and experiences. Thus a person – a Lockean person, a subject of experience

Galen Strawson

who is a Person – is different every day and indeed every moment, on Locke's view, so far as its *Personal identity* or *Personhood* is concerned. And this is of course not so given the standard person₁ use or the standard person₂ use of 'person' according to which a person's personal identity remains unchanged through time.

4. '"Person" a forensic term'

Plainly there is scope for confusion. I hope things will become clearer in what follows. One can put the point by saying that there's a sense in which 'person' is indeed a property term, a term for a *moral quality*, in Locke's text, in spite of its natural use as a thing term. Throughout the seventeenth century, as Thiel observes,

> 'person' most commonly referred to an individual human being: it was simply a term for the individual human self, as it is today. But in some philosophical discussions 'person' referred to a particular aspect, quality, or function of the individual human being (1998, 868–9)

This second use of the word derives from Roman law, in which '*persona*', which originally meant 'mask', refers 'to the individual human being specifically in so far as he or she stands in a relationship to legal matters' (ibid.).

J. L. Mackie generally reads Locke well, and he's right when he says that Locke's theory 'is ... hardly a theory of personal identity at all, but might be better described as a theory of action appropriation'. This, after all, is exactly what Locke says himself. But Mackie then goes on to claim that 'Locke seems to be forgetting that "person" is not only "a forensic term", appropriating actions and their merit, but also the noun corresponding to all the personal pronouns, i.e. a thing term' (1976, 183). But Locke isn't forgetting this. He's chosen to use the word 'person' in a less common but time-honoured way which, for all that it is forensic, can still correspond to the personal pronouns. He's well aware that his use of 'person' is non-standard. He says so himself: 'Person, *as I take it*' – 'Person', *as I am taking the word* – 'is a forensic term' (§26).

5. The Field of Responsibility and the Field of Concernment

'Person ... is a forensic term appropriating actions and their merit' (§26). It applies to subjects of experience who are 'intelligent agents' (§26), i.e. subjects of experience whose mental capacities are such that they qualify as Persons by Locke's definition. Consider S, a subject of experience who is suitably complex and so qualifies as a Person. Given the forensic sense of 'person' the question of *what S's Personal identity consists in* considered at some particular time is simply the question of what S is morally or legally responsible for at that time.[5] This is the force of 'forensic'. One could put the point by saying that the question of which or what Person S is is a question about S's overall *field* of responsibility at that time.

A little more accurately, one could say that it is a question about S's overall field of *concern or concernment* at that time. The adjustment is needed because one's field of concernment is wider than one's field of responsibility. One's field of concernment contains everything that one is intimately involved in in such a way that it can be a source of one's 'pleasure or pain; i.e. happiness or misery; beyond which we have no concernment' (4.11.8). It therefore extends beyond matters of specifically moral or legal concern – to one's mind and body and toothache. One's field of responsibility falls wholly within one's field of concernment because what one is responsible for has vast consequences for one's happiness or misery both here on earth and on and after the Day of Judgement, but the field of responsibility is not coextensive with latter field of concernment because many pains and pleasures have nothing to do with responsibility.

What is the extent of a person's concernment? As we ordinarily understand concern, one can be concerned for or in or about many things: one's family, one's possessions, one's business concerns, the fate of the world, the baggage retrieval system at Heathrow. In his *Essay*, however, Locke focuses on a much narrower notion of concernment which I'll mark with a capital letter – *Concernment*. He makes the scope of Concernment clear by tying it tightly to consciousness in his special sense of 'consciousness' which I'll also flag with a capital letter – *Consciousness* – except when it appears in quotations. He holds that Consciousness entails Concernment: 'concern for happiness [is] the *unavoidable concomitant* of consciousness' (§26); 'self is that conscious thinking thing ... which is sensible or conscious of pleasure and pain, capable of happiness or misery, and *so* is concerned for itself, *as far as that consciousness extends, and no farther.*' (§17).

---

[5]   It may (somewhat confusingly) be rephrased as the question of *which Person S is* considered at some particular time, or (slightly less confusingly) as the question of which *forensic* Person S is at some particular time.

Galen Strawson

6. 'Consciousness'

To understand the precise scope of Concernment, we have to know exactly what Consciousness is. Fortunately the matter is straight-forward: to be Conscious of x is to experience x *in a certain immediate kind of way* – whether x be one's actions and experiences, one's mind, or one's body. One's awareness or consciousness of one's present actions and experiences is the paradigm case of such immediacy (for illustrative quotations, see page 20 below). It's the immediacy of the way in which we experience our own pains, to take a familiar example. Our present-day use of the word 'conscious' allows that we can be said to be conscious of other creatures' experiences but we don't think that we are or can be conscious of others' experiences in the immediate kind of way in which we are conscious of our own.

One may say that to be Conscious of x is to experience x *as one's own* in a certain immediate kind of way, but one does then run the risk of being misunderstood. To avoid misunderstanding one needs to stress that this kind of experiencing something as one's own is found in all sentient beings; it doesn't require any sort of express self-consciousness of the sort characteristic of human beings, any sort of explicit conceptual representation of x as one's own, although it does also involve this in the special case of a Person, since a Person is a fully self-conscious creature that 'can consider itself [specifically] as itself' (§9).[6]

This is what Locke means by 'consciousness'. It's not an elaboration or variation of what he means. To be Conscious of x is to experience x in a certain immediate kind of way. It is in fact the way in which a subject of experience S can experience an action or experience or mind or body only if it is in fact S's own action or experience or mind or body.

We can now ask why Consciousness of x entails Concernment about (or in or for) x. The answer is simple. Locke takes it, reasonably enough, that one is necessarily concerned for oneself. One is necessarily concerned for what is one's own in the narrow sense of being part of oneself, the Person one is; where this crucially includes, on his view, one's actions and experiences in addition to one's substantial realization (material or otherwise).

In taking it that the converse is also true, i.e. that Concernment entails Consciousness (see the last three words of the last section),

---

[6]   Grice agrees: consciousness 'for Locke means "consciousness of ... as one's own"' ('Personal identity', *Mind* **50** (1941), 341).

Locke makes it clear that he's focusing on a notion of concernment –
Concernment – which is narrow in precisely the following sense.
One's Concernment (one's capital-C Concernment) extends *only to
whatever one experiences (as one's own) in a certain immediate kind of
way.* That is, it extends only to whatever one is Conscious of in his
sense of 'conscious'. That is, it extends only to oneself, the Person
one is, where 'the Person one is' includes one's actions and experiences – since this notion of Person is a forensic notion – in addition
to one's current substantial realization, material or otherwise.[7]

7. The Field of Consciousness

The notion of experiencing something as one's own is crucial when it
comes to the forensic consequences of Consciousness for subjects of
experience who are Persons. Briefly (and to anticipate) if you genuinely
no longer experience something as your own in the required immediate
kind of way then you're no longer Conscious of it. It follows that you're
no longer genuinely Concerned in it. It follows in turn that it's no
longer part of your Personal identity, i.e. your forensic identity. It
follows in turn that you are no longer properly held responsible for it.
One is of course (lower-case) concerned for one's family members or
possessions, on Locke's view, but one is not (upper-case) Concerned
for them. One's field of Concernment is restricted to oneself – so that
it is at any given time identical with one's field of Consciousness at
that time, which, to repeat, includes one's body[8] in addition to one's
mind and one's actions and experiences.

[7]   For a qualification see Strawson, *Locke on Personal Identity* (2014),
38–9. The general notion of concern or concernment is taken as given, and
the scope of the special restricted notion – capital 'C' Concernment – is
fixed by reference to Consciousness. The effect of the restriction is clear:
whatever one's wider concerns, one is only *Concerned* for oneself. Locke
had already tied concernment tightly to the notion of Personal identity in
the first edition of the *Essay*: 'if we take wholly away all consciousness of
our actions and sensations, especially of pleasure and pain, and the *concernment* that accompanies it, it will be hard to know wherein to place personal
identity' (2.1.11). He has it always in mind that one's eternal fate subsequent
to the Day of Judgement must always be one's greatest Concern(ment).
[8]   This may be doubted, for it implies that Locke is dramatically extending the then standard notion of consciousness, which restricted consciousness to knowledge of one's own mental goings-on. See further n. 25
below; see also Strawson, *Locke on Personal Identity* (2014), 31–2, 39n.

Galen Strawson

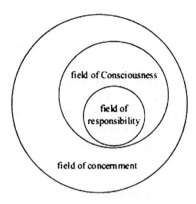

Figure 1. The fields of responsibility, Consciousness and concernment[9]

Lockean Consciousness isn't memory, contrary to what so many commentators have supposed, although memory can certainly involve Consciousness. If one still feels immediately 'personally involved' in or with one's past actions and experiences in remembering them, if one feels about them rather as one does about one's present actions and experiences, which are the paradigm cases of what one is Conscious of, then one is still Conscious of them. But memory as such – even autobiographical memory – needn't involve any Concernment. Nor therefore need it involve any Consciousness – any experiencing of what is remembered as one's own in the immediate kind of way that Locke has in mind in talking of Consciousness. I'll return to this in section 11.

Nor need being Conscious of one's experiences – experiencing them as one's own – involve any sort of express conscious second-order apprehension of them as one's own, any more than experiencing one's mind or body as one's own does. In the case of one's present experiences, which are always and paradigmatically Conscious, it never involves this. It's just a matter of what it is like to have the experiences, a matter of their 'immediate givenness'. Locke makes this plain when he says that Consciousness is

> inseparable from thinking, and as it seems to me essential to it: it being impossible for any one to perceive, without perceiving, that he does perceive. When we see, hear, smell, taste, feel, meditate,

[9]   If one capitalizes the word concernment in the diagram, so that it represents Lockean Concernment, the outer circle shrinks on Locke's view to become identical to the field of Consciousness circle.

or will anything, we know that we do so. Thus it is always as to our present sensations and perceptions (§9).

This passage is enough to settle the point that Consciousness is not an explicit second-order matter, in Locke's view. If one thing is certain it is that Locke – that most sensible of philosophers – doesn't think that we spend our whole lives having explicit second-order thoughts about all our first-order experiences.[10]

We can vary the characterization of Consciousness by using the expression 'from the inside'.[11] Subject of experience S's field of Consciousness is identical with S's *field of from-the-inside givenness*. If, however, it is allowed that past events can be given from-the-inside in memory in a way that is empty of affect or personal 'identificatory involvement' (Concernment), then we will need to say rather that S's field of Consciousness, in Locke's sense of 'consciousness', is identical with S's *field of morally-affectively-concerned from-the-inside givenness*. This is a pretty barbarous expression so I won't use it again. The point is that Locke has in effect built moral-affective Concernment into Consciousness: (Lockean) Consciousness is essentially accompanied by Concernment: 'self' or Person, he says, is that conscious thinking thing … which is sensible or conscious of pleasure and pain, capable of happiness or misery, and *so is concerned for itself, as far as that consciousness extends*'.

8. The Reach of Consciousness

One's field of from-the-inside givenness, one's field of Consciousness, isn't just a matter of whatever one is now aware of

---

[10] Locke uses 'thought' in the Cartesian sense to cover all conscious mental goings on, as this passage shows (see also n. 25 below); I'll use the word 'experience' instead. Note also that Locke takes 'action' to cover mental goings on as well as larger-scale bodily actions (it covers anything that is morally assessable).

[11] Coined, as far I know, by Sydney Shoemaker ('Persons and Their Pasts', *American Philosophical Quarterly* **7** (1970), 269–85). The difference between remembering something from the inside and remembering it only from the outside is the difference between *remembering falling* out of the boat, the water rushing up to meet you, and so on (memory from the inside) and *remembering that you fell* out of the boat, something that might be all that you have left in the way of memory of the event, and something that someone other than you might equally well remember (memory from the outside).

in occurrent thought or sensation or memory. It also, and crucially, has a dispositional aspect. In addition to containing all the experiences one is having now, together with any past experiences one is at present explicitly recalling, it contains all of those past experiences, and in particular actions, that one *can* remember from the inside.

How far into the past does this 'can' reach? The brief answer is that Locke takes it to reach beyond what one can now bring back to mind unaided (and perhaps also beyond what one can remember when suitably prompted or shocked) to all of those past actions that one is Conscious of in one's conscience or heart (§22). What one is Conscious of in one's heart may not be fully known or accessible to one now but on the Day of Judgement 'the secrets of all hearts will be laid open' (§§22, 26). On that alarming day you'll recall things that you are in fact still morally-affectively involved in, in such a way as to be properly held responsible for them, even if they've slipped beyond recall in your ordinary everyday life.[12]

One's Consciousness doesn't reach back to early childhood, though – if only because of the phenomenon of 'childhood amnesia'. Nor does it reach back to most of the actions of childhood. On one natural reading of Locke it needn't reach back to these actions even if they're remembered, because one can remember one's past actions while no longer experiencing them as one's own in the required immediate way or feeling morally-affectively Concerned about (or in) them. Nor does it reach back to the bulk of one's past life. When Locke imagines a 'spirit wholly stripped of all its memory or consciousness of past actions, as we find our minds always are of a great part of ours', he indicates the sense in which *most of one's past actions are not actions of the (forensic) Person one is now*.[13]

---

[12] Can one be responsible for a past action that one remembers *that* one did, although one no long remembers doing it *from the inside*? It may be thought that Locke can't allow this, because he says that Consciousness of a past action requires being able to 'repeat the idea of [the] past action with the same consciousness [one] had of it at first' (§10), which requires rich 'from-the-insideness'. To this extent his theory seems to give a wrong result, for one can feel responsible for an action that one knows one did although one no longer has any memory of doing it from the inside. One can accommodate the case by arguing that the mere fact that one still feels responsible for it shows that one is still Concerned in it, Conscious of it, in the required way.

[13] §25. It's not helpful to take this simply as a huge understatement on Locke's part, i.e. as the claim that we are not at any given time *occurrently* Conscious of a great part most of our past actions.

Thomas Reid tells the story of a young boy who becomes an officer who is Conscious of something the boy did, and then a general who is Conscious something the officer did but has wholly forgotten – and is no longer Conscious of – what the young boy did.[14] Following Berkeley in the insensitivity of his reading of Locke, Reid objects that on Locke's account of personal identity

(i)   the general may be the same person as the young officer, because he's Conscious of some experience had by the young officer,

(ii)   the young officer may be the same person as the boy, because he's Conscious of some experience had by the boy,

while

(iii) the general may not be the same person as the boy, because he's not Conscious of the experience of the boy.

Reid's objection is that the conjunction of (i), (ii), and (iii) contradicts the principle of the transitivity of identity and that Locke's theory is therefore inconsistent.

The conjunction of (i), (ii), and (iii) does contradict the principle of the transitivity of identity but this isn't an objection to Locke's account of personal identity. It's a perfect illustration of its fundamental and forensic point – the plausible idea (it's plausible relative to the story of the Day of Judgment) that human beings won't on the Day of Judgment be responsible for all the things they've done in their lives but only for those that they're still genuinely Conscious of – still genuinely morally-affectively Concerned in, implicated in. What they'll be responsible for will in practice be a bundle of actions dating from many different periods of their lives.

Butler misses Locke's point as spectacularly as Berkeley and Reid. In speaking of Locke's 'wonderful mistake' he makes a wonderful mistake. Ignoring Locke's explicit statement that he's using 'person' specifically as a forensic term, and Locke's definition of Consciousness in terms that have nothing to do with memory, Butler takes Locke to mean memory by the word 'consciousness' and writes as follows:

> to say, that [consciousness] makes personal identity, or is necessary to our being the same persons, is to say, that a person has not existed a single moment, nor done one action, but what he can

[14]   I'm putting aside the point that Reid wrongly takes Locke to mean 'memory' by 'consciousness'.

remember; indeed none but what he reflects upon. And one should really think it self-evident, that consciousness of personal identity presupposes, and therefore cannot constitute, personal identity; any more than knowledge, in any other case, can constitute truth, which it presupposes (1736, 440–41)

One should really think it self-evident that this isn't any sort of objection to Locke's theory. It's a statement of its central point. As a subject of experience you have a lifetime of actions and experiences behind you – most of which you've completely forgotten. The ones that are part of your Personal identity, i.e. the ones that constitute your forensic identity, i.e. the ones that *constitute the Person you are*, considered as a moral being, a forensic entity, are simply those which you're still Conscious of, hence still Concerned in: those that you still experience as your own in the crucial moral-affective way.

It's worth stressing that the Lockean question of Personal identity is always a question raised about a subject of experience S *considered at a particular time*. The particular time at which the question is raised (now, say, or on the Day of Judgement) is crucial because S's Personal identity or Personhood is differently constituted every day, on Locke's view. This follows immediately from the fact that S's field of Consciousness, and in particular the overall field of things S is responsible for, changes each day and indeed every moment. This is so for no other reason than that S has done more things a day later. But it may also be so for other reasons. S may for example have ceased to be Conscious of certain things that S was Conscious of yesterday.[15]

9. Locke's Definition of 'Person' 1

Although Berkeley, Butler and Reid are largely to blame for the misunderstanding of Locke, 'marvellously mistaken', as Law observes (1769, 21), Locke isn't blameless. Part of the misunderstanding stems from the fact that he offers a definition of 'person' that is independent of his definition of it as a forensic term. I'll now consider this definition, and offer a general statement of what Locke takes a Person to be.

I'm an individual agent, a thinking being, a persisting human subject of experience, very much as I think I am. All good. But what am I in so far as I am a Person – according to Locke? This still doesn't seem clear.

---

[15]   In *Locke on Personal Identity* I raise the question of how *repentance* can change one's field of responsibility. Note that Butler's addition of 'indeed none but what he reflects upon' is particularly aggressive (and stupid).

The first answer we can give is terminological: the *Person* that I am is the *self* that I am: 'Person, as I take it, is the name for this self. Wherever a man finds what he calls himself, there, I think, another may say is the same person' (§26). This is one of many places where the terms are equated.

The second answer is more substantive. It's the answer to the first of the four questions listed in section 1 above, question **[A]**: what does a subject of experience that qualifies as a Person consist of, ontologically speaking, considered at any given time? The answer is that the self or Person that I now am – the individual, persisting, morally accountable subject of experience that I am – considered at any given particular time *t*, consists, literally consists, of the following things. First

[1]   my living body at *t*

for as Locke says 'any part of our bodies vitally united to that, which is conscious in us, makes a part of our selves' (§25); all the particles of our bodies

> whilst vitally united to this same thinking conscious self, so that we feel when they are touched, and are affected by, and conscious of good or harm that happens to them, are a part of our selves: i.e. of our thinking conscious self. Thus the limbs of his body are to everyone a part of him self: he sympathizes and is concerned for them (§11).[16]

What else is part of the Person I am? Well, if I have an immaterial soul – which may be doubted, as Locke observes – then the person that I am at *t* consists also of

[2]   my soul at *t*

the immaterial soul-substance in which my thinking goes on; for 'any substance [now] vitally united to the present thinking being, is a part of that very same self which now is' (§25), be it material or immaterial.

---

[16]   Note that Locke is using 'ourselves' ('our selves') in a sense directly related to his use of the word 'self', not in some more indeterminate or generic way. To quote more fully from §25: 'Thus any part of our bodies, vitally united to that, which is conscious in us, makes a part of our selves: but upon separation from the vital union, by which that consciousness is communicated, that, which a moment since was part of our *selves*, is now no more so, than a part of another man's self is a part of me: and 'tis not impossible, but in a little time may become a real part of another person' (§25).

Galen Strawson

That **[1]** and also **[2]** are literally part of the self or person I am at t (assuming that materialism is false and that **[2]** is therefore to be included) is explicitly stated by Locke. The third and for many purposes central component consists of everything else (everything other than **[1]** and **[2]**) of which I am Conscious at t, i.e.

[3]   all the experiences (thoughts and actions, past and present) of the individual-persisting-subject-of-experience that I am of which I am now occurrently or dispositionally Conscious at t.[17]

Consciousness of the past is thus a fine-grained matter, in Locke's view. For I may still be Conscious of one thing I did on my birthday twenty years ago and not be Conscious of a thousand other things I did on that day, things I've completely forgotten and am no longer 'Concerned in' in any way.[18] In that case they're no longer any part of the Person I am, for it is only 'that with which the consciousness of this present thinking thing can [now] join itself' that 'makes the same person, and is one self with it'. The present thinking being that I am

> attributes to itself, and owns all the actions of that thing, as its own, as far as that consciousness reaches, and no farther;[19]

> if there be any *part* of [an immaterial substance's] existence, which I cannot upon recollection join with that present consciousness, whereby I am now myself, it is *in that part of its existence* no more myself, than any other immaterial being. For *whatsoever any substance has thought or done, which I cannot recollect, and by my consciousness make my own thought and action*, it

---

[17]   When Locke says that 'anything united to the ... present thinking being ... by a consciousness of former actions, makes also a part of the **same** self, which is the same both then and now' (§25) the scope of 'anything' is only 'former actions'. It's not as if the material particles that made you up ten years ago when you performed a certain action of which you are now conscious are (thereby) still part of the person you are now.

[18]   It's even more fine-grained than Parfitian psychological connectedness, which also picks and chooses. See section 13 below.

[19]   §17. In full the passage reads 'that with which the **consciousness** of this present thinking thing can join itself, makes the same person, and is one self with it, and with nothing else; and so attributes to itself, and owns all the actions of that thing, as its own, as far as that consciousness reaches, and no farther'. It may help understanding to remove the last two commas: the present thinking being acknowledges 'all the actions of that thing as its own as far as [its] consciousness reaches and no further'. It acknowledges the actions of that thing as its own *only* as far as its present consciousness reaches them.

126

will no more belong to me, whether [or not] a part of me thought or did it, than if it had been thought or done by any other immaterial being anywhere existing.[20]

So when Locke says that Consciousness of one of Nestor's actions would make one 'the same person with Nestor' he doesn't mean that one would be the same person as Nestor with respect to all Nestor's actions. In the case imagined one's Consciousness doesn't reach any further into Nestor than that one single action, 'that part of [Nestor's] existence', and one is the same person as Nestor only so far as that action is concerned.[21]

This, then, is a Person ontologically considered, a person in Locke's special sense of the word. This is the answer to question **[A]**. A Person is a **[1]** ± **[2]** + **[3]**.[22] This is the ontological core. Now we need to answer question **[B]**: what mental capacities must a subject of experience have in order to qualify as a person? We need to list the defining characteristics of Personhood, the properties that distinguish Persons from other subjects of experience that have bodies and experiences and act (and even perhaps have immaterial souls), but aren't Persons.

10. Locke's Definition of 'Person' 2

The first thing to record is that Persons are essentially

[i]   capable of a law, and happiness, and misery (§26)

---

[20]   §24. Locke is here focusing on the case of an immaterial substance, but the point is for him quite general. Note how the 'and' in this passage distinguishes memory and Consciousness.

[21]   §14. Here I disagree with Garrett ('Locke on Personal Identity, Consciousness, and "Fatal Errors"'). Note that even if one were supposed to connect with the whole forensic Person that Nestor was at the time he performed the action in question one would surely not connect forensically with any actions that he had at that time not yet performed.

[22]   Locke takes an orthodox Christian position in holding that we can't be said to exist as persons unless we're embodied. Like almost everyone else at the time, he agrees with Boethius that a person consists essentially of 'soul and body, not soul and body separately' (Boethius, *De Trinitate*, in *The Theological Tractates and The Consolations of Philosophy* (trans. H. F. Stewart and E. K. Rand) (Cambridge, MA: Harvard University Press, c510), 11). A disembodied soul would not be a person. See Thiel 'Personal Identity' (1998), 870.

where to say that something is 'capable of a law' is to say that it is capable of grasping the import of a law in such a way that it can understand itself to be subject to it *and can thereby be subject to it*. Given that this is an essential part of Locke's definition of 'person' as a forensic term, it's regrettable that it occurs several pages after his famous more narrowly cognitive-functional definition of 'person' in §9 according to which a Person is

> a thinking intelligent being, that has reason and reflection, and can consider itself as itself, the same thinking thing, in different times and places; which it does only by that consciousness, which is inseparable from thinking, and as it seems to me essential to it...(§9)

The trouble is (and Locke must take some of the blame) that this part of his definition tends to be cited in isolation from the point that a Person is also essentially 'capable of a law, and happiness, and misery' (§26) and the intimately connected point that 'person' is for Locke an essentially 'forensic' term (§26).

Regrettable – but there it is. What does the cognitive-functional definition say? It's very clear. Capacities for

[ii]   thought (experience)

[iii]   intelligence

[iv]   reason

and

[v]   reflection

are essential preconditions of being a Person.[23] But they're not sufficient, nor are they the central focus of the definition. The crucial further cognitive-capacity condition is a Person's

[vi]   capacity to consider itself as itself, the same thinking thing in different times and places

'which it does only by that consciousness which is inseparable from thinking, and, as it seems to me, essential to it'. This condition fits tightly with the requirement of being 'capable of a law', for on Locke's view one can reward and punish intelligent beings for what

---

[23]   In *Locke on Personal Identity* (2014) (pages 62–4), I argue that Locke specifies four separate conditions by the words 'thinking' (used in the wide Cartesian sense – see note 10), 'intelligent', 'reason', and 'reflection'. There is no redundancy.

they've done because and only because they possess this cognitive capacity, which keeps them in touch with their past actions, and makes it possible for them to be aware that these actions are their own.[24] To see this, imagine a thinking, intelligent, reasoning, reflecting being that is 'capable of a law' (it might act out of morally good or bad intentions in the moment of action), but has no memory at all. It makes no moral sense to punish or reward it for its past actions. It has no personal identity in Locke's sense – given that personal identity is an essentially diachronic notion.

There's a further and connected problem that arises from restricting one's attention to the famous part of Locke's definition in §9. The famous part specifies Consciousness in a merely cognitive way that makes no explicit mention of the essential connection between Consciousness and Concernment (Concernment is mentioned in §11, two paragraphs later). To see this imagine an utterly emotion-lacking subject of experience that fully satisfies the famous part of the definition. It is a cognitively highly sophisticated, fully memory-equipped subject of experience that qualifies as Conscious inasmuch as it possesses the mental reflexivity that is in Locke's view essentially constitutive of all 'thinking' (i.e. all experience) and is in addition fully and explicitly self-conscious in the way that human beings are and dogs and foxes aren't, so that it can consider itself specifically as itself in the past and future. It has, however, no capacity for happiness or misery and therefore no Concernment, nor any grasp of a law. Such a subject of experience is certainly not a Person on Locke's view.[25]

---

[24]   Compare Leibniz *New Essays on Human Understanding*, (ed. and trans. J. Bennett and P. Remnant) (Cambridge: Cambridge University Press, 1704/1996), §34, 2.27.9.

[25]   Some, perhaps, have supposed that Locke means something merely cognitive by the word '*thinking*', and so has only the cognitive aspect of memory in mind when considering Consciousness of the past. As already noted, however, Locke uses 'thinking' in the wide Cartesian sense, as is shown by the immediate continuation of the famous passage: 'it being impossible for any one to perceive, without perceiving, that he does perceive. When we see, hear, smell, taste, feel, meditate, or will anything, we know that we do so. Thus it is always as to our present sensations and perceptions: and by this every one is to himself, that which he calls self... consciousness always accompanies thinking, and 'tis that, which makes every one to be, what he calls self' (§9). It's a pity that many encounter the famous passage only lifted out of context and quoted in a truncated form.

11. Consciousness isn't memory

It's already clear that Consciousness isn't the same as memory. But this is not just because Consciousness is essentially accompanied by Concernment, in addition to its purely cognitive features. The principal point is much simpler: the primary case of Consciousness involves no memory at all, according to Locke, for it's the Consciousness that one has of one's own experience and action in the present. It's the Consciousness that is 'inseparable from thinking' (i.e. experience), 'essential to it', essentially constitutive of it. 'Thinking consists in being conscious that one thinks', Locke writes, just as 'hunger consists in that very sensation' (2.1.19). One could be fully Conscious in this fundamental way throughout one's life and have no memory at all, or only a few seconds' worth.[26] The case of Consciousness of *past* actions and experiences, which does of course involve memory, is explicitly explained and characterized by reference to the primary and fundamental case of present Consciousness. Personal identity 'extends itself beyond present [conscious] existence' (where Consciousness is certainly in place, because it is essentially constitutive of the very existence of experience)

> only by consciousness, whereby it becomes concerned and accountable; owns and imputes to itself past actions, *just upon the same ground, and for the same reason, that it does the present* [actions] (§26).

> As far as any intelligent being can repeat the idea of any past action with the same consciousness it had of it at first, and with *the same consciousness it has of any present action*; so far it is the same personal self. For it is by the consciousness it has of its present thoughts and actions, that it is self to itself now, and so will be the same self as far as the same consciousness can extend to actions past or to come' (§10).[27]

The fundamental reference point for all attributions of Consciousness is the subject considered in the present moment.

It may be said that Consciousness *of the past*, at least, is the same as memory, on Locke's view. Or rather, it may be said that Locke

---

[26]   Such cases are found in clinical neurology; see e.g. Damasio *The Feeling of What Happens: Body and Emotion in the Making of Consciousness* (New York: Harcourt Brace, 1999), and 'Interview', *New Scientist* **165** (2000), 46–49.

[27]   Note that 'with the same consciousness it had of it at first' makes this, at least on one reading, an implausibly strong requirement.

wouldn't have felt any need to distinguish memory and Consciousness if he had restricted attention to autobiographical from-the-inside memory. But he might have rejected even this identification if he had thought (as I do) that there can be from-the-inside memory without Concernment.[28] One can identify Consciousness of the past with from-the-inside memory only if one accepts that from-the-inside memory is truly inseparable from moral-affective Concernment.

Some years ago, Schechtman observed that almost all commentators on Locke think of Consciousness as merely

> a faculty of *knowing*, and this makes the interpretation of consciousness of the past as memory almost irresistible. This is not, however, the aspect of consciousness that Locke most emphasizes in his discussion of personal identity. Instead he stresses the *affective* side of consciousness. (1996, 108)

She put a very good question: if Locke means memory when he talks of Consciousness, why doesn't he say so? Why doesn't he simply talk of memory? Why does he 'never *say* ... that memory connections constitute personal identity if this is what he means?' (1996, 107). There's an extended discussion of memory in 2.10 of the *Essay*, and Locke uses the word many times in his discussion of personal identity, and yet 'when he tells us what personal identity consists in, which he does many times throughout the chapter, he *always* talks about extension of consciousness and *never* about memory connections' (ibid.).

The principal reason for this has been given: Consciousness has nothing essentially to do with memory. But the point Schechtman stresses is also important – the fact that 'we extend [Lockean] consciousness back in time to some past action or experience by caring about it in the appropriate way' (ibid., 109). Certain 'past events can become part of present [Lockean] consciousness by affecting us in the present along the dimension of pleasure or pain' (ibid., 112). That said, it should be noted that caring or affective concern (Concernment) is not strictly part of Consciousness, on Locke's view, only an inevitable accompaniment of it. It's also arguable that one may be Conscious of a past experience in the present simply in so far as one experiences it as one's own, while having no particular

---

[28]   See e.g. Strawson '"The Self"' in *Models of the Self* (ed.) S. Gallagher & J. Shear (Thorverton: Imprint Academic, 1997/1999), §8, 'Against Narrativity' in G. Strawson *Real Materialism and Other Essays* (Oxford: Oxford University Press, 2004/2008), §4.

feelings of pleasure or pain with regard to it; just as one can be Conscious of a part of one's body as one's own while having no particular present feelings of pleasure or pain with regard to it. One may also, perhaps, remember stealing plums and being flogged as a boy with some amusement, and hence with whatever pleasure and emotion is inseparable from amusement, while no longer being Conscious of it in the accountability-engaging sense.

Another case involves a complication Locke didn't consider, and which arguably raises a doubt about the adequacy of his account. Suppose one is given to guilt. It seems plain that one can continue to feel guilty about an action performed as a child although one is *not* in fact still related to it – emotionally implicated in it – in an accountability-engaging way. Guilt, however, is a form of Concernment, and entails Consciousness in Locke's sense, and Consciousness entails Personal identity or same-Personhood, and same-Personhood entails present accountability and punishability. So it seems that a current feeling of guilt entails accountability and punishability even when the feeling is inappropriate or absurd.

A quick answer to this in the spirit of Locke's theory is that one will be all right on the Day of Judgement, because one's conscience on that awesome occasion will get things in proportion and excuse one (§22) for one's childish misdeed. One will see how things are and no longer feel guilty. Alternatively one may suppose that one's childish misdemeanour will indeed feature on the long list of things for which one is *accountable*, simply in so far as one is Conscious of it, but that it certainly won't follow that one will actually be *punished* for it. (God, for one, wouldn't dream of doing such a thing.)

12. Personal Identity: The Canonical Question

I'll take these issues a little further below. First consider the canonical personal identity question mentioned in section 1: What are the necessary and sufficient conditions of the truth of the claim that a person considered at time t_1 – whom we may call P_1 – is the same person as a person considered at a different (later) time t_2 – whom we may call P_2? What has to be true if it is to be true that P_1 is indeed the same person as P_2? The present claim is that Locke doesn't address this question – or not as it's ordinarily understood. He simply assumes – takes it for granted – that he's dealing with a continuously existing thing, a continuously existing subject of experience, a continuously existing 'consciousness' (in the special count-noun use of 'consciousness' in §23) that is of such a kind that it

132

qualifies as a Person. Having taken the existence of continuously existing subjects of experience for granted, and having specified what they have to be capable of to qualify as Persons (= answering question **[B]**), and what they consist of ontologically, at any given time (= answering question **[A]**), he raises question **[D]**: the question of what the *Personal identity* – i.e. the forensic identity – of such entities consists in.[29]

He also raises and answers question **[C]**: the question of what sorts of substantial changes subjects of experience like S that qualify as Persons can undergo while continuing to exist. He argues that, as far as we know, they may possibly survive complete replacement of any parts that substantially realize them at any time – whatever those parts are. S may for example survive a complete change of body or body parts (**[1]** parts), and/or a complete change of immaterial soul (a **[2]** part). In telling us what sorts of changes and replacements he thinks Persons can survive, Locke makes it clear that he's conceiving of them as things whose continuing existence essentially involves the continuing existence, through all possible changes of substantial realization, of *something that remains in possession of psychological capacities [i]–[vii] – the psychological capacities specified in answer to question [B]*.[30]

I'll repeat this. Locke is simply *assuming*, and operating with, a conception of *continuously existing psychological-capacity-preserving subject-of-experience-hood* that allows that a single persisting subject of experience may survive replacement of all its substantially realizing parts. He's not giving an account of what the continuity of this same-subject-of-experience-hood consists in (as most accounts of personal identity aim to do) in giving his special forensic account of Personal identity. He's assuming the existence of entities like S that have this sort of continuity, and taking it that we are ourselves things of this kind, in order to raise the issue that then concerns him: the issue of the Personal identity of such things, including most notably ourselves; that is, the question of the *moral standing* – the *forensic identity* – of such things; that is, the question of which parts of their past still count as theirs forensically speaking; and

[29] He doesn't have much to say about what might preserve the identity of subjects of experience between death and resurrection. See further note 23.
[30] Here there is an interesting connection to Dainton's conception of the self: 'a subject', he says, 'is essentially a continuous potential for consciousness' (*The Phenomenal Self* (Oxford: Oxford University Press, 2008), 251); 'the essence of subjects is the *capacity to be conscious*' (*Self* (London: Penguin, 2013), ch. 6).

therefore still count as part of the Person they are. Equivalently: he's asking which parts of the past of the continuing *subjects of experience* that they are *no longer* count as part of the continuing *Persons* they are.

This is the point at which these things' capacity for Concernment-involving Consciousness of their past actions and experiences becomes crucial – because it provides the answer to question **[D]**. But there's no sense in which possession of this capacity constitutes one of these subjects of experience, say S, as a continuously existing thing. The subject of experience S is simply given as a continuously existing thing that possesses this capacity, and it would continue to exist as the same *subject of experience* even if it lost this capacity, and so ceased to be a full *Person*. Nor does the set of things of which S is Conscious at any given time, in virtue of its possession of this capacity (i.e. **[1]** ± **[2]** + **[3]** – pages 15–16), constitute it as a continuously existing thing. Its material and immaterial parts (**[1]** and **[2]**) may completely change, compatibly with its continuing to exist. As for **[3]**, the past actions and experiences of which it is Conscious, these do not in fact constitute a temporally continuous series. The subject of experience, once again, is simply given as a continuously existing thing. Some but certainly not all of the subject of experience's past actions and experiences are still part of the Person it is.

So Locke doesn't answer the canonical personal identity question. But he does give a full account of what one is considered specifically as a Person: **[1]** ± **[2]** + **[3]**. Why is **[1]** ± **[2]** literally part of what constitutes one, considered specifically as a Person, in spite of the fact that it's the persistence of one's psychological capacities that is essential to one's persistence as a Person? Two answers are possible and correct: [i] because **[1]** ± **[2]** is situated in the field of one's Consciousness, and hence in the field of one's Concernment; [ii] because one is (one's actions and experiences apart) what actually substantially constitutes one at any given time.

The first answer is primary for Locke: *one is constituted as a Person by whatever lies in one's field of Consciousness.*[31] That's it. And that's the answer to question **[D]**, although it's only **[3]** (the set of actions and experiences one is Conscious of) that matters, not **[1]** and **[2]** (one's substantial realization), when it comes to **[D]**, the question of responsibility. Locke's famous claim that 'Consciousness makes personal identity' (§10) is not in any sense a claim that something merely mental or psychological constitutes Personal identity in the

---

[31] Nothing can lie in the field of Consciousness of more than one person.

sense of making up its whole being. It is rather and precisely the theoretically elegant claim I've just italicized. Given a subject of experience, a thinking intelligent agent, considered at a particular time t, it's the reach of that subject of experience's Consciousness at t that wholly determines and settles the question of which or what Person that subject of experience is at t; where this includes, of course, the question of what constitutes the Person substantially speaking (materially ± immaterially). Everything that one's Consciousness touches or 'can join itself...with', everything that is 'comprehended under' one's Consciousness in this sense, is a part of the person one is.[32] This and only this settles the question of the subject of experience's Personal identity, or Personhood, which is also (given [3]) question [D], the question of its forensic identity, at t. Certainly one needn't know exactly what is comprehended under one's Consciousness. (One may not for example know something Locke knew himself not to know, i.e. whether an immaterial substance is comprehended under one's Consciousness, or whether instead materialism is true.)

I hope the picture is now clear. The material ± immaterial substance that actually makes you up now, substantially, is literally part of what constitutes you, the Person you are now. What about the past? Which parts or aspects of the past of you-the-continuing-subject-of-experience are now part of the Person you are? None of the material particles that have previously constituted your body are, given that they no longer lie in your field of Consciousness (or Concernment). Only those that are now part of your body do so. The same goes if there has been any change in your immaterial substance. Only the immaterial soul or soul-substance that is currently part of you lies in your field of Consciousness (and Concernment) and is therefore part of the Person you now are.

So far as its substance is concerned, then, a subject of experience S who is a Person consists of S's present substantial realization – which may be wholly different from S's substantial realization at some

---

[32]   Note that this includes one's body, in Locke's account, even though Consciousness is standardly and primarily defined as a reflexive property of experience. See e.g. §11: 'cut off a hand, and thereby separate it from that consciousness, we had of its heat, cold, and other affections; and it is then no longer a part of that which is *himself*'. See also §17: 'thus every one finds that, whilst comprehended under that consciousness, the little finger is as much a part of himself as what is most so. Upon separation of this little finger, should this consciousness go along with the little finger, and leave the rest of the body, it is evident the little finger would be the person, the same person'.

previous time. One may certainly say, in spite of this, that S is a dia-chronically extended entity, but one must cancel any implication that diachronic extension implies any kind of same-substance-involving diachronic continuity. Most essentially, S is a diachronically continu-ous stream of memory-and-disposition-rich mental being ('a con-sciousness' in the count-noun use). S is always carried by something, substance-wise, but it doesn't matter what substantial realization S has at any given time. It doesn't matter what substantial realization S has although S must of course always have some sub-stantial realization or other in order to exist at all. For on the one hand S may have switched bodies, according to Locke, as in the case of the cobbler and the prince; on the other hand S's whole mental being (memory, Consciousness, personality, and so on) may have transferred from one portion of soul-substance to another, as in the case Locke considers in §13.[33] S is indeed – as ever and without qualification – a whole single subject of experience, meta-physically speaking, and it is as such that S will report for inspection, fully embodied, on the Day of Judgement. But there's also a *sense* in which S may be said to be a gappy entity metaphysically speaking, when considered as a Person, because the temporally scattered actions and experiences that S is still Conscious of are literally part of what constitutes S as a Person so far as S's (forensic) Personal iden-tity is concerned. In this forensic respect, one's Consciousness-constituted Personal identity resembles the contrail of an aeroplane most of whose parts have faded to nothing while some indelibly remain.

Suppose we draw an unbroken line (Fig. 2) to represent my actual life as a subject of experience, from my first coming into existence as a human being. We may then consider the segment from t_1 a moment ten years ago, to t_2, a moment five years ago:

We can now add a line above my basic lifeline (Fig. 3) to represent schematically the *Person* that I am at t_2 considered specifically with respect to [3] my actions and experiences between t_1 and t_2.[34] This will be a broken line and will look something like this:

---

[33] This is part of Locke's campaign against those of his contemporaries who argue that belief in Resurrection requires belief in an immaterial soul because personal identity between death and Resurrection requires the per-sistence of single continuing substance.

[34] And so not considered with respect to my substantial composition between t_1 and t_2, insofar as this involves more than the existence of the rele-vant actions and experiences.

Figure 2. My life from t_1 to t_2

The dashes of the fragmented upper line represent pieces of the lower line: action-and-experience-involving pieces of which I am now Conscious. The curving lines represent the fact that I am at t_2 Conscious of some of the periods of time between t_1 and t_2. The line from t_2 to t_2 represents my present Consciousness of my currently occurring experiences at t_2 ('thinking consists in being conscious that one thinks', 2.1.19).

Now consider the view of t_1–t_2 from t_3, the present moment (Fig. 4), and see what the passing of time has done.

The view from t_2 is represented as before by the gappy line above my continuous lifeline; the view from t_3 is represented by the gappy line below it. (The vertical line cutting the continuous horizontal lifeline marks the Person I was at t_2.) The key change in my (forensic or [3]-related) Consciousness from t_2 to t_3 – the change so far as the period from t_1 to t_2 is concerned – is marked by the fact that the lower gappy line is sparser than the higher gappy line. This represents the fact that I am at t_3 Conscious of fewer of the experiences that occurred between t_1 and t_2 than I was at t_2. So the Person that I am at t_3, the moral unit that I am, has changed not only because I've performed new actions and undergone new experiences between t_2 and t_3 but also because I'm no longer Conscious, at t_3, of some of the actions and experiences that occurred between t_1 and t_2 of which I was still conscious at t_2.

The diagram represents a considerable thinning of the lower dotted line relative to the higher one, and may not be accurate in

Figure 3. The view of t_1–t_2 from t_2; my (forensic) Consciousness at t_2 with respect to t_1–t_2

Galen Strawson

[3]

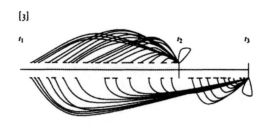

Figure 4. The view of t_1–t_2 from t_3; my (forensic) Consciousness at t_2 and t_3 with respect to t_1–t_2

this respect. For I may at t_3 still be Conscious of almost all the things I was Conscious of at t_2. If we slightly redefine 'Conscious' so that it doesn't pick up everything that I'm still Concerned or emotionally implicated in, such as happy memories of morally neutral experiences, but only picks up morally relevant items, then it may be that not much has changed at t_3, Consciousness-wise, when it comes to the period between t_1 and t_2. In particular, it may be that not much has changed in my 'heart' – all of whose secrets will be 'laid open' on the Day of Judgment. I think that Locke doesn't expect the field of my Consciousness to change much from t_2 to t_3 so far as the morally important events in my life prior to t_2 are concerned.

That said, it's important that his view allows change in the content of my field of Consciousness over time, relative to the actions and experiences of any period of past time. I may for example steal plums between t_1 and t_2 and no longer be Conscious of this action at t_3 – and so no longer be properly punishable for it at t_3 (which may be the Day of Judgment). A Person's Consciousness may contain an involuntary natural mechanism that operates somewhat like a statute of limitations. One may forget many things precisely because they can appropriately be forgotten, because one is no longer Concerned in them (rather than ceasing to be Concerned in them simply because one has irretrievably forgotten them and is therefore no longer Conscious of them). And one may perhaps *remember* things although one is no longer *Conscious* of them in the relevant sense, no longer Concerned in them in the moral-responsibility-engaging sense. One may not have to ask for 17,033 other minor offences to be taken into consideration on the Day of Judgment, when receiving one's doom (i.e. all the offences of the human subject of experience = person$_1$ one is). For even if one then

138

remembers them one may no longer be Concerned in many of them. One may hope that Reid's general will not be punished by God on the Day of Judgement for stealing plums when he was a boy,[35] for he neither remembers nor is Conscious of the theft, and the theft is therefore not part of the Person he is, on the Day of Judgement. In fact he won't be punished for it even if he does *remember* it – so long as he isn't still *Conscious* of it, i.e. so long as he isn't still morally or affectively concerned or implicated in it. For in this case it will again not be part of the Person he is: 'whatever past actions [he] cannot reconcile or appropriate to that present self by consciousness, [he] can be no more concerned in, than if they had never been done' (§26).

It seems to me that the general shouldn't be punished even if he not only remembers it but still feels bad about it, and is to that extent still Concerned in it in such a way that it is still part of the Person he is. For in childhood we have not yet attained the 'age of responsibility', and this is a fact to which divine law will surely not pay less attention than human. There are vicious eschatologies that demand punishment of young children and of all wrong acts performed in childhood, but what will presumably happen on the Great Day, as remarked earlier, is that the general's conscience, enlightened by the grandeur of the occasion, will excuse him, and so surely and in any case will God.

It may help to introduce the notion of one's *account* – the bill, the tab, the list of chargeable items that the subject of experience that one is will have on the Day of Judgement.[36] Only things (actions) that are on one's account will be punished or rewarded. What is on one's account will be a function of what one is Conscious of, where Consciousness (as always) brings with it moral-emotional Concernment.[37] To work out one's Personal account one starts out from the complete set of the past actions of the continuing subject of experience one is, i.e. – in our own case – the human person$_1$ that one is. Plainly not all of these actions are on one's account. In fact very few of them are. The question, question **[D]** (familiarly

---

[35]   Even leaving aside the fact that he was at the time soundly flogged for doing so.

[36]   At one point Locke imagines a thinking being losing all consciousness of its past, 'and so as it were beginning a new account from a new period' (§14).

[37]   One might say, in other terms, it will be a matter of what one still identifies with in the past, where this identification is not necessarily a matter of having a positive attitude to something, nor a matter of choice or intentional action.

Galen Strawson

by now), is this: which of these actions does one still feel involved in, involved in in such a way as to feel that it is something that *one* did – where this '*one*' in italics denotes the Person one is now or if you like the person$_2$ one is now? This tiny subset of the actions of the person$_1$ that one is contains all the actions that are on one's account and that actually constitute the Person one now is so far as one's past actions are concerned (i.e. so far as **[3]** rather than **[1]** ± **[2]** is concerned): 'that with which the **consciousness** of this present thinking thing can join itself, makes the same person, and is one self with it, and with nothing else' (§17). And although being on one's account is a necessary condition of attracting punishment or reward, it is not a sufficient condition, for many things – like warm memories – will be morally neutral; and God has a reputation for mercy.

13. Psychological Connectedness

The point can be re-expressed in Parfitian terms, according to which a person P_7 at t_7, e.g. now, is (directly) *psychologically connected* to a person P_1 at some past time t_1 if – to take the case of memory – P_7 can now remember having some of the experiences that P_1 had at t_1; while P_7 is *psychologically continuous* with P_1 if there is an overlapping chain of such direct connections (e.g. P_7 is psychologically connected to P_6, P_6 to P_5, P_5 to P_4, and so on unbrokenly back to P_1). Clearly P_7 can be psychologically continuous with P_1 even if P_7 is not psychologically connected to P_1. Equally clearly, P_7 can be psychologically connected with P_1 even if not psychologically continuous with P_1.[38]

In these terms we may say that Locke isn't interested in the (transitive) relation of psychological continuity when it comes to the question of personal identity. He's only interested in the (non-transitive) relation of psychological connectedness. It is accordingly misleading to call those who seek to give an account of personal identity principally in terms of psychological continuity 'neo-Lockeans'. It's true that Locke gives an essentially psychological account of the conditions of Personal identity (an account in terms of Consciousness) but the resemblance between Locke and the neo-Lockeans ends there.

The psychological connectedness that matters to Locke is furthermore narrower – more fine-grained – than psychological connectedness as ordinarily understood; and this isn't simply because

[38] Cf. Parfit *Reasons and Persons* (Oxford: Clarendon Press, 1984), 205–206.

Consciousness isn't the same as memory (it's not the same as memory even when we restrict attention to Consciousness of the past). The point was made in section 10 but it's worth repeating. Suppose P_1 performs two actions a_1 and a_2 at the same time at t_1.[39] Locke's position, which is clearly correct given the constantly reiterated point of his account of Personal identity, is that P_7 at t_7 can be Conscious of a_1, and so psychologically connected to P_1 at t_1 as the performer of a_1 in such a way as to be the same Person as P_1 at t_1, and so morally responsible for a_1, while not being Conscious of a_2 – not psychologically connected to P_1 at t_1 as the performer of a_2 in such a way as to be the same Person as P_1 at t_1. Plainly, then, P's Consciousness connection at t_1 to P_1 at t_1 is not a connection to P_1 at t_1 *überhaupt*, for if it were this would yield a contradiction. The Consciousness connection is to the doing of a_1 at t_1 and not to the doing of a_2. On Locke's theory it doesn't matter that there is only one human being involved. P can be the same Person as P_1-doing-a_1 ('P_{1a1}') and not the same Person as P_1-doing-Y ('P_{1a2}').

Objection. 'This isn't possible. P_{1a1} is not only the same *human being* as P_{1a2} but also the same *Person*, because she is (we may suppose) fully Conscious of what she is doing at t_1. And this means that we can generate a contradiction. For even if we allow ourselves for purposes of argument to treat P_{1a1} and P_{1a2} as potentially different Persons, in spite of the fact that there's only one human being, so that P_7 at t_7 can be the same Person as P_{1a1} and not the same Person as P_{1a2}, still P_{1a1} and P_{1a2} must be the same Person *by Locke's own Consciousness criterion*, given that P_1 is fully Conscious of what she is doing at t_1; so P_1 can't be identical with P_{1a1} and not also with P_{1a2}.'

Reply. There is perhaps no better way to understand Locke's theory of personal identity than to realize that is not any sort of objection to it. 'Person ... is a forensic term, appropriating actions and their merit'.[40]

The University of Texas at Austin
gstrawson@austin.utexas.edu

---

[39] 'Do an action' seems incorrect in modern English, outside philosophy, but I follow Locke's usage.

[40] In *Locke on Personal Identity* (2014), I go into more detail. I also analyse the 'fatal error' passage in §13 of Locke's chapter. I'm grateful to Ruth Boeker and Mohan Matthen for comments on a draft of this paper, and to audiences at Reading University, the American University of Beirut, and the Royal Institute of Philosophy.

Selfless Persons: Goodness in an Impersonal World?

LYNNE RUDDER BAKER

Abstract

Mark Johnston takes reality to be wholly objective or impersonal, and aims to show that the inevitability of death does not obliterate goodness in such a naturalistic world. Crucial to his argument is the claim that there are no persisting selves. After critically discussing Johnston's arguments, I set out a view of persons that shares Johnston's view that there are no selves, but disagrees about the prospects of goodness in a wholly impersonal world. On my view, a wholly objective world is ontologically incomplete: Persons have irreducible first-person properties. My aim is to show that we can (and should) reject selves, but that we can (and should) retain persons and their essential first-person properties as ontologically significant.

In a fascinating – indeed, mesmerizing – book, *Surviving Death*, Mark Johnston aims to secure the ideal of goodness in a naturalistic world. According to the worldview of naturalism that Johnston endorses, reality is wholly objective and impersonal: there are no irreducible first-personal facts. Johnston wants to show that the ideal of goodness – which he takes to be radical or impersonal altruism – can survive in such a naturalistic world.

Here's the problem that Johnston poses: Naturalism seems to make reality indifferent to the distinction between the good and the bad. Death, the great leveler, engenders the threat that, since everyone – the good and the bad alike – goes down to oblivion, the good never get their just deserts. Hence, 'the distinction between the good and the bad is less important. So, goodness is less important.'[1] Johnston aims to ward off this threat to goodness from naturalism. His argument for goodness in a naturalistic world moves from a denial that persons have selves to the conclusion that the good survive death in the 'onward rush of humankind' by forsaking their egocentric concerns and re-making themselves in light of impersonal altruism.[2]

Although I agree with Johnston that there are no selves (distinct from whole embodied persons), I disagree with his supposition that

---

[1] Mark Johnston, *Surviving Death* (Oxford: Oxford University Press, 2010), 5.

[2] Johnston, *Surviving Death*, 49.

doi:10.1017/S1358246115000028   ©The Royal Institute of Philosophy and the contributors 2015

Royal Institute of Philosophy Supplement **76** 2015   143

Lynne Rudder Baker

reality is wholly objective or impersonal.[3] My goal here is twofold: first, to show both that what Johnston takes to be impersonal altruism, in fact, presupposes that the world is *not* wholly objective or impersonal; and second, to show that Johnston's conception of goodness is anemic. The upshot is that, while rejecting selves, we can (and should) retain persons and their first-personal properties as ontologically significant. First, let us turn to Johnston.

1. Johnston's Project

Johnston aims to show, without recourse to any supernatural means, that, as Socrates hoped, 'there is something in death that is better for the good than for the bad'.[4] Although I cannot hope to do justice to Johnston's extremely complex view, I want to discuss three arguments that lend support to his central claim. Let me apologize in advance for the rather rigid way that I introduce Johnston's ideas by means of deductive arguments. The reason that I approach his discussion this way is that I find it extremely complicated, with multiple ideas in play at once, and I want to extract a single continuous strand of thought from them.

2. For Impersonal Altruism

The first part of the continuous strand is an argument for impersonal altruism. Its first premise is that there are no persisting selves worth caring about.[5] Selves are supposed to provide independent justification for seeking premium treatment for oneself. Johnston defines a

---

[3]   Also, I do not follow neo-Lockeans, who take persons not to be substances, but rather to be 'cross-time bundles' (Johnston's term), 'which do not have all their essences present at each moment the exist'. (Johnston, *Surviving Death*, 53–54).

[4]   Johnston, *Surviving Death*, 13.

[5]   Selves, according to Johnston, are to provide independent justification for seeking premium treatment. Johnston takes Kant's claim that we are radically evil to be the manifestly true claim 'that there is something at the root of human nature that disposes each one of us to favor himself or herself over the others'. This is why his thinking of 'Johnston as me, as the one at the center of this arena, makes him appear privileged, even if he is actually just one human being among the others'. (Johnston, *Surviving Death*, 158) In contrast to Johnston, I think of the asymmetry between myself and others to be a matter of the first-person perspective, not a matter of thinking of myself as the center of an arena. And I think of exemplifying

144

self as the center of an arena of presence, an all-inclusive psychological field, a sort of container for all your conscious experiences, a bed for your stream of consciousness. But, he argues, it is indeterminate whether an arena of presence considered at one time is identical to an arena of presence considered at a different time. There is no fact of the matter about whether someone '*continue*[s] to be at the center of this arena of presence'.[6] Johnston says: 'There need be no determinate content to the prospective subjective question, the question of whether such and such a human being in the future *will* be me.'[7] So, an arena of presence, in terms of which a self is defined as its center, is only an intentional object, like Macbeth's dagger.[8] And 'given that the identity over time of a merely intentional object is a matter of how things strike the subject, so too is the identity over time of a self!' Hence, there are no persisting selves.[9]

Johnston goes on to argue that, in the absence of selves, all reasons for doing anything derive from impersonal reasons: If there are no selves, he argues, all first-personal reasons depend on impersonal reasons applied to one's own case.[10]

The way that he puts this point is to say there are no non-derivative or basic de se practical reasons.[11] (Since 'de se' is a technical term, I'll

---

the robust first-person perspective as having ontological import, not moral import.

[6] Johnston, *Surviving Death*, 168.

[7] Johnston, *Surviving Death*, 175. This question seems to me to be rooted in Johnston's discussions with Parfit. I myself *never* pick out a person in the future and ask if it will be me. Never.

[8] Johnston, *Surviving Death*, 169

[9] Johnston, *Surviving Death*, 231. Johnston's aim in denying that there are persistent selves is to show that self-concern is irrational. Here is an argument:

1. What really matters is to be me, not to be this human being.
2. To be me is to be at center of this arena of presence, self.
3. I – this self – am defined only relative to this arena of presence.
4. This center of presence is an intentional item, a virtual item at which perspectival modes of presentations appear to converge – and not a feature of the world.

∴5. This self is not a feature of the world.
∴6. It's irrational to care about this self.

[10] Johnston, *Surviving Death*, 238.

[11] Johnston also calls the first-personal reasons '*de se*' reasons. Johnston characterizes de se thought as 'thought about oneself *as oneself*', thought that one typically expresses in the first person. (Johnston, *Surviving Death*, 189)

Lynne Rudder Baker

replace it with 'first-personal'.) Johnston agrees that we *have* first-personal reasons for acting; they are just derivative from impersonal reasons. For example, John Perry's messy shopper does not look into his shopping cart to find the leaking sugar until he realizes, 'Oh, it's me who's making a mess!' At that point, he may have implicitly reasoned, 'It's my mess, so I should clean it up.'[12] If so, his first-personal reason is derived from an impersonal reason, perhaps derived from 'Everyone has reason to see that the mess he makes in public places is cleaned up.'[13] Johnston explicitly includes not only moral and prudential reasons in the category of practical reasons, but also reasons of etiquette.[14]

Johnston says that basic first-personal practical reasons – reasons that derive only from one's own interests – have 'no force because they depend for their coherence on the persistence of a self worth caring about'.[15] If there is no persisting self worth caring about, there is nothing (no self) that that can be 'a rational object of special concern'.[16] So, all practical reasons 'are derived simply from the structure of impersonal reasons'.[17] In that case, 'the premium or excess that self-concern expects...cannot represent a reasonable demand or expectation'. So, impersonal altruism – the disposition to absorb the legitimate interests of others – is required by the structure of reason.[18]

---

[12] I should mention that Johnston distinguishes between two forms of 'I' thought: one merely indexical to register information about the person who tokens it, and the other truly subjective, 'mediated by thinking of oneself as some person or other *qua* at the center of an immediately given arena of consciousness'. (Johnston, *Surviving Death*, 193) On his view, however, the second form of 'I' thought is illusory. I make no such distinction between merely indexical 'I' thoughts and truly *de se* 'I' thoughts. A child, who uses 'I' in a merely indexical way (if there are such), simply hasn't completely mastered the use of the first-person pronoun.

[13] Johnston, *Surviving Death*, 189.

[14] Johnston, *Surviving Death*, 9. Even my special attachment to friends and family, because they are *my* friends and family derives 'from an objective point of view, *anyway* owed to family members, friends and others'. (Johnston, *Surviving Death*, 191).

[15] Johnston, *Surviving Death*, 236.

[16] Ibid., 48.

[17] Ibid., 235.

[18] Nevertheless, self-concern may be bequeathed to us by natural selection. If survival and reproduction are built-in goals, then when I can conceive of the difference between *my* survival and *others'* survival, I seem to have a reason to seek premium treatment for myself.

Here's a sketch of Johnston's argument from the structure of reasons as I understand it:

(1)   There are no persisting selves worth caring about.[19]

(2)   If (1), then there is no ME (in the relevant subjective sense) that could be 'a rational object of self-concern'.[20]

(3)   If (2b), then there are no first-personal (de se) practical reasons that derive only from one's own interests.[21]

(4)   If (3b), then all practical reasons 'are derived simply from the structure of impersonal reasons'.[22]

(5)   If (4b), then impersonal altruism is required by the structure of reason.[23]

∴(C1)   Impersonal altruism – the disposition to absorb legitimate interests of others – is required by the structure of reasons.

If Johnston is right, the command to cease considering oneself as an entity of special concern is the command of agape – the New Testament command of universal love. The command of agape is not merely a moral command;[24] it is rather the command 'to live in accord with the practical reasons that there actually are. And that is all "goodness" in the practical realm can reasonably be to taken to mean.'[25]

This argument from the structure of practical reasons, to which I'll turn critically later, paves the way for the discussion of how to become a good person, an impersonal altruist.

3. How We Can Become Good

The discussion of how to become good shifts the focus from the self, which depends on a merely intentional object (an arena of presence), to 'the person I presently find myself to be'.[26] This person is an embodied human being, with an individual personality. Johnston offers a 'radical reversal' of the idea of personal identity over time.

---

[19]   Johnston, *Surviving Death*, 178.
[20]   Ibid., 48.
[21]   Ibid., 48, 179.
[22]   Ibid., 235.
[23]   Ibid., 238.
[24]   Self-regard, Johnston argues, is not rational. (Johnston, *Surviving Death*, 49) Johnston has Kantian overtones throughout: The impersonality of nonderivative reason, goodness as a good will.
[25]   Johnston, *Surviving Death*, 296.
[26]   Ibid., 241.

Lynne Rudder Baker

The naive intuitive view that Johnston wants to reverse is that 'the relation of personal identity independently justifies certain future-directed dispositions'.[27] According to the radical reversal, personal identity does not justify certain future-oriented dispositions, but rather the reverse. The radical reversal is that personal identity itself is determined by a certain future-directed disposition that we can alter, thereby altering the changes we can survive.[28] That is, we can change the conditions under which we can survive.

How is it that we can change our conditions of survival? Well, we are Protean.[29] The 'essence-characterizing kind for [you and me]', says Johnston, 'is the kind Protean Person'.[30] He continues, 'The fact that we are *Protean*, namely, *that the terms of our survival depend on our dispositions*, is an independent and essential fact about our natures as persons.'[31] To be Protean implies that if 'we could refigure our identity-determining dispositions then what we are... *capable of surviving* would change'.[32] The way in which we implement personal identity is response-dependent. The identity-determining disposition 'determines what kind of thing, with what temporal extent, counts as the person in question'.[33]

The good person is disposed to regard the legitimate interests of all present and future persons as on a par with her own. She acquires the disposition to 'absorb the anticipatable interests of future persons into [her] present practical outlook, so that [she is] now disposed to promote those interests'.[34] How might the disposition to be impersonally altruistic be acquired? '[O]ne's basic practical dispositions can change as a result of self-examination, modeling, and training. The process is more like becoming an extraordinary pianist than like choosing to see things a different way.'[35]

By refiguring my dispositions to identify with the interests of others, I see that there is nothing special about my individual personality, or anyone else's. Each of us is just one person among many. We simply 'implement personal identity in such a way that we would

27 Johnston, *Surviving Death*, 274.
28 Ibid., 272.
29 The term 'Protean' pertains to the shape-changing god Proteus. A Protean entity is extremely variable, like an actor play who has multiple roles in a play.
30 Johnston, *Surviving Death*, 284.
31 Ibid., 285.
32 Ibid., 284.
33 Ibid., 278.
34 Ibid., 275.
35 Ibid., 327.

survive wherever and whenever interests are to be found. We would, quite literally, live on in the onward rush of humankind.'[36] In a naturalistic world, if one gives up seeking 'premium treatment', one encounters herself objectively as just another person and arrives at a 'thoroughly objective relationship with the human being [she] finds [herself] to be'.[37]

Here is a reconstruction of of Johnston's argument How to Become Good:

(1)   We are Protean persons – i.e., the terms of our survival depend on our dispositions.

(2)   If we are Protean, then we can re-figure our identity-determining dispositions in a way that makes us good persons – i.e., we can become disposed to absorb the legitimate interests of persons at all times at which we take them to exist.[38]

∴(C2)   We can become good persons – i.e., we can become disposed to absorb the legitimate interests of persons at all times at which we take them to exist.

4. How the Good Literally Survive Death in a Naturalistic World

A good person – at least an extremely good person – alters her identity-constituting dispositions by giving up concern with any individual personality and becoming impersonally altruistic.[39] In *any* naturalistic world, 'death obliterates one's individual personality'. Nevertheless, 'if there are extremely good people, they are not only able to face down death, that is, face the obliteration of their own individual personality without feeling it to be a tragic loss, they are also able literally to survive death'.[40] '[I]n identifying fundamentally with the interests of the arbitrary other', Johnston says, 'you will have become something that is present whenever and wherever individual personality is present.'[41]

[36]   Johnston, *Surviving Death*, 296.
[37]   Ibid., 14.
[38]   Ibid., 284, 295, 296.
[39]   Ibid., 49.
[40]   Ibid., 318.
[41]   Johnston, *Surviving Death*, 350. To *identify with* someone is to be disposed to 'take [certain] anticipated future interests as default starting points in our practical reasoning'. (Johnston, *Surviving Death*, 295) Earlier, Johnston explained 'identification with' as 'caring for [the good of

Lynne Rudder Baker

The good can live on in the lives of countless others because they are Protean. Johnston offers an analogy: Protean people are higher-order individuals like species – e.g., The tiger is a sub-kind of the kind *Panthera*. The species, constituted by a succession of organisms, admits not only variable constitution but also multiple constitution.[42] (That is, a species is constituted by different organisms at different times, and by many organisms at once.) If a Protean person becomes good, then 'he becomes generally embodied; his constitution is made up of the constitution of all present and future beings with interests'. This 'shared embodiment'[43] is how, when death brings the destruction of his initial individual personality, he continues in the onward rush of humanity – or, more precisely 'as living on with those that are not closed to goodness'.[44] On the other hand, a Protean person who 'firmly sticks to selfishness', and does not become good, 'will cease to exist when the human organism that embodies [him] dies'.[45]

When a good person survives death, Johnston insists, it is not 'merely a surrogate or spectral form of survival without consciousness, deliberation or action'.[46] If persons are Protean, then 'a person is conscious at a time if at that time he is constituted by a body that is then a site of consciousness'.[47] After death, when you become partly constituted by numerous conscious people, you will be conscious without realizing that you are conscious. (Similarly for deliberating and acting.) In this way, 'One quite literally lives on in the onward rush of humankind.'[48]

This, Johnston says, is the 'reward' of *agape*.[49] Noting that '*anastasis*' is the Greek word that the Apostle Paul used for resurrection, Johnston says, '*[A]gape* constitutes the *anastasis* of the good, their rising up to acquire a higher-order identity, an identity as a thing that is present wherever and whenever others are present.'[50] 'If we are Protean', says Johnston, 'then *agape* is identity-constituting in a

---

people] in a non-derivative way'. (Johnston, 'Human Concerns Without Superlative Selves', in *Reading Parfit,* Jonathan Dancy, ed. (Oxford: Blackwell Publishers (1997), 149–179. Quotation is on 157.)

[42] Johnston, *Surviving Death*, 319.
[43] Ibid., 336.
[44] Ibid., 335.
[45] Ibid., 331.
[46] Ibid., 350.
[47] Ibid., 350.
[48] Ibid., 49.
[49] Ibid., 350.
[50] Ibid., 351.

way that makes for survival in the onward rush of humankind'.[51] In this way, Johnston says that he vindicates Socrates' hope that 'there is something for us in death [that is...] better for the good than...for the bad'.[52]

Here is a sketch of how the good literally survive death in a naturalistic universe:

(1)   Good persons alter their identity-constituting dispositions by 'identifying fundamentally with the interests of the arbitrary other', and become disposed to absorb the legitimate interests of other persons (who are not closed to goodness) in the present and in the future.[53]

(2)   If (1), then the good are (and will be) present wherever and whenever good people are present.[54]

(3)   If (2b), then the good can be multiply constituted by the bodies of others whenever and wherever they are.[55]

(4)   If (3b), then the good survive death (in the onrush of humankind).[56]

∴.(C3)   The good survive death.

To sum up my reconstruction of the three arguments: The thread of the argument moves from 'no self' to 'no basic de se [or first-personal] practical reasons' to impersonal altruism as a rational requirement. Then, on a revisionary conception of personal identity and a Protean view of persons, personal identity is a matter of our identity-determining disposition. An extremely good person, whose identity is determined by her identifying herself with personality as such, survives her own death. If these are Johnston's three conclusions – (C1), C2), and (C3) – then his overall argument lacks only the conditional premise: If (C1), (C2), and C3), then in a naturalistic world, the ideal of goodness is not obliterated.

5. A Critical Look at Johnston's Arguments

Still, I do not believe that Johnston has shown that the ideal of goodness is not obliterated in a naturalistic world. Let's look at the arguments again.

[51]   Johnston, *Surviving Death*, 49.
[52]   Ibid., 361.
[53]   Ibid., 275, 335.
[54]   Ibid., 350.
[55]   Ibid., 13, 351.
[56]   Ibid., 350.

Lynne Rudder Baker

Is the argument for (C1) – the argument from 'no self' to impersonal altruism sound? The argument is valid, but, I think, unsound. I'll
not challenge the first premise, that there is no persisting self worth
caring about. However, there seems to be a dialectical oddity in
Johnston's 'no-self' strategy. In order for the illusoriness of the self
to play its intended role, Johnston must first characterize a self in
such a way that there *seem* to be selves as well as persons: Johnston
must assume that many or most of us take selves to exist.[57]
The self is supposed to be something with a subjective principle of
unity: same arena of presence, same self. But there are no selves for
the reason that there is no sense to the notion of 'same arena of presence'. Johnston introduced the distinction between selves and
persons only to discredit the reality of selves.[58] However, if my
view – which we'll consider later – is correct, we are no more committed to centers of arenas of presence than we are to Dennett's Cartesian
Theatre. Such a Cartesian approach is a nonstarter. Nevertheless, I
agree that there are no selves in addition to persons – despite the dialectical oddity.
The premise of the argument for (C1) that I want to challenge is
premise (3): While I agree that there are no selves (albeit on different

[57]   Johnston distinguishes self-identity from personal identity. 'Self-
identity, the identity that guarantees the coninuation of one's immediately
available arena of presence over time, is more basic in its importance than
personal identity, the identity over time of the public person who happens
now to be at the center of one's arena of presence.' Johnston picks out his
(hylomorphic) self as 'the self that I am is constituted by a potential succession of persons united by the following cross-time unity condition – that
they be successively at the center of this arena of presence'. (Johnston,
Surviving Death, 204) This self is 'presently constituted by Johnston.
Johnston presently has the property of being me'. (Johnston, *Surviving
Death*, 206) There's *prima facie* evidence that we trace selves, he says, 'by
bringing to bear a salient subjective unity conditions, rather than tracking
persons by offloading onto the most salient substance in the vicinity'.
We're haunted by thoughts of an afterlife in which we come to be things different from human beings, or we come back as another person. (Johnston,
Surviving Death, 212).
[58]   It is only because Johnston equates *being me* with being at the center of
this arena of presence and action that he can say that 'the idea that there is
nothing real to being *you*, when properly grasped, is even more terrifying
than death'. (Johnston, *Surviving Death*, 164) 'Perhaps the key to deathless-
ness is the realization that YOU, in the relevant sense, could not possibly be
real – are anyway, not *real enough* to justify a temporally extended pattern of
self-concern, which manifests itself in your everyday egocentrism and in
your special fear of your own(most) death.' (Johnston, *Surviving Death*, 179).

152

grounds from Johnston's), and hence no 'rational object of special self-concern', I also believe that there are non-derivative first-personal practical reasons. So, let me propose four candidates for basic first-personal practical reasons – that is, for reasons for acting that derive only from one's own interests and not from impersonal reasons:

First, there are free-rider cases. If I break in line, because I don't want to waste my time waiting, I am thinking of myself as a whole person, standing there, not a self that I agree is nonexistent. The absence of a self seems irrelevant to my reason for breaking in line, which seems not irrational, even if immoral.

Second, suppose that the reason that I'm wearing widow's weeds is that my dear husband died and I want to mourn him this way. (Not everyone whose dear husband dies does or should wear widow's weeds; it's not part of our culture to wear them.) Johnston himself says that it would be 'ham-fisted and obscene' to interfere with someone's mourning the death of a beloved other.[59] Well, yes – although that opinion seems to me completely at odds with impersonal altruism. (The mourner is not treating the dead beloved as an arbitrary other.) It seems otiose to insist that the reason that one grieves in one way rather than another must be derived from the structure of impersonal practical reasons.

Third, suppose that I'm in a spy ring and I want to alert my contact that I'm now in the vicinity without alerting anyone else. Suppose that I habitually wear an unusual shade of lipstick, and that I know that my contact is familiar with my lipstick preference. I dab a bit of the lipstick on a tissue and drop it beside my contact's car. The reason that I left the lipstick-dabbed tissue beside that car is that I wanted my contact to know that I was there without tipping off anyone else. This reason depends only on my knowledge of another person's knowledge of my use of a shade of lipstick; it seems not to derive from any impersonal structure of reasons.

Fourth, the phenomena associated with love for another person seem to be rife with basic first-personal reasons for acting. Suppose that I give my loved one a deliberately mismatched pair of socks. I reason, 'I love him deeply, and want to give him something that always reminds him of me. That's why I gave him the unusual pair of socks.' This seems like a totally idiosyncratic reason to give mismatched socks, untethered to the structure of impersonal reasons.

I submit that all four of these examples give basic first-personal (or *de se*) reasons for acting – reasons that do not derive from impersonal reasons. Johnston may object: 'Baker is talking about self-concern of

---

[59] Johnston, *Surviving Death*, 50.

persons; I, Johnston, am talking about self-concern of selves; so, the counterexamples are irrelevant.' I would respond that there is no non-question-begging reason to suppose that my special self-concern pertains to my nonexisting self rather than to *this* existing person. So, I stick by the counterexamples, each of which provides a rational motivation for acting.

It would just be a contrivance, a work-around, to look for impersonal rules from which to derive these reasons. Even if all *moral de se* (or first-personal) reasons are derivative from impersonal moral rules, it is not the case that all *practical* reasons – reasons for acting – are moral reasons. (Johnston seemed to agree that not all reasons are moral reasons when he mentioned rules of etiquette as reasons for acting.[60] So, I conclude that Johnston's argument that we are called to impersonal altruism by the very structure of reasons is not sound. In that case, Johnston has not succeeded in showing that the ideal of goodness fits into a wholly impersonal ontology.

Now turn to the argument for (C2) – for How We Can Become Good. Is it sound? I think that Johnston's argument is bold and stunning. But I cannot endorse it. I am unconvinced by Johnston's radical reversal of the notion of personal identity. It is difficult to see how a good person can change her persistence conditions, in effect, by changing her dispositions. This picture of goodness challenges credulity.

Be that as it may, there is also a more direct criticism of the argument for (C2). I do not believe that Johnston's view of goodness can be implemented in a wholly objective world as pictured by naturalists. To be good, Johnston says, is to identify 'fundamentally with the interests of the arbitrary other'.[61] However, to identify with the interests of the arbitrary others is to 'take [their] anticipated future interests as default starting points in our practical reasoning'.[62] I cannot take someone else's anticipated future interests as a starting point in my practical reasoning in a wholly objective and impersonal world.

This is so, for two reasons: (1) I cannot even consider another person's future interests as a starting point in *my* practical reasoning unless I can conceptually distinguish myself from others, and distinguishing myself from others requires a first-person perspective. It's not just a matter of distinguishing this from that; it's a matter of distinguishing me (in the first person) from others. (2) I cannot attempt to change my own dispositions unless I have a *robust* first-person perspective. I have a robust first-person perspective if and only if I have a

[60] Johnston, *Surviving Death*, 9.
[61] Ibid., 350.
[62] Ibid., 295.

capacity to conceive of myself and know that it is myself I am conceiving of, without any informative criterion for being me.[63]

The closest that Johnston comes to discussing a robust first-person perspective is to mention in passing 'a person's....capacity to take him- or herself as a topic of thought and talk'.[64] But this is equivocal, because there are two distinct ways to make oneself the topic of thought and talk. One can conceive of oneself in the first-person or in the third-person.[65] And it is only when one conceives of oneself in the first-person that she manifests a robust first-person perspective.

Suppose that I want to become a good person by becoming disposed to absorb the future interests of other people. In that case, I want myself (conceived of as myself in the first person) to become disposed to absorb the interests of others; I don't just want Baker to become so disposed. So, it's difficult to see how in a wholly impersonal world, anyone could become a good person in Johnston's sense. To become good, in Johnston's sense, I really must manifest a robust first-person perspective – that is, I must exercise a capacity to conceive of myself as myself in the first person in order even to try to align my interests with the interests of an arbitrary other. So, the premises of the argument for (C2), if true, presuppose that robust first-person perspectives are exemplified.

Ontologically speaking, there is no place in a wholly objective world for a robust first-person perspective. So, either one of the premises in the argument for (C2) is false, or the universe is not wholly objective. Either way, Johnston has not shown that his conception of goodness can be realized in a wholly impersonal and objective universe.[66] A similar argument holds for the first premise of the argument for (C3).

---

[63]   Trenton Merricks, 'There are no Criteria of Identity Over Time', Noûs **32** (1998), 106–124.

[64]   Johnston, *Surviving Death*, 268.

[65]   I am relying here on the important work of Hector-Neri Castañeda (Castañeda, 'Indicators and Quasi-Indicators', *American Philosophical Quarterly* **4** (1967), 85–100; Castañeda, 'He: A Study in the Logic of Self-Consciousness', *Ratio* **8** (1966), 130–157.

[66]   And even when Johnston makes no obvious first-person reference, what he says presupposes first-person perspectives. For example: Johnston says that a good will 'is a disposition to absorb the legitimate interests of any present or future individual personality into one's present practical outlook, so that those interests count as much as one's own'. (Johnston, *Surviving Death*, 332) No one can count the interests of others as much as her own unless she can conceive of herself as herself in the first

Lynne Rudder Baker

As impressive as I think Johnston's argument is, I do not think that it succeeds in showing how the ideal of goodness can survive in a wholly objective and impersonal world.

Now, let me turn briefly to my own account of persons that also denies the existence of selves, but still holds to irreducible first-personal properties.

6. Persons and the First-Person Perspective

My view is similar to Johnston's up to a point: Persons are essentially embodied but they do not essentially have the bodies that they in fact have.[67] Rather, persons are constituted by bodies with which they are not identical.[68]

Here is where I part ways with Johnston: I don't think that persons can be scattered objects, as Johnston's Protean persons seem to be. Moreover – and central to my view – persons essentially have first-person perspectives, which have two stages, rudimentary and robust. At the rudimentary stage, a first-person perspective is a non-conceptual capacity shared by human infants and (some) nonhuman animals. It is the capacity of a conscious subject to perceive of and interact with entities in the world from a first-personal 'origin'. At the robust stage, a first-person perspective is a conceptual capacity displayed by language-users; it is the capacity to conceive of oneself as oneself from the first person.[69]

Born with a rudimentary first-person perspective and a remote (or second-order) capacity to acquire a robust first-person perspective, a human person gets to the robust stage in the natural course of development. As she learns a language, a person acquires numerous

---

person. A world with such first-person perspectives is not the wholly object-ive and impersonal world of naturalism.

[67] I also agree with Johnston that we do not use any sufficient conditions for personal identity over time to reidentify people. (Johnston, *Surviving Death*, 59; Lynne Rudder Baker, 'Three-Dimensionalism Rescued: A Brief Reply to Michael Della Rocca', *Journal of Philosophy* **110** (2013), 167)).

[68] I use the word 'constitution' somewhat differently from Johnston; see, for example, *The Metaphysics of Everyday Life*. (Lynne Rudder Baker, *The Metaphysics of Everyday Life: An Essay in Practical Realism* (Oxford: Oxford University Press, 2007).

[69] And a first-person perspective has nothing to do with justifying 'a certain temporally extended pattern of special self-concern'. (Johnston, *Surviving Death*, 176).

concepts, among which is a self-concept that she can use to conceive of herself as herself in the first person. On acquiring a self-concept, a person gains a robust first-person perspective – an in-hand capacity to conceive of herself as herself in the first person, without identifying herself by a name, description or third-person demonstrative. This capacity is exhibited throughout one's life in characteristically human activities – from making contracts to celebrating anniversaries to seeking fame by entering beauty contests.

Metaphysically speaking, to have a first-person perspective (rudimentary or robust) is to exemplify a dispositional, non-qualitative property. A human infant, with only a rudimentary first-person perspective, exemplifies a dispositional property that she continues to exemplify in different ways as she learns a language and gets to the robust stage of the first-person perspective, and indeed, exemplifies as long as she exists. What makes you the same person that you were when you were an infant is that there is a single exemplification of the dispositional property of having a first-person perspective both then and now – regardless of the vast differences in its manifestations over the years.

Let me emphasize that a first-person perspective is not something that 'exists only when it is experienced'.[70] It is a property – a dispositional property that is not manifested at every moment that it is exemplified. (You continue to have a first-person perspective even when you are sleeping soundly.)

Johnston suggests that 'a perspective, as understood by Baker, is not a property but an individual item of some sort, and a perspective is first-personal just when the one that occupies the perspective thinks of herself as occupying that perspective'.[71] That is not my view. In the first place, on my view, a perspective is not something that one occupies. To have a first-person perspective is to exemplify a dispositional property – a property that I exemplify or instantiate, and in virtue of exemplifying it, I (essentially a person) exist. I do not occupy a property; I exemplify it, and my exemplification of this property is unique.[72]

---

[70]   This expression is John Searle's characterization of subjective phenomena. (John R. Searle, 'Consciousness', *Annual Review of Neuroscience* **23** (2000), 561).

[71]   Johnston, *Surviving Death*, 221.

[72]   The property of being a person is the property of exemplifying a first-person perspective essentially. The property of being me is the property of being this exemplifier of a first-person perspective essentially. There is no informative noncircular definition of 'x and y have the same first-person

Lynne Rudder Baker

So, I do not first exist and then come to have a first-person perspective. I (the person) cannot exist *without* exemplifying a first-person perspective: I came into existence when the fetus that came to constitute me could support a first-person perspective. In short, the first-person perspective is not thought of as a 'center of presence' that can be illusory. Hence, a first-person perspective is not a Johnstonian self or any other 'individual item'.

In contrast to Johnston, for me, there are no Protean persons, only individual persons, who are seats of individual personality. Persons have their persistence conditions – continued exemplification of a first-person perspective – essentially, and they survive (or not) individually.

7. A Last Word on Goodness

I'd like to finish by suggesting that Johnston's conception of goodness cannot stand on its own. As I argued earlier, Johnston's strategy for becoming a good person seems to violate his view that the world is wholly objective. Indeed, is goodness, as construed by Johnston, even desirable? If Johnston is right, then if I were a truly good person, it seems that I would not love my husband for himself in his particularity, but only as representative of humanity. No good person would love anyone, in his or her particularity, for being the person he or she is. This seems to me a rather bleak view of reality.

One last thought: The people whose legitimate interests we are supposed to align ourselves with are all the human beings who are not permanently closed to goodness. It seems possible to not be permanently closed to goodness while believing that, say, the entire bourgeoisie should be eliminated – even if one included oneself in that group. That is, one need not be permanently closed to goodness to believe that the entire bourgeoisie (including oneself) should be eliminated. If so, then, for all that's been said, we should align

---

perspective' inasmuch as any such definition must characterize persons in nonpersonal terms. Since I believe that we are not reducible to nonpersonal or subpersonal items, of course I can not give a definition of what makes us persons in nonpersonal terms. Persons are fundamentally different kinds of beings from anything else in the natural world. If this metaphysical claim is correct, then what I say about human persons does not – cannot – be a noncircular informative definition. (I think that this meets van Inwagen's objection.)

ourselves with that person's legitimate interests. Ah, but no, you might object. Eliminating the bourgeoisie is not a *legitimate* interest. I agree, but then you need a more substantive view of goodness to rule out eliminating the bourgeoisie as a legitimate interest. If so, then Johnston's conception of goodness as it stands is anemic.

Conclusion

I agree with Johnston that there are no selves.[73] But eliminating selves does not leave us ontologically with only objective and impersonal reality. On my view, there are persons, constituted by bodies, who have first-person perspectives essentially. I applaud Johnston's aiming to show that nobody deserves special treatment – religious people of many persuasions officially agree – but I do not think that seeking special treatment depends on any illusions about mental substances. Moreover, a robust first-person perspective is not tied to seeking special treatment, but is a capacity whose exercise is presupposed by a great variety of human activities.

Ontologically, we all are selfless persons: there are no selves, but there are persons with first-person perspectives. Morally, only those few who never seek special treatment are selfless. To be selfless in either sense entails that first-person perspectives, first-person dispositional properties, are exemplified. If I am right, then the very existence of selfless persons insures that reality is not wholly objective. And if reality is not wholly objective, where does that leave naturalism?

University of Massachusetts, Amherst
lrbaker@philos.umass.edu

---

[73]   But I strenuously disagree with Johnston that there are no subjects of experience, that there are only modes of presentation and mental acts of accessing them. If x is accessed, then there is a y who accesses x. The human brain makes accessing possible, but it is not the accessor. The accessor is a subject of experience (a human person) Where there are acts, there are agents. But there are no arenas.

From Phenomenal Selves to Hyperselves

BARRY DAINTON

Abstract

The claim that we are *subjects of experience*, i.e. beings whose nature is intimately bound up with consciousness, is in many ways a plausible one. There is, however, more than one way of developing a metaphysical account of the nature of subjects. The view that subjects are essentially conscious has the unfortunate consequence that subjects cannot survive periods of unconsciousness. A more appealing alternative is to hold that subjects are beings with the *capacity* to be conscious, a capacity which need not always be exercised. But this view can itself be developed in more than one way. The option I defend here is that subjects are nothing more than capacities for consciousness, a view I call the 'C-theory'. Although the C-theory supplies us with a potentially appealing account of the nature of subjects (and hence ourselves), there are challenges to be overcome. Olson has argued that identifying ourselves with what are, in effect, *parts* of human organisms leads to a variety of intolerable problems. I suggest that these problems are by no means insuperable. Bayne and Johnston have argued that identifying subjects with experience-producing systems is confronted with a different difficulty. What if these systems can produce multiple streams of consciousness at once. Whatever else they may be, aren't subjects the kind of thing that can have *just one* stream of consciousness at a time? In response I argue that this is true in one sense, but not in another. Once this is appreciated, the notion that a subject could have several streams of consciousness at once no longer seems absurd, or impossible.

1.

The metaphysical thesis that we are *subjects of experience* is in many ways an appealing one. Or at least, I have generally found it so, and when it comes to assessing philosophical accounts of our own nature, this is of no little importance. When I engage in a philosophical inquiry into the nature of the self, what I am seeking is an answer to the question 'What sort of thing am I?' For an answer to this question to be maximally credible it needs to be metaphysically coherent – it needs to make sense philosophically – but it also needs to be as intuitively plausible as possible. So in assessing a putative answer to the question if I ask myself 'Could I really be a thing of *that* sort?' I want to be able to respond 'Yes, of course, very easily

doi:10.1017/S1358246115000065   ©The Royal Institute of Philosophy and the contributors 2015

Royal Institute of Philosophy Supplement **76** 2015   161

indeed'. The claim that what I am, fundamentally, is a subject of experience meets this requirement fully.

By a 'subject of experience' I mean simply this: a thing whose sole essential property is the ability to enjoy unified states and streams of consciousness. If I know anything about myself right now – or whenever I am awake and capable of thinking anything at all – it is that I am having some experiences, and these experiences form parts of a continuous, flowing stream of consciousness. My experiences may be misleading me as to the real character of other aspects of reality, but I can't seriously doubt that I'm really having the experiences I currently seem to be having. By virtue of this fact, if subjects of experience exist then I obviously qualify as one simply by virtue of being one of the things that is currently having experiences. Moreover, since the only requirement on subjects is their ability to have experiences, should it turn out that appearances are *very* misleading it need not and should not affect how I conceive of myself. Perhaps I am in fact a non-human entity on some distant planet who (for some reason) is suffering a series of vivid hallucinations. Since this alien is having experiences it too qualifies as a subject of experience.

Taking myself to be a subject has further advantages. In my search for an account of my own nature that I can readily believe, one of the things I am looking for is an account which makes it possible for me to survive undergoing changes or transformations which it seems obvious (to me) that I would in fact survive, if they were to occur. A key advantage of taking myself to be a subject is that I would then be able to survive readily conceivable transformations which would *not* be survivable if I were an entity of a different kind.

Vampires are non-human creatures of the night, who have the ability to turn ordinary human beings into vampires by feeding them their blood (according to some tales anyway). Suppose I have just imbibed some vampire blood, and am in the midst of the – quite agonizing – transformation. Do I survive? If the stream of consciousness that I currently enjoying continues on without any interruption in the felt flow of thoughts, perceptions and feelings – and we can stipulate that this is the case – it seems clear to me that I do survive this transformation. The idea that the stream of consciousness that is now mine could continue on, without interruption, but fail to take *me* with it, is not one I can take seriously. But this has a significant consequence. Since by the end of the transformation I am no longer a human being (even though I outwardly resemble one) it seems that I am not essentially a human being. For no human being can survive being transformed into something that is very definitely not a human being.

Radical physical transformations needn't involve change of species. Why is it so easy for me to imagine myself existing in the form of an envatted brain? For two reasons. First, because like many others I assume that all my mental capacities and faculties – my capacities for consciousness included – reside solely in my brain. Provided it is kept in a healthy fully-functioning condition, a human brain doesn't need the rest of a human body in order to sustain a conscious human mind. (It might, of course, require its sensory nerves to be stimulated in appropriate ways if it is to enjoy anything resembling normal perceptual experience.) Second, because it seems obvious to me that provided these mental capacities continue to exist then *I* will continue to exist, even if I end up losing the rest of my body. I'm glad that in actual fact I have the rest of my body – I'd be sorry to lose it – but lose it I could. In being reduced to the condition of an envatted brain my existence as a subject would not be threatened in the slightest, for if my brain retains the ability to sustain a fully conscious mind it also retains the ability to sustain a subject in existence.

Or at least, it wouldn't be threatened provided the surgery does not damage the brain. Certain forms of damage would be inconsequential so far as my continued existence is concerned. Damage to neural tissues which are not relevant to the production of experience would not threaten my existence as a subject of experience. But if, say, some of my brain's visual systems were damaged, leaving me entirely incapable of visual experience, then I would be touched – diminished – at my very core, since a form of experience I was previously able to enjoy is no longer available to me. Even so, since I retain the capacity for other forms of experience, I continue to survive, my identity entirely undiluted and unimpaired. However, should my brain suffer damage which permanently obliterates its ability to produce experience in any shape or form, then I too would have ceased to exist. Once again, taking myself to be a subject of experience allows me to make sense of how a range of possible changes could have precisely the effects on *me* that I believe they would in fact have.

Consider a different case, one where the envisaged transformation is psychological rather than biological. Let's suppose – let's not enquire why – that I am about to be subjected to a radical brainwashing, a procedure which over a period of an hour or so will remove all my memories, my values, my personality traits, my likes and dislikes, my hopes and fears, and replaces them with quite psychological traits that are quite different. Provided my current stream of consciousness continues on without interruption – provided I continue to have a unified stream of sensory and emotional experiences throughout, even though my thought processes become fragmented and inchoate – it seems absurd to me to suppose that this process would be fatal to me. This fact alone suggests that accounts of the self which require a strong degree of psychological continuity if we are to persist through time – and here the contemporary neo-Lockean view comes to mind – cannot be right. In contrast, if we are subjects of experience, there is no psychological constraint on our persistence at all. Provided we remain capable of experiencing – experiencing anything we remain in existence.

2.

There is more to be said about all the scenarios briefly outlined above, but we have seen enough for this at least to be clear: the notion that we are each of us, fundamentally, subjects of experience has considerable appeal, at the intuitive level. But we mustn't overlook the other half of the equation: can we make philosophical sense of this concept? From a metaphysical perspective, what *are* subjects of experience? Out of what are they constructed? What does it take for a single subject to persist through time?

There are different ways of answering these questions Although the doctrine that subjects are immaterial substances whose essential nature is to be conscious has a long and venerable history, it holds little appeal for those who believe that their conscious states are entirely the product of physical activity in our brains. The Cartesian view also has the unfortunate – or at least implausible – consequence that subjects are by their nature conscious throughout their lives, and so cannot survive periods of unconsciousness. Since few of us contemplate periods of dreamless sleep with the sort of dread which would accompany a visit to the dentist's chair, let alone the executioner's chamber, it seems most of us do not believe that periods of unconsciousness are invariably fatal – or that we are the kind of thing which cannot emerge from such periods unscathed.

In fact, the difficulties confronting the Cartesian view are of little import, for in making metaphysical sense of subjects of experience we do not need to appeal to immaterial substances of any sort. There are other possibilities, and of these some look to have considerable promise.

One option is to hold that subjects are things which essentially possess the *capacity* to be conscious. The notion that subjects and capacities for experience are intimately linked is itself venerable. Locke certainly appreciated the connection, criticizing Descartes' position thus:

> ... the perception of ideas being (as I conceive) to the soul, what motion is to the body; not its essence, but one of its operations. And therefore, though thinking be supposed never so much the proper action of the soul, yet it is not necessary to suppose that it should be always thinking, always in action. ... We know certainly, by experience, that we sometimes think; and thence draw this infallible consequence, that there is something in us that has a power to think. But whether that substance perpetually thinks or no, we can be no further assured than experience informs us.[1]

As Locke clearly realized, holding that subjects are essentially possessors of capacities for consciousness has a very significant advantage. Capacities can be active during some periods and entirely dormant during others. A car has the capacity for self-powered motion, but most cars only exercise this capacity from time to time. Nevertheless, a well-maintained car continues to possess its capacity for self-powered motion even when it is not exercising it. Consequently, if we say that a particular subject continues to exist for as long as its capacities for consciousness exist, the notion that subjects can survive periods of complete unconsciousness is no longer problematic. A subject persists through such periods provided their capacities for consciousness continue to exist, completely dormant though they be.

Recognising that subjects and capacities for experience are intimately related is an important step, but there remains the task of establishing precisely what kind of thing subjects are. One option is to hold that subjects are *physical objects*, albeit of a distinctive kind: they are material things which possess capacities for consciousness. A position along these general lines has been elaborated and defended at considerable length by Peter Unger in *Identity, Consciousness and Value* (1990), and more recently – and succinctly – by Christopher Peacocke in *The Mirror of the World* (2014).[2]

---

[1] John Locke, *An Essay Concerning Human Understanding*, ed. P. Nidditch (Oxford, Oxford University Press, 1690/1975), Book II, chapter 1, §10.

[2] Peacocke holds that a subject of experience x is identical with a subject y if and only if x and y have the same S-generator – or in his terms 'same material integrating apparatus' (*The Mirror of the World*, 66). But he does not claim that a subject is numerically identical with an integrating

Our own mental capacities reside in our brains, but straightfor-wardly equating subjects with *human* brains is not an appealing step to take. After all, we know that there are (very) many non-human brains with the capacity to produce unified streams of con-sciousness – the brains of monkeys, dogs and dolphins, for example – and these non-human brains all sustain subjects of experience. Since it might be possible for subjects to be sustained by non-biological physical systems – some advanced form of computer, perhaps – it would also be a mistake to equate subjects with purely biological organs of any kind. What we need is a more general notion. Accordingly, let's use the term *S-generator* to refer any physical object or system that in its current form is capable of generating a single unified streams of consciousness. With this more refined concept in hand, should we take ourselves to *be* S-generators?

This position has its advantages. It can encompass subjects of many different shapes, sizes and constitutions. Also, a system with the capacity to produce two streams of consciousness – as may well be the case with human split-brain patients – will support two S-gen-erators, and hence two subjects, which seems the right result. But this position also suffers from some serious drawbacks, at least in the form defended by Unger and Peacocke.

The latter both hold that the persistence conditions of S-genera-tors, and hence ourselves, are broadly similar to those of other complex physical objects, such as cars, computers and caravans. Just as a car (or biological brain) can survive a complete changes in its constituent parts provided the changes don't occur too quickly – over a period of several days or weeks, say – so too can S-generators. But equally, just as a particular car (or biological brain) cannot survive if its parts are replaced very rapidly – in a matter of minutes or seconds, say – the same applies in the case of S-generators.

To see why this last claim is problematic, it's useful to consider a spectrum of cases. At one end of the spectrum we have a brain all of whose parts get changed in a gradual fashion – atom by atom, neuron by neuron – over a period of five years. At the other end of

---

apparatus, since the latter possess properties (such as being spatially loca-lized in the brain) that the subject does not – he takes subjects to be meta-physically basic entities. But for present purposes what matters is that he does hold that 'the identity of a subject over time consists in the identity of the apparatus that integrates states and events in such a way that a single subject has, or may have, perceptions, sensations, thoughts, action-awareness, and the rest, both at a time and over time.' (Ibid., 65)

the spectrum, we have a brain all of whose parts are all replaced very rapidly indeed: near-instantaneously.[3] In between these extremes there is a vast range of intermediate cases, where the part-replacement happens more or less quickly. Importantly, in *each* of these cases in our spectrum, or so we stipulate, the mental life that is produced by the physical system(s) in question is subjectively indistinguishable: during their waking hours the subject(s) involved enjoy streams of consciousness that are as continuous as the stream you are currently enjoying.

Now, because they want subjects to have the same general persistence conditions as any other compound material object, proponents of the S-generator view are committed to the claim that somewhere along this spectrum of cases, the part-replacement is fatal to the original subject. If the replacement is carried out over a couple of days or weeks, for example, there is no problem: the subject survives; but if the replacement is carried out over a couple of seconds, the subject most definitely does *not* survive.

It is this last claim which I find incredible. If my own brain were suffer the envisaged part-substitutions, given that in *all* the cases along the spectrum, the flow of my consciousness – or at least, the consciousness being produced by the physical systems in question – would be entirely unperturbed, I find it impossible to believe that in *some* of these cases I would survive, but in others would cease to

---

[3]   Achieving an instantaneous change of parts would be impractical using anything resembling standard surgical techniques, but this does not mean it is physically impossible, just rather improbable. Cosmologists have recently started worrying that the most numerous conscious subjects in the universe might be *Boltzmann brains*, i.e. brain-like physical systems that are produced by random quantum fluctuations; these systems only enjoy a brief period of experience: shortly after their creation they vanish again, as their particles disperse. The spontaneous creation of experience-sustaining brains is immensely improbable, but if the universe is infinite – as currently seems likely – there will nonetheless be vast numbers of these entities overall. If Boltzmann brains *are* physically possible, then there is no obvious reason why these same processes couldn't cause a brain at a certain time and location to suddenly vanish, and then – a moment or so later – be replaced by an exact duplicate (this newly created brain does *not* vanish straight away, but endures). Needless to say, this sequence of events is far less probable than the simple creation of a single briefly-existing Boltzmann brain, but improbable is not the same as impossible. If the universe is infinite, it probably happens from time to time. For more on Boltzmann brains, see Sean Carroll, 'Boltzmann's Anthropic Brain', *Discover*, August 1, 2006.

Barry Dainton

exist. Given that the physical alterations to brain have no impact whatsoever at the experiential level, they do not threaten my existence in the slightest.

A variant of this scenario reveals a further potential difficulty for the S-generator approach. Consider a case in a region of the cell-replacement spectrum where the entire process takes place in around half an hour. We have been assuming thus far (albeit tacitly) that whenever a cluster of neurons gets ever-so-carefully removed from my brain it is simply discarded. Let's suppose that this is not the case. Instead, when each cluster of neurons is removed, it is (ever-so-carefully) frozen. Let's further suppose that a couple of days after the replacement procedure has been completed the frozen neurons are carefully un-frozen and re-assembled, to yield a fully functioning brain – a brain that is composed of the same particles – the same flesh and blood – as my original brain possessed, before the cell-replacement treatment commenced. Let's call the latter the 'original matter' or *OM-brain*, and the brain which is composed of new matter but which remains continuously functional throughout the *CF-brain*.

This scenario is of course a neural variant of the classic 'Ship of Theseus' puzzle. The latter puzzle concerns the relationship between material objects and their constituent parts. So far as the 'What happens to the original ship?' question goes, although there are different views as to what the correct answer is, it is generally accepted that our intuitions are pulled in both directions. It seems plausible to think that the CF-ship (as we can call it) is the original, but it can also seem plausible to hold that the OM-ship is the original. Now, if the fundamental premise of the S-generator view is correct, and (a) we are subjects of experience, and (b) subjects are themselves material objects, then we should experience a similar divergence of intuitions in the neural variant. It should seem perfectly intelligible to suppose that the original subject lives on sustained by the CF-brain, but the claim that the original subject is in fact the OM-brain should also seem entirely plausible. The latter, after all, is composed of the same matter in the same configuration as the pre-replacement-process brain. Peacocke for one agrees with this. Discussing such cases he writes 'we are liable to have conflicting intuitions about identity in any case that is structurally analogous to that of Theseus' ship'.[4]

However, as far as I can see, this is not plausible in the least. Given that the CF-brain exists, and continuously sustains a capacity for

---

[4]   Peacocke, *The Mirror of the World*, 69.

conscious – a capacity which could conceivably be exercised without interruption for the entire period – the claim that this subject is one and the same as the original subject is completely compelling. In contrast, the claim that the original subject – or something with a strong claim to be such – pops back into existence when the newly re-constituted OM-brain starts to sustain consciousness does not seem remotely plausible. The tiny brain-fragments that are removed from the CF-brain and then deep-frozen do not posses any capacity for consciousness, singly or collectively, and so manifestly do not constitute a subject. When the fragments are thawed and re-assembled into a working brain, the latter does sustain a subject. But this subject's claim to be numerically identical with the original subject is negligible compared with the strength of the subject sustained by the CF's brain's claim to this status. There is no ambiguity or lack of certainty here – it seems *just obvious* that these verdicts as to what happens to whom are true. In this respect at least, subjects do not seem to be the same kind of thing as compound material objects such as ships, trees or houses.

3.

Evidently, the S-generator approach is seriously problematic, at least as an intuitively appealing account of what subjects of experience are. It is perverse, to put it mildly, to suppose that an uninterrupted (and non-branching) stream of consciousness could fail to belong to a single unique subject, but as we have just seen, the S-generator approach delivers precisely this result.

Is it possible to do better? I believe so. In *The Phenomenal Self* I elaborated an account of subjects which is as naturalistically oriented as the S-generator view, but which does not identify subjects with material objects of any kind – and so does not suffer from the deficiencies we just encountered.[5] On this alternative view – which I called the 'C-theory' – subjects are what I call *C-systems*, and C-systems are *collections of experiential capacities* that possess some highly distinctive attributes. The C-system of a typical human subject (or so it is natural to think) is composed of a sizeable number of different sorts of experiential capacities. Although these capacities are for very different forms of experience – visual, auditory, bodily sensations, conscious thoughts, and so forth – the capacities

[5]   Barry Dainton, *The Phenomenal Self* (Oxford: Oxford University Press, 2008).

which belong to just one subject at a given time have a distinctive feature. If these capacities are active, all the experiences they are producing are *co-conscious*, i.e., they form parts of a single unified conscious episode. If at the time in question these capacities are not active – and typically, the bulk of our experiential capacities at any one time fall into this category – they nonetheless have a distinctive feature: they are such that if they *were* active, all the experiences they would be producing *would* be co-conscious with one another. In short, at any given time, it is the ability to contribute to a single unified state of consciousness which distinguishes experiential capacities which belong to a single subject from those which don't.

It is very plausible to think that this criterion for assigning experiential capacities to subjects at-a-time works well for human subjects. It is no less plausible to think that it works equally well for *all* subjects, irrespective of whether their C-systems are more complex than those of the typical human, or less complex.

Experiential capacities which belong to the same subject needn't exist at the same time. If this were the case, subjects would be condemned to a strictly momentary existence, which would be unfortunate! Happily, the C-theory does not curtail our anticipated lifespans. The solution is simple: C-systems which exist at different times belong to a single subject if their constituent capacities have the ability to contribute experiences to a single continuous *stream* of consciousness. Our streams of consciousness have a distinctive form of unity which exists both at and over time, a unity which is experiential in character: just think of the way each brief phase of a typical stream of consciousness flows – *is experienced* as flowing – into the next. Since experiences which belong to a single stream of consciousness obviously belong to a single subject, it seems equally obvious that capacities for experience which can together produce a single stream of consciousness, whether simultaneously or successively, should also belong to a single subject.

We can call C-systems which have this distinctive property *directly stream-related*. There may well be some subjects who are capable of remaining conscious throughout their entire life-spans, whether this be measured in hours, weeks, years or centuries. Since all the experiential capacities of subjects of this kind are capable of contributing to a single uninterrupted stream of consciousness, these capacities are all directly stream-related. But since our own experiential capabilities are more limited – we cannot stay continuously awake for more than a day or so – a typical human subject possesses experiential capacities which are not directly stream-related (e.g. those which are separated by a few week, or months, or years). This does not affect the fundamentals. We need simply say that experiential capacities belong to the same C-system, and hence subject, if they are either directly or *indirectly* stream-related. Experiential capacities are indirectly stream-related if they are not directly stream-related to one another, but they are connected by an overlapping chain whose successive members consist of experiential capacities which are directly stream-related.

There are a number of further complications which I need not enter into here, but for present purposes all that matters is the basic picture, and this is an appealingly straightforward one. Subjects of experience are defined by their capacity to enjoy unified states and streams of experience – this capacity is the *only* essential property subjects possess. According to the C-theory, the distinguishing feature of experiential capacities which belong to a single subject is precisely their ability to contribute to unified states and streams of consciousness. Moreover, by taking subjects to *consist* of capacities for consciousness we strip away everything that is inessential to a subject's existence, and isolate precisely what all subjects have in common.

Last but not least, if we equate subjects with C-systems, the problems encountered by the S-generator view simply vanish.

Suppose some immensely powerful entity is tampering with your matter in your cranium. Over the past ten minutes it has been annihilating your brain every thirty seconds, and replacing it on each occasion with an exact duplicate; but as previously, this massive material disruption has had no experiential consequences: the succession of brains in your skull has been sustaining a fully continuous stream of consciousness throughout. Depending on how we opt to individuate experiential capacities, this process may well have resulted in the destruction of your original experiential capacities, and their replacement by qualitatively indistinguishable duplicates. So far as the C-theory is concerned, although you are a subject, and subjects are composed of experiential capacities, since the affected capacities have been producing experientially continuous streams of consciousness throughout, this sequence of events poses no threat to your continued existence. In contrast, as we have already seen, proponents of the S-generator account are committed to holding that you cease to exist, even though your stream of consciousness flows serenely on.[6]

---

[6] The identity of an experiential capacity depends on three elements: the kind(s) of experience it produces when triggered, the conditions which trigger it, and the particular *ground* or *base* it has. If our own experiential capacities are properties of our brains, then their bases will, I take it, be neural systems of one kind or another. Whether or not the very rapid

The C-theory delivers a similarly plausible verdict in the neural variant of the 'Ship of Theseus' case. If the gradual replacement of the neurons in the CF-brain does not interfere with its capacity to produce unified streams of consciousness – and this is what we are assuming – then the outcome of the procedure is intuitively obvious: you remain in existence throughout, and *your* experience is wholly the product of that brain. The C-theory concurs with this verdict: since the CF-brain possesses a single uninterrupted experiential potential throughout, it sustains a single subject (in this case, you). Prior to its thawing and re-construction, the OM-brain, consisting as it does of scattered frozen chunks of neural tissue, is wholly incapable of sustaining any consciousness whatsoever, and so it does *not* constitute or sustain a C-system or a subject.

One of the most appealing aspects of Locke's writings on personal identity and the self is his modesty, open-mindedness, and lack of dogmatism. Since he took the view that we had a great deal still to learn about the nature of matter and consciousness, Locke remained resolutely agnostic on the issue of whether conscious minds are material or immaterial in nature. What's more, his own account of personal identity is generally thought to be perfectly compatible with both hypotheses. Three centuries later, most would agree that we still have a great deal to learn about the real nature of the physical world, and how it is related to conscious experience. Accordingly, the fact that the C-theory is also entirely neutral on this issue is a very definite advantage. The claim that we are subjects, and subjects are composed of capacities for consciousness, can stand irrespective of whether these capacities are possessed by entities that are material or immaterial in nature, or whether experiences themselves are material or immaterial. Even if it should turn out that our own experiential

---

replacement of one's neurons with exact duplicates leads to a replacement of one's experiential capacities depends on the relationship between capacities (or dispositional properties) in general and their bases. If they are distinct, as some hold, then the original capacities may survive; if they are identical, as others hold, this won't be possible. But irrespective of which of these views is correct, the original subject's existence is not threatened provided there remains in existence an uninterrupted potential for fully continuous consciousness. (By way of analogy, think of the 'third' power-carrying rail of a transit system; there can be a continuous electrical potential between two locations x and y irrespective of whether the track in between consists of a single long piece of track, or several shorter laid end to end.) We will be looking at the relationship between capacities and their bases in more detail later on.

capacities are housed in immaterial substances, it could easily remain the case that we are numerically distinct from these substances. The only way we subjects could be identical with immaterial substances is if the latter are composed of *nothing but* experiential capacities, and if the latter were the case, it is not obvious why the substances in question should be taken to be immaterial in nature at all.

4.

As I hope is now clear, the C-theory offers a promising account of what we fundamentally are. Or to be more accurate, it offers a promising *framework* for thinking about this issue, one which can be developed in different ways.

The C-theory rests on the claim that our streams of consciousness possess an inherent unity and continuity that is entirely experiential in nature. On other occasions I have defended the view that synchronic and diachronic phenomenal unity should both be understood in essentially the same way. On this view, streams of consciousness consist of (experiential) parts that are experienced together, or *co-conscious*, both simultaneously and successively. Co-consciousness in its synchronic and diachronic forms is a primitive inter-experiential relationship, or so I argue.[7] Although I believe this account has advantages over the alternatives, anyone who (for whatever reason) subscribes to a different account of the unity of consciousness – whether synchronic or diachronic – can still adopt the C-theory. All the latter requires is for our streams of consciousness to possess a genuine unity, of an experiential kind, both at and over time. The C-theory is not beholden to any one account of how this unity is best understood.

Similarly, whether or not consciousness essentially involves some form of *self-consciousness* continues to be debated. Locke famously held that a person is something which possesses the ability to *think about* itself as a persisting conscious being. To be capable of such thoughts a being requires a good deal of cognitive sophistication, and it seems very plausible that there might be subjects of experience – e.g. non-human animals, human infants – who lack this degree of

---

[7] See my *Stream of Consciousness* (London: Routledge, 2000/2006) for further elaboration. I respond to some recent challenges to my account of diachronic unity in 'Flow, Repetitions and Symmetries: Replies to Lee and Pelczar', in N. Oaklander (ed.) *Debates in the Metaphysics of Time* (London: Bloomsbury, 2014), 175–212.

Barry Dainton

sophistication. Does the experience of even these quite primitive subjects involve some form of minimal self-consciousness? Some say yes, while others are more skeptical.[8] While the outcome of this debate is relevant to the forms of experience that are open to subjects, as far as I can see they do not impact at all on the ability of the C-theory to give us a believable account of the existence and persistence conditions of subjects.

Other relevant but as yet unresolved questions are metaphysical rather than phenomenological in character. There are, for example, very different accounts of the nature of dispositional properties, and the outcome of *these* debates will obviously influence how we think of our own natures, or at least they will if we are constituted of nothing but experiential capacities – which, after all, are a particular species of dispositional property. We encountered one example of this in the previous section, and we will be encountering another later on.

There are also issues of a more empirical or scientific kind which will influence the overall picture. One of the advantages of the C-theory, particularly over its Cartesian rival, is that it allows us to survive periods of complete unconsciousness. According to it, you will survive your next period of dreamless sleep provided your capacities for consciousness remain in existence during this period, in a dormant state. It certainly seems plausible to suppose that our brains retain their capacities for consciousness during periods of dreamless sleep – we can, after all, be woken in a second or two, and when it comes to their neural structures, waking brains and (dreamlessly) sleeping brain are really quite similar. Even so, we will have to wait for advances in neuroscience before we have a clear understanding of precisely what is involved in a sleeping – or anaesthetized – brain retaining its capacities for consciousness. Although advances are being made, the sleeping brain is largely as mysterious as its waking counterpart.

Although issues such as these are interesting and important, I will not be focusing on them here. Instead, I want to concentrate on some

---

[8] Following Brentano (and ultimately Aristotle) many classical phenomenologists have endorsed the doctrine that consciousness necessarily involves some form of self-consciousness, recent advocates include D. Zahavi, *Subjectivity and Selfhood* (Cambridge: Cambridge University Press, 2005); U. Kriegel *Subjective Consciousness: A Self-Representational Theory* (Oxford: Oxford University Press, 2009). For some skeptical doubts see Peacocke, *Mirror of Nature,* chapters 1–3, and Dainton, *The Phenomenal Self* , §2.4, §8.2.

important challenges of the metaphysical variety, challenges which will have to be overcome if the C-theory is to prove viable. Unless these foundational challenges *can* be overcome, expending further work on developing the C-theory will simply not be worth the time or trouble.

5.

If we are subjects of experience, and subjects are C-systems, then it looks very much as though we are not human beings. A human being is a complex biological organism, with the corresponding synchronic and diachronic identity conditions. Spelling out precisely what these identity conditions are is a non-trivial task, but will involve details relating to body shape and size, chemical structure and constitution, genetics, and so forth. A C-system is a collection of capacities for unified states and streams of consciousness. These are obviously very different kinds of thing. Although the experiential capacities of human subjects are (very probably) grounded in their brains, as we have already noted, there are easily conceivable circumstances in which subjects and their organisms can go their separate ways. The bite of a vampire would terminate the life of the human animal I am currently housed in, but it would not put an end to *me*. Alternatively, I might be reduced to the condition of some envatted consciousness-sustaining brain-parts. I could not continue to exist in the absence of my biological organism if I were numerically identical with it.

So much seems clear, but questions remain. If I am not numerically identical with my human animal or organism, just how am I related to it? There remains a story to tell about this. Moreover, my non-identity with my organism is itself a source of difficulties. My organism may be an animal rather than a subject of experience, but it has an impressively wide range of properties. It can walk, run, sleep and digest, but it can also read and write, talk, think thoughts, remember its past, feel emotions and perceive the world around it. By virtue of having a brain, my organism has a mind, and by virtue of having a mind my organism has an array of cognitive and experiential capabilities. Indeed, it looks to have exactly the same cognitive and experiential capabilities that I have! But if so, we are confronted with a worrying problem. If I am a thinking, experiencing being, and my organism is a thinking, experiencing being, then if I and my organism are distinct things we have *two* thinking experiencing beings. Since the same applies to every human subject, the world's population of thinking, experiencing beings is double what we have previously assumed. And while this is bad enough, there is worse to come. What makes me so sure that the thinker of *these* thoughts is the subject, rather than the organism? If I can't rule this out, how can I rule out the possibility that I am the organism after all, rather than the subject?

In recent years this objection to variants of the Lockean approach to selfhood has been forged into a potent weapon by a number of philosophers, among whom Paul Snowdon and Eric Olson have been particularly prominent.[9] Much-discussed in the literature, it goes by a variety of labels, e.g. the 'too many thinkers problem' or the 'too many subjects issue'. Whatever label we choose, the problem *is* potentially a serious one. Any account of the self which leads to a doubling of the number of experien*cers* without a corresponding doubling in the number of experien*ces*, is in very serious trouble.

There are a number of ways of countering this overpopulation menace, but my preferred solution has long been a mereological one. On this view, subjects, in the form of C-systems, are related to their human organisms as parts to wholes. This is a very natural position to adopt; after all, there is a lot more to a typical human organism than a collection of experiential capacities. It also allows us to respond to the overpopulation problem as follows:

> Can human organisms have thoughts and experiences? In one sense it's true to say that they can, but in another it's not. Organisms have experiences in the way that a car can tell the time: by having a *proper part*—in the form of a clock on the dashboard, say—that can tell the time. The vast bulk of a car (its engine, its chassis, the seats and wheels and so forth) is entirely irrelevant to its time-keeping capacity, which is wholly located in one small part, the clock. To register this difference we can say that the whole car possesses the capacity to tell the time in a *secondary* way, the clock possesses this capacity in a *primary* way. Analogously, a human organism only possess experiential capacities in a secondary way. The primary or non-derivative possessor of these capacities is the subject of experience, in the form of a C-system, which is in turn located in the organisms brain.

9   Paul Snowdon, 'Persons, Animals and Ourselves', in C. Gill (ed.), *The Person and the Human Mind* (Cambridge: Cambridge University Press, 1990), 83–107. Eric Olson, *The Human Animal* (Oxford: Oxford University Press, 1997); 'An Argument for Animalism', in J. Barresi and R. Martin (eds), *Personal Identity* (Oxford: Blackwell, 2003).

If we take this line, the overpopulation problem is dissolved at a stroke. Recognizing that human organisms possess experiential capacities in a secondary way does not increase the number of primary possessors of these capacities. There remains just one primary possessor – and hence subject – per organism. Nor does it increase the number of experiential capacities or experiences. Human organisms possess the capacity to metabolize alcohol in a secondary way, by virtue of possessing a part – the liver – which possesses this capacity in a primary way. There is just *one* metabolic capacity per animal, possessed in two different ways.[10]

6.

In his recent paper, Derek Parfit has espoused a solution to the overpopulation problem along just these lines, and for (largely) these reasons.[11] More recently still, Olson has discussed this alleged solution. He calls it *thinking-subject minimalism*, or just 'minimalism' for short, characterizing it as the view that an organism cannot think 'because it has a smaller part that *really* thinks'.[12] Olson goes on to argue that although this view may seem to have its attractions, when examined more closely it turns out to be deeply troubled.

One of the problems to which Olson draws our attention runs thus. According to minimalism, a being thinks or experiences in the primary non-derivative sense only if all of its constituent parts are directly involved in its thinking and experiencing. This is why, after all, an entire organism only possesses experiences or experiential capacities in a secondary or derivative manner. But can we draw, in a principled way, a boundary between those parts of an organism that

[10] For a fuller exposition see *The Phenomenal Self*, §7.7; I also suggest a solution along these lines in my 'Review of Eric Olson's *The Human Animal*, in *Mind* **107**, (1998), 679–82. Galen Strawson adopts the same position in 'The Self and the SESMET', *Journal of Consciousness Studies*, **6**:4, (1999), 99–135.

[11] D. Parfit, 'We Are Not Human Beings', *Philosophy*, **87**:1 (2012), 5–28.

[12] E. Olson, 'The Nature of People', in S. Luper (ed.) *The Cambridge Companion to Life and Death* (Cambridge University Press 2014, 30–46); also his 'On Parfit's View That We Are Not Human Beings', in A. O'Hear (ed.), *Mind, Self and Person* (Cambridge University Press, forthcoming)

are directly involved in experiencing, and those which are not? Consider the case of walking or eating, and imagine what it would be like trying to specify which of the atoms in your body are 'directly' involved in these activities. How would you go about it? Some parts of your body are *more* involved with walking than others (e.g. your feet), but even here there are some parts of your feet (e.g. your toe-nails) that aren't obviously involved at all. So in these cases, Olson suggests, the idea that some parts of a person are 'directly involved' in their walking is simply confused: there are no such parts. Moreover, he argues, precisely the same applies in the case of thinking or experiencing.

Transferring these considerations into a C-theoretical key, is Olson right in claiming that it is impossible, even in principle, to specify which parts of an organism are directly responsible for the capacities for consciousness it possesses? I cannot see that he is. Olson is right that it isn't easy to specify which parts of an organism are specially relevant to its capacity for walking. The ability to walk (in a normal fashion) involves host of different factors: muscular and skeletal conditions must be met, but a functioning nervous system and brain (or some of it) are required too. In assessing the minimalism approach to subjects of experience a better analogy would be functions or capacities that are localized in a single organ, such as the ability to pump blood round an organism's body (which our hearts accomplish), or extract oxygen from the atmosphere (our lungs are good at this). The experiential capacities relevant to subjecthood are, after all, localized in a similar fashion in our brains – if they weren't, we wouldn't be able to enjoy a subjectively normal life while reduced to a (functioning) brain-in-a-vat.

There is no reason why things must stop there. As neuroscience progresses, we may well learn more about precisely which neural systems are the minimal causal bases for the different kinds of experience we can enjoy. These minimal bases will no doubt overlap considerably, but not completely. It is already clear, for example, that different parts of the brain are involved in vision, hearing, taste and smell. Moreover, if certain aspects of the brain's functioning are destined to remain mysterious there is every reason to think that there *exist* minimal causal bases for different experiential capacities, even if neuroscience proves incapable of discovering their exact contours. We should also bear in mind that the task of isolating these minimal causal bases may be easier for some subjects than others. Subjects whose experiential capacities are grounded in digital computers, for instance – if there be such – will no doubt prove less troublesome in this regard.

7.

Olson finds minimalism problematic for a second reason. Let's suppose – as Olson is prepared to grant, for the sake of argument – that our different mental capacities have distinct (but partially overlapping) causal bases. The neural systems which constitute the causal base for your capacity to remember faces will be different from your capacity to see faces, or hear the sound of a trumpet, feel sensations of warmth on your skin or think conscious thoughts. Each of these systems is a distinct physical thing, directly responsible for a different form of experience. In the context of the C-theory, embracing minimalism amounts to equating subjects with only those parts of an entire organism which are directly involved in the production of experience. If we follow this minimalist maxim, Olson argues, it looks very much as though a human organism sustains not *one* subject, but *many*. There will be the subject that consists of the neural system that is responsible for your ability to remember faces, another that consists the system responsible for your ability to hear trumpet-sounds, another for the system responsible for your ability to feel warmth, and so on, and on. As Olson observes, the result is a disaster: 'What we take to be a person able to perform all sorts of mental operations is really many beings, each able to perform only one. If, as Locke said, a person is by definition both intelligent and self-conscious, then there are no people, and we do not exist.'[13]

Subjects of experience (as I am construing them here) are not Lockean persons, since they do not essentially possess high-level cognitive abilities required for full self-consciousness in Locke's sense. Nonetheless, if each our experiential capacities turns out to constitute a distinct subject, in the way Olson suggests, the C-theory would be in very serious trouble. In fact, this is not the case.

As I have already indicated, the C-theory is based on a simple but compelling criterion for allocating experiential capacities to individual subjects. At any given time, experiential capacities which have the ability to produce co-conscious experiences belong to the same subject, and those that lack this ability belong to different subjects. Accordingly, if at any given time the neural systems in your brain that are responsible for your ability to see faces, hear trumpet-sounds and feel sensations of warmth are such that when active and producing experience, the experiences they produce all belong to a single unified conscious state, then these systems – or rather, the experiential capacities they possess – all belong to the same

---

[13] 'On Parfit's View That We Are Not Human Beings', this volume.

C-system and hence the same subject, in this case you. In contrast, if when exercised simultaneously the experiences these capacities produce do not exist within the same unified stream of consciousness, they do *not* all belong to the same C-system or subject.

For Olson's argument to get off the ground, it would have to be plausible to suppose that group of experiential capacities could be such that (a) they all belong to a single C-system, and (b) each capacity in the group also constitutes a distinct subject in its own right. But as far as I can see, it is not remotely plausible to suppose this could be the case. By virtue of being able to produce co-conscious experiences when active together, experiential capacities which belong to the same C-system are manifestly *not* distinct and separate subjects in their own right. The ability to contribute experiences to the same stream of consciousness is surely the defining trait of capacities which are unambiguously constituent part of a *single* subject's mind. The situation is altogether different in the case of experiential capacities which, when active simultaneously, produce experiences which are not co-conscious with any other experiences, and which lack the ability to contribute to unified conscious states which include the contributions of other experiential capacities. These entirely isolated capacities might very well constitute distinct subjects in their own right.[14] But isolated capacities such as these are also very different from capacities which are integral parts of C-systems – i.e., capacities which, when active together, can and do contribute to fully unified conscious states.

There is a more general lesson here. When considering the circumstances in which one or more experiential capacities constitute a single subject it isn't sufficient to consider solely the forms of experience *these* capacities taken in isolation can produce when active; one must also consider their relationships with *other* experiential

---

[14]   In *The Phenomenal Self* (§8.1–8.3) I broach the question of how simple a subject of experience could possibly be. Could there be a subject with a mind so primitive that it possesses the capacity for just a single simple form of sensation? An issue anticipated by Hume: 'We can conceive a thinking being to have either many or a few perceptions. Suppose the mind to be reduc'd even below the life of an oyster. Suppose it to have only one perception, as of thirst or hunger. Consider it in that situation' (*A Treatise of Human Nature*, (ed.) Selby-Bigge, Oxford: Clarendon Press, 1739/ 1978: 634) I argue that such minds may well be (logically) possible. If so, then the entirely isolated experiential capacities envisaged by Olson *would* constitute subjects of experience in their own right – or at least, they would if (as we are assuming) each produces an entirely separate stream of consciousness.

capacities. Provided minimalists do not forget this, they have nothing to fear from Olson's objection.

8.

Olson's third main criticism of the minimalist approach tacks in a different direction. In rejecting the claim that we are animals minimalists avail themselves of a solution to the overpopulation problem, but they also incur a debt: just what are we, if we are not organisms? One option is to say that we are identical with our brains. However, as Olson points out, holding that we *are* a biological organ has highly counterintuitive consequences. After your (bodily) death, your brain might be pickled in formaldehyde and preserved, completely lifeless, in a jar for decades. If you are your brain, then that's *you* in pickling-jar. Needless to say, this is not a very plausible result, particularly for anyone who believe that continuing to have some form of mental continuity is essential to their continuing to exist, and most minimalists fall into this category. However, all is not lost. There is an alternative view, which Olson suggests might prove appealing to minimalists: we identify ourselves not with brains *per se*, but with brains which possess the capacity to sustain a mental life of some specified kind or level. Olson calls this the 'functioning brain' view.

In effect, the functioning brain view is a variant of the 'S-generator' doctrine I considered earlier. It is also vulnerable to the objections I leveled against that doctrine: a rapid replacement of parts will be fatal to a functioning brain, but not to the subject it sustains, provided the brain(s) capacities for experience remain intact, and capable of producing unified states and streams of consciousness. Olson puts his finger on a different problem. If we say we are functioning brains, we are confronted with an awkward fact: our *ordinary brains* haven't gone away. As biological organs, with the persistence conditions of such, our ordinary brains are capable of doing things that functioning brains can't do, such as survive being kept lifeless for years in a pickling jar – or more simply, continuing to exist without being able to sustain any sort of mental life. But equally, under normal circumstances, when normally connected to healthy human bodies, our ordinary brains are capable of doing everything that a functional brain can do. Just as functional brains are capable of sustaining a conscious mental life, so too are ordinary brains. So if functional brains are subjects, by virtue of this ability, why aren't ordinary brains? We are confronted once more with the overpopulation problem.

For advocates of the functional brain view this is a very real difficulty. However, consisting as they do of nothing more than capacities for experience, C-systems are a quite different kind of entity. From the perspective of the C-theory, subjects – in the form of C-systems – are nothing more that *dispositional properties* of both ordinary brains and functional brains. More specifically, C-systems are properties of the minimal causal basis of a brain's experiential capacities mentioned earlier. Although there is much yet to be discovered about the neural correlates of consciousness, given what we do know it seems very unlikely that our *entire* brains are involved in the production of consciousness – damage to certain brain regions has no effect on our experiential capacities at all. We can thus appeal once again to a version of the mereological solution to the threatened doubling of subjects: both ordinary and functional brains possess experiential capacities in a derivative or secondary way, whereas the primary possessor is the C-system itself. Since there is just *one* primary possessor of experiential capacities in the picture, the overpopulation problem simply doesn't arise.[15]

9.

The thesis that we are subjects of experience, where subjects are entities whose defining trait is their capacity to have conscious experiences may be an appealing one, but there is troublesome scenario, of a rather exotic kind, which suggests that it is fatally flawed, or so Tim Bayne and Mark Johnston have both argued.

In his *Surviving Death* (2010), Johnston envisages the following sequence of events. First of all, we are to suppose that a subject whose experience has hitherto been qualitatively quite similar to your own, becomes convinced – correctly, it turns out – that their experience is not veridical, but hallucinatory. What's more the beings who are in control have the power to provide the subject

---

[15] The issue of precisely how C-systems are related to brains is bound up with several very general metaphysical questions concerning (a) the relationship between objects and their properties, and (b) the nature of dispositional properties. To illustrate, for anyone inclined to identify dispositional properties with their physical bases it will be an option to maintain that in the human case, experiential capacities are identical with certain neural systems. On the resulting view, C-systems will almost certainly be *proper parts* of human brains, rather than properties of them. But irrespective of whether C-systems are parts of brains, or properties of them, it remains the case that they are *less* than entire brains, and so not identical with them.

with any form of experience they choose. (In fact, it is by exercising this power that they manage to convince the subject that their experience is in fact hallucinatory.) This subject then receives the following message from the controllers:[16]

> We have had the ability to create artificial conscious beings for centuries, and we enjoy experimenting on our creations in all sorts of ways. However, despite being in possession of vast psychophysical knowledge, in all these centuries we have never managed to achieve the goal of one physical realizer of consciousness to one stream of consciousness. What we know of psychophysics tells us that physical realizers always produce streams of consciousness (qualitatively identical) in batches of seven. What's more, our best psychophysics strongly suggests that this problem cannot be overcome. So there is in fact no single physical system that is especially causally responsible for any one of the seven distinct streams of consciousness in which these words are now appearing.

Johnston goes on to argue that if you were to find yourself in these circumstances, there is only one conclusion that you should draw: contrary to what you have doubtless assumed thus far, you do not in fact exist. In the envisaged circumstances, there is no *you* thinking your thoughts. Or at least, this is the conclusion you should draw if you are inclined to equate subjects with physical systems possessing the capacity for consciousness.

Bayne introduces an imaginary case along the same lines, one which involves single physical system producing several simultaneous streams of consciousness. He goes on to spell out precisely why this 'multiplicity scenario' (as I will call it) poses a problem for anyone who wants to equate selves or subjects with 'the underlying substrate that is responsible for generating the stream of consciousness – the *machinery* in which consciousness is grounded.'[17] If we know anything about subjects it is that they are the kind of thing which possess a single stream of consciousness. In other words, at any one time a subject who is conscious will have just *one* synchronically unified state of awareness. Hence the problem. The multiplicity scenario shows us that there is no *a priori* guarantee 'that a single consciousness-generating mechanism will produce

[16] Here I paraphrase a passage from Johnston's *Surviving Death* (New Jersey: Princeton University Press), 143.
[17] T. Bayne, *The Unity of Consciousness* (Oxford: Oxford University Press, 2010), 288.

only one stream of consciousness' at a given time.[18] If consciousness-generating mechanisms can produce several streams of consciousness at once they cannot *be* subjects, they're just the wrong kind of thing.

Although the C-theory identifies subjects with systems consisting of *capacities* for consciousness, not consciousness-generating mechanisms, it is difficult to see that this suffices to circumvent the problem. In our own case at least, C-systems are (very probably) grounded in our brains. If a single brain can produce multiple streams of consciousness at once, what are we to make of the situation? Does the brain possess one C-system or several? If the latter, then – by the lights of the C-theory – this brain sustains several subjects, and since each of these subjects possesses a single stream of consciousness there is no problem. But if there is just a single C-system involved we are in trouble, for Bayne is right: it is difficult to see how a single subject could have multiple streams of consciousness at any one time. In these circumstances it looks very much as though we would be obliged to say that the brain in question does not sustain a subject at all, even though it possesses experiential capacities, and is in fact generating several streams of consciousness. So we are left confronted with this question: just how many C-systems *does* such a brain possess?

10.

Bayne and Johnston's multiplicity scenario leaves the C-theory in an awkward position, for it gives rise to questions for which there are no easy or obvious answers. These questions only need be addressed if the scenario itself is really possible. But is it? The envisaged state of affairs is certainly very exotic indeed, and I am by no means certain that it is logically possible. But equally, I am not certain that it isn't.

So far as I can see, we would have to know a good deal more about the way in which conscious experience is related to the physical world before we would be in a position to answer this question with any confidence. There are certainly some positions on this relationship which leave the multiplicity scenario looking very dubious. Suppose consciousness is wholly material in nature, and that our ordinary conscious states extend through almost the entire volume of our brains – as might be the case, for example, if different forms of experience are constituted by different modes of excitation in some physical field generated by neural activity. In this case, supposing that a single

[18]   Ibid., 288.

brain could produce seven streams of consciousness would be as absurd as supposing that a single pint class could contain seven pints of water.

But on other views of the nature of consciousness, the multiplicity scenario looks a good deal less problematic. Suppose, for example, that a form of property dualism is true. Experiences are non-physical particulars that are nomologically correlated with certain patterns of physical activity – the sort of view which David Chalmers has sympathetically explored on various occasions.[19] In our world (or so we generally assume), the psychophysical laws are such that human brains produce just one stream of consciousness, but in other possible worlds the psychophysical laws may be such that the brains that are physically indistinguishable from ours produce two streams of consciousness, or seven, or seven hundred. So far as I can see, there is nothing metaphysically incoherent in these multiplicious states of affairs. Since the additional streams of consciousness are non-physical, they do not exist in physical space, and so are not competing for room – the situation is very *unlike* squeezing several pints of water into a pint glass. The fact that these experiences lack a spatial location might itself be a source of trouble. If, as I have been assuming, all of the multiple streams of consciousness produced by a given brain over a given interval are qualitatively indistinguishable, what individuates them? What makes it the case that there are seven streams (say), rather than just one? However, provided that the property dualist takes experiences to be basic particulars, there is no difficulty here either. The identity and individuality of an experience, and hence of the streams of consciousness they compose, would be as autonomous and secure as that of any material object – or even the entire physical universe.

There may well be other possibilities compatible with the multiplicity scenario. Perhaps consciousness is wholly physical in nature, but in some physically possible universes it exploits the 'hidden' spatial dimensions that string theorists believe to exist. In which case, a three-dimensional brain might sustain multiple streams of consciousness which are located in these additional spatial dimensions. I am not suggesting that this is very likely. The lesson, rather, is that when it comes to the relationship between the physical and phenomenal realms, at present we are confident of very little. So much so that we cannot, with any confidence, deem the multiplicity scenario to be metaphysically impossible.

---

[19] Such as his *The Conscious Mind* (Oxford: Oxford University Press, 1996).

Barry Dainton

11.

So we are left with the task of working out how to make best sense of
Johnston and Bayne's hypothetical state of affairs. For anyone who
takes the view that subjects of experience are *identical* with their
streams of consciousness – Galen Strawson defends this line – there
is no difficulty here.[20] If your brain is producing seven streams of
consciousness, it is sustaining seven subjects of experience, and you
are one of these seven. But the C-theory I have been defending
does not equate subjects with streams of consciousness. Instead, it
equates them with the clusters of capacities for consciousness. We
are thus returned to the question posed earlier. If a brain is producing
seven streams of consciousness, does it possess seven C-systems, or
just one? If the latter, the brain in question is sustaining a single
subject, one possessing seven streams of consciousness. If the
former, the brain is managing to sustain seven subjects, each with
their own stream of consciousness. The idea that a single subject
could have several entirely distinct streams of consciousness at the
same time looks to be problematic: as Bayne rightly stresses, subjects
are the kind of thing that have just one unified consciousness at any
given time. So the situation would be easier – for the would-be C-theorist at any rate – if we can say that in the envisaged circumstances the
brain is sustaining seven C-systems, rather than one. But is such a
state of affairs really intelligible? Before attempting to answer this
question it will help if we take a closer look at the properties from
which C-systems are built.

An experiential capacity is a particular species of dispositional
property. A typical physical object – a glass vase, say – has a great
many properties of this sort. If filled with water, it will not leak (provided it is oriented the right way); if dropped, it will shatter (provided
the surface it falls on is sufficiently strong and rigid), and so on.
Objects have the dispositions they do because of their particular
natures, or more precisely because of their causally relevant features.
If an object O possesses the dispositional property D to produce an
effect of type E under conditions C, it is because O possesses some
feature F that is causally relevant to occurrence of E. In the not incon-
siderable literature on the nature of dispositional properties, feature F
is known as the 'ground' or 'base' of the disposition D. This is all

---

[20] G. Strawson, *Selves* (Oxford: Oxford University Press, 2009).
Strawson, notoriously, also holds that subjects only last a fraction of a
second, as measured by clock time – but this is because he believes that
our streams of consciousness are much briefer than most of us tend to think.

relatively uncontroversial.[21] However, when it comes to the precise relationship between dispositions and their bases, there is a significant divergence of views, one that is very relevant to how the multiplicity scenario should be interpreted.

One view, associated with Armstrong (1969) and Mellor (2000) is that dispositions and their bases are identical: D and F are simply one and the same property.[22] Taking this stance has its advantages. If we adopt it, there is no mystery as to how dispositions can be causally efficacious. A particular kind of berry is *poisonous* because some of the damaging effects some of the chemicals in it have on the human body, and these same chemicals constitute the disposition's base. Also, since we don't have to recognize dispositional properties over and above the base-properties, the Armstrong-Mellor view is parsimonious. However, in the eyes of some it is also problematic. Many different foods and liquids possess the property of being poisonous-to-humans, and in many cases the chemicals involved are themselves different, e.g. with holly berries the toxic agent theobromine, in yew berries the prime culprit is taxine. If we hold that dispositions and their bases are identical, then the property *poisonous* doesn't exist. What exists are the (very) many different specific chemical compounds that produce unpleasant or fatal effects in people when ingested.

To circumvent this unwelcome (to some) consequence, Prior, Pargetter and Jackson (1982) argued that it is a mistake to identify dispositional properties with their bases.[23] Instead, dispositions should be viewed as second-order properties of *having a first-order property which plays a causal role of a particular sort*. On this view, something has the property of being poisonous if it possesses a first-order property (containing the compound potassium cyanide, say) which has the relevant causal consequences (ingestion proves troublesome to humans). When construed in this 'functionalist' way, a dispositional property *has* a causal base, but it is not identical

[21]   It is not *completely* uncontroversial. There are those – causal structuralists, for example – who hold that there can be capacities or dispositions which are not grounded in properties of a non-dispositional sort. Whether 'bare dispositions' are possible is an interesting question, but as far as I can see it is largely irrelevant to the present issue – for reasons which will emerge.
[22]   D. Armstrong, 'Dispositions are Causes', *Analysis* **30** (1969), 23–6; H. Mellor, 'The Semantics and Ontology of Dispositions', *Mind*, **109** (2000), 757–780).
[23]   E.M. Prior, R. Pargetter, F. Jackson, 'Three Theses about Dispositions', *American Philosophical Quartely*, **19** (1982), 251–257.

with this base. This approach has its advantages, but it too has its critics. Heil (2003), for example, complains that it renders dispositions themselves causally impotent, since all the causal work is done by the first-order properties.[24] Another option, defended by Mumford is to opt for token-identities between particular instances of dispositions and instances of their bases.[25] There are many ways of being poisonous, and so many different bases, but each instance of this dispositional property is identical with some particular base.

The debate on the nature of dispositions is very much alive, and this brief survey does not do justice to its intricacies, but we have what is needed for present purposes. The question we were considering was this: if a particular brain sustains seven streams of consciousness at the same time, how many C-systems are involved, seven, or just one? Since there is just one brain involved, and this brain is in all non-experiential respects similar to an ordinary brain which sustains just a single consciousness (or so we are supposing), the causal base is going to be precisely the same in both cases. Appreciating the significance of this will be easier if we focus on a simple example.

Let's begin with a single experiential capacity, call it P1, whose causal base F is such that it produces an single token E-type experience when triggered in circumstances of type C. Let's now suppose that the psycho-physical laws are different, and that when F is a triggered in the same way it produces not one, but two token E-type experiences. In this case, can we hold that F is grounding two distinct experiential capacities, P1 and P2, each for E-type effects? If so, then there is no obstacle to our supposing that an otherwise ordinary brain which is sustaining seven simultaneous streams of consciousness is also sustaining seven C-systems.

Here the different views on the nature of dispositions in general enter the scene. If we follow Armstrong, Mellor and Mumford in holding that dispositions are identical with their causal bases, in either type- or token-specific ways, we immediately encounter a problem. The hypothesis that P1 and P2 are numerically distinct powers is simply incoherent. Since P1 and P2 are identical with the same (token) base, on this view of dispositions they must be identical with one another. If this view of dispositions is correct, a single brain can sustain just one C-system at a time.

For proponents of the higher-order functionalist account, the situation is less cut-and-dried. Since the causal base F we are considering

---

[24]   J. Heil, *From an Ontological Point of View*, (Oxford: Oxford University Press, 2003).
[25]   S. Mumford, *Dispositions* (Oxford: Oxford University Press, 1998).

can produce two E-type experiences, rather than just one, there is a case for holding that it grounds two numerically distinct capacities for single E-type experiences. Since on this view dispositional properties are not identical with their bases, the fact that these capacities – if they existed – would have a common base does not entail that the capacities themselves must be identical.

However, before concluding that the multiple C-system interpretation of the multiplicity scenario is viable, at least if we construe dispositions in the Prior-Pargetter-Jackson way, there a hurdle to be overcome. Although we can interpret the case as involving two capacities, each for an E-type experience, we could also interpret it as involving a single capacity for *two* E-type experiences. Since each of these hypotheses fits all the facts equally well, it is difficult to see why we should prefer the two capacity interpretation simply because it makes life easier for the C-theory. Certainly, the facts of the matter do not seem to *compel* us to adopt the two capacity interpretation. Indeed, the fact that the one- capacity interpretation is more economical might be a reason for preferring it over the rival two-capacity view.

In the light of these considerations, the multiple capacity – and hence multiple C-system – interpretation looks to be on very shaky ground. Firstly, because it is only intelligible at all on the 2nd-order view of dispositions, a view which many find problematic. Second, because even if the 2nd-order view proves to be correct, the issue of whether or not a brain is sustaining a single subject or many looks to be grounded on nothing more solid than a *decision* to describe matters in one way rather than another, a decision that is in no way compelled by the underlying facts. Many will find it objectionable to suppose that the issue of how many distinct subjects of experience a given brain is supporting at a given time could be conventional in this sort of way – I certainly do.

12.

Since the alternative has proved unsatisfactory, it looks as though we should accept that if a brain is producing seven streams of consciousness it possesses just one C-system. This means, of course, that if we equate subjects of experience with C-systems, there is just a single subject present, one which is enjoying seven streams of consciousness at once.

Since this can easily seem completely absurd, one option open to the C-theorist is to subscribe to a more restricted position. Yes, subjects are C-systems, but only when the C-system in question can produce a single stream of consciousness. C-systems which can produce multiple streams of consciousness do not constitute subjects. Imposing this restriction has a clear rationale – subjects with multiple streams of consciousness *are* bizarre – and it provides the C-theorist with an effective counter to the Bayne-Johnston multiplicity objection: just because *some* possible C-systems are not subjects it doesn't necessarily follow that *no* C-systems are subjects. There is no obstacle at all to taking well-behaved single-stream C-systems to be subjects.

But while this response is adequate, it may not be the best. Another, more radical option is available. We are all familiar with ordinary cubes. They possess six square sides of equal size, which meet at right-angles and extend through three spatial dimensions. For most of human history, the notion that there could be *hypercubes* possessing more than six sides, and extending through more than three dimensions, would have seemed absurd. Yet thanks to the efforts of mathematicians over the past couple of centuries, we know that 4, 5, 6, 7 ... *n* dimensional cubes are perfectly possible, mathematically, and the properties have been successful explored. Since our imaginations are confined to three dimensions, we cannot mentally picture such entities, but this does not prevent our recognizing that they are possible. Analogously, perhaps *hyperselves* are possible: subjects of experience possessing more than a single stream of consciousness at a time. Since we cannot our imagine more than a single consciousness at a time – doing so is incompatible with the unity of our streams of consciousness – we cannot imagine (fully) what it would like to be such a subject, but we already know that reality is not confined to what we are able to mentally picture. A single C-system with the ability to generate multiple streams would clearly qualify as a hyperself, provided of course that we continue to equate C-systems and subjects of experience.

There is, of course, a problem that is still to be overcome. As Bayne points out, it is plausible to suppose that a subject of experience is the kind of being whose consciousness is fully unified at any given time. This constraint on the mental life of subjects can be formally stated like this:

> *Subject-Unity Principle*: at any one time, the experiences of a single subject *S* are all synchronically co-conscious, and necessarily so.

A hyperself, if it were to exist, would clearly fail to conform to the Subject-Unit Principle. Although some of its experiences at any

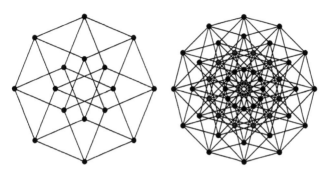

The shadows cast by 4 and 6 dimensional hypercubes onto a 2 dimensional surface.

given time are co-conscious (those existing within individual streams of consciousness) many of its experiences are very definitely not co-conscious (those found in different streams). However, deeming hyperselves to be impossible would be premature.

Why does the Subject-Unity Principle seem plausible? The answer, I take it, is that (a) under normal circumstances our own streams of consciousness are fully unified, as far as we can tell, and (b) we assume that we are not hyper-selves, and have only one stream of consciousness at a time. Anyone wishing to defend the possibility of hyperselves might be tempted to put pressure on (b). Can you really be certain that you are not in fact a hyperself? Since the multiple stream of consciousness of such a subject are experientially self-contained, the qualitative character of each stream is just as it would be if the other streams did not exist. But while this is true, there is of course no reason to believe that our brains *are* producing multiple streams at any one time, so there is no reason to take this exotic possibility very seriously. Moreover, and more importantly, anyone who believes the notion of a hyperself to be incoherent will follow Bayne and Johnston, and argue that if our brains are in fact producing multiple streams of consciousness, then these streams do not belong to a single subject – in effect, there is no subject on the scene at all. The Subject-Unity Principle demands that we interpret the situation thus.

Have we reached a stand-off? I think not, for the Subject-Unity Principle itself is not beyond question. This is because there are easily conceivable circumstances in which it fails to hold at all. In science fiction tales – not to mention philosophical thought-experiments – featuring time travel, it is by no means unusual to find tales which involve a time-travelling protagonist who meets up with their earlier (or later) self. In the 2012 movie *Loopers*, the complex plot revolves around precisely this possibility. The eponymous loopers are assassins who hide their victims bodies in the past, and when young they are hired to kill (unknowingly) their older and no-longer-quite so-deadly selves: we thus find Bruce Willis spending much of the movie trying to avoid the efforts of his younger self to kill him.[26] Now, when a time traveller spends a period co-existing with an earlier or later version of themselves, we have a single person, at different stages of their life, existing twice-over at the same time. Although Young-Willis and Old-Willis are one and the same person, during those periods when they co-exist, they each have their own entirely distinct and separate streams of consciousness. When Young-Willis punches Old-Willis, the pain in the jaw felt by the latter is not felt by the former; when Old-Willis retaliates and hits back – hard – the same applies, but in reverse. We thus have a situation in which it is not the case that all the experiences of a single subject at a given time are all mutually co-conscious.

Opinions differ on the issue of whether or not time travel is really a genuine logical or nomological possibility. (Complicating the issue still further, travel through some forms of time – e.g. a block universe – may be easier than in others – e.g. a presentist universe – and there is nothing approaching agreement as to which of these competing views of the nature of time is correct.) For present purposes, however, I am not sure this matters much. The fact that the relevant time travel scenarios are so easily conceivable surely suggests that the Subject-Unity Principle cannot true, or at least, not without emendation or qualification.

As for the way in which this constraint needs qualifying, we need look no further than the literature on time travel. Suppose a time traveler spends an hour in their time machine travelling a thousand years into the past. Their trip might seem paradoxical: the traveler arrives both an hour *after* setting off, and a thousand years *before* setting off. But there is really nothing paradoxical here at all. As Lewis argued, if we are to make sense of time travel we need to recognize a distinction between two forms of time: ordinary objective world-time, and the

---

[26] The complexity of some of the time travel scenarios devised by philosophers easily match the complexity of those devised by most Hollywood scriptwriters. In his 'Who was Dr Who's Father?' MacBeath defends the logical possibility of a case (devised by Jonathan Harrison) which implies 'that a man can be his own father, that he can eat himself (that is, eat himself up), and that he can die before he is born.' See MacBeath 'Who Was Dr Who's Father?', *Synthese* **51** (1982), 397.

personal or *subjective* time of the time traveler.[27] It is with respect to ordinary objective time that the traveler arrives a thousand years before setting off, and with respect to their subjective time that they arrive an hour later.

Lewis himself took subjective time to be determined by physical, psychological and causal factors: 'First come infantile states. Last come senile ones. Memories accumulate. Food digests. Wristwatch hands move. The assignment of coordinates that yields this match is the time travelers personal time'.[28] There is nothing wrong in allowing factors such as these determine someone's subjective time if these same factors also determine that person's persistence through time. Unless subjective time and personal identity are guaranteed to march in step circumstances might arise in which episodes in the person's life are not assigned any location in their subjective time at all (or the wrong one). Since Lewis believed that personal identity is determined primarily by psychological and causal factors, it was natural for him to characterize subjective time in the way he did. But if, as I have been arguing, we should trace our existence through time in terms of experiential continuity – both actual and potential – rather than physical or psychological continuities, we will need to think about subjective time in a different way. According to the C-theory, we are essentially subjects of experience, and a subject remains in existence for a given interval of time if throughout that interval it is either continually conscious or retains the capacity for consciousness. If such a subject can survive dramatic ruptures in psychological and/or physical continuity – as we saw at the outset, there are reasons for thinking this is the case – if subjective time were determined solely by psychological and/or physical factors then such ruptures would terminate the subject's subjective time, even though the subject continues to exist.

Fortunately, we needn't look very far for an alternative way of generating subjective temporal orderings. At the heart of the C-theory is a simple idea: over short periods all and only those experiential capacities which have the ability to contribute to unified states and streams of consciousness belong to the same subject. As a moment or two's introspection reveals, a typical stream of consciousness is experientially continuous: each brief phase is experienced as flowing seamlessly into the next. (Think of what it is like to hear a sound *continuing on*, or the sky *remaining resolutely blue* as you stare

[27] D. Lewis, 'The Paradoxes of Time Travel', *American Philosophical Quarterly* **13** (1976), 145–152.
[28] Ibid., 70

Barry Dainton

up at it.) Given this, we can say of two experiential capacities C1 and C2, that C1 is *subjectively earlier* than C2 if the experiences C1 can produce would be experienced as flowing into the experiences C2 can produce. C1 and C2 are *subjectively simultaneous* only if the experiences they can produce would be experienced together as synchronically co-conscious. In this sort of way the relationships which bind experiences into unified streams – i.e. co-consciousness, in its synchronic and diachronic forms – can be used to define a subjective temporal ordering for a collection of experiential capacities (or phases of such) distributed through ordinary objective time.[29]

According to the Subject-Unity Principle, in the form given above, at any given time the experiences of a single subject are necessarily all mutually co-conscious – in effect, a subject is confined to just one stream of consciousness at a time. However, while on the face of it the Principle is a very appealing one, it runs into trouble: there are easily conceivable time travel scenarios in which a single subject enjoys two (or more) streams of consciousness at a given time. Having acknowledged the distinction between objective and subjective time, there is a natural and appealing way of relieving this tension. Let's return to the case of the time-travelling Young-Willis and Old-Willis, who are engaged in a fist-fight with one another during one of the periods during which they coexist. At any moment during this interval the experiences of Young-Willis and Old-Willis are simultaneous with respect to ordinary objective time, but non-simultaneous in their respective subjective times. Given the way we are now thinking of subjective times, the experiences of the two Willis' would have to be co-conscious if they were to be subjectively simultaneous, but evidently they aren't.

There is a more general lesson to be drawn from this case, and it's a simple one. The problematic constraint on the relationship between subjects, time and experience should be reformulated along these lines:

Subject-Unity Principle: at any given moment in the **subjective time** of a subject S, the experiences of S are all mutually synchronically co-conscious, and necessarily so.

---

[29]   For two experiences E1 and E2 to be synchronically co-conscious it is not enough for them simply to be experienced simultaneously, i.e. be experienced at the same moment of ordinary objective time. E1 and E2 are only synchronically co-conscious if they are *experienced together*, i.e. unified in the same distinctive way as the current contents of your stream of consciousness.

Bayne, it will be recalled, insists that there is a constitutive *a priori* connection between subjecthood and the unity of consciousness: a subject is the kind of thing whose nature is such that at any one time its consciousness is fully unified. I too find this plausible. This connection is not abandoned in the revised Subject-Unity Principle, it is simply relativized to locations in subjective time, rather than objective time. What's more, if we conceive of subjective time in the way I have suggested, we now have a fuller understanding of why this constitutive connection exists in the first place. Since subjective simultaneity is *defined* in terms of synchronic co-consciousness, it simply makes no sense to suppose that the experiences a subject is having at a given location in its personal time could be anything other than synchronically co-conscious. Experiences which aren't related in this must either belong to a different subject altogether, or to the same subject, but at different locations in its subjective time. The *a priori* link between phenomenal unity and subjecthood is thus not only retained, it is explained.

13.

This is all very well, you may by this point be thinking, but hyperselves are not time travelers, they are beings of a seemingly paradoxical sort. From the vantage point of the C-theory, a hyperself looks very much as though it constitutes a single subject. The C-theory equate selves with subjects, and subjects with materially (or immaterially) grounded capacities for experience, in the form of C-systems. Since in the case of a hyperself there is just one material (or immaterial) base – a single brain-like system, say – as we saw earlier, there is a strong case for holding that in these circumstances there is just a single C-system involved, and hence a single subject. However, there's a problem: how can a single subject possess more than one stream of consciousness at a time? Travelling through time to co-exist with one's earlier or later self is one way of achieving this, but time travel is of no assistance in the case of hyperselves, whose multiple streams of consciousness exist at the same location in their personal time as well as ordinary world-time.

While this is true, it is also not the end of the story. If a seven-streamed hyperself suffers a headache at precisely noon, the pain will exist in each of its seven streams of consciousness. Do these seven pains exist simultaneously? In one sense, yes: so far as world-time is concerned, they all occur at noon. However, from the perspective of this hyperself's subjective time the situation is altogether

195

different. Since each pain occurs within a distinct stream of consciousness, they are not synchronically co-conscious with one another, and hence are not related in the way experiences have to be related if they are to be subjectively simultaneous. What goes for these pains goes for *all* the experiences in the seven separate streams of consciousness: these experiences are simultaneous with experiences occurring in the same stream, but not simultaneous with any of the experiences occurring in the other streams.

Given these facts, a way of interpreting the envisaged state of affairs almost imposes itself: a hyperself is a single subject, but one whose experience unfolds in multiple *parallel* dimensions of subjective time. Here 'parallel' time-dimensions are those where (a) every distinct moment in each dimension occurs before or after every other moment, (b) no moments in different dimensions are temporally related in any way to any moments in any of the others. If Lewis' concrete possible worlds exist, the events in each such world unfold in a different parallel objective temporal dimension. If a hyperself were to exist, the experiences in each its streams of consciousness unfold in a different parallel subjective temporal dimension. As far as I can see, these scenarios are equally possible, metaphysically speaking.

There is an important difference, however. Lewis' worlds are entirely isolated from one another. The experiences which occur in a hyperself's various streams of consciousness at a given (objective) time are experientially isolated from one another, but nonetheless intimately related by virtue of their belonging to a common subject of experience. But we already know how *this* is possible. It is possible because the experiences are being produced by a single C-system, one possessing a single material (or immaterial) dispositional base.

There is a second point of divergence. Lewis' parallel universes each constitutes (or is located within) a different objective time-system. A hyperself's multiple parallel subjective temporal dimensions all exist within a single objective time-system. However, this does not mean that the experiences in these streams at a given objective moment all *really* exist simultaneously. Viewed from the vantage point of one temporal framework they do exist simultaneously, viewed from the perspective of another – perfectly valid – temporal framework they don't. In the time travel case, the distinction between objective and subjective times forces itself upon us because genuinely temporal relations which cannot be accommodated in objective time alone. If you are about to travel a thousand years into the past, there is a legitimate sense in which the experiences you have after you arrive (one subjective hour from now) will occur in your future, even though they are also located in the objective past. In this sort of case, we are compelled to recognize the existence of subjective time because objective time cannot satisfactorily accommodate the temporal relations which exist between the different phases of a time traveller's life. The situation is the reverse of this in the case of hyperselves. Here we are led to acknowledge subjective temporal dimensions because events that are clearly simultaneous from the objective temporal perspective are clearly *not* simultaneous from the subjective perspective. The events in question, are of course, the experiences a hyperself would enjoy, if one were to exist.[30]

University of Liverpool
bdainton@liverpool.ac.uk

[30]   For comments on earlier drafts and discussion of the ideas therein, my thanks to Thomas Jacobi, Galen Strawson and Tom Winfield.

An Intellectual Entertainment

The Nature of the Mind

P. M. S. HACKER

Participants:
Jill: a philosopher in her early thirties, dressed in an elegant but informal manner.
Richard: a middle-aged Oxford philosopher of the mid-twentieth century, dressed in cavalry twill slacks, waistcoat and tie, and well-cut jacket.
Descartes: in sombre Dutch mid-seventeenth century dress.
Frank Craik: A contemporary American neuroscientist, casually dressed in jeans and pullover, with open necked shirt.
Aristotle: In Greek dress
The author

The setting is a garden in Elysium. The sun is shining. A rich verdant lawn is surrounded by flower beds and flowering bushes, with a grove of magnificent trees behind. Beyond, a large lake and in the distance high mountains. Five comfortable garden chairs are placed in the shade of some trees. There is a low table on which are placed a wine decanter and glasses, three of which are half full. Richard, Jill and Frank are deep in discussion.

Richard: But you must admit that it is very puzzling that we speak of *having* a mind and *having* a body. I mean, if I have a mind and also have a body, then who and what am I that has these two things?

Jill: Well, it seems obvious enough. After all, you just said '*I* have a mind' and '*I* have a body'. It is you, the 'I', the Ego, the Self, that has a mind, on the one hand, and a body, on the other.

Richard: But, Jill, what on earth is this 'I' or 'Ego' or 'self'? Surely I'm a human being.

Frank: Sure. And if you're a human being, then you can't be an Ego or Self. Unless human beings are selves.

Jill: All right. But then I surely *have* an Ego or Self. Human beings *have* selves.

doi:10.1017/S1358246115000156   ©The Royal Institute of Philosophy and the contributors 2015
Royal Institute of Philosophy Supplement **76** 2015

P. M. S. Hacker

Frank: No, no. Do I have a self? I've never come across it! I'm sure I'm sometimes selfish, but that doesn't mean that I have a self. And as for an Ego, that's just a fancy way of saying that I have an 'I'. It may sound better in Latin, but it's just baloney. Look, talking of *an 'I'* is just plain ungrammatical. I mean, y'don't talk of the you, the she or the it. Well, it's just as ungrammatical to talk of an I, of the I, or of my I.

Richard: [*chuckles*] Oh, my eye!

Jill: [*A little hotly*] All right. I grant you the ungrammaticality. Perhaps all this talk of '*an* "I"' and '*the* "I"' is ill-advised. But it doesn't follow that there is no such thing as a self, does it? After all, we speak, perfectly intelligibly, of our better self, and Polonius advised Laertes 'to thine own self be true' – you can't say that that's baloney, Frank.

Richard: [*pouring oil on troubled waters*] Take it slowly. We really need some clarity here... No one is going to quarrel with the statement that we have a mind and that we have a body. Some people want to insist, as Jill does, that we also have a self, and others like you, Frank, disagree. Let's shelve the disagreement for a moment and try to let some light in. In the first place, who is it that has a mind, a body, and perhaps also a self?

Jill: Well... It's me, *this* living human being.

Richard: So it's human beings who have minds, and have bodies, and have perhaps selves. So we're human beings, and we possess a mind, possess a body, maybe also possess a self. What about the soul. Do you also have a soul, Jill?

Jill: Well, I'm not sure. That smacks a bit of religion, doesn't it?

Frank: It's just pre-scientific mythology. Look, you, your joys and your sorrows, your memories and your ambitions, your sense of personal identity and free will, are in fact no more than the behaviour of a vast assembly of nerve cells and their associated molecules.

Richard: That's a bit quick, Frank. In the first place, we aren't behaviour. And our joys and sorrows, our memories and ambitions, are not behaviour either, although they are *manifest* in behaviour. But they're manifest in *our* behaviour, not in the behaviour of our nerve cells. Secondly, we're flesh and blood – living animals constituted of a vast array of different kinds of cells. And, like all other organisms, we are also constituted of a variety of chemical elements, variously combined to form hugely complex molecules. But we are not identical with the stuff of which we're made, any more than we're identical with the ever changing assemblage of cells of which we consist.

Frank: Why not? Why aren't we identical with the matter – the material stuff – of which we're made?

Richard: The natural replacement over time of the cells of which a living organism is constituted does not change the identity of the organism. These mighty trees [*he waves at the trees beyond the garden*] are the same organisms as the little seedlings from which they grew, are they not? But neither the matter of which they are made nor the cells of which they are constituted are the same.

Frank: OK... Yeah ... I can see that. I'm not a philosopher, and I'm not sure how to respond to your point. But it surely doesn't follow that you're a soul and that you're identical with your soul. That's just religious mythology. Y'don't *have* a soul. Souls don't exist.

Jill: And yet we do speak perfectly intelligibly of someone's being a soul in torment or of being a gentle soul.

Richard: And we also speak of someone losing their soul and of selling their soul, to the devil or to the company store, as the case may be. So, on your view, Jill, is the soul something we *are* or something we *have*?

Jill: It looks as if we both have a soul and are a soul. But that *is* paradoxical. I mean the owner cannot be identical with what she owns, can she? This is very odd. How is the soul related to the mind? And how is it related to the self? And how is the mind, the soul, or the self related to the body one has? Does my mind belong to my body?

Richard: What would a body do with a mind? And if your body turned to stone, Jill, would your soul then belong to the stone statue?

Jill: Oh! . . . All right. So does my body belong to my mind?

Richard: And not to you? Is it really your mind that has a body? If that is right, then who on earth is it that has a mind?

Jill: Well, it's obviously me – *I* have a mind.

Frank: OK, OK. But now we're just going round in circles.

Descartes strolls out of the trees.

Descartes: *Bonjour, mes amis.* I could not help hearing you conversing as I was taking my afternoon stroll. The topic about which you are discoursing is a deep and important one. Your ardour is *admirable*, although your reasoning may be questioned.

Richard: Well, please do join us here, sir. This lady is Jill.

Descartes: [*bows and doffs his hat*] *C'est un honneur et un plaisir, Madame.*

Richard: This is Frank, a brain scientist [*Descartes smiles and raises his eyebrows*] and my name is Richard. I'm a philosopher.

Descartes: [*bows*] *Messieurs.*

Richard: We should be delighted if you were to join us, sir. Do sit down. Would you care for a glass of wine? [*He pours a glass of wine and hands it to Descartes.*]

Descartes: *Merci, merci.* [*He takes a deep drink*] Ah, *très bien*. It would be most *agréable* to sit here under the trees and join your debate. I gather from what I heard that you are concerned with the relation between the mind and the body, *n'est-ce pas*?

Jill: Yes, that's right. We were trying to get clear about what exactly we are, whether we're minds or egos or selves.

Richard: The question, I think, is what a human being is. I mean we speak of having a mind, and of having a body. And it seems as if the entity that has the mind and has the body is the 'I'. But now what exactly is this 'I'. Is it a self? And what is the human being? Is it a self attached to a mind and a body. Or is the self the mind? But if the self *is* the mind, how can we speak of it's *having a mind*? I'm afraid we are confused.

Frank: [*chuckles*] Y'know, when the Lone Ranger and his Indian sidekick Tonto get captured by some Apaches, Lone Ranger says to Tonto 'We're in real trouble', and Tonto replies, 'Who's we, white man?' [*Descartes looks puzzled*] . . . Well, I'm not so sure as my friends that *we're* confused. I just think that *they're* confused. I think that the mind *is* the brain, and that the activities of the mind just are the activities of the brain.

Look, sir, it was you who taught us that we can explain everything about living bodies by reference to the same general principles that govern physics – that the sciences of life are no different in principle from the physical sciences. Life, and the functions of living things, can be explained by reference to broadly speaking mechanical principles. That was a great insight. It freed neuroscience – the study of the brain and nervous system – from futile investigations of psychic pneuma, and from the ancient ventricular doctrine that located the physiological root of psychological functions in the ventricles of the brain.

Descartes: I am grateful to you for your compliments, Monsieur Frank. I agree with you that it was indeed an achievement of some moment. Now, *mes amis*, if you think carefully and methodically about your questions, it is not too difficult to discover the truth of the matter. It should be evident that you are not your body. For it is possible to doubt whether your body exists, but you cannot doubt whether you exist. And since that is so, you cannot be your body. If you were your body, then the fact that you cannot doubt that you exist would also mean that you cannot doubt that your body exists. But you can doubt whether your body exists.

Frank: But what about the brain. I can't doubt that I have a brain – I have a brain, and so does every other animal.

Descartes: *Non, non.* You, who know that you exist merely by trying to doubt whether you exist, are not something you have. And can you really not doubt whether you have a brain? After all, you have never even seen or touched your brain. Of course, you have one. But that is hardly the soundest and most certain of knowledge, *n'est-ce pas?* You can, provisionally, in the course of your search for truth, doubt whether you have a brain, just as you can doubt whether you have a body.

Frank: [*a bit puzzled and out of his depth*] Well, I'm not sure how to answer you. I'm not a philosopher; just a scientist. But do go on, sir.

Descartes: *Bien!* The first step towards true knowledge – *scientia* – that is absolutely certain is to say to yourself 'I doubt, that is to say: I think, therefore I am'. This establishes an indubitable truth concerning something that exists: *I* exist. Now ask yourself what is this 'I' by which you are what you are. It is a thing that thinks, is it not?

Jill: But I not only think, I affirm and deny, I want and intend, and many other things too.

Descartes: *Mais certainement!* But these are all modes of thought. By 'thought', I understand everything of which we are conscious as happening within us, in so far as we are conscious of it. So thinking is not merely reflecting, but also understanding, willing, imagining, as well as sensory experience in general – that is, the experience of seeing, hearing and so forth, irrespective of whether one is dreaming, hallucinating or actually perceiving. All these I deem forms of consciousness.

Jill: So you are claiming that thinking belongs to our essence?

Descartes: *Exactement!* You are a mind or soul, the essence or nature of which is to think – to be conscious of what passes within you. The mind is a substance the essence of which is to think, just as body is a substance the essence of which is to be extended.

Jill: But even if it is true that thinking is the essence of the mind, it does not follow that *only* thinking is the essence of the mind.

Descartes: I admit that what you say is true. But since I have a clear and distinct idea of myself in so far as I am simply a thinking, non-extended thing, and, on the other hand, I have a clear and distinct idea of body as an extended unthinking thing, I know with certainty that I am distinct from my body.

Richard: So you are essentially a thinking substance?

Descartes: *Mais oui.* I am not a thought or collection of thoughts, as my friend David 'ume supposes. Thoughts demand a substance in which to inhere. One cannot have thoughts floating around like so many phantasms flitting through the air! I am a thinking substance.

Jill: But Hume argues that when, as he put it, he 'entered most intimately' into what he called *himself*, he always stumbled upon some particular perception or other – roughly speaking, what you call 'thoughts' – but could never perceive *a self*, a mental substance that persisted through time.

Descartes: *Le pauvre David! Certainement* he could not. The self is not something we perceive or experience. It is what thinks and perceives, imagines and wills. That thoughts inhere in thinking substances is not a matter of fact that we discover by experiences, it is presupposed by all thought and experiences. It is something that we clearly and distinctly perceive to be true by the natural light of reason.

Richard: So the self, in your view, is the same as the mind or soul and indeed the same as the 'I'.

Descartes: What you say is very true. And my mind is entirely distinct from my body, even though it is very closely intermingled with it.

Richard tops up all the glasses, and thoughtfully takes a sip himself.

Richard: Well, I have some qualms. In the first place, you have simply by-passed the question we raised earlier, namely: how can I be something I have. I have a mind, of course, but by the same token I can't be the mind I have.

Descartes: *Mais Richard*, that is merely a trivial idiom. It can have no bearing on deep metaphysical questions.

Richard: Really? I'm not so sure...

But let's pass over that one. I *suppose* I can't doubt whether I exist – although, I confess, I am not sure what the form of words 'I doubt whether I exist' mean. And for the sake of argument let me grant you that we can doubt whether our bodies exist, although I have qualms about that too – I mean, I don't even know how I'd go about doubting that I have a body. But even if I grant you all that, does it really show that I am distinct from my body? I mean, if a child knows what a triangle is, he cannot doubt that it has three angles, but he can doubt whether the sum of its angles equals two right angles. But *we* know that it is necessarily so. The child still lacks an adequate understanding of the nature and essence of triangles. Perhaps we lack an adequate understanding of mind and body and do not grasp that they are necessarily united and cannot exist one without the other.

Descartes: But, my friend, you are no child, and you do know what the nature of matter is, namely a substance the whole essence of which is to be extended. And you know what the nature of mind is, namely: it is a thinking substance. Reflect moreover that the body, being an extended thing, is divisible – but the mind is utterly indivisible. When I consider myself in so far as I am merely a thinking thing, I am unable to distinguish parts within myself. I understand myself to be something quite single and complete.

Richard: Are you? Since you hold that you are your mind, surely your mind is divisible into different faculties – faculties of sense, of passion, of understanding and reason, of memory, and so forth. And indeed you can lose one of these faculties, as when you suffer from amnesia. When you have lost your memory, you have lost a part of your mind.

Descartes: I think that I can easily get round this objection. We must distinguish between the faculty and what possesses the faculty. It is one and the same thinking substance that reasons and reflects, that senses and remembers. If you lose your memory, it is still one and the same thinking substance that before had the faculty of memory and now has lost it. Loss of a faculty does not imply divisibility of the thinking substance that previously possessed it. This one argument concerning the divisibility of the body and indivisibility of the mind would be enough to show me that the mind is completely different from the body.

Jill: But surely the mind and the body are united in each human being? I'm not just a non-spatial mind temporarily embodied in a female human body.

Descartes: *Mais naturellement*, your body is not merely the vehicle for your soul. You are united with your body. You are, so to say intermingled with it. Embodiment is not like being a sailor in a ship, who

P. M. S. Hacker

has to look to see whether the vessel in which he dwells is damaged. But you *feel* your sensations just *as if* they were located in your body.

Jill: But pains, itches and tickles *are* located in our bodies. We have head-aches, stomach-aches and back-aches.

Descartes: *Non, non,* Madame Jill, you feel them *as if* they were in the body. But careful reflection on phantom limb pain shows that pain in the hand is felt by the soul not because it is present in the hand but because it is present in the brain. We feel pain *as it were* in the hand or foot, but that does not show that pain exists outside the mind in the hand or foot.

Frank: Yeah, that's right. Common sense tells us that a pain in the foot is really there in the physical space of the foot. But, just as you said, sir, we now know that's wrong. The brain forms a body image, and pains, like all bodily sensations, are parts of the body image. The pain-in-the-foot, as John Searle has written, is literally in the physical space in the brain. But the way it appears to consciousness is just as if it were in the foot.

Descartes: What you say is very true, *Monsieur*. This judgement was already made by the author of *Principia Philosophiae*. I am delighted that truth has prevailed.

Richard: I'm not convinced that what has prevailed in neuroscientific and in some philosophical circles too is the truth. The fact that an amputee can hallucinate that the pain he feels is in his foot when he has no foot does not show that when one feels a pain in one's foot when one *does* have a foot, the pain is not in the foot.

Descartes: But the pain is not located in the foot at all, *mon ami*. It is not in physical space as the foot is. And if you examine the foot you will not find a pain in it. The pain, in one sense, is in the brain, and in another sense, it is in the mind.

Frank: Yeah, that's dead right.

Richard: Well, I am afraid I disagree with both of you. It is the foot that hurts, not the mind. As Aristotle taught us, and as our language shows us, we have a sensitive body – our head may ache, our back may tickle, our leg may itch and our feet may hurt. The human body is not an insensate machine, but a living organism.

Descartes: I am very grateful to you, Monsieur Richard, for the objection. But as Monsieur Frank observed, the author of *Traité de l'Homme* showed quite clearly that living organisms are no more than machines. And if you reflect further, you will note that our head does not have a head-ache, rather we do; our back does not

206

have a back-ache, rather we have an ache that sensibly seems to us to be in the back; and so too, we may feel a pain that seems to us to be in the tooth, but the pain is caused by the decaying tissue in the tooth, which sends signals to the brain, which presents them to the mind in the form of toothache.

Jill: You mean that we have toothache in the brain? That seems a very odd thing to say, Monsieur Descartes. When I have a toothache, it is my tooth that aches, not my mind.

Descartes: [*condescendingly*] Well, Madame, you may speak with the vulgar, but you should think with the learned. Sensation is a confused mode of awareness which arises from the union and as it were the intermingling of the mind with the body. Furthermore, hunger and thirst, pleasure as well as pain, perception as well as sensation, likewise arise from the union of mind and body. For this 'I' whereby I am what I am, is entirely distinct from the body. Nevertheless, a human being is an *embodied* soul or mind. It is not the accidental union of the two, but a substantial union. For a human being is an *ens per se*, in which mind and body form a unity. But sensation is not a part of my essence, that is, of the essence of my mind.

Jill: [*indignantly*] And how is this 'intermingling', as you call it, effected, Monsieur Descartes? How can an immaterial non-spatial substance interact with, let alone intermingle with, a material substance that constitutes our body? You say that acts of will cause the transmission of animal spirits to the muscles, so making them contract or extend. And you say that the impact of light waves and sound waves on our nerves causes the movement of animal spirits from the sense organs to the brain, where they cause perceptual thoughts. But you don't explain how this can be.

Descartes: Madame Jill, you should read *Principia Philosophiae, la Dioptrique* and *Les Passions de l'Ame*. The author there explains that it is the soul that sees, not the eye; and it does not see directly, but only by means of the brain. Furthermore, the seat of the soul or mind – the point where it affects and is affected by the body – is not the whole brain, but the pineal gland that lies within the ventricles between the two hemispheres of the brain. Insofar as we do not see double or hear everything twice, there must necessarily be some place where the two images coming from the two eyes or the two ears can come together in a single image or impression before reaching the soul, so that they do not present to it two objects rather than one.

Frank: Well, sir, that is not persuasive, y'know. First of all, animals other than us have a pineal gland too. But on your view they do not

P. M. S. Hacker

have the thought that things sensibly seem to them to be this or that, because they don't have any thoughts at all. Moreover, the pineal gland isn't located in the passage between the anterior and posterior ventricles and so can't affect the flow of 'animal spirits' between the ventricles. So your metaphor of the mind's being like the water engineer who turns the taps that control the flow of water to the fancy fountains at the Royal gardens is inappropriate. The pineal gland isn't in the ventricular fluid, and neuro-transmission isn't by means of animal spirits, as you supposed – it's electro-chemical. Secondly, your identification of the functional localization of what you call 'the soul' or 'the mind' is, *as a matter of scientific fact*, mistaken. It is the cortex that is the varied locus of mental functions, not the pineal body. We now know that different psychological functions have different cortical localizations. Vision, for example, has its functional localization in the 'visual' striate cortex, whereas thinking is associated with the prefrontal cortices.

Jill: Moreover, sir, your reasoning is flawed. Even if it were the mind that sees, then unless it sees the alleged image on the pineal gland, it does not matter whether there is one image there or two or none at all. For whatever is there, if anything, *is not an object of vision*. It is not as if two objects would cause double vision! As you yourself pointed out, there is not another pair of eyes within the brain with which to see the representations you hold to be on the pineal gland – or, for that matter, on the visual striate cortex. Moreover, it is neither the brain nor the mind that sees and hears, smells and tastes. It is the creature as a whole, no matter whether man or animal.

Richard: Whoa! Slow down. We needn't confront the matter of animal thinking and perceiving now. The central *philosophical* point we are advancing in criticism of your system, Monsieur Descartes, is that you have not given any explanation of *how* thinking immaterial substance can interact causally with unthinking and extended material substance. You insist, unlike your successors Malebranche and Geulincx, that they *do* interact. But you have not explained how that is possible – saying that the soul interacts with the body via the pineal gland simply shifts the problem back another stage, for now you must explain how the unextended immaterial soul can interact causally with the extended material pineal gland, or, as we should say, with the cortex.

Descartes: Ah, *je suis mortifié*. Her Highness, the Princess Elizabeth of Bohemia, once sapiently asked me how the soul, being only a thinking substance, can determine the animal spirits to bring about voluntary actions. I replied to her that the question

208

she posed is the one which can most properly be put to me in view of my published writings. Everyone invariably experiences in himself, without philosophizing, the union of soul and body. I concede to you that the human mind is not capable of forming a very distinct conception of the distinction between the soul and the body and also of their union. For to do this it is necessary to conceive them as a single thing and at the same time as two things. This is an *absurdité*. But everyone *feels* that he is a single person with both body and thought so related that the thinking mind can move the body, and the mind can also feel the things that happen to it.

Frank: Well, Monsieur Descartes, now y'really have blown it. If reasoning comes up with one thing and feeling with the opposite, then one may be right and the other wrong, or both may be wrong, but they can't both be right.

Richard: Moreover, the issue is not so much *whether* our mind and our bodies interact. We are not asking you to persuade us of that, sir. What you owe us is an explanation of *how* they can interact.

Descartes: I am not in the habit of crying when people are treating my wounds, and those who are kind enough to instruct me and inform me will always find me very docile. I cannot answer your question, *Messieurs*. But before I take my leave, I wish to remind you of one further point. We all *feel* the unity of soul and body – this you will surely not deny. And *we* are all here *in Elysium* – so the soul and the body *must be* separable, for our mortal remains have long since turned to bone and dust. But our souls, being indivisible are therefore also indestructible, and hence immortal – unless, of course, reduced to nothingness by God. So I must surely be right, even though it is beyond my powers to explain how it is that I am right. Perhaps, as my follower Noam Chomsky says when he encounters what he calls 'Descartes's problem' of how we can utter sentences we have never encountered before, it is beyond the powers of the human mind to comprehend such matters. [*He rises to his feet, picks up his hat, and bows to the others*]
Au revoir, Madame Jill, Au revoir, Messieurs. [*He leaves*]

Frank: Well, that was kind of interesting, but I don't think it helped much. The idea that the mind is an immaterial substance interacting with the brain is just hopeless. But he did make a point that floored me. What d'you make of the idea that the mind is immortal since it is indivisible, Richard?

P. M. S. Hacker

Richard: Well, assuming that all destruction is disintegration or decomposition, then if the mind were indivisible, it would be indestructible. But although one might say that the mind is not divisible, one must admit that it is not indivisible either.

Frank: What d'you mean?

Richard: Well, it is not as if you cannot divide a mind no matter how hard you try. It's rather that there is no such thing as dividing a mind, just as there is no such thing as dividing red. Minds, like colours, are neither divisible nor indivisible. So I wouldn't hang any hopes of immortality on that argument.

Frank: I see. Yeah. I always thought that dualism is a false theory. Y'know physics has disproved it.

Richard: What on earth do you mean?

Frank: Well, if my mind could move my body, that would violate the law of conservation of momentum.

Richard: No, no, Frank. That objection was already advanced by Leibniz, but it is wholly misconceived. No scientific discovery and no scientific theory can resolve a philosophical or conceptual problem.

Frank: [*annoyed*] What the hell do you mean?

Richard: There's no need to get hot under the collar, old boy. You grant, I trust, that no discovery in physics and no law of physics can contribute to the resolution of a problem in pure mathematics, let alone confirm or infirm a mathematical proof. After all, it's not as if Newton's physics confirmed the theorems of the differential calculus.

Frank: [*still resentful*] OK, sure. So what?

Richard: Well, that's because mathematics is concept-formation by means of proofs. And philosophy is, among other things, concept-clarification by means of linguistic description. Conceptual clarification is not answerable to facts and theories of physics. Concepts, including the concepts of physics, create the logical space within which physics can determine facts and formulate theories concerning matters of fact.

Frank: OK. But even if I give you that, it still seems to me that if Descartes were right, then the mind's making the body move by acts of will *would* violate the laws of physics, in particular the law of conservation of momentum.

Richard: No, *if* the mind could move matter, it would show definitively that the law of conservation of momentum is false. But this

210

hypothesis can only be true or false if the statement that the mind moves the body by acts of will makes sense. And that would make sense only if the idea of an immaterial substance made sense, and if we could render intelligible the supposition that an immaterial thing can have causal powers and could bring about change by acting *on* a material thing.

Jill: You mean the idea of an immaterial mind is nonsense?

Richard: Just so. There is no such thing as individuating substances independently of their being material space-occupants. Abstract material constitution, and with it spatial location and a spatio-temporal path through the world, and we would have no principle of individuation or criteria of identity.

Jill: I don't follow.

Richard: The deep trouble with Cartesian minds is that they lack criteria of synchronic identity. We cannot distinguish between one mind having a thought, and a thousand different minds having the very same thought. And, as Kant pointed out, they lack criteria of diachronic identity too, since we cannot distinguish between one mind persisting over time and having fresh thoughts from a thousand successive minds, each with the same thoughts as its predecessor with the addition of one more thought. So every time one has a thought, a different mental substance springs into being, possessed of all the thoughts of the prior substance together with a new thought – just like one billiard ball passing its momentum on to another on impact.

Jill: But that's absurd!

Richard: Of course it is. But that's no thanks to Descartes's tale, since on his account it cannot be excluded. The very notion of an immaterial mental substance makes no sense.

Frank: That's OK by me! I told you that the answer is clear. Dualism in any shape or form is just plain wrong. We have to opt for straightforward materialism: *the mind is the brain*. I have a brain, and *that is what it is* to have a mind. Because all the mental functions of perceiving, thinking, imagining, deciding and willing are brain functions. Descartes was right to think that the body is a machine. He was only wrong to think that the mind is an immaterial substance that interacts with it.

Richard: You mean it's not elephants all the way down, as Russell's old lady thought, but it's machinery all the way up!

Frank: [*chuckles*] Yeah, that's right. The fact of the matter is that although we feel ourselves to be in control of our actions, that feeling is the product of our brain, whose machinery has been designed, on the basis of its functional utility, by means of natural selection. We are machines, but machines so wonderfully sophisticated that no one should count it an insult to be called such a machine.

Jill: Oh come on, Frank. You can't really believe that!

Frank: Why not? I do believe it.

Jill: Well, because machines are neither conscious nor unconscious. They take no pleasure in what they do and suffer no pain. They neither love nor hate. They do not deliberate on courses of action and then decide what to do on the basis of reasons. Machines don't know the difference between right and wrong, they have no obligations and they have no rights either. It's no insult to call a machine a machine, but it certainly is an insult to call me a machine! Do you think that I have no moral sense? Or are you suggesting that I have no rights and duties?

Frank: No, no.

Jill: Moreover, the fact that in one sense everything we think, feel and do depends upon the activity of our brain, as you say, does not show that it is the brain that thinks and feels, makes decisions and acts.

Frank: Why not? We perceive because the brain forms an internal image on the basis of the information it receives from the senses. That's scientific fact. All y' have to do is look it up in any decent textbook of neuroscience. We know that the brain makes decisions before you're even conscious of it. Benjamin Libet showed that decades ago. And it's the brain that makes our hands and legs move and do things. In fact, we are our brains. As Chris Frith says, we are nothing more than 1.5 kilograms of sentient meat that is our brain.

Richard: No. That isn't scientific fact, it's scientific confusion. For heaven's sake, Frank, you weigh more than one and a half kilos, and you're taller than seven inches. To be sure, you have a brain, but you're not what you have, and your brain doesn't have a brain, it is one. Your brain is in your skull, but you are not enskulled. You can't seriously believe such nonsense. Moreover, there is no such thing as a brain's forming images on the basis of information it receives from the senses. When we observe the world around us, what we see are objects and their properties, the unfolding of events and the obtaining of states of affairs. We don't see images, unless we are in a picture gallery. Nor does the brain *receive information*, in the sense in which you or I might receive information about lectures and concerts here by reading the *Elysian Gazette* or the *Heavenly Herald*.

Frank: Y'mean that the theories of Nobel prize winners like Eric Kandel, Francis Crick, Gerald Edelman, as well as the theories of world renowned scientists like Michael Gazzaniga, Antonio Damasio and Horace Barlow, are plain false? I mean, what scientific work have you ever done, Richard?

Richard: None at all, my dear fellow. But I am not saying that their theories are false.

Frank: [*irritated*] You're just advancing your opinion against theirs. There is a whole group of representationalists in cognitive science and the philosophy of cognitive science who think it is perfectly OK to attribute – for example – memory to cognitive subsystems. It is, to put it mildly, provocative to suggest your view as if it were a settled fact that they are wrong. That's just opinion presented as fact.

Richard: My dear chap, it is no more an opinion than it is an opinion that red is a colour or that nothing can be both round and square at the same time. Nor am I saying that it is a matter of fact that brains don't think or remember or form images. If something is a matter of fact, then things are so, but they might have been otherwise. But this is a matter of logic, not of fact. It makes no sense to say that the brain thinks or remembers. And that is why these theories are not false. They are nonsense.

Frank: [*spluttering with indignation*] Who the hell are *you*, Richard, to say that the work of these distinguished scientists is all rubbish? That's just outrageous.

Richard: Calm down, Frank. I didn't say their work was rubbish. I said their claims about the brain that we just mentioned are nonsense – that they lack sense. It makes *no sense* to say that the brain thinks, re-members, and perceives, constructs hypotheses and guesses what is, as your friends misguidedly put it, 'out there'. It is senseless to say that the brain decides and wills. These are forms of words that are simply excluded from language, like 'black whiteness' or 'square roundness'.

Frank: I don't see why. That's the way neuroscientists talk. What's wrong with it? It may be excluded from folk-psychological language, but it sure isn't excluded from scientific language. And who the hell are you to tell scientists how they should talk?

Richard: Frank, they may talk as they please. If they want to talk nonsense, let them talk nonsense. I'm not a linguistic policeman. All I am pointing out is that if you chaps want to speak *of yourselves* as thinking and reasoning, perceiving and feeling, deciding and acting in the received sense of these terms, then you cannot coherently *also* say that *your brain* thinks and reasons, perceives and feels, and so forth, *in the same sense.*

Frank: I don't follow you.

Richard: It is actually straightforward, once you orient yourself correctly, Frank. Look, you don't say that the table feels things, do you.

Frank: No, I'm not stupid, y'know.

Richard: No, of course your not. You're one of the most intelligent scientists I know, old chap. Now, you don't think that the trees and roses over there can see or hear, do you.

Frank: [*a bit mollified*] No, of course not.

Richard: Why not?

Frank: Why not? Well, for one thing, they don't have eyes.

Richard: Quite so. And they don't duck when you throw a rock at them. Nor do they look at things or move closer to observe things better.

Frank: Yeah. OK. So?

Richard: Well, does the brain have eyes? Does it look at things that catch its interest? Does it move its eyes to follow what it's looking at? Does it rub its eyes when there's a glare, and shield them when it's too bright?

Frank: No. If it has no eyes, it can't engage in visual behaviors.

Richard: That's right. There is no such thing as *a brain* exhibiting visual behaviour. Increased neural activity in the 'visual' striate cortex is not a form of behaviour. Moreover, even if, as you suggest, brains see and hear, think and remember, how would that help *you* to see and hear, think and remember?

Frank: Well, my brain informs me.

Jill: But, Frank, how can your brain inform you of anything if it cannot speak English? Or are brains language-users? Do brains have voices? And how would you listen to your brain when it talks to you? With an inner ear? It is schizophrenics that hear inner voices, you know.

Frank: Yeah, OK. I see what you're driving at. So, how does all this add up?

Richard: How it adds up is this: It only makes sense to ascribe vision to beings that have eyes with which to see, and that exhibit – manifest – their visual powers in their behaviour. An animal that sees avoids obstacles in its pathway, it goes around them or steps over them. It examines and scrutinizes anything it sees that rouses its curiosity, and it flees from dangerous things it perceives. It's not false that trees see. If it were false, then it might have been true but doesn't happen to be. But trees aren't blind either. Nor are brains – they can neither see, *nor are they blind*. It *makes no sense* to ascribe seeing or overseeing or not seeing to them. Brains don't make decisions, and they're not indecisive either. It simply lacks sense to say that my brain decided to do something. And the brain doesn't *make* your hands and legs move, rather it makes it possible for you to move them at will.

Frank: So what you're saying is that cognitive neuroscientists are making a conceptual mistake here.

Richard: Exactly. That's why I said that they're talking nonsense. I don't mean that they're talking sheer rubbish, what I mean is that they're transgressing the bounds of sense and that they're putting words together in a way that's excluded from the language. They're committing a mereological fallacy.

Jill: What's a mereological fallacy, Richard?

Richard: It's the fallacy of ascribing to a part of a thing properties that can only intelligibly be ascribed to the thing as a whole. Look, an aeroplane can't fly without its engines, but it isn't its engines that fly, it's the 'plane. An antique bracket clock can't keep time without a fusée, but it's the clock that keeps time, not the fusée. So too, an animal cannot walk or run, talk or sing, without a brain, but its not the brain that walks and talks, it is the animal as a whole.

[*Silence for a moment*]

Frank: OK. You're a clever beggar, Richard. I see what y'mean.

Jill: But then Descartes was equally misguided to say that it is the mind that thinks and perceives, imagines and wills. It isn't my mind that thinks – I think. And it isn't my mind that perceives or enjoys sensible experience – I do. And it isn't my mind that decides and acts – I decide and act.

Richard: Exactly. That's why neuroscientific materialism is a degenerate form of Cartesian dualism. It just replaces ethereal minds with grey glutinous stuff and leaves everything else intact. It replaces mind/body dualism with brain/body dualism.

Frank: Hey, wait a minute. The brain is just as material as the rest of the human body. There can't be any such thing as brain/body dualism. Both the brain and the body are material.

P. M. S. Hacker

Richard: Of course. But you neuroscientists leave intact the whole structure of Cartesian dualism. You think that the only thing wrong with it is that it introduces a mental substance as the subject of all psychological attributes. You think that perceiving is the generation of mental images in the brain by the impact of material things and of sound or light waves on our sense organs. That is senseless. You think that voluntary movement is movement caused by the brain's deciding to move. And that is nonsense too. And you imagine that thinking is information processing by the brain, whereas it is nothing of the sort. Frank, the trouble about you neuroscientists is not that you are anti-Cartesian, it is that you are not nearly anti-Cartesian enough.

Frank: OK. I get the message. But where does that leave us?

Jill: It means that there aren't enough 'or-s' in your battle-cry: Either dualism or materialism.

Frank: OK. So what's the new deal?

Jill: Yes. What is the third way, Richard? We haven't even scratched at answers to the questions we started out with. I mean: What is the mind? What is the self? What is the Soul? What am I, and who or what is it that has a mind, a self or a soul? And how is the mind related to the body? And who is it that has a body? And ...

Frank: Enough already. You're swamping us. We need some help.

Richard: Yes, a *deus ex machina* would come in useful.

A dignified, good-looking, late middle age gentleman strolls in from the trees, wearing ancient Greek dress. He has a well-cut beard, flecked with grey, and greying hair. They all recognize Aristotle, and the men rise to their feet.

Aristotle: Good day. May I join you for a short while. I think I may be able to help you a little.

Richard: We are honored that you should choose to join our modest symposium here, sir. May I introduce my friends? This is Jill; this is Frank; and my name is Richard. May I offer you some wine? [*He pours Aristotle a glass of wine and hands it to him.*] It comes from an excellent cellar: the *Nectarian*. Please sit down. [*Aristotle takes a seat.*] We have been struggling to clarify the nature of the mind.

Aristotle: Your difficulties are quite reasonable. For among the many, and even more among the wise – including Plato – there is division of opinion and obscurity of statement concerning the mind.

216

Jill: Well, we certainly have plenty of difficulties. We had a long discussion with Monsieur Descartes, and examined his view that the mind is a separate substance from the body and that its essential nature is thought, construed as consciousness of what passes within us. But there were many objections to this dualist view. And we examined Frank's view that the mind is just the brain and that all the attributes of the mind are in effect attributes of the brain. But Richard showed us that this view too is unacceptable. We really are at a loss.

Aristotle: But that is already progress, madam. It is the height of madness not merely to be ignorant but not to realize that you are ignorant, and therefore to assent to false conceptions and to suppose that true conceptions are false.

Jill: But there are so many competing reasons that it is difficult to know where to begin.

Aristotle: I agree with you, madam. But you must bethink yourself that some people offer reasons that are irrelevant or unsound, and often get away with it. Some people do this in error. Others are sheer charlatans. By such arguments even thoughtful people may be caught out by those who are lacking in the capacity for serious theoretical reflection.

Richard: So where do we begin?

Aristotle: Most of the controversies and difficulties will become clear if we offer an appropriate explanation of how to think of living beings. Living beings are organisms. Where we have living beings, beings that may prosper and flourish or deteriorate and die, we have welfare and ill-fare. Where we have organisms of developed form, we have organs. Where we have organs, we have function and purpose. Where we have function and purpose, welfare and ill-fare, we have varieties of the good. For we have the goodness of health, the goodness of organs, the goodness of their exercise, the good of the being that has organs, and the goodness of that which is conducive to the good of the being. From this it is evident that one of the roots of axiology is biology.

Jill: So you mean that the sciences of life are inseparable from the study of the good?

Aristotle: But of course. No one in his right mind could think otherwise. However, let us focus upon our task, which is to clarify what is distinctive of all living beings.

Frank: Well, I guess it's that they all ingest nutriment from their environment, they all grow and reproduce, giving rise to the next generation.

P. M. S. Hacker

Aristotle: I agree. We must begin our investigation by noting the *archē*, the distinctive principle, of the lower forms of life – the plants. It is evident that they have the powers of metabolism, growth, and reproduction. This is characteristic of all species of living things, is it not? These nutritive or vegetative powers constitute the form of botanical life. Indeed, we may say that they *inform* the organism, constituting the essential powers of botanical organisms that have organs. And we may characterize this form as the nutritive or vegetative *psuchē*.

Richard: But that is not how Plato thought of the *psuchē*? He thought that the soul is something that resides temporarily in the body and that will leave the body on death.

Aristotle: Indeed. Like many others, Plato joined the *psuchē* to a body, or placed it in a body, without explaining the reason for their union or the bodily conditions required for it. He thought that the *psuchē* is *embodied*. But that is absurd. For it is not as if *any psuchē* could be conjoined with *any* body – the *psuchē* of a man with the body of a tree, or of a bean – as the Pythagoreans supposed. This is not a helpful way of thinking about the soul. We should not conceive of the *psuchē* as a being – a secondary substance of a strange kind – but rather as the form of living things. The *psuchē* is not embodied, rather the organic body – the body with organs – is *empsuchos*, ensouled. The *psuchē* is constituted by the distinctive powers that *inform* living beings and in virtue of which they are the kinds of beings they are. Thinking thus, we have a far more powerful way of conceiving of natural life in general and of ourselves as part of nature – albeit partaking of the divine or blessed.

Frank: Hey, slow down. What do you mean 'partaking of the divine'?

Aristotle: Mankind possesses nothing divine or blessed that is of any account except what there is in us of mind and understanding. We are born for two things, understanding and action, and we fully realize our nature in the exercise of our understanding in the noble endeavour to understand the world in which we pass our lives, on the one hand, and in the excellence of our actions in accordance with virtue. To achieve this to the best of our abilities is what I mean by 'partaking of the divine'.

Frank: I see. So you don't mean that the mind or soul, or the *psuchē* as you call it, is *a part* of a living animal? If it was a part, it might be separated from the body – and that's surely just a fiction.

Aristotle: The *psuchē* is the form of living things. Where there is no living thing, there can be no *psuchē*, for the being of such forms is to inform matter. Now, we can say that a substance has parts in many

218

different senses. It is clear that the *psuchē* is not a part of a body that potentially has life as wheels are a part of a chariot. The *psuchē* stands to the organism somewhat as the shape of a statue stands to the marble of which the statue is carved. That is why it is absurd to ask whether the body and soul are one or two. That is like asking whether the wax and its shape are one or two. From this it is clear that the *psuchē* is inseparable from the body. It is the principle of life characteristic of kinds of living beings, for its distinctive powers are what make a living being with organs the kind of being it is.

Jill: So according to you, sir, the *psuchē* explains the nature of life?

Aristotle: It is a notion that belongs to the sciences of life, but not after the manner of those who conceive of the soul as corporeal and originative of movement, and identify it with hot breath or hot blood, thinking of these as the principle of life. The *psuchē* characterizes organic life by reference to its powers. Of course, we can study the powers of living things only by studying their behaviour, for activities and actions are logically prior to potentialities. But let us not jump ahead of ourselves as a steed jumps before it has reached the correct distance from a wall. We must proceed methodically, in the correct order. So, the nature of the nutritive *psuchē* by which all living things are informed has been outlined. Now, what further powers characterize *animals*?

Frank: Well, I guess they can perceive their environment, they have desires and they can move about to get what they want.

Aristotle: Quite so. Animal life, over and above the powers of the nutritive *psuchē*, is characterized by sensibility, of which the primary form is touch and hence taste. Where there is sense, there is the capacity for pleasure and pain. Where these are present, there too must be appetite. Otherwise even the most primitive of sea animals could not nourish themselves and distinguish what is beneficial from what is detrimental to them. Certain kinds of animal also possess powers of locomotion, and further senses of sight, hearing and smell. Where there is sensibility and self-movement, there too must be desire and aversion, and action for the sake of a goal.

Frank: Y'mean that animals have two of these *psuchē*-s – two souls. That seems weird!

Aristotle: Not weird, absurd. What I mean is that the distinctive set of powers of animate creatures *includes* the essential powers of vegetal forms of life, namely: powers of nutrition, growth and reproduction, but incorporates further distinctive powers that constitute, in one sense of the word, the essence of animal life. And, of course, we classify different kinds of animals according to their distinctive powers and the distinctive organs by means of which they exercise them.

Jill: But still, there is something distinctive of us humans in virtue of which we conceive of ourselves as having a mind.

Aristotle: Of course. We possess rational faculties. Animals lack the powers of reason, calculation and reflection. And it must be born in mind that thought is found only where there is also reason. What distinguishes us within the realm of nature is the possession of a rational *psuchē*, over and above the nutritive and sensitive *psuchē*. It is this that you may think of as *the mind*, which is distinctive of mankind. The power of reason is the ability to apprehend the transition from premisses to the conclusion that they determine, and hence too the power of understanding the manifold 'because-s' that answer the question 'Why?'. Only beings that can answer the question 'Why?' can be answerable for their deeds, and know the difference between virtue and vice. Rationality is exhibited in drawing inferences from premisses and in deriving conclusions from evidence. It is manifest in deliberating, in rational choice, and in sensitivity to reasons.

Richard: I don't follow that. I'm not sure what you mean by 'sensitivity to reasons'. Since sensitivity is itself a potentiality, not an actuality, I am not sure what you mean by saying that mind is exhibited in a potentiality, given that you also want to say that it *is* a potentiality.

Aristotle: You must realize that there are many different kinds of 'can' and different sorts of potentiality. Because mankind is endowed with reason and understanding, we can understand something as warranting thought and action. We can apprehend a 'this is so' as a justification for acting thus-and-so, or as a warrant for concluding that things are so. But we may know something to be a reason, just as we know something to be so, even when we are asleep. Or we may apprehend something to be a reason while we are awake, and yet not take notice of it. Or we may take notice of it and act immediately without deliberation, as when we catch someone who is about to fall. Or we may apprehend something as a reason, and deliberate on what is to be done, and later do it for that reason. What is clear is that in all or some or one of these ways, we, unlike all other animals, are sensitive to reasons.

Frank: I don't see how this 'rational *psuchē*' or mind can interact with the body if it isn't a part of the body, like the brain is. I mean if the nature of the rational *psuchē* is to be sensitive to reasons, how does it make the body move?

Aristotle: We are speaking of powers, my dear sir, not of things. The ability of an axe to cut is not a part of the axe. Nor does it interact with the axe, or make the axe cut. We cannot see without eyes, but eyesight is not a part of the eye. It is not the eye that sees, it is the animal with eyes. Without eyes, there is no eyesight, but eyesight does not make the eyes see. So too, it is the human being that reasons and deliberates for reasons and acts on account of reasons and for the sake of rationally chosen ends. It is not the mind or rational *psuchē* that reasons, infers, and comes to conclusions. It is the human being. To say that the *psuchē* reasons or deliberates is like saying that the *psuchē* weaves or builds. Surely it is better not to say that the *psuchē* pities, learns or thinks, but that the man does these things with his *psuchē*.

Jill: You mean one does things with one's mind or rational *psuchē* just as one sees with one's eyes and walks with one's legs?

Aristotle: No, my dear lady, not at all. The *psuchē* is not a part of a living being and so the rational *psuchē* is not an organ of a human being like the legs and eyes. One does things with one's *psuchē* in the sense in which one does things with one's talents.

Jill: Ah, I see. So the very question of how the mind is related to the body is itself a misguided question?

Aristotle: Of course. It is akin to the question of how the potter is related to his ability to throw a pot, or of how the eye is related to eyesight. These are not relations at all. We have capacities and abilities, liabilities and susceptibilities, but while *having an axe* is a relation between an owner and his possession, having powers is no relation. You must think of the peculiarities of the idea of *having*. For we speak of *having* in a number of different ways: of having knowledge, which is akin to possessing abilities; or of having courage, which is a trait of character; of having a height or length, as well as of having a cloak or tunic, as when one covers oneself after exercise in the palaestra. And we speak of having a ring on one's finger, as when one wears a ring on a part of oneself. We speak of the jar as having wine in it, when it contains wine. And there is an even stranger way of having, as when we speak of having parents – which means that one's parents are alive, and of having a wife, which signifies no more than that one is married to her.

Richard: Yes, I read that in your *Categories*. But you wrote there that you had made a pretty complete enumeration of the different ways 'having' is spoken of. But you didn't speak of having a mind, of having something in mind or having something at the back of one's mind. Nor did you extend your remarks to such forms of *having* as having a thought, having a reason or having a goal. But that surely is a most fruitful way of pursuing further your idea of conceiving of the mind, the *rational psuchē*, in terms of having first- and second-order abilities and exercising them. For here too we must examine carefully what lies behind all this *having*.

Aristotle: But of course. I wrote three carefully composed pages of notes in Chapter 15 of the *Categories*, which made the matter quite clear. You don't mean to say that you stopped before the end?

Richard: Well, no. I read right to the end, but Chapter 15 consists only of one brief paragraph.

Aristotle: [*agitated*] You mean that those concluding pages have been lost?

Richard: Well, yes, I suppose they must have been.

Aristotle: [*jumping to his feet*] This is grievous indeed. I did not realize that the complete notes have not survived. Pray excuse me now. I must see whether there is a decent copy in the Library here. [*he pauses and collects himself*] But before I go, let me suggest to you how to pursue matters further for yourselves. Bear in mind that if you begin with things that are said in a manner that is true but unenlightening, you will make progress towards enlightenment by constantly substituting more perspicuous expressions for the ones that are more familiar but confusing. But now I must go and try to find Theophrastus and Neleus to see whether they can throw some light on this loss. Farewell. [*He leaves*]

Jill: Oh what a shame! That was wonderful. And we were just about to get to the heart of the matter.

Frank: Who are these guys Theophrastus and Nellyus?

Richard: Neleus. Theophrastus took over the Lyceum after Aristotle died, and so he inherited all of his manuscripts, and he passed them on to his nephew Neleus of Skepsis, one of Aristotle's last pupils, for safe keeping.

Frank: Ah! . . . Well, that was some display of fireworks. He sure did leave dualism in tatters.

Jill: But also reductive materialism, Frank. What he's offering us is naturalism without reduction − a conception of the mind that is neither dualist nor materialist.

Richard: Yes. What we now have to do is apply the schema he's given us to our normal discourse about the mental. We need to examine the use of such phrases as 'having a thought at the back of one's mind', 'having a thought cross one's mind', ' having something in mind', 'making up one's mind' and . . .

Frank: Hey, wait a minute. If he's right, then it makes no sense to speak of the mind being separable from the body.

Richard: Yes, that seems eminently plausible to say the very least. Surely you must find that idea congenial?

Frank: Yeah, sure. But then how do you reply to Descartes's parting shot? I mean, we *are* here y' know, and our bodies must have turned to dust by now. So maybe we do survive without the bodies we once had.

Richard: My dear chap, did it never occur to you that we might simply be characters in someone's dream?

There is a roll of thunder and flash of lightening, and all goes black. When light returns the scene has changed. The author is lying on a chaise longue in which he has dropped off to sleep. He sits up and rubs his eyes.

The author: What an amazing dream! How extraordinary. [*He rises to his feet*] I must go and write it all down before I forget.

St John's College, Oxford
peter.hacker@sjc.ox.ac.uk

The sequel to this dialogue is 'A Dialogue on Mind and Body', in Philosophy 89 (2014), 511–535, in which Jill, Frank and Richard continue their discussion in Elysium with Peter Strawson and Alan White.

Acknowledgements: Hanoch Ben-Yami; Dan Robinson; John Cottingham; David Wiggins; Hans Oberdiek.

Power, Scepticism and Ethical Theory

THOMAS PINK

Abstract

It is often thought that as human agents we have a power to determine our actions for ourselves. And a natural conception of this power is as freedom – a power over alternatives so that we can determine for ourselves which of a variety of possible actions we perform. But what is the real content of this conception of freedom, and need self-determination take this particular form? I examine the possible forms self-determination might take, and the various ways freedom as a power over alternatives might be constituted. I argue that though ordinary ethical thought, and especially moral blame, may be committed to our possession of some capacity for self-determination, the precise nature of this power is probably ethically underdetermined – though conceptions of the nature of the power that come from outside ethics may then have important implications for ethics.

1. Freedom and Scepticism

Ethical theory has often appealed to the idea that as agents we have a power of self-determination – a power to determine our action for ourselves. The immediately natural conception of self-determination seems to be as freedom, a power that leaves it up to us whether we do A or refrain – a power of *control* over which actions we perform. Central to the idea of freedom, then, is power over alternatives. This involvement of alternatives is picked out by the 'up to me whether' construction, which is completed by specification of alternatives by way of actions and outcomes within my power; freedom is the power to determine for ourselves which alternative occurs.

Belief in our possession of such a power is especially naturally reported by talk of what we do being 'up to us'. And put in such terms, belief in the power is very general. It is easy to think of its being up to me whether I go out or stay in, raise my hand or lower it.[1] But there has long been scepticism about the reality of such a

---

[1]   'Freedom' is very much a philosopher's term, and the origins of its use to pick out a form of power seem to lie in the transference to metaphysics of what was an initially political and ethical term. I discuss elsewhere the connexions between metaphysical, ethical and political uses of the term 'freedom' – see 'Thomas Hobbes and the ethics of freedom', *Inquiry*, **54** (2011) 541–63.

doi:10.1017/S1358246115000119

power among philosophers. This scepticism often begins nowadays from the supposed link of our conception of freedom to incompatibilism. Incompatibilism about freedom is the doctrine that the possession and exercise of the power is incompatible with the causal determination of our action by prior occurrences outside our control. Sceptics such as Galen Strawson have viewed incompatibilism as supposedly both implied by our present concept of freedom, and dooming that concept to non-application.

Strawson allows for a weak kind of compatibilistically acceptable self-determination involving a power of our passive motivations to determine how we act. This power is what Thomas Hobbes called voluntariness – the power of motivations, of desires or other pro attitudes towards action, to cause the action motivated. Hobbes took voluntariness to constitute the very definition of human action, which by its very nature (in his view) involved doing things as an effect of our wanting to do them. Strawson goes further, and takes voluntariness to provide not just action, but a metaphysically unproblematic form of self-determination – a power on our part to determine action:

> A naturalistic explanation of this sense of self-determination would connect it tightly with our sense, massively and incessantly confirmed since earliest infancy, of our ability *to do what we want in order to (try to) get what we want,* by performing a vast variety of actions great and small, walking where we want, making ourselves understood, picking up this and putting down that. We pass our days in more or less continual and almost entirely successful self-directing intentional activity, and we know it. Even if we don't always achieve our aims, when we act, we almost always perform a movement of the kind we intended to perform, and in that vital sense (vital for the sense of self-determining self-control) we are almost entirely successful in our action.

> This gives rise to a sense of freedom to act, of complete self-control, or responsibility in self-directedness, that is in itself compatibilistically unexceptionable, and is quite untouched by arguments against true responsibility based on the impossibility of self-determination. But it is precisely this compatibilistically speaking unexceptionable sense of freedom and efficacy that is one of the fundamental bases of the growth in us of the compatibilistically impermissible sense of true responsibility. To observe a child of two fully in control of its limbs, *doing what it wants to do with them, and to this extent fully free to act in the compatibilist sense of the phrase,* and to realise that it is precisely such

unremitting experience of self-control that is the deepest foundation of our naturally incompatibilistic sense of true-responsibility-entailing self-determination, is to understand one of the most important facts about the genesis and power of our ordinary strong sense of freedom.[2]

Bernard Williams too talks of our primitive conception of self-determination as being Hobbesian voluntariness, or 'action unimpeded' in the execution of one's will; a conception which he describes as 'seed' to the 'plant' of any more developed or demanding conception of self-determination as incompatibilist freedom.[3]

The supposedly original conception of self-determination locates the power as a power of our motivations, conceived as passive in that they precede any doing by us, to cause actions that would satisfy them. And of course this conception of self-determination is entirely compatibilist. The operation of the power is not only consistent with the causal determination of our action by occurrences outside our control, but actually involves just such causation. The introduction of an incompatibilist conception of the power requires, then, a wider transformation in our understanding of it. The power must no longer attach to passive desires, but be exercised by us independently of our desires. And if action must by its very nature involve motivating attitudes, then these attitudes cannot be passive determinants of what we do, but arise as themselves aspects or parts of what we do. The motivation for our action is relocated to a mythical and inherently self-determined faculty of will – a faculty that involves inherently active motivations of decision that operate apart from ordinary desire.

We tend to think we have a will (a power of decision) distinct from all our particular [passive] motives.[4]

If freedom as we have currently come erroneously to conceive it, as a power exercised apart from ordinary desires, does not really exist, how has such a conception of power entered our psychological belief? An obvious line of thought involves an error theory – the intrusion of defective ethical conceptions into psychology. The culprit is some erroneous model of blame and moral responsibility. We begin with incompatibilism, not about freedom, but about moral responsibility. The actions for which we are morally

---

[2]   Galen Strawson, *Freedom and Belief* (Oxford University Press, 1986), 110–111 (my emphases)
[3]   See 'Saint-Just's illusion', in his *Making Sense of Humanity*, (Cambridge University Press, 1995), 136.
[4]   Galen Strawson, *Freedom and Belief*, 113

responsible must not be determined causally by prior conditions for which we are not responsible. So a new power is introduced to base that moral responsibility that likewise rules such causal determination out – a power of libertarian or incompatibilist freedom.

This theory of a development in the understanding of self-determination – a development from an unobjectionably compatibilist 'seed' to an extravagantly incompatibilist 'plant' – faces a number of questions. First, the transformation is hard to understand as a development of one conception of self-determination from another, just because the initial power, Hobbesian voluntariness, looks so unlike genuine self-determination. Instead of determination of action by the self, we have determination of an action by a passive motivation – a desire that happens to the agent and that is not of their own doing. Indeed as we shall see, Hobbes certainly did not suppose that voluntariness involves a form of self-determination – a power by which we determine for ourselves what we do. He saw voluntariness as nothing more than the determination of action, as one motion in matter, by passions as just other motions in matter. For reasons that we shall be examining, he denied the very possibility of self-determination, and gave it no role in his ethical theory.

Secondly, we might question the centrality given to incompatibilism as an element of our ordinary conception of freedom. Incompatibilist intuitions are very widespread. But they are not universal. And they arguably have to do, not with the nature of freedom as a power in itself, but with the power's relation to – its compatibility with – another case of power, namely antecedent causation. More central to our conception of freedom or control, and what distinguishes it as freedom, just is its involvement of alternatives – the very up-to-us-ness of how we act. The particular way in which alternatives are involved in our idea of freedom, it will emerge, distinguishes freedom as a power very sharply from Hobbesian voluntariness. But the way we understand freedom to involve alternatives may have very little to do with incompatibilism. And it may not be easily explicable just in terms of some intrusion of ethical theory into psychology. The way freedom involves alternatives certainly feeds into our ethical belief. But it may not be entirely ethical in origin.

2. Self-determination and moral responsibility

We can criticize someone ethically or by standards of reason without implying their possession of some power of self-determination. We can criticize someone as selfish without implying any power on their part to determine that they are selfish or unselfish. Similarly we can criticize someone for some failure of reason without implying that they had a power to determine for themselves whether the failure occurred. Failures of theoretical reason, for example, may occur without any power on the believer's part to determine or prevent their occurrence. A degree of selfishness, or some imperfection in one's capacity for reason, can perfectly well be built in.

For this reason, philosophers from Hobbes and Hume to our own day have striven to detach ethics from any presupposition of some metaphysically problematic power of self-determination by assimilating moral blame, the holding of someone as morally responsible, to some more general form of ethical criticism. For Hume, such blame is no more than a pronouncedly negative evaluation – an evaluation that can as much be of passive attitudes and dispositions as of actions. For Scanlon, moral blame is rational criticism that is distinctive only as coming with a sting, a special significance for us, not as presupposing any distinctive, moral responsibility. And precisely because it occurs simply as rational criticism, Scanlonian blame, too, can be for attitudes as much as actions:

> …"being responsible" is mainly a matter of the appropriateness of demanding reasons…For this reason, one can be responsible not only for one's actions but also for intentions, beliefs and other attitudes. That is, one can properly be asked to defend these attitudes according to the canons relevant to them, and one can be appraised in the light of these canons for the attitudes one holds. The "sting" of finding oneself responsible for an attitude that shows one's thinking to be defective by certain standards will be different in each case, depending on our reasons for caring about the standards in question. But the basic idea of responsibility is the same.[5]

But moral blame is more distinctive than that. It involves more than criticism of someone as defective in their actions or attitudes. Blame does not just report a deficiency in the person blamed. It further states that this deficiency was the person's fault – that they were 'to blame' for it. The attribution of something not only as a fault, but as someone's fault, the fault of the person blamed, is essential to anything recognizable as genuine blame.

For suppose someone is subject to ordinary rational criticism. Suppose, for example, that they have committed some error of

---

[5]   T.M. Scanlon, *What We Owe to Each Other* (Harvard University Press, 1998), 22

reasoning. It is always a *further* question whether that they made this error was their fault. Are they responsible and to blame for the fact that they made it? – or did they make the mistake through no fault of their own? They were certainly being foolish or less than sensible; it is, after all, their reasoning which was bad. But we can still ask whether it was through their own fault that they reasoned incorrectly. The question of one's responsibility for one's attitudes remains open, even when one's rational appraisability for those attitudes is admitted. In which case Scanlon must be wrong. The kind of responsibility assumed in blame does not reduce to the appropriateness of rational appraisal.

R.M. Adams similarly confuses moral blame with more general ethical criticism. In his 'Involuntary sins' Adams has suggested that when people are criticized for being selfish, such criticism amounts to blame:

> Perhaps for some people the word 'blame' has connotations that it does not have for me. To me, it seems strange to say that I do not blame someone though I think poorly of him, believing that his motives are thoroughly selfish. Intuitively speaking, I should have said that thinking poorly of a person in this way is a form of unspoken blame.[6]

But the selfishness of someone's motivation does not of itself settle the question which is raised in blame – namely their responsibility for the motivation they possess. Their selfishness is one thing. It is still a further question whether their possession of such a character is their fault. There is no inconsistency at all in criticizing someone as having a selfish character, while wondering or doubting whether their possession of this character really is their fault. Just as someone can be criticized as poor at reasoning without this being supposed to be their fault, so they can be criticized as selfish without this being supposed to be their fault.

In moral blame, the agent is not merely criticized for some fault in their actions and attitudes. The fault is put down to them as their fault. And this putting a fault down to someone as their fault is essential to the content of blame. And it is at this point that a power on the agent's part comes in. Why should a fault on the agent's part be their fault unless they had a power to determine its occurrence – or a power to prevent its occurrence which, though possessed by them, they failed to exercise?

---

[6]   R. M. Adams, 'Involuntary Sins', *Philosophical Review*, **94** (1985), 1–35.

3. The Nature of Power

Many philosophers write as if power were a rather uniform phenomenon. It is often claimed, for example, that power is by its very nature a causal phenomenon – a claim that, as we shall see, was importantly made by Hobbes, but which is still very current today:

> In the first place, the notions of power or disposition are already causally laden notions and it can thus reasonably be argued that unless one already has a grasp of causation, one cannot have a grasp of power. Powers, indeed, are often called causal powers.[7]

Certainly, one very intuitive case of power is the very familiar kind that is involved in causation, and that is possessed and exercised, not by causes and effects indifferently, but specifically by causes. This is the power of stones to break windows or the power of fire to boil water – the power that causes have to produce their effects. But it is useful to step back, and raise the question why causation itself is so widely viewed as involving power – and, more specifically, a power possessed and exercised by causes over what they affect?

Power involves a kind of capacity. Causal power constitutes, after all, a capacity to produce effects. But, of course, it is not the mere presence in them of a capacity that makes it true that causes possess power. And that is because the idea of a capacity extends far wider than that of power. For example, there are capacities not to cause and affect, but to be affected. But the capacity to be affected hardly constitutes any kind of power over anything, and the process of being affected is hardly the exercise of power. The contrary is true: to be affected is to be subject to power that is possessed and exercised by something else. Contrast my view with John Locke's.[8] Locke divides power into active and passive. Active is defined as the power to make a change, passive is the power to receive it. As an account of power this is certainly defective. For, of course, Locke ignores powers to prevent change from occurring. But more importantly, Locke's 'passive power' involves the opposite of any exercise of genuine power. It is a form of powerlessness – subjection to the power of another.

---

[7] Rom Harre and Edward Madden, cited with approval in Stephen Mumford and Rani Anjum, *Getting Causes from Powers* (Oxford University Press, 2011), 7.

[8] See John Locke, *An Essay Concerning Human Understanding*, ed. P.H. Nidditch (Oxford: Clarendon Press, 1975), Book 2, chapter 21 'Of power', §10, 234

Thomas Pink

Power, then, is a very special capacity. And what, I conjecture, is common to power in all its forms is a capacity to produce or, at the upper limit, to outright determine the occurrence or non-occurrence of outcomes. It is this capacity to produce or determine outcomes that causes possess, but which their effects lack. Causes determine the occurrence of their effects, and not vice versa.

If a power is a capacity to produce or determine outcomes, a causal power must be a capacity to produce or determine outcomes causally. And that might suggest the possibility, at least at the conceptual level, of power that is not causal. A power that is not causal is going to be a power the exercise of which determines outcomes, but without determining them causally. And that in turn raises the question of whether the power involved in self-determination is conceived by us as a straightforwardly causal power. Is it conceived as determining outcomes as ordinary causes do?

4. Hobbesian Scepticism about Self-determination

Thomas Hobbes denied the very possibility of self-determination. He mounted his assault on the very idea of self-determination as part of a radical programme to detach ethical and political theory from reliance on the notion. The moral and psychological theory for this programme was principally expounded by Hobbes in a dialogue – the *Questions concerning Liberty, Necessity and Chance* – with an opponent, a defender of Aristotelian scholasticism, the Anglican Bishop Bramhall.[9]

How does Hobbes propose to detach ethics from self-determination? Some of the time, Hobbes does what Hume will do later as well – which is to treat moral blame as no more than negative evaluation:

> [Why do we blame people?] I answer because they please us not. I might ask him, whether blaming be any thing else but saying the thing blamed is ill or imperfect...I answer, they are to be blamed though their wills be not in their power. Is not good good and evil evil though they be not in our power? And shall I not call

---

[9] See *The Questions Concerning Liberty, Necessity and Chance, clearly stated between Dr Bramhall Bishop of Derry, and Thomas Hobbes of Malmesbury* (London, 1656). An edition by me of the *Questions* is forthcoming for the Clarendon edition of the works of Thomas Hobbes.

them so? And is that not praise and blame? But it seems that the Bishop takes blame not for the dispraise of a thing, but for a prae-text and colour of malice and revenge against him that he blameth.[10]

In other contexts Hobbes seems to allow for a distinctive responsibility for how we act:

The nature of sin consisteth in this, that the action done proceed from our will and be against the law.[11]

But the responsibility here involves a kind of legal responsibility – according to a view of that responsibility which avoids appeal to self-determination. Holding someone responsible, in Hobbes's view, seems to involve no more than holding them to sanction-backed directives on the voluntary – something that presupposes no more than their rational responsiveness to such directives. To be morally responsible, on this model, we have merely to be legally governable. But, for Hobbes, that only requires that we be capable of performing or avoiding actions on the basis of a desire so to do, as a means to avoiding sanctions. And this presupposes nothing more than action in the form of Hobbesian voluntariness – something that Hobbes thought had nothing to do with self-determination.

Freedom, for Hobbes, consisted not in a power of agents over alternatives, but in something quite different: namely, in an absence of obstacles to the satisfaction of an ordinary causal power – the power of a motivation to cause its satisfaction. Freedom consists, for example, in the absence of external constraints, such as chains, or sanction-backed laws, that might prevent my desires from causing movements by me that might satisfy them:

Liberty is the absence of all impediments to action, that are not contained in the nature, and in the intrinsecal quality of the agent.[12]

Hobbes's opponent Bramhall was effectively a spokesman for the ethical and psychological theory of the late scholastic Francisco Suarez. And it is Suarez who is the ultimate target of much of Hobbes's writing in this area. In Suarez the idea of freedom really is the idea of a special kind of power – a power that, though still for Suarez a form of causation, is causation of a quite distinctive kind.

---

[10]   Hobbes, *Questions concerning Liberty, Necessity and Chance,* 40
[11]   Ibid., 185
[12]   Ibid., 285

Freedom is causal power in what he describes as *contingent* form.[13] As a free agent I am not a necessary cause as causes in wider nature are – a cause that under any given circumstances can operate in only one way. A massive brick that strikes a window can determine but one outcome – that the window breaks. Whereas, by contrast, I have a power, freedom, by which in one and the same set of circumstances I could equally well determine any one of a range of alternative outcomes. So under a given set of circumstances I have the power, say, to lower my hand or to raise it – and my nature as possessor of the power leaves it contingent how I will exercise it, and so which action I shall perform.

Hobbes denies that such a contingent power is possible, because it is unrecognizable as causal power. For Hobbes's scepticism about freedom is based on a clear view of the only form that power can take in nature. The only possible form that power, the capacity to produce or determine outcomes, can take, in Hobbes's view, is as ordinary causation – the kind of power that bricks, or motions involving them, possess and exercise to break windows.

It is tempting to think that Hobbes's problem with freedom is mainly with what I shall call *multi-wayness*. Freedom or control of what we do involves alternatives. To have control of whether one does A is to be capable of determining either that one does A or that one refrains. And it is very natural to view this control as a single power that could be employed in more than one way – hence multi-wayness – to produce either the outcome that I do A or the outcome that I refrain. That is the nature of control as a power: to leave it up to me which I do, and to be employable in doing either. Hobbes's case, on this reading of him, is simply that there cannot be such a thing as a multi-way power – a power that can, under a given set of circumstances, be used in more than one way, to produce one of a variety of outcomes.

However we should beware of this tempting assumption. It should not be assumed that freedom, understood as its being up to me to determine a range of alternatives, need involve multi-wayness as just defined – a single power employable in more than one way, to produce any one of these alternatives. And in any case, I shall suggest, even if freedom did not involve multi-wayness, it would still involve a form of power which Hobbes denied.

[13]   See Francisco Suarez, *Metaphysical Disputations*, disputation 19: *On causes that act necessarily and causes that act freely or contingently; also, on fate, fortune, and chance* in *Francisco Suarez S.J. on Efficient Causality*, (ed.) Alfred Freddoso, (Yale University Press, 1994).

Moreover, it seems there could be cases of multi-way power that were not at all like freedom, but much more like (possibly slightly unusual) cases of ordinary causal power. True, much ordinary causation seems not to be multi-way – as the case of the brick hitting the window reminds us. Causation here seems to take one-way form. In a given set of circumstances, when the massive brick hits the window, the brick or its motion can exercise its power to produce but one effect – that the window breaks. But need this be true universally? Can there not be probabilistic causes with a power that could, under certain circumstances, operate in more than one way, to produce a range of outcomes? Perhaps the power of one particle to accelerate another could produce in the other particle, with some probability, one acceleration; or perhaps, with another probability, another slightly different acceleration instead. This would still be recognizable as 'ordinary' causal power. And it would not involve the causing particle's possession of freedom. It would not be up to the particle which acceleration it produced; that would not be something that the particle 'determined for itself'.

Hobbes was, of course, a determinist. Probabilistic causation is not a possibility on his metaphysics of causation. He thinks that a cause's power operates, under any given circumstances, to produce but one outcome. But the issue of multi-wayness – the possibility of a causal power's operating under given circumstances in more than one way, to produce more than one possible outcome, is not what is fundamental to Hobbes's scepticism about the very reality of freedom, or indeed of self-determination in any form at all. Hobbes's scepticism has more to do with something that can be detached from multi-wayness, and that radically distinguishes freedom from ordinary causation. I shall call this factor *contingency of determination*; and it has to do with how the possessor of a power, such as a cause, *determines* an outcome when it does.

In Hobbes's view, if an entity has the power to determine a specific outcome, and the circumstances required for the successful exercise of the power are all met – then the power must be exercised. The determining entity's very presence, with its power, must necessitate the occurrence of the outcome it has the power then to determine. It follows on this view that an entity cannot really possess the power to determine, under one and the same set of circumstances, more than one alternative outcome. For an entity really to be capable of determining each outcome, Hobbes argues, it must simultaneously produce each outcome. Referring, abusively, to Suarez's contingent cause as an 'indetermination', Hobbes writes:

But that the indetermination can make it happen or not happen is absurd; for indetermination maketh it equally to happen or not to happen; and therefore both; which is a contradiction. Therefore indetermination doth nothing, and whatsoever causes do, is necessary.[14]

Suarez was right about one thing. Contingent determination is part of our ordinary understanding of freedom, and distinguishes freedom from ordinary causation. In the case of freedom, the power-bearer may have the power to determine the occurrence of a particular outcome, and all the circumstances required for the power's successful exercise may be met – without the power being exercised to produce that outcome. Freedom can involve the power to determine alternatives, only one of which can actually be produced, only because this is so.

Suppose by contrast an ordinary cause has under given circumstances, the power to produce a range of possible effects. The cause is probabilistic: any one of these effects might with some probability occur, or it might not. In such a case the cause does not count as determining the effect that it produces. A probabilistic cause at most influences the occurrence of that effect, but without determining it in a way that removes all dependence of the final outcome on simple chance. Whereas we do think of the free agent as determining that he does what he does, but without the action's performance being guaranteed just by his presence as a free agent with the power then to determine it.[15]

Contingency of determination distinguishes a free agent from any cause – including a probabilistic cause. But so too does something else – something which involves not the power's relation to outcomes, but the agent's or power bearer's relation to the power.

Consider again ordinary causes. Either their operation is predetermined by the very nature of the power and the circumstances of its exercise: in those circumstances their power is to determine one particular outcome, an outcome which they will then produce. Or, as in the case of probabilistic causes, how the cause will operate is undetermined, that is, dependent on mere chance. But what seems importantly to distinguish freedom, as ordinarily conceived, is that this is not so. It is neither predetermined nor merely chance and

---

[14] Hobbes in *Questions Concerning Liberty, Necessity and Chance*, 184
[15] This important distinction between freedom and ordinary causation, and the problem it poses for a view of freedom as a straighforwardly agent-*causal* power, was discussed earlier in my *Free Will: A Very Short Introduction* (Oxford University Press, 2004), 114–15.

undetermined which way a free agent exercises their power. The agent determines for himself how he exercises his power. It is up to the agent whether he exercises his power to produce this outcome or that. If the power of freedom is indeed multi-way, a power employable in more than one way to produce more than one outcome, then in relation to that power there is what we might term a *freedom of specification*: it is up to the bearer which outcome the power is exercised to produce.

Hobbes is very well aware of this element to our conception of freedom as a power. The idea of the agent's determining his exercise of the power is arguably central to self-determination – to the very idea of determining outcomes *for oneself*. In Hobbes's view, this idea of a determination of how the power is exercised is viciously regressive.

> And if a man determine himself, the question will still remain what determined him to determine himself *in that manner*.[16]

The very idea of self-determination, for Hobbes, is incoherent. And that is because it viciously involves the idea of a power to determine, the exercise of which has first to be determined.

But it is not obvious that Hobbes is right about the regress. The regress is vicious only if the way in which the exercise of the power is determined – to produce this outcome or that – involves a prior exercise of power distinct from the exercise of the power determined. But this is not obviously what we ordinarily suppose.

There is in the case of freedom a *conceptual* distinction between (a) the power's relation to outcomes – the power can operate to produce more than one outcome – and (b) the power's relation to me, namely that I determine for myself what way it operates. But we do not suppose there to be any corresponding *ontological* distinction between distinct exercises of power – one exercise of power by me to produce outcomes, and a prior exercise of power to determine that exercise. Multi-wayness and determination of the mode of exercise by me are simply conceptually distinct features of a single exercise of control. In exercising control over outcomes I *ipso facto* determine for myself how the control is exercised. That is what control is – a power to produce outcomes the manner of exercise of which I determine for myself. In one and the same exercise of power I produce one outcome rather than another, and I determine how the power is exercised.

[16] Hobbes in *Questions concerning Liberty, Necessity and Chance*, 26 (my emphasis)

Thomas Pink

Scepticism about freedom has often been directed at freedom conceived in incompatibilist terms. We saw this in Galen Strawson; but such scepticism was strongly expressed long before, by writers such as David Hume. Hume thought that incompatibilist or libertarian freedom was impossible, and impossible because by detaching freedom from prior causal determination – from prior necessity – it reduced freedom to nothing more than the operation of chance. To remove prior necessity – to reduce the influence on the agent of prior causes or remove causal determination – is to leave the final outcome dependent on mere chance.

> … liberty, by removing necessity, removes also causes, and is the very same thing with chance.[17]

Certainly with ordinary causes, if it is not determined in advance what effect a given cause will produce, the outcome must indeed depend, to a degree, on simple chance. If causation is the only power in play, take away prior necessity and you certainly are left with mere chance – chance and nothing else. So to the extent that a cause is merely probabilistic, what effect it will produce depends to a degree on mere chance. But to suppose that in all cases the alternative to necessity is mere chance is to assume that there can be no such power as freedom as we ordinarily understand it – a power involving contingency of determination. For even if the outcome is not already causally predetermined – so that it is initially chancy how the agent will act – freedom, as ordinarily understood, may prevent the final outcome from depending on simple chance. Freedom allows the outcome still to be determined – by the agent. It is arguable, then, that the real target of Hume's scepticism is not freedom conceived in incompatibilist terms, but freedom in a form that involves contingency of determination.

And contingency of determination is not a specifically incompatibilist notion. To say that a power involves contingency of determination, is not itself to say anything about the power's compatibility with causal determinism. All that contingency of determination expressly asserts, is that an agent might possess the power to determine an outcome in the circumstances – and yet still not exercise the power to produce that outcome. It is quite another question whether, compatibly with his possession of the power, the agent's exercising or failing to exercise it could itself be causally determined.

---

[17] David Hume, *A Treatise of Human Nature* ed. P. H. Nidditch (Oxford: Clarendon Press 1978) book 2, part 3, section 1, 'Of liberty and necessity', 407

Where freedom is concerned, there are two forms of scepticism. There is scepticism from the supposed conceptual truth of incompatibilism. But there is also scepticism from freedom's basic identity as a power over alternatives distinct from ordinary causation. The second scepticism denies the very possibility of such a power, not because of any incompatibilist theory of it, but because as ordinarily understood, as a power over alternatives, freedom is too radically unlike the causation found in wider nature. It is this second form of scepticism that may prove the most serious. Indeed, it looks as though, as in Hume's case, some of the first kind of scepticism might really depend on the second. Freedom is indistinguishable from chance only if there can be no such thing as a power that is distinct from ordinary causation – a power to determine alternatives that can operate even in cases where the final outcome is initially undetermined causally.

5. Freedom and Reduction

We have been examining freedom as a basis of moral responsibility, and what seems distinctive, and metaphysically problematic perhaps because so distinctive, about power so conceived. But need freedom be so metaphysically distinctive? What of theories of freedom that instead of distancing freedom from ordinary causation, appeal to ordinary causation to explain what freedom is, and especially its involvement of alternatives?

Classical post-Hobbesian English language compatibilism adopted such an account. In that intellectual tradition, self-determination as power to determine alternatives, and so to determine otherwise, was not dismissed as Hobbes dismissed it, but was instead simply constructed from Hobbes's theory of action – out of voluntariness. Hobbes had rejected this as a possible theory of self-determination: but the English language philosophical tradition that followed him, and which was deeply influenced by him in other respects, did not. Was this whole compatibilist tradition misconceived; or should it have followed Hobbes's more radical example of abandoning self-determination altogether?

Classical English-language compatibilism explains freedom in terms of a combination of distinct cases of voluntariness as involving ordinary one-way causal power. So the account of freedom is *ontologically reductive*. The power to determine alternatives is not a single multi-way power that can be used to determine more than one outcome, but is explained as constructed out of a combination of distinct one-way powers. And the account is *conceptually reductive*. No appeal is made to any conceptually primitive notion of freedom or up-to-us-ness to characterize the agent's relation to the power.

For it to be true that it is up to me whether I do A, on this theory, the following must then be true:

if I were motivated to do A, that would causally determine me to do A.

if I were motivated to refrain, that would causally determine me to refrain.

The ontological reduction of freedom's involvement of alternatives in terms of a combination of distinct cases of one-way causal power is very important in its implications for ethics and moral responsibility. It explains why in our own day so many philosophers, and principally Harry Frankfurt, have come so readily to assume the irrelevance of freedom to moral responsibility. Defining freedom in terms of voluntariness profoundly changes our view of what is going on when an agent exercises freedom to determine what he does, and in a way that detaches moral responsibility from freedom as a power to determine alternatives by way of action – as involving a power to act otherwise.

The distinctive feature of freedom or control as a power over action, we have supposed, is its involvement of alternatives. To be free is to have control over whether one does A or not. And I have said that it is natural to understand this involvement of alternatives in terms of multi-wayness – a single power that could under given circumstances be used to produce more than one action or outcome. One and the same power could be exercised either to do A, or to refrain. To do A through exercising this power is to do A through the exercise of a power to do otherwise – a power, control of which action one performs, that could equally have been used to omit doing A. To possess that power of control with respect to an action's performance is, equally, to possess it with respect to the action's omission.

Whereas voluntariness is obviously quite different. To do A voluntarily is to do A because one decides or wants to. But this capacity to do A on the basis of wanting to do it would in no way be involved in refraining to do A. Voluntarily to refrain from doing A would involve the quite distinct power to refrain from doing A on the basis of wanting to refrain. And the powers really are distinct, in that each power can be possessed without the other. To use Locke's example: I can possess and be exercising a power to stay in my room on the basis of wanting to; but, unbeknown to me, the door may be locked, and I altogether lack the power to leave should I so want.[18] Moreover, as distinct, the two powers are exercised quite separately: each of these two powers is exercised without any exercise of the other – we obviously cannot at one and the same time both be doing A on the basis of our power voluntarily to do A, and refraining from doing A on the basis of our power voluntarily to refrain.

Voluntariness can only be used to provide an account of freedom, then, by appealing to an agent's possession of both these two distinct voluntary powers – both a power to do A voluntarily and also a power voluntarily to refrain; and by then claiming that the agent is exercising his freedom whenever he is exercising one of these powers. Instead of a single power that is inherently multi-way, we have a combination of two distinct one-way powers. But if freedom is indeed just a combination of two distinct powers for voluntariness, then freedom will surely drop out as a distinct condition on moral responsibility. And that is because, on this classic reductive account of freedom, the only power of self-determination we ever exercise is voluntariness. Freedom as a power to do otherwise is left a power that is never exercised at all.

On the classical English-language compatibilist reduction, whenever I do A, the power of self-determination which I am exercising is the power to do A voluntarily. But this, very evidently, is not a power to act otherwise. Any power to act otherwise – to refrain – that I may possess is quite distinct. It is the power voluntarily to refrain from doing A. And even if this power does happen to be possessed, it is certainly not being exercised. It is quite inert. Its absence would make no difference to the power I am actually exercising, since the two powers are distinct and independent of each other. In which case, the presence or absence of this unexercised power to act otherwise must be irrelevant to my moral responsibility for what I do. How can moral responsibility ever depend on a kind of power that is never actually exercised to determine what we do? But that, on this reductive account of freedom, is precisely what the power to do otherwise becomes.

Our moral responsibility for action depends on the fact that we ourselves determine how we act. The question then is what kind of self-determining power we really exercise. For that will provide the true basis of our moral responsibility. Is it that we are exercising a power to act otherwise? Or is that we are acting as we will and

---

[18]   See John Locke, *An Essay Concerning Human Understanding*, (ed.) P.H. Nidditch (Oxford: Clarendon Press, 1975), Book 2, chapter 21 'Of power', §10, 238

Thomas Pink

because we so will? Which matters – control or voluntariness? The idea of freedom as a complex case of voluntariness is an attempt to combine both conceptions. But it is a deeply unstable compromise, and control is surely going to be the loser. And this is because the power to act otherwise is never actually being exercised to determine action – only a power to act as one wills. The power to act otherwise is present, but as a dummy that plays no active role at all. Why make moral responsibility depend on it, if it is irrelevant to any power that the agent actually exercises over how he acts?

It is this transformation in the theory of freedom that left it so easy for Frankfurt to think that moral responsibility must be independent of any freedom to do otherwise:

> When a person acts for reasons of his own, and is guided entirely by his own beliefs and preferences, the question of whether he could have done something else instead is quite irrelevant to the assessment of his moral responsibility. Analyses purporting to show that agents do invariably have alternatives are simply not to the point, when there is no reason to suppose that having those alternatives affects the decision or conduct of the agents in any way.[19]

It might seem initially puzzling why Frankfurt should say this. Suppose the power I exercise over how I act, and that bases my moral responsibility for how I act, is an inherently multi-way power of freedom that could equally be used to do A or to refrain. Then surely the presence or absence of an alternative to whichever I actually do, which comes with the presence or absence of the power to determine that alternative, would imply a difference to my actual decision or conduct in one crucial respect. It would betoken the very presence or absence of power on my part to determine what I do. But now it is clear why Frankfurt is denying this. For he is assuming that as a power over alternatives, freedom is not an inherently multi-way power.

He is assuming that the apparently multi-way power of freedom decomposes into two distinct cases of one-way power: a power to do A and a further and distinct but otherwise like kind of power to refrain. This one-way power that is used to construct and compose freedom and that, in effect, replaces it, is supposed to be recognizably a power of self-determination, sufficient to base the agent's moral

[19]   Harry Frankfurt, 'Some thoughts concerning the principle of alternate possibilities' in *Moral Responsibility and Alternative Possibilities*, (eds) David Widerker and Michael McKenna (Ashgate, 2003), 340

responsibility for what he does. And when we exercise our power to determine our actions for ourselves, it is only ever this one-way power that we exercise. There really is no inherently multi-way power of self-determination that could be exercised instead. Granted this account of self-determination, the presence or absence of a freedom to act otherwise would make no difference to the power being exercised by the agent over what he does – and so it would indeed be of no relevance to the agent's moral responsibility for what he does.

Of course it is far from obvious that the power by which we actually determine what we do really is a composite of distinct one-way powers. Whether we are incompatibilists or compatibilists, why not suppose that freedom is what it appears to be – a multi-way power that leaves it up to us, within our control, which action we perform? And in fact our conviction that freedom is of immediate relevance to moral responsibility suggests that our understanding of freedom is of a single multi-way power. As far as intuition is concerned, its being up to me which action I perform provides immediate support for how I act being my responsibility; and my lacking control over which action I perform provides equally intuitive support for my not being responsible. And that suggests that our ordinary conception of freedom does not allow for its reduction into distinct cases of one-way power.

Frankfurt has of course claimed to *prove* that moral responsibility does not depend on any freedom to act otherwise. In his 'Moral responsibility and alternate possibilities' he asks us to consider examples where, he argues, an agent Jones is deprived of the freedom not to perform some action A, not by anyone else actually intervening to make him do A, but by the mere possibility of their so intervening.[20] Someone very knowledgeable and powerful, Black, is monitoring Jones to check that he really is going to do A. Should he show any sign of acting otherwise Black would certainly act to ensure that Jones did indeed still do A. Hence, thanks just to Black's potent but inactive presence, Jones lacks the freedom not to do A. But Black does not have to intervene, since Jones goes ahead and does A 'off his own back' and independently. In fact he does A in just the same way that he would have done had Black not been present, so that he remained free not to do A. Jones does A anyway, independently of Black.

---

[20]   'Alternate possibilities and moral responsibility' in Harry Frankfurt, *The Importance of What We Care About* (Cambridge University Press, 1988), 1–10.

Since Black's presence and the concomitant lack of a freedom to do otherwise make no difference to what Jones does and why he does it –

> Indeed everything happened just as it would have happened without Black's presence in the situation and without his readiness to intrude into it.[21]

– they can make no difference to Jones's moral responsibility. The presence or absence of freedom must in itself be irrelevant. Jones must be morally responsible whether or not he is free to act otherwise.

Frankfurt is taking cases where his opponents would already accept that the agent is morally responsible – which *ex hypothesi* are cases where the agent is free to act otherwise; and hopes to show that these cases can be transformed into examples where the agent is not free to act otherwise, but without change in any features of the case that might be relevant to the agent's moral responsibility. The removal of the agent's freedom to act otherwise must make no difference to how the agent acts and to the power deployed by him to determine how he acts. That's why Frankfurt is so keen to emphasise that, with the removal of Jones's freedom

> Indeed everything happened just as it would have happened without Black's presence in the situation and without his readiness to intrude into it.

If Black's potent but inert presence does indeed make no difference, someone who believes in Jones's moral responsibility given his freedom to do otherwise and Black's concomitant absence, will remain committed to admitting Jones's moral responsibility even given Black's presence – and even given the consequent lack of any freedom to act otherwise. Having admitted Jones's moral responsibility initially, they must go on admitting it even when Black is introduced into the story.

But this strategy will only work if the removal of a freedom to act otherwise does make no difference to how the agent acts and to the power deployed by him to determine how he acts. And that will only be true if agents do determine how they act by exercising power in one-way form, and not in a form that is inherently multi-way. The problem for Frankfurt is that those who believe that moral responsibility does depend on a freedom to do otherwise cannot accept his view that human self-determination is exercised only in one-way form. They are committed to maintaining the opposite – that human self-determination is only ever exercised

---

[21]   Harry Frankfurt, 'Alternate possibilities and moral responsibility', 7

through a power of freedom that is inherently multi-way. Why else would moral responsibility depend on the freedom to do otherwise? For if self-determination were exercised in one-way form, then the irrelevance of a freedom to do otherwise to moral responsibility would follow immediately – as we have already seen, and without having to appeal to complicated Frankfurtian thought-experiments.

Frankfurt's opponents cannot be expected to admit that the presence or absence even of a Black who does not actually intervene is irrelevant to Jones's moral responsibility. For in so far as the presence of Black, willing and able to intervene, and with consequent control over Jones's action, did imply the absence in Jones of any power to act otherwise, Black's presence would – in their view – also mean that Jones lacked any power to determine for himself how he would act. And lacking that power, Jones would lack moral responsibility for his actions. Thanks to what Black's intentions and ability to determine Jones imply for Jones's own powers, Jones simply cannot be determining his action as he might in a world where Black were absent.[22]

The work is all done, then, by Frankfurt's assumption that self-determination is exercised only in one-way form. And the Frankfurt cases are irrelevant to the argument. They do no actual work themselves. For once we grant that self-determination is only ever exercised in one-way form then, as we have seen, Frankfurt's claim of the irrelevance of freedom to moral responsibility follows immediately, and without the need to appeal to complex Frankfurt-cases. On the other hand, without this assumption, the Frankfurt-cases cannot be used to prove freedom's irrelevance anyway. For Black's presence or absence can no longer be assumed to imply no

[22]   Robert Kane endorses what he calls 'a powerful intuition': 'we feel that if a Frankfurt-controller [such as Black] never actually intervened throughout an agent's entire lifetime, so that the agent always acted on his or her own, then the *mere presence* of the controller should not make any difference to the agent's ultimate responsibility.' Robert Kane, *The Significance of Free Will* (Oxford University Press, 1998), 143. But what is crucial is the implications of that presence for the agent's power. If Black is not only intent on preventing the agent from acting otherwise, but is fully able to prevent him from so acting, and if (as is supposed) Black's presence equipped with such an intention and such a power over the agent is enough to imply the agent lacks all power to act otherwise, then that may be very relevant to the agent's ultimate responsibility. It will be relevant if the agent can determine his actions for himself only through exercising an inherently multi-way power to act otherwise.

difference in Jones's power to determine for himself what he does. When Frankfurt expressly asserts

> Indeed *everything* happened just as it would have happened without Black's presence in the situation and without his readiness to intrude into it.

that claim can only be true if the power exercised over Jones's action to determine what he does is one-way and not multi-way. And that is just the point at issue.

6. One-way Self-determination

The classical compatibilist reduction of freedom to a complex form of voluntariness looks unhappy – but not just because it denies multi-wayness. The denial of multi-wayness makes the reduction implausible as an account of the power of freedom that we ordinarily take ourselves to possess, because inconsistent with the ethical significance we ordinarily accord the freedom to do otherwise. But the reduction contains other features that are problematic in more fundamental ways – that make the reduction implausible as an account of self-determination in any form at all.

There are two related difficulties. The first is that a compatibilist conception of moral responsibility is being built into the theory from the outset. Self-determination is being explained in terms of the determination of action by some entity that is distinct from the agent, and that, as prior to what the agent is responsible for, is not itself the agent's responsibility. But this obviously presupposes that the self-determined character of action must be compatible with the action's determination by factors for which the agent is not responsible. The problem is clear. Apparently competent users of concepts of moral responsibility and blameworthiness disagree about whether compatibilism about moral responsibility is true. But that makes it implausible that compatibilism about moral responsibility, even if it proves to be true, should follow immediately and trivially from our very concept of the power that leaves us responsible.

The worry is reinforced, and in a way that does not involve any assumption of incompatibilism, by the distinctive nature of moral blame – the criticism that asserts moral responsibility. As we have already noted, ordinary rational criticism operates at just one level. It criticizes the person by reference to some deficiency in a state or occurrence in the life of that person. We criticize someone as irrational because they hold or are disposed to hold attitudes that

246

are irrational. The criticism is of defective states and of the person just as possessing those defective states. Blame, on the other hand, does not simply criticize someone for deficiencies in their attitudes or other states but puts their possession of such states down to them as their fault. This supposes something more – a problem not simply with events and states in the agent's life, but with the agent as determiner of those events and states. But explaining such determination in terms of voluntariness removes this distinctive element. The supposed problem with the agent as determiner is turned back into a problem that primarily involves an event or state within their life, such as a motivation, and the agent just as possessor of the event or state. In which case, what is left of the idea that the agent is especially responsible, in a way that goes beyond ordinary criticizability?

But none of this is necessarily to reject one fundamental theoretical ambition of Frankfurt's, which is to establish that moral responsibility can be detached, at least *conceptually*, from being based on any power to determine alternatives by way of action. Frankfurt may not have proved that, as things are, our moral responsibility does not actually depend on a freedom to act or determine otherwise. But it may still be at least conceptually possible that moral responsibility should have been independent of such a freedom.

Our ordinary conception of self-determination takes it to involve a multi-way power – a power to produce more than one outcome – and this multi-wayness is fundamental to the ethical significance of its involvement of alternatives. It is this multi-wayness, if anything does, that leaves moral responsibility dependent on a freedom to act otherwise. But multi-wayness is not obviously essential to self-determination, nor what distinguishes self-determination most fundamentally from ordinary causal power. For we saw that probabilistic causation could perhaps involve multi-way causal power: one and the same power could operate, under a given set of circumstances, to produce a variety of possible outcomes, such as different rates of acceleration. Even the thought, arguably essential to self-determination, that the bearer of the power must be the self, the agent, and not a mere occurrence, does not obviously differentiate self-determination from ordinary causation. Ordinary causal power has often been understood to be a power not, or not simply, of occurrences, but a power of substances too. The cause of the window's breaking may be understood to be not just the event of the brick's hitting it, but the brick itself, when it hits the window.

What is most distinctive of self-determination as a power, and most sharply distinguishes it from ordinary causal power? What is

Thomas Pink

distinctive flows from the basic thought that in exercising the power the agent must really be determining outcomes *for himself*. The agent is the determiner of what he does, and in a way that does not subordinate his role either to prior determining factors for which he is not responsible or to simple chance. It is this aspect of self-determination that makes incompatibilism about the power, and about the moral responsibility that rests upon it, at least an initial theoretical possibility, and so – as it clearly is – a matter for real debate, rather than something ruled out by the very nature of the power. The alternative to the action's determination by factors for which the agent is not responsible is not, as Hume alleged, the operation of mere chance.

This is missing from ordinary causation. To the extent that an ordinary cause determines an outcome, this involves prior factors, the circumstances under which the cause is found together with its own causal power – what in the circumstances it is capable of determining – ensuring that it operates to produce that very outcome. How the cause will operate is already predetermined, and not left up to the cause. If the cause's operation is not so predetermined – if what outcome it operates to produce is not already settled by its powers and circumstances – then the cause can at most influence and not determine what will happen. And its operation, far from being determined by it or by anything else, will depend on mere chance.

What prevents this being true where self-determination is concerned? We have seen that two related factors are crucial. There is contingency of determination, which leaves it open whether an agent with the power to determine a given outcome will so exercise his power. The agent's exercise of action-determining power is not *ipso facto* predetermined by factors for which he need not be responsible. The second factor is freedom – not in relation to outcomes, but in relation to the agent's very exercise of power. The agent's exercise of power is not undetermined, but up to the agent, so that the agent determines that exercise for himself.

This involvement of the agent as determinant of his own exercise of power is what Hobbes objected to in his attack on the very idea of self-determination. But we can detach this aspect of self-determination from multi-wayness – the identity of freedom as a power to determine more than one outcome. For there could be a one-way power the exercise of which was up to the agent. Obviously if the power were one-way – under given circumstances there is only one outcome its exercise can produce – it could not then be up to us *how* we exercised it, to produce this outcome or that. In relation to a one-way power, there could be no room for what we have termed a freedom of *specification*.

248

But it could still be up to us whether we exercised the power at all. There is room, then, for our possession, even in relation to a one-way power, of a *freedom of exercise* – a freedom to use the power or not. Self-determination could involve the exercise of a power to determine but one outcome, where it was up to the agent, not which outcome he determined – that is fixed by the one-way nature of the power – but whether he exercised the power at all.

If self-determination did take this one-way form, we could still possess freedom as its being up to us which actions we perform. For alternatives to be left up to the agent it would be enough that the agent should possess each of a power to determine that he does A and a distinct power to determine that he refrains – and a freedom of exercise in relation to each of these powers. That would leave it up to the agent which power he exercised and so whether he did A or not – just as freedom requires. But since no multi-way power would be involved in the determination of action, no power to do otherwise – to determine alternative actions or outcomes – would ever be exercised by the agent in the determination of what he actually does. In which case the power to do or determine otherwise would remain an inert extra. It might be lacking without making any difference to what the agent is actually doing, or to the power actually exercised by him to determine what he does. In which case the power or freedom to act otherwise – freedom as a power over alternatives by way of action – would be irrelevant to moral responsibility, just as Frankfurt supposes.

Such an account of freedom as power over alternatives by way of action would be ontologically reductive. Freedom would no longer be characterized as a multi-way power – a power to determine more than one outcome. It would be decomposed into a combination of distinct one-way powers. But the theory of freedom would no longer be conceptually reductive. A primitive notion of freedom would still be deployed within the theory, to characterize the agent's relation to the power itself, as involving a freedom of exercise.

We now see that we can appeal to one-way self-determination to provide a theory of freedom that is very close to our ordinary understanding of it, but which abandons the multi-wayness that is so clearly an element of that ordinary understanding. On this theory the bearer of the one-way power is the agent, and not some other entity for which the agent has no responsibility; and it is genuinely up to the agent whether he exercises the power. The power of self-determination involved is plainly sufficient to base moral blame as we ordinarily understand it. So it looks as though there is certainly no conceptual dependence of moral responsibility on a freedom of

Thomas Pink

alternatives at the point of action. It is conceptually perfectly open that an agent be morally responsible for what they do, without possessing a freedom to act otherwise. On that specific issue, Frankfurt seems to be right.

Frankfurt supposes, though, that from the conceptual possibility of moral responsibility without the freedom to do otherwise, it follows that our moral responsibility is actually independent of the freedom to do otherwise. But that is a simple mistake, and does not follow. Our moral responsibility may still actually depend on a freedom to do otherwise, but without this following from the very concepts of moral responsibility and self-determination. For it might be a non-conceptual or a contingent truth, but a truth nonetheless, that the only power that we actually possess and exercise to determine how we act is a multi-way power, and even one additionally involving a freedom of specification in relation to the manner of its exercise. In the absence of this power, we would be simply incapable of self-determination in any form. In the absence of a freedom to do otherwise, we would not be morally responsible at all. There is nothing in Frankfurt's arguments to rule out the possibility that we are actually capable of self-determination only in this multi-way form.

Our belief in freedom does seem to be a belief in our possession of a multi-way power to determine alternatives. But because it is at least conceptually open that we could be morally responsible without such a power, this raises a doubt about the hypothesis that entirely locates the origin of our belief in multi-way freedom in a theory of blame. The hypothesis, a sceptical one, was that our belief in multi-way freedom is not based on anything genuinely in human nature, or even on the way that human nature and human action is represented in experience to us. Instead it comes from an intrusion of ethics into psychology. We postulate the power only because forced into it by our belief in our moral responsibility and by our practice of blaming people, and putting their faults down to them as their fault.

This hypothesis is put in doubt because it now appears that we could intelligibly hold people morally responsible for what they do without any belief in freedom as a multi-way power. We have just established that we could operate a theory of moral blame and moral responsibility that justifiably puts faults in the agent down to the agent as their fault, and even left room for an incompatibilist conception of that responsibility and the power that based it, but which did not involve a conception of that power as multi-way, and that consequently did not treat the agent's responsibility as depending on the power to do otherwise. Belief in the multi-wayness of self-determination and in a freedom of specification in relation to that power seems strictly inessential to our ordinary understanding of moral blame. In which case it may well come from elsewhere.

The problem of free will and moral responsibility is often thought to be a conceptual problem. Our concept of moral responsibility is supposed by itself to fix the nature of the power of self-determination that bases it; or the concept of freedom as involving a power over alternatives is supposed to fix the properties of the power in other respects, such as its compatibility with determinism. But now we see that this may not be so. The concept of moral responsibility places some demands on self-determination[23] – but not to the extent of demanding power over alternatives by way of action. And the very idea of power over alternatives does not even fix the composition of that power.

We might wonder then if the relation of freedom to other powers, such as prior causation, is conceptually determined either. After all, why should relations of compatibility or otherwise between powers always be conceptually determined? We would not usually assume that for distinct cases of causal power. But that is another topic.[24]

Kings College, London
tom.pink@kcl.ac.uk

[23] How extensive these demands may be is not entirely obvious. Frankfurt's arguments oppose a dependence of self-determination, and so of moral responsibility, on the freedom to act otherwise, that is on the availability of alternatives in respect of what that power determines – actions and their outcomes. But does the very possibility of self-determination depend on freedom at a more primitive level – freedom in relation to the very exercise of power? That may depend on whether the idea of the agent's power to determine outcomes *for himself* – the idea to which Hobbes took such exception – needs to be unpacked in terms of freedom at least in relation to the power.

[24] This topic, and the general argument of this paper, is taken further in my *The Ethics of Action*, volume 1 *Self-Determination* (Oxford University Press, forthcoming)

The Mental States of Persons and their Brains

TIM CRANE

Abstract

Cognitive neuroscientists frequently talk about the brain representing the world. Some philosophers claim that this is a confusion. This paper argues that there is no confusion, and outlines one thing that 'the brain represents the world' might mean, using the notion of a model derived from the philosophy of science. This description is then extended to make apply to propositional attitude attributions. A number of problems about propositional attitude attributions can be solved or dis-solved by treating propositional attitudes as models.

1. Does the Brain Think?

Consider a picture of a domino with an arrangement of apparently concave and convex circles. The same picture rotated through 180 degrees makes the concavity and the convexity appear reversed. Why does this happen? Why does the very same picture, the same arrangement of pixels or ink on a page, appear so different when turned upside down? Chris Frith gives the following answer in *Making Up The Mind*:

> The light of the sun comes from above ... this means that concave objects will be dark at the top and light at the bottom, while convex objects will be light at the top and dark at the bottom. Our brain has a simple rule built into its wiring. It uses this rule to decide whether an object is concave or convex.[1]

Frith claims that the brain has a rule built into it and uses this rule to makes decisions about how things seem. Taken literally, saying that the brain 'uses' a rule, as opposed to merely behaving in a rule-governed or law-like way, implies that the brain somehow represents the content of the rule. And saying that the brain makes decisions implies that the brain is something like a thinker; in short, the brain thinks.

---

[1]   Chris Frith, *Making Up the Mind* (Oxford: Wiley-Blackwell 2007), 128.

doi:10.1017/S1358246115000053

Tim Crane

For those like Frith, the idea that the brain represents the world (or 'thinks'), should be accepted as part of the orthodox ideology of cognitive science or cognitive neuroscience. Others say that the question is totally confused.[2] For them, this kind of talk embodies a mistake; or even worse, a fallacy (and not all mistakes are fallacies). M.K. Bennett and P.M.S. Hacker have argued that it is an instance of what they call the 'mereological fallacy': the 'mistake of ascribing to the constituent parts of an animal attributes that logically apply only to the whole animal'.[3] In this they take themselves to be following Wittgenstein, who famously said that 'only of a human being and what resembles (behaves like) a living human being can one say: it has sensation; it sees, is blind; hears, is deaf; is conscious or unconscious'.[4] A brain doesn't resemble a living human being; it doesn't even resemble something that resembles a living human being. A chimpanzee at least resembles something that has thoughts; the brain does not even resemble a chimpanzee.

Bennett and Hacker think it's not empirically or straightforwardly false that the brain represents the world. Rather, it is a conceptual truth 'that perception, thoughts and feelings are attributes of human beings, not of their parts – in particular not of their brains'.[5] So it is a fallacy to say something which is incompatible with this conceptual truth. But the supposed fallacy cannot derive from any conceptual principle that you cannot, in general, attribute things to the parts of a system that you would also attribute to the whole. There are many cases where you can do this (e.g. weight, colour etc.) which of course Bennett and Hacker will not deny. So if there is a fallacy here, it must be to do with the use of the terms 'thought' or 'sensation' or 'consciousness' or 'thinking' or 'deciding': mental terms in general.

It is true that the paradigm applications of the concepts of thought, decision, sensation and so on are to organisms: things like human beings and those animals which it makes sense to describe as conscious or thinking. But often we extend the use of words creatively beyond their paradigm applications, to illuminate or illustrate some significant feature of the thing described. Stephen Mulhall makes this point in a recent discussion of the concept of a picture.

---

[2]   See M.R. Bennett and P.M.S. Hacker, *Philosophical Foundations of Neuroscience* (Oxford: Wiley-Blackwell, 2003).
[3]   Ibid., 72.
[4]   Ludwig   Wittgenstein,   *Philosophical   Investigations*   (Oxford: Blackwell, 1953), §281.
[5]   M.K. Bennett and P.M.S. Hacker, *Philosophical Foundations of Neuroscience*, 3.

The Mental States of Persons and their Brains

In considering what he calls the 'projectability of language', Mulhall writes,

> The word 'picture' denotes, among other things, abstract paintings, representational paintings and films, i.e. motion pictures. Although abstract paintings and films each have something in common with representational paintings, there seem to be no relevant features common to a Jackson Pollock drip painting and a projected image of Humphrey Bogart, and yet we have no inclination – do we? – to say that the word has one meaning in a conversation about *Casablanca* and another when the talk turns to *Lavender Mist*.

He continues,

> If someone were to construct such a pattern of use from scratch, we might find it rather puzzling. But if we see it as a process of historical development, the puzzle dissolves. In the case of 'picture', the original focus on representational painting naturally licenses an extension of the term's use to photographs and thence to motion pictures; and developments in painting also made natural a different extension of the term to include canvasses of a non-representational sort.[6]

As the use of the word develops across time, we can extend its use by applying it intelligibly to other things. We find it very natural to extend the use of a word beyond some original or initial contexts, without the word changing its meaning in any strict sense. Another simple example is the concept of flying. Suppose a child asks, can a person fly? Of course people can't fly, we might reply; Superman can't really fly, it's only a story. So what is it to fly? Perhaps we might say something like this: to be propelled through the air, by using the motion of wings (as a bird flies) or some other kind of mechanism attached to the flying object (as a rocket flies).

But what if I tell you that I am flying to Turin in a few weeks' time? Then we should give another answer to the question 'can people fly?'. Of course people can fly: travelling in an aeroplane is flying. It would be at best a bad joke to respond to the question 'did you fly here, or did you come by train?' by saying 'no, I can't have flown here, because to fly is to propel yourself through the air using wings or some other kind of mechanism'. And yet, as Mulhall says about

---

[6] Stephen Mulhall, Stanton lectures 2014, University of Cambridge (unpublished).

Tim Crane

pictures, there should be no temptation to say that the word has one meaning in the first conversation and a different meaning in the second. Just as developments in painting led to the natural extension of the word 'picture' to Pollock's work, so developments in aeronautical technology led to a natural extension of the word 'fly' to what people do when they go somewhere by plane: in this sense, people can fly. When we focus on the historical development of the use of the word, any puzzlement we felt about giving different answers in the two scenarios should vanish.

As Mulhall says, this possibility of words having uses which extend across many different kinds of case, without being ambiguous or polysemous, is something to which Wittgenstein drew attention:

> I can think of no better expression to characterise these similarities than 'family resemblances'; for the various resemblances between members of a family: build, features, colour of eyes, gait, temperament, and so on and so forth – overlap and crisscross in the same way. – And I shall say: 'games' form a family.[7]

The relationship between the different uses or meanings of the words 'picture' and 'fly' in our scenarios seems to be a kind of family resemblance of the sort Wittgenstein talks about. To say this is not to propose or defend any particular theory or account of meaning; it is simply to draw attention to a phenomenon. But once we have recognised this phenomenon, we thereby open up the possibility of making sense of the idea that the brain thinks or represents the world.

However, some may object at this point that the meaninglessness of saying that the brain thinks is underwritten by the well-established distinction between the personal and sub-personal levels of psychological explanation and description. The concepts of thought, decision, and so on belong to the personal level, and we should not extend them to the sub-personal level. Before explaining what I think it means to say that the brain thinks, I need to put this objection to one side.

Daniel Dennett introduced the personal/sub-personal distinction in *Content and Consciousness* in the context of a discussion of pain:

> When we've said that a person has a sensation of pain, that he locates it and is prompted to react in a certain way, we have said all there is to say within the scope of this vocabulary. Since the introduction of unanalysable mental qualities leads to a premature end to explanation, we may decide that such an

---

[7] Wittgenstein, *Philosophical Investigations*, §67.

introduction is wrong, and look for alternative modes of explanation. If we do this, we must abandon the explanatory level of
people and their sensations and activities, and turn to the sub-
personal level of brains and events in the nervous system.[8]

As Dennett's remark about 'alternative modes of explanation' indicates, the personal and sub-personal are two modes of explanation
of the one cognitive system. The personal mode of explanation
appeals to concepts like *sensation* and then *behaviour*, *location* and
reaction; and the alternative explanatory level of the sub-personal
appeals to brains, nerves, neurones, synapses and events in the
nervous system.

Dennett points out that the lesson about the personal/sub-person-
al distinction has occasionally been misconstrued 'as the lesson that
the personal level of explanation is the *only* level of explanation
when the subject matter is human minds and actions'.[9] Now a
strict and literal reading of Wittgenstein's remark about 'only of a
human being and what resembles a living human being...' would presumably entail this claim that the personal level is the only level of
explanation that matters when the subject matter is human minds
and actions. But this is not Dennett's view. In his commentary on
Bennett and Hacker's idea of a mereological fallacy, he writes,

> we don't attribute fully-fledged beliefs to the brain parts. That
> would be a fallacy but we attribute an attenuated sort of belief
> to these parts, stripped of many of its everyday connotations.
> Just as a young child can sort of believe that her daddy is a
> doctor, without full comprehension of what a daddy or a
> doctor is, so a robot, or some part of a person's brain can sort
> of believe that there is an open door a few feet ahead... far from
> being a mistake to attribute hemi-semi-demi-proto-quasi-
> pseudo-intentionality to the mereological parts of persons, it is
> precisely the enabling move that lets us see how on earth to get
> the whole wonderful persons out of brute mechanical parts.[10]

Dennett's view is clearly that the distinction between the personal
and the sub-personal levels of explanation is clearly compatible
with two ideas: (i) that we might extend to the sub-personal level

[8]   Dennett, *Content and Consciousness* (London: Routledge and Kegan
Paul 1969) 95.
[9]   Ibid., 95.
[10]   Daniel C. Dennett, 'Philosophy as Naive Anthropology: Comment on
Bennett and Hacker' in *Neuroscience and Philosophy* (New York: Columbia
University Press, 2007), 87–9.

words whose paradigmatic application is at the personal level; (ii) that we might use this extension to help us explain how intentionality at the personal level is possible. One could reject either or both of these ideas, but this rejection is not implied by the very distinction between the personal and the sub-personal.

So this brings us back to our question, what does it mean to say that the brain thinks, or represents the world? I take Frith's comments quoted above as representative: many cognitive neuroscientists and others are perfectly happy to talk in terms of the brain representing the world. Given this, Hacker's approach leaves us with a mystery: how is it that so many people, apparently highly competent in their use of language and highly knowledgable about the empirical facts, fall so easily into such a simple fallacy? What is more, why is it that they are so resistant to recognising that they have made this apparently simple mistake?

I will argue in the rest of this paper that in fact it is not a mistake, and I will attempt to explain what it means to say that the brain represents the world. Just as it makes perfect sense to say that people fly, and it makes perfect sense to say that a Jackson Pollock painting is a picture, so similarly it makes sense to say that the brain represents the world, or even that it thinks. If we allow for words to extend their meaning through a historical process, then we can see how this is not obviously meaningless. In fact, on broadly Wittgensteinian grounds, we should accept that such transfers and extensions of meaning are part of the essence of our language, and there is nothing in principle stopping the talk of neuroscientists being such a case. But how should we spell out this idea that the brain represents?

2. Contents as Models

One answer to this question, going back to the 1970s, is that representation in the brain involves there literally being symbols written in your brain: there are symbols which represent the contents of your beliefs and other personal mental states, or your sub-personal states, or both. These symbols are part of what's known as a 'language of thought'; this view was defended by Jerry Fodor in 1975.[11] Fodor

---

[11] Jerry A. Fodor, *The Language of Thought* (Hassocks: Harvester 1975). For a critical overview, see Susan Schneider, *The Language of Thought* (Cambridge, Mass.: MIT Press 2011).

argued that there can't really be beliefs unless there are representations in the brain.

The main problem with the Language of Thought hypothesis, to be blunt, is that there is no reason to believe there is such a thing as the Language of Thought. Some people hypothesise that there might be such a thing for the sake of argument, but few of those who say this never defend the idea that it really exists (and even Fodor himself is sceptical these days[12]). As Frances Egan remarks: 'There isn't much empirical support for this view. It's a very elegant picture but it's not likely to be the way that minds developed naturally, as a product of evolution, in fits and starts'.[13]

Instead of speculating about the inner structure of the brain, or simply denying that representation in the brain makes any sense, we should ask instead of what it is that people are doing when they attribute representations to the brain – when they say things like 'the brain knows that light comes from above'. What is it that those who attribute intentional states are actually doing in this kind of case?

The interpreter is the theorist – the neuroscientist or psychologist – who is trying to provide the best explanatory structure to account for how the system moves from one state to the next. The system, in the cases we are considering, is the brain, and what the theorist is trying to do is to explain why the system moves from one state to another. There are states of the system which the theorist can then map on to what I'm going to call its contents. The content might be something like the rule that *if the object is light at the top and dark at the bottom then this is a convex object*, for example. Contents are related to the intrinsic or non-intrinsic states of the system by a *mapping* provided by the theorist; that is to say, a correlation between the states of the system and the content. I suggest that we think of the content as part of a *model* of the system, in the sense in which this word is used in the philosophy of science.

It is a familiar claim in recent philosophy of science that scientific theories are 'collections of models'; but given the variety of things the word 'model' has come to mean, some clarifications are needed. The original proposal that theories should be thought of in terms of models is normally traced back to Patrick Suppes's work in the 1960s, subsequently developed by Bas van Fraassen.[14] Suppes and

---

[12] Jerry A. Fodor, *LOT2* (Oxford: Oxford University Press, 2008).
[13] Frances Egan, http://www.3ammagazine.com/3am/meaning-as-gloss/.
[14] Patrick Suppes, 'A Comparison of the Meaning and Uses of Models in Mathematics and the Empirical Sciences' *Synthese* **12** (1960), 287–301;

Tim Crane

van Fraassen used the word 'model' in the sense of model theoretic semantics; a model of a theory is a collection of objects which renders true the claims of the theory. Hence the association of the idea of a theory as a collection of models with the label 'the semantic view of theories', contrasted with the 'syntactic' view of theories defended by the logical empiricists. 'Semantic' is appropriate because scientific models were being conceived of in terms of model theory, the standard semantic framework for formal languages.

Later work on models by Ronald Giere and others emphasised something quite different: the use of simplified mathematical structures (e.g. equations describing ideal populations), imagined comparisons (the atom is like a solar system) or even concrete objects (the actual wire and wood construction which represents the double-helix structure of DNA).[15] All these things are classified as models by scientists, and philosophers of science attempted to make sense of them. But models in this second sense look very different from the models of model theory, as a number of writers have emphasised.[16]

In model theory, a model is collection of objects and operations on these objects – a set-theoretic structure – which makes the sentences of a theory true. (Nothing metaphysically weighty is meant by 'making true' here; this is just a standard definition of a model.) Even if model theory can be used to illuminate scientific theorising, as Suppes and van Fraassen argue, it is plain that a model-theoretic model does not look much like Rutherford's solar system model of the atom. For the solar system does not make true any claims about atoms; and nor does the comparison between the solar system and the atom make this true. Rather, the solar system is used to represent an aspect of how things are with the atom, just as equations describing an idealised population in biology is used to represent an aspect of how things are with some real population. Neither the equations

---

Bas Van Fraassen, *The Scientific Image* (Oxford Oxford University Press, 1980).

[15] See e.g., Ronald N. Giere, 'Using Models to Represent Reality' in *Model-Based Reasoning in Scientific Discovery*, (ed.) L. Magnani, N. J. Nersessian, and P. Thagard (New York: Kluwer/Plenum, 1999), 41–57.

[16] See Stephen Downes, 'The Importance of Models in Theorizing: a Deflationary Semantic View' in Hull D, Forbes M, Okruhlik K (eds) *PSA* 1992, vol. 1. Philosophy of Science Association, East Lansing (1992), 142–153; and Martin Thomson-Jones 'Models and the Semantic View' *Philosophy of Science* **73** (2006), 524–535.

nor the idealised population can be described as making true the claims about the real population.

The model-theoretic conception of models makes more sense if we think of the model as the *comparison* between the solar system and the atom. Here we might consider the model to be the mapping itself (sometimes described as an isomorphism, as it is by Suppes) between aspects of the real-world system and those of the object used to represent it. Whether this is a good way to understand models in science is much discussed in the philosophy of science; but what is clear is that it is a different idea from that of those who talk of one system being a model of another. Peter Godfrey-Smith puts this point well:

> Representation of a real-world system involves two distinct relations, the specification of a model system and some relevant similarity between model system and the world itself. So the word 'model' tends to be ambiguous here, between what we can call the model system and the model description.[17]

In what follows, I will talk of models as being what Godfrey-Smith calls the 'model system', and not as the 'model description' (i.e. the description mapping the system to the real-world system under investigation). To the extent, then, that the semantic conception of theories is tied up with the model-theoretic conception of models, we should avoid talking about 'the semantic conception' of theories here.

Models, in the sense I intend, are used to understand the behaviour of real-world systems by being used to represent how things are with those systems at a time, or how they evolve across time. Typically, the models are simpler than the real-world systems under investigation. They may involve idealisations (frictionless planes), or even empirical falsehoods (rational actor models in economics), and they may be unspecific in certain respects (a model of a cell may leave out information relating to what kind of cell it is).[18] The point of the model is to facilitate understanding of the real-world system by examining the behaviour of the model system: it is what Michael Weisberg calls an 'indirect theoretical investigation of a real-world phenomenon'.[19]

[17] Peter Godfrey-Smith 'The Strategy of Model-Based Science' *Biology and Philosophy* **21** (2006), 725–740; 733.
[18] See Downes, 'The Importance of Models in Theorizing: a Deflationary Semantic View', 145–6.
[19] 'Who is a Modeler?' *British Journal for the Philosophy of Science* **58** (2007), 207–233; 208.

Tim Crane

If we apply this to the case of the brain, the following picture emerges. The brain is the system under investigation (the 'real-world system') and the theorist attributes to it certain states, in order to predict or explain certain outputs. The theorist models these states by relating them to the abstract objects which are what I call the contents of the system. They expect to give a better understanding of the transitions between states of the brain by relating these states to contents than they would by merely citing neurochemical interactions, say, or gross external behavioural changes. This is what is going on when Frith claims that 'the brain has this simple rule built into its wiring; it uses this rule to decide whether an object is concave or convex'. The rule is that because light generally comes from above, concave objects will be dark at the top and light at the bottom; convex objects will be light at the top and dark at the bottom. That doesn't mean that those words are written in the brain, that those words are written in English or any other language, or even in the Language of Thought. The attribution of content is, rather, an abstraction away from the activity of the brain in a way that can help you with predicting and explaining what's going on. The claim, then, is that the process in the brain is understood by modelling it with a rule relating shading to convexity and concavity.

As Giere has emphasised, modelling works by exploiting relations of similarity.[20] What is similar to what, in the case of the brain? It's not that the brain state, whatever it is, resembles an abstract object, any more than a population resembles the equations used to model its growth. It's rather that the movement between states is similar to the stages of an explicit inference from the rule about concrete objects, plus the input from the image, to the conclusion about how the object looks. Inferences relate propositions; so the claim is that what is going on in the brain resembles a relationship between propositions. The appropriate comparison here is between modelling the brain with an inference, and modelling some target system by using a mathematical model.

Notice that this idea contains an echo of Fodor's famous argument for the Language of Thought based on the nature of mental processes.[21] I agree with Fodor that there is this similarity; but I resist the jump to the conclusion that this gives us a reason to say that there are symbols in the brain. Once equipped with a proper

---

[20]   See Giere, 'Using Models to Represent Reality'.

[21]   See Tim Crane, *The Mechanical Mind* (London: Routledge, 2003) chapter 4, for an exposition of this argument.

understanding of models, there is no need to move to this more out-landish hypothesis.

This does however raise an important question. What is the differ-ence between a theory which models the transitions among states of the brain by relating them to representational contents (i.e. treats the states as representations) and one that merely treats the transitions as law-governed processes? When looking at the Kanizsa triangle, for example, normal perceivers see a white triangle as occluding seg-ments of three black circles at its corners. Some neuroscientists and psychologists talk about the representation being 'completed' in the visual system by means of it making certain 'assumptions' about objects and how they normally relate to one another. On this under-standing, the brain is conceived of as making an inference: in moving from state to state, its states are modelled by contents. But on another understanding, the brain is simply a law-governed system which pro-duces certain visual outputs by being governed by a law about how objects normally look. On this view, there is no reason to call this an inference, not least because an inference must be rationally sensi-tive to further information, and this one isn't: no matter what you know, what you see will not change.

To determine whether it is correct to model a brain process by relating it to an inference will depend on the details of the case. My aim here is not to defend any particular hypothesis that treats the brain as making an inference; my aim is only to argue that it makes sense, and to say something about what kind of sense it makes.

3. The Propositional Attitudes

My discussion so far has been about things going on the sub-personal level; but does the modelling picture apply to the states of the whole person? In particular, does it apply to beliefs, desires, hopes and the other propositional attitudes? Some philosophers may agree that the modelling picture makes sense applied to sub-personal states but not to personal-level states; perhaps because these states have 'original' rather than 'derived' intentionality.[22]

Here I want to resist this objection. In the remainder of this paper, I will argue that ascriptions of propositional attitudes employ propo-sitions as models in a similar way that ascriptions of sub-personal states employ contents as models. But I don't say this because I

[22] For this distinction, see John R. Searle, *Intentionality* (Cambridge: Cambridge University Press, 1983).

Tim Crane

reject the distinction between original and derived intentionality. Rather, I would draw the significant distinction in this area not between sub-personal states and personal-level propositional attitudes, but between intrinsically intentional states of consciousness and all the other mental states. However, I cannot defend this further thesis in this paper; so I will confine myself to the claim about models.[23]

Contemporary philosophy of mind contains two influential views about the propositional attitudes. The first is that the concept of intentionality, the mind's representation of the world or direction upon its objects, should be understood entirely in terms of the propositional attitudes. This is a thesis that's been held by many people – Donald Davidson and many others. I call it 'propositionalism'.[24]

The second view – which I will call the 'relational thesis' – is that the propositional attitudes should be thought of as (literally) relations to propositions: a propositional attitude like *believing that the sun is shining* is a relation between the person and the thing believed, namely, the proposition that the sun is shining. When you believe that the sun is shining you have one kind of relation to it, and when you hope that the sun is shining you stand in another kind of relation to it. The conjunction of propositionalism with the relational thesis implies that intentionality should be understood in terms of relations to propositions.

For a long time the relational thesis has been something of a dogma in analytical philosophy of mind. Fodor made his argument for this thesis a cornerstone of his intentional realism: 'Believes looks like a two place relation so it relates two things the thinker and the proposition and it would be nice if our theory of belief permitted us to save the appearances'.[25] And in a famous paper, Hartry Field said a similar thing: 'propositional attitude attributions appear to relate people to non-linguistic entities called propositions' and he then claims that this fact is a problem for materialists.[26] The picture we are given is of a real relation to a proposition – the proposition is the thing you believe, and your belief state is a relation to it.

---

[23]   For defences of the latter thesis, see John Searle, *The Rediscovery of the Mind*, and Galen Strawson, *Mental Reality*.

[24]   See Donald Davidson, 'Mental Events' in *Essays on Actions and Events* (Oxford: Oxford University Press, 1982). In chapter 4 of *The Objects of Thought* (Oxford: Oxford University Press 2013) I offer a critique of propositionalism which is independent of the present paper.

[25]   Jerry A. Fodor, 'Propositional Attitudes' *The Monist* **61** (1978) 501–23.

[26]   Hartry Field, 'Mental Representation' *Erkenntnis* **13** (1978) 9–61, 10.

The Mental States of Persons and their Brains

Before deciding whether this claim is true, there is a prior question: what does it mean? What does it mean to say that you're 'related to a proposition by the relation of believing', if that is not just another way of saying that you believe it? What's the point of saying that you stand in a 'real relation' to a proposition?

The picture I want to reject is that it is a basic psychological or metaphysical fact, something that needs to be explained, that people are related to propositions. But this does not mean that it is not true. Rather than being something that needs to be explained, it is rather part of the theoretical explanation or description of your state of mind. In other words, we should think of the ascription of propositional content to a person – placing someone in a relation to a proposition – as a way of modelling their mental state.

When we say that someone believes that p, or thinks that p, what we are doing is picking out a feature of their state of mind – their whole psychological outlook, or world picture – by relating it to this abstract object, the proposition p. The proposition serves to pick out part of the way the subject represents the world. We use a sentence to express the proposition, but we shouldn't think of the belief simply as a relation to a sentence, since the same feature of the state of mind can be expressed by different sentences (in the same or different languages). So for example, if we say that someone thinks Scotland should be an independent country, we are picking out an aspect of their world view, by relating them to the proposition expressed by the sentence 'Scotland should be an independent country' and all sentences that mean the same.

It is not plausible that someone could believe this without believing, for example, that some countries should be independent; this is an instance of the well-known 'holism of the intentional', which should be accepted by everyone. This means that if we attribute the first belief we should also attribute the second, unless we have some countervailing reason not to. Why this is so, is a question which divides theories of mind and intentionality: 'inferentialists' take these facts to be the *basis* of intentionality, 'representationalists' take them to be *explained* by facts about intentionality. Here my aim is not so much to contribute to this debate but to point to the role of 'the proposition' in describing beliefs and the relationships between them.

In identifying a belief by using a proposition, we are exploiting the logical and conceptual relationships between propositions to reflect the holism of the intentional. The fact that if you are ascribed the belief that Scotland should be an independent nation means that you can also be ascribed the belief that some countries should be independent mirrors the fact that the proposition that *Scotland should be an independent nation* entails that *some nations should be independent*. I presuppose here that propositions stand in logical and conceptual relationships – they are inconsistent, they entail one another, they support one another and so on. On the assumption that we have a fairly good understanding (or at least an agreement) about which logical and other relationships hold between propositions, we can then use this understanding or agreement to underpin our conjectures about propositional attitudes. It is because we understand that A entails B that we can use this understanding to say that 'if someone believes that A then they will/should believe that B'.

This is why I say that the relation to a proposition is a way of modelling a belief. Just as Rutherford used our antecedent understanding of the structure of the solar system to model or picture something we are trying to understand – the atom – so we can use our antecedent knowledge of the relations between propositions to model the relationships between beliefs, and thus various aspects of the beliefs themselves. This is one feature of models: they use something which is in some way already understood to enlighten us about something that is less understood. Models do this by idealisation. If you say that someone believes that Scotland should be an independent nation, you do not thereby say everything about their conception of Scotland, nations and independence. They may have a very complex conception which is not easily summarised by a single sentence; yet it may still be perfectly true that they believe this, and in that sense the proposition models what they believe. As Robert Cummins puts it, 'attributing a belief is going to be a bit like attributing a point of view to an editorial'.[27] You can attribute a point of view to an editorial even if in doing so, you don't actually pick out a sentence that is contained in that editorial.

I mentioned above that when we attribute a belief, we typically commit ourselves to attributing certain related beliefs; or rather, we commit the believer to having certain related beliefs. This is the holism of the intentional. But of course, people do not always believe the logical consequences of what they believe, and our belief ascriptions should reflect this fact. Thinking of propositions as modelling beliefs captures this situation: the model is an idealisation. We say that if someone believes A then they should believe B but that may be because proposition A entails proposition B, or because it gives strong inductive support to B, or because it provides some other

[27]   Robert Cummins, *Meaning and Mental Representation* (Cambridge, MA: MIT Press, 1989), 144.

kind of reason for believing B. We might expect that a thinker will have the second belief if they have the first; this is a reasonable idealisation. But there might be all sorts of reasons why they don't have the second, and if so we would have to revise our model in the light of other things we find out about them. (I do not mean to imply here that thinkers are obliged to believe all logical consequences of what they believe, only that there are some cases where they do have an obligation to believe some of the consequences.)

There are two central questions about the propositional attitudes which this modelling approach answers. The first concerns what kind of objects propositions themselves are; the second concerns which specific propositions (however conceived) actually are the contents of any particular belief.

The first question is about the metaphysics of propositions. Some philosophers (Russellians) think that the constituents of propositions are objects and their properties; some (Fregeans) say that the constituents of propositions are senses or 'modes of presentation'; others (Lewisians/Stalnakerians) say that a proposition is a set of possible worlds.[28] Which view is right? Which objects are thinkers related to in their propositional attitudes?

There are things to be said in favour of each view. For example, sets of possible worlds are formally tractable – relations of entailment (etc.) can be understood set-theoretically. But there are also aspects of the possible worlds view of propositions which are very bad for representing distinctions between mental states. As has been observed many times, if a proposition is a set of possible worlds, then a necessarily true proposition is the set of all possible worlds. So all necessarily true sentences express the same proposition; and all necessary false sentences express the same proposition. We could take this to be a *reductio ad absurdum* of the view, but I don't think we should do this. Rather, I think what it shows is that propositions as sets of possible worlds constitutes a partial model of certain states of mind. It is a model which is good for some things and not for others.

A similar thing can be said about the view that propositions are Russellian. This too is a partial model. It might express the fact that the object of your thought is that *very particular object* you are thinking about, and no other object will do. Similarly the Fregean view that distinguishes propositions (*Gedanken*) more finely than objects and properties may be used to express a finer-grained perspective on a subject's mental life. But we should resist the idea

---

[28] For a recent contribution to this debate see Jeffrey C. King, *The Nature and Structure of Content* (Oxford: Oxford University Press, 2007).

Tim Crane

that only one of these views is correct in giving the content of some-one's belief, that *this* and not *that* is the proposition they are related to. The modelling picture allows that people can be related to proposi-tions of all these kinds; in other words, objects of all these kinds can be used to pick out their beliefs.

In a recent insightful discussion of this subject, Ian Rumfitt says:

> It is pretty clear that the maxims we ordinarily go by in reporting the speech and beliefs of others do not place people in relation either to Fregean *Gedanken* or to Russellian propositions; for that reason, there is little mileage in discussing whether *Gedanken* or Russellian propositions best match our pre-theoretic notions of saying or believing the same thing. These entities are better conceived as constructs, postulated for various theoretical purposes in philosophy, linguistics and psychology. The proper topic of debate, then, is whether a given construct serves a specified theoretical purpose. It is entirely possible that Fregean *Gedanken* might best serve one such purpose, Russellian propositions another, and indeed Stalnakerian propo-sitions (i.e. sets of possible words) a third.[29]

Unlike Rumfitt, I am happy to say that ordinary belief and speech reports do place thinkers in relation to propositions, since I think that ascribing a belief is modelling, and this places the thinker in a relation to a proposition, in a metaphysically innocuous sense. But this is a minor disagreement; if we read Rumfitt as saying that our ordinary maxims for reported speech and belief do not *determine* that one kind of proposition rather than another are the objects of belief or speech, then his remarks here get the matter exactly right.

The second question which the modelling picture answers is about which specific proposition actually is the content of a given belief, once we have settled on a general type of proposition. How specific or determinate should the content of a belief be, for example? And how should we identify the concepts which a thinker employs when they have a given belief? These questions arise particularly starkly in connection with animal belief. Consider Norman Malcolm's example of whether a dog believed that a cat went up a certain tree.[30] Some say that if the dog believes that the cat ran up the tree, this requires that the dog has the concept of a tree, and this requires

[29]   Ian Rumfitt, 'Truth and Meaning' *Proceedings of the Aristotelian Society, Supplementary Volume* **88** (2014), footnote 6.

[30]   Norman Malcolm, 'Thoughtless Brutes' *Proceedings and Addresses of the American Philosophical Association* **46** (1973), 5–20; cf. Donald

that it can think of a tree as something living, and the tree has leaves and the tree is made of wood ... Most or all of these things we believe about trees. But how can a dog believe any or all of those things? The same applies to the beliefs of children. When a child believes – to use Dennett's example – that her father is a doctor, what exactly does she believe? If beliefs are determinate states of subjects, then surely there must be an answer to this question.

The modelling view gives an answer. The child and the dog have a conscious perspective on the world, a point of view. What we do when we ascribe them a belief is to attempt to make sense of their behaviour (running towards the tree, saying 'Daddy is a doctor') by identifying some feature of their point of view. This feature we pick out using a proposition. The proposition can truly describe part of that point of view – after all, it is a *tree* that the dog is thinking about, and it is *being a doctor* that the child ascribes to her father. But that does not require that the dog or the child means *tree* or *doctor* in exactly the same sense that we do. The relation to the proposition is a partial model.

And the same applies to more sophisticated thinkers. There is normally not just one sentence that expresses what you believe – in other words, there are many propositions that characterise your belief in different ways. As you struggle to express your beliefs, what you're trying to do is fix on what is the most appropriate way of expressing them. This does not mean that there is no fact of the matter about what you believe, that it is 'simply' a matter of interpretation. I say there is such a fact; but it is often a very complex fact, because of the holism of the intentional. Even where the simplest beliefs about your perceived environment are concerned, what you believe about here depends on so many beliefs about other things, that we should not expect that one sentence can adequately capture it all. It might be replied that a very *long* sentence could do it; maybe, but the suggestion is practically worthless when it comes to understanding real belief ascriptions.

It should be obvious that the view I am defending here owes a lot to Daniel Dennett's views about intentionality and belief-ascription.[31] But this does not mean that the view is some sort of anti-realism or instrumentalism about the mental (regardless of where Dennett himself stands on this vexed issue). On the contrary; I claim that my view involves a robust psychological realism. There is a

---

Davidson, 'Thought and Talk' in *Inquiries into Truth and Interpretation* (Oxford: Oxford University Press, 1984).
[31]   See in particular, 'Beyond Belief'.

Tim Crane

psychological reality out there: this is the reality that you're attempting to model by using propositions in these various different ways. And just as the modelling conception of the atom is compatible with a hard-headed realism about atoms, so the modelling conception of the propositional attitudes is entirely compatible with realism about the psychological. Psychological reality is precisely that which we are trying to model in our personal and sub-personal psychological ascriptions.[32]

(new)*University of Cambridge*
tc102@cam.ac.uk

----

[32] Thanks to Ali Boyle, Dan Brigham, Katalin Farkas, Anthony O'Hear and Michael Weisberg for discussion, to members of the audience at the Royal Institute of Philosophy for helpful comments at the RIP meeting in February 2014, and to Stephen Mulhall for permitting me to quote from his unpublished work. An earlier version of this talk was given at the University of London's Institute of Philosophy in June 2012, at a workshop on Dennett's personal/sub-personal distinction; thanks to Dan Dennett for his comments on that occasion.

Actual Consciousness: Database, Physicalities, Theory, Criteria, No Unique Mystery

TED HONDERICH

Abstract

(i) Is disagreement about consciousness largely owed to no adequate initial clarification of the subject, to people in fact answering different questions – despite five leading ideas of consciousness? (ii) Your being conscious in the primary ordinary sense, to sum up a wide figurative database, is initially clarified as *something's being actual* – clarified as *actual consciousness*. (iii) Philosophical method like the scientific method includes transition from the figurative to literal theory or analysis. (iv) A new theory will also satisfy various criteria not satisfied by many existing theories. (v) The *objective physical* world has specifiable general characteristics including spatiality, lawfulness, being in science, connections with perception, and so on. (vi) *Actualism*, the literal theory or analysis of actual consciousness, deriving mainly from the figurative database, is that actual consciousness has counterpart but partly different general characteristics. Actual consciousness is thus *subjectively physical*. So physicality in general consists in objective and also subjective physicality. (vii) Consciousness in the case of perception is *only* the dependent existence of a subjective external physical world out there, often a room. (viii) But cognitive and affective consciousness, various kinds of thinking and wanting, differently subjectively physical, is internal – subjectively physical representations-with-attitude, representations that also are actual. They differ from the representations that are lines of type, sounds etc. by being actual. (ix) Thus they involve a subjectivity or individuality that is a lawful unity. (x) Actualism, both an externalism and an internalism, does not impose on consciousness a flat uniformuity, and it uniquely satisfies the various criteria for an adequate theory, including naturalism. (xi) Actual consciousness is *a* right subject and is a necessary part of *any* inquiry whatever into consciousness. (xii) All of it is a subject for more science, a workplace. (xiii) There is no unique barrier or impediment whatever to science, as often said, no want of understanding of the mind-consciousness connection (Nagel), no known unique hard problem of consciousness (Chalmers), no insuperable difficulty having to do with physicality and the history of science (Chomsky), no arguable ground at all of mysterianism (McGinn).

1. Need for Adequate Initial Clarification of Consciousness?

You are conscious just in seeing this room you are in, conscious in an ordinary sense. That is not to say what is different and more, that you

doi:10.1017/S1358246115000077   © The Royal Institute of Philosophy and the contributors 2015

Royal Institute of Philosophy Supplement **76** 2015   271

are seeing or perceiving the room, with all that can be taken to involve, including facts about your retinas and visual cortex. To say you are conscious just in seeing this room is not itself to say, either, what is often enough true, that you are also *attending* to the room or something in it, fixing your attention on it.

You are now conscious, secondly, in having certain thoughts, about what you are reading.

Likely you are conscious, thirdly, in having certain feelings, maybe the hope that everything is going to be clear as a bell in the next half-hour, maybe in intending to say so if it isn't.

What are those three states, events, facts or things? What is their nature? What is the best analysis or theory of them? What is what we can call perceptual consciousness, cognitive consciousness, and affective consciousness?

There is also another question, as pressing. What is common to the three states, events or whatever? What is this consciousness in general? What is the kind of state, event or whatever of which perceptual, cognitive, and affective consciousness are three parts, sides, or groups of elements? As I shall be remarking later in glancing at existing theories of consciousness, the known main ones try to answer only the general question. But can you really get a good general answer without getting a particular answer or two?

These are the questions of a line of inquiry and argument in a large book which sure asks for a very dogged reader,[1] a book of which this lecture is the short story. We can ask the three particular questions and the general question, as we shall, in mainstream philosophy. That in my view is certainly not ownership of, but a greater concentration than that of science on, the logic of ordinary intelligence: (i) clarity, usually analysis, (ii) consistency and validity, (iii) completeness, (iv) generalness. Is it safe enough to say, then, that philosophy is thinking about facts as distinct from getting them?

Another preliminary. There are ordinary and there are other related concepts of things, ordinary and other senses of words – say stipulated or technical ones. Let us ask, as you may have taken me to have been implying already, what it is to be conscious generally speaking in *the primary ordinary sense*, in what a good dictionary also calls the *core meaning* of the word – and what it is to be conscious in each of the three ways in the primary ordinary sense. Do you ask if that is the right question? Assume it is and wait for an answer in the end.

---

[1]   Honderich, T. *Actual Consciousness* (Oxford University Press, 2014).

We have what John Searle rightly calls a common sense definition,[2] something he calls unanalytic, of what seems to be this ordinary consciousness – presumably must be of ordinary consciousness since it *is* common sense. This consciousness in the definition is states of *awareness* that we are in except in dreamless sleep. That has the virtue of including dreaming in consciousness, which surprisingly is not a virtue of all definitions, notably an eccentric Wittgensteinian one.[3] But how much more virtue does Searle's common sense definition have? *Awareness* obviously needs defining as much as *consciousness*. Certainly there seems to be uninformative circularity there.

Each of us also has something better than a common sense definition. Each of us has a *hold* on her or his individual consciousness. That is, each of us can recall now the nature of something a moment ago, perceptual consciousness of the room, or a thought, or a feeling. I guess that is or is part of what has been called introspection, and doubted because it was taken as a kind of inner seeing, and people or subjects in psychology laboratories being asked to do more with it than they could. Forget all that. We can be confident right now that each of us can recall that event or state of consciousness a moment ago, say the look of a thing or a passing thought or an urge, say of psychology laboratories.

There are lesser and greater pessimisms about our answering the general question of consciousness. Greater pessimists have included Noam Chomsky,[4] Thomas Nagel,[5] David Chalmers[6] – and Colin McGinn,[7] who began by saying we have no more chance of getting

---

[2]   Searle, J. *The Rediscovery of the Mind* (MIT Press, 1992), 83–4; *Consciousness and Language* (Cambridge University Press, 2002), 7, 21.

[3]   Malcolm, Norman, *Dreaming* (Routledge, 1962).

[4]   Chomsky, N. *Reflections on Language* (Pantheon Books, 1975); *Rules and Representations* (Columbia University Press, 1980); otherwise unpublished material in Lycan, W. 'Chomsky on the Mind-Body Problem', in Antony and Hornstein, *Chomsky and His Critics* (Blackwell, 2003).

[5]   Nagel, T. 'What is it Like to be a Bat', *Philosophical Review* (1974); 'Conceiving the Impossible and the Mind-Body Problem', *Philosophy*, (1998).

[6]   Chalmers, D. 'Facing Up To the Problem of Consciousness', *Journal of Consciousness Studies* (1995); 'The Puzzle of Conscious Experience', *Scientific American* (1995); *The Conscious Mind: In Search of a Fundamental Theory* (Oxford University Press, 1996).

[7]   McGinn, C. 'Can We Solve the Mind-Body Problem?', *Mind* (1989); 'Consciousness and Content', in *The Problem of Consciousness: Essays Towards a Resolution* (Blackwell, 1991); *The Mysterious Flame: Conscious*

Ted Honderich

straight about consciousness than chimps have of doing physics, but ended up by seeming to say a lot less.

Here is a first question for you, a first piece of this lecture. Are those pessimisms and also, more importantly, the great seeming disagreement about what consciousness is, a pile of conflicting theories in philosophy, neuroscience, cognitive science and psychology, owed at least significantly to one fact? Are they owed to the fact that there has not been agreement on what is being talked about, no adequate initial clarification of the subject matter, but people talking past one another, not asking the same question? In a sense, of course, that is not disagreement at all, but a kind of confusion.

So far and still more hereafter, by the way, indeed as before now, this lecture is a sketch of a sketch – a bird's-eye view with the bird flying high and fast. I worry that someone once said to Professor Quine of Karl Popper that Popper lectured with a broad brush, to which Quine mused in reply that maybe he thought with one too.

2. Five Leading Ideas of Consciousness

I say there are five leading ideas of consciousness. They are about qualia, something it's like to be a thing, subjectivity, intentionality, and phenomenality. Fly over them with me.

Qualia. Dan Dennett says qualia are *the ways things seem to us*, the particular personal, subjective qualities of experience at the moment.[8] Nagel says qualia are features of mental states.[9] Very unlike Dennett, he says it seems impossible to analyse them in objective physical terms, make sense of them as objectively physical. Ned Block has it that they include not only experiential properties of sensations, feelings, perceptions, wants, and emotions.[10] They are also such properties of *thoughts*, anyway our thoughts that are different from the sort of thing taken to be the functioning of unconscious

---

Minds in a Material World, (Basic Books, 1999); *The Making of a Philosopher* (Harper Collins, 2002); *Consciousness and Its Objects* (Oxford University Press, 2004); 'All Machine and No Ghost?', *New Statesman* (2012).

[8] Dennett, D. 'Quining Qualia', in Marcel and Bisiach, *Consciousness in Contemporary Science* (1992).

[9] Nagel, T. 'What Is It Like To Be a Bat?', *Philosophical Review*, (1974)

[10] Block, N. 'On a Confusion About a Function of Consciousness', *The Behavioral and Brain Sciences* (1995), 380–1, 408.

computers – computation or bare computation.[11] Others disagree in several ways with all that.

Do we get an adequate initial clarification of the subject of consciousness here? No. There is only what you can call a conflicted consensus about what qualia are to be taken to be. In this consensus, worse, one thing that is very widely assumed or agreed. Qualia are *qualities of* consciousness, not what has the qualities, consciousness itself, maybe its basic or a more basic quality. Another thing mostly agreed is by itself fatal to the idea of an adequate initial clarification – that qualia are only part of consciousness. There's the other part, which is propositional attitudes – related or primarily related to my cognitive consciousness.

Something it's like to be a thing. That idea of Nagel in his paper 'What It's Like To Be a Bat' (1974), however stimulating an idea, as indeed it has been, is surely *circular*. Searle in effect points to the fact when he says we are to understand the words in such a way that there is nothing it is like to be a shingle on a roof.[12] What we are being told, surely, is that what it is for something to be conscious is for there is something it is like for that thing *to be conscious*. What else could we being told? Also, you can worry, no *reality* is assigned to consciousness here. Can there conceivably be reality without what Nagel declined to provide in his paper, an assurance of physicality?

Traditional or familiar subjectivity. Here, whatever better might be done about subjectivity, and really has to be done, and as we can try to do, there is circularity. Consciousness is what is *of a subject*, which thing is understood as a bearer or possessor *of consciousness*. There is also obscurity. Further, a subject of this kind is a metaphysical self. Hume famously saw off such a thing, didn't he, when he reported that he peered into himself and could not espy his?[13]

Intentionality. The idea was brought into circulation by the German psychologist Brentano in the 19th Century and has as its contemporary defender and developer Tim Crane. It is sometimes better spoken of as *aboutness*, where that is explained somehow as also being the puzzling character of lines of type, spoken words and images. There is the great problem that when intentionality is made clear enough by way of likeness to such things, it is evident that it is only

[11]   Ibid.
[12]   Searle, J. *The Rediscovery of the Mind* (MIT Press, 1992), 132; *The Mystery of Consciousness* (New York Review Book, 1999), 42.
[13]   Hume, D. *A Treatise of Human Nature,* (ed.) L.A. Selby-Bigge (Oxford University Press, (1888)), 252.

Ted Honderich

part of consciousness. As is often remarked, it leaves out aches and objectless depression. Crane argues otherwise, valiantly but to me unpersuasively.[14]

Phenomenality. Block himself speaks of the concept of consciousness as being hybrid or mongrel, and leaves it open whether he himself is speaking of consciousness partly in an ordinary sense.[15] He does concern himself, certainly, with what he calls *phenomenal consciousness*, as does David Chalmers.[16] This is said by Block, not wonderfully usefully, to be 'just experience', just 'awareness'. Circularity. I add in passing that he takes there to be another kind of consciousness, *access consciousness*, which most of the rest of us recognise as an old and known subject, what we still call unconscious mentality, only dispositions, maybe related brain-workings. Here, I remark in passing, is a first and striking instance of philosophers or scientists definitely not meaning the same thing in speaking of consciousness as other philosophers or scientists. Nagel sure wasn't on about access consciousness – or what has it as a proper part. How many more instances do we need in support of that idea about what disagreement about consciousness is largely owed to?

A last remark or two about the five ideas. It is notable that Chalmers takes them all to come to the much the same thing, one thing, to pick out approximately the same class of phenomena.[17] He is not alone in that inclination. But evidently the ideas are different. Certainly the essential terms aren't what he calls synonyms. And is it not only the case that none of the five ideas provides an adequate initial clarification of consciousness, but also that a comparison of them in their striking variety indicates immediately the absence and lack of a common subject?

---

[14]   Crane, T. 'Intentionality as the Mark of the Mental', in Anthony O'Hear (ed.), *Current Issues in the Philosophy of Mind* (Cambridge University Press, 1998); *Elements of Mind: An Introduction to Philosophy of Mind* (Oxford University Press, 2003), 4–6; 'The Intentional Structure of Consciousness', in Quentin Smith & Alexander Jokic (eds), *Consciousness: New Philosophical Perspectives* (Oxford University Press, 2003), 33.

[15]   Block, N. 'Functionalism' in *Consciousness, Function, and Representation, Collected Papers*, Vol. 1 (MIT Press, 2007), 159, 180–1.

[16]   Chalmers, D. *The Conscious Mind: In Search of a Fundamental Theory* (Oxford University Press, 1996).

[17]   Ibid., 4–6, 9–11.

3. Something's Being Actual

Is confession good for a philosopher's soul? Well, it might help out with your getting an early idea of a lecture.

I sat at in a room in London's Hampstead some years ago and said to myself stop reading all this madly conflicting stuff about consciousness. *You*'re conscious. This isn't Quantum Theory, let alone the bafflement of moral and political truth. Just answer the question of what your being conscious right now is, or for a good start, more particularly, just say what your being conscious of the room is, conscious just in seeing the room. Not thinking about just seeing, or attending to something in it. Not liking it or whatever. You know the answer in some sense, don't you? You've got the hold.

The answer in my case, lucky or unlucky, was that my being conscious was the fact of *the room being there*, just the room being out there. Later on, as you will be hearing, I preferred to say that *a* room was being there.

You will be more reassured, I'm sure, to hear that that I do not just discard all that philosophy and science of mind just glanced at – the five leading ideas, and a lot more. On the contrary, it must be that there is something in it all. It's hard to have a view about the value of consensus in philosophy, or in science, about what you can call democracy about truth. But who can say there isn't any value at all? If you go through the philosophy on qualia, what it's like, subjectivity, intentionality, and phenomenality, you can get to what is the first of the main things in this lecture.

You find all those philosophers and scientists using certain terms and locutions – certain conceptions. Suppose, as you very reasonably can, that they or almost all of them are talking about consciousness in the primary ordinary sense. They think about it in a certain way, have certain concepts, use certain language for it. Further, and of course very importantly, this is shared with philosophers and scientists otherwise concerned with consciousness and with what they call the mind. I am pretty confident that it is shared with you.

If you put together the terms and locutions you get what we can certainly call *data*. You get a *database*. It is that in the primary ordinary sense, in any of the three ways, your being conscious now is the following:

the *having* of something, something being *had* – if not in a general sense, the general sense in which you also have ankles,
hence something being held, possessed or owned,
your seeing, thinking, wanting in the ordinary *active* sense of the verbs,

277

hence the experience in the sense of the *experiencing* of something,
something being in contact, met with, encountered, or undergone,
awareness of something in a primary sense,
something being directly or immediately in touch,
something being apparent,
something *not* deduced, inferred, posited, constructed or otherwise got from something else,
something somehow existing,
something being *for* something else,
something being *to* something,
something being in view, on view, in a point of view,
something being open, provided, supplied,
something to which there is *some* privileged access,
in the case of perception, there being the world as it is for something,
what at least involves an object or content,
an object or content's coming to us, straight-off,
something being *given*,
hence something existing and known,
something being present,
something being presented, which is different,
something being shown, revealed or manifest,
something being transparent in the sense of being unconveyed by anything else,
something clear straight-off,
something being open,
something being *close*,
an occurrent or event, certainly not only a disposition to later events,
something real,
something being vividly naked,
something being right there,
in the case of perception, the openness of a world.

That, I say to you, *is* data, and I sure bet you it exists in other languages than English. We can await reassurance from the Germans and no doubt even the French. Probably Latvians. It *is* a database. To glance back at and compare it to the five leading ideas, it's not a mediaeval technical term in much dispute, or a philosopher's excellent *aperçu* but still an *aperçu*, or a familiar or traditional idea or kind of common talk, or an uncertain truth based on a few words and images, or an uncertainty about a consciousness that seems to slide into unconsciousness.

Without stopping to say more about the database, except that in character it has to do with both existence and a relationship, is both ontic and epistemic, we can of course note that certainly it is figurative or even metaphorical. To say consciousness is *given* is not to say it's just like money being given.

There is an equally figurative encapsulation of it all, which I will be using. It is that being conscious in the primary ordinary sense is *something being actual* – which certainly isn't open to the objection of circularity. We can also say that what we have is an initial conception of primary ordinary consciousness as being *actual consciousness*. Can we follow in the history of so much science by starting from but getting beyond metaphor and the like?

This start immediately raises two general questions. *What* is actual with this consciousness? And what is it for whatever it is *to be actual*? And, remembering that this consciousness has three parts, sides or groups of elements, there are the questions of what is actual and then what the actuality is with each of perceptual, cognitive and affective consciousness.

So the first two criteria – of eight – for an adequate theory or analysis of ordinary consciousness, for a literal account of its nature, is the theory's giving answers to those questions about (1) what is actual and (2) what its being actual comes to. Certainly we have to get to the absolutely literal.

We will get to better answers, however, if we look at a few other things first.

Functionalisms, Dualisms

It is prudent, whether or not required by a respect for consensus, for democracy about truth, to consider existing dominant theories of anything. If you take the philosophy and science of consciousness together, certainly the current philosophy and science of mind, you must then consider *abstract functionalism* and its expression in cognitive science – computerism about consciousness and mind, which of course might be or anyway might have been right.

Could it be that abstract functionalism is usefully approached in a seemingly curious way, approached by way of what has always been taken as an absolute adversary, traditional dualism, including spiritualism, which goes back a long way, to before Descartes? This dualism, often taken as benighted, is the proposition that the mind is not the brain. That, in a sentence only slightly more careful, is to the effect that all consciousness is not physical. There are, of course, reputable and indeed leading philosophers and scientists of mind who are in

279

Ted Honderich

some sense dualists. Chalmers is one.[18] There are other more meta-physically explicit dualists, including Howard Robinson.[19] Has Block been a fellow traveller?[20]

You may excuse me saying of dualism, since I have a lot of my own fish to fry, that it has the great recommendation of making consciousness *different in kind*, which it sure is. And that it has the great failing of making it *not a reality*. It shares that fatal failing with abstract functionalism. The old metaphysics and the reigning general science of the mind fall together. But your being conscious, rather, for a start, is something with a history that began somewhere and will end somewhere. Who now has the nerve to say it is out of space? It is now *real*. It now *exists*. It's *a fact*. Evidently all this is bound up with the clearer and indeed dead clear truth that consciousness has physical effects, starting with lip and arm movements. This is only denied in Australia, where the sun is very hot. Elsewhere there is the *axiom* of the falsehood of epiphenomenalism. But, however, to go back to the first point, as the dictionary says mind is somehow different from matter – or from some or much matter.

There is no more puzzle about what, in general, abstract functionalism is, even if the elaboration of it in cognitive science has been rich. Abstract functionalism is owed to a main premise and a large inspiration.

The large inspiration is that we do indeed identify and to an extent distinguish types of things and particular things in a certain way – by their relations, most obviously their causes and effects. We do this with machines like carburettors, and with our kidneys, and so on, and should do it more with politicians and our hierarchic democracy. The premise, more important now, is the proposition that one and the same type of conscious state somehow goes together with or anyway turns up with different types of neural or other physical states. This is the premise of what is called *multiple realizability*. We and chimps and snakes and conceivably computers can be in exactly the very

[18]   Chalmers, D. *The Conscious Mind: In Search of a Fundamental Theory* (Oxford University Press, 1996); 'Verbal Disputes', *Philosophical Review* (2009).
[19]   Robinson, H. (ed.) *Objections to Physicalism* (Oxford; New York: Clarendon Press, 1993); 'Some Externalist Strategies and their Problems', *Croatian Journal of Philosophy* (2003).
[20]   'On a Confusion About a Function of Consciousness', *The Behavioral and Brain Sciences* (1995); *Consciousness, Function, and Representation, Collected Papers*, Vol. 1 (MIT Press, 2007).

same pain that goes with quite different physical states. You can doubt that. I sure do, for several reasons.

But my own short story of abstract functionalism, my own objection, is that a conscious state or event is *itself* given no reality in this theory that allows it to be *only* a cause of actions etc. It does go together with traditional dualism in this respect, and is therefore to me as hopeless. There is a place within other and very different theorizing for what you can call *physical functionalism*, which is better, partly because it puts aside multiple realizability, which has been too popular by half. But that too is not a subject for right now.

5. Other Theories, More Criteria

There are more existing theories and sorts of theories of consciousness than dualism and abstract functionalism. Note that like dualism and abstract functionalism, they make the nature of consciousness uniform or at least principally or essentially or primarily uniform as, incidentally, do the five leading ideas – despite our own initial division of consciousness into the perceptual, cognitive and affective kinds, sides, or groups of elements.

My own list of existing theories and sorts of theories has on it Non-Physical Intentionality and Supervenience, notably the work of Jaegwon Kim,[21] Donald Davidson's Anomalous Monism,[22] the mentalism of much psychology and science as well as philosophy that runs together conscious and unconscious mentality, Block's mentalism in particular, naturalism, the dominant representational naturalism of which there are various forms, such aspectual theories as Galen Strawson's panpsychism and double aspect theory, Bertrand Russell's Neutral Monism, the different physicalisms of Searle, Dennett, and of neuroscience generally, the Higher Order Theory of Locke and David Rosenthal, the audacity of the Churchlands seemingly to the effect that it will turn out in a future neuroscience that there aren't any beliefs or desires,[23] the wonderful elusiveness of quantum theory consciousness, which is certainly a case of the explanation of the obscure by the more obscure, and the

---

[21] Kim, J. *Physicalism, Or Something Near Enough* (Princeton University Press, 2005).

[22] Davidson, D. *Essays on Actions and Events* (Oxford University Press, 1980).

[23] Churchland, Patricia. *Neurophilosophy* (MIT Press, 1986); Churchland, Paul, *Matter and Consciousness* (MIT Press, 1988).

Ted Honderich

previous externalisms – Hilary Putnam,[24] Tyler Burge,[25] Alva Noe,[26] and Andy Clark.[27]

I save you consideration of and incidental objections to these existing theories of consciousness, and say only a few things.

One is that while all of these theories are crucially or at least centrally concerned one way or another with *the physical*, physical reality, they do not slow down to think about it. They do not come close to really considering what it is, going over the ground. Was that reasonable? Is it reasonable? Shouldn't we get onto the ground, walk around there for a while? Be pedestrian?

And just in passing, for the last time, do these theories concern themselves with the same question? For a start, was Non-Physical Supervenience about the same question of consciousness that representational naturalism or neuroscientific physcalism was about? Surely not.

A third thing is important, indeed crucial, for anyone who believes, as I do, despite such original tries as Frank Jackson's,[28] there are no *proofs* of large things in philosophy, which is instead a matter of comparative judgement between alternatives. The thing is that a good look through those various theories gives us more criteria for a decent theory or analysis of consciousness – additional to answers to the questions you've heard of (1) what is actual and (2) what the actuality comes to. Also criteria additional to two others already announced to you, that a decent theory of consciousness will indeed have to recognize and explain (3) the *difference* of consciousness from all else and (4) the *reality* of consciousness and the connected fact of its being causally efficacious – maybe several-sided difference and several-sided reality.

A further condition of adequacy is (5) something just flown by so far in this talk – *subjectivity*, some credible or persuasive unity with respect to consciousness, something quite other than a metaphysical self or homunculus. Another condition is (6) the *three parts, sides or*

---

[24] Putnam, H. *Mind, Language and Reality: Philosophical Papers,* Vol. 2 (Cambridge University Press, 1975).
[25] Burge, T., *Foundations of Mind* (Oxford University Press, 2007); *Origins of Objectivity* (Oxford University Press, 2010).
[26] Noe, A. *Action in Perception* (MIT Press, 2006); *Out Of Our Heads: Why You Are Not Your Brain, and Other Lessons from the Biology of Consciousness* (Hill and Wang, 2009).
[27] Clark, A. *Being There: Putting Brain, Body and World Together Again* (MIT Press, 1997).
[28] Jackson, F. *Mind, Method, and Conditionals: Selected Essays* (Routledge, 1986).

kinds of elements of consciousness. It is surprising indeed that the existing general theories of consciousness do not include in their generality the distinctness of perceptual, cognitive and affective consciousness, as psychology did in the past and still does in practice – and indeed as philosophy itself does when it is not focussed on the general question, but, say, thinking about perception. Another requirement (7) is that of *naturalism*, essentially a relation to science. A last one (8) is of course *the relation or relations* of consciousness to a brain or other basis and to behaviour and also other relations.

Something else I should provide here, since I know where this lecture is going, is a scandalously speedy reminder of the theories that are the externalisms. Putnam said meanings ain't in the head but depend on science. Burge cogently explained by way of arthritis in the thigh that mental states are individuated by or depend on external facts, notably those of language. Clark argued that representation with respect to consciousness is a matter of both internal and external facts – minds are extended out of our heads. Noe theorizes that consciousness partly consists in acting.

There is a very different externalism.

6. The Objective Physical World

To make a good start on or towards the theory we will call *Actualism*, think for just a few minutes, whether or not you now suppose this is a good idea, about the usual subject of the physical, the objective physical world. The existing theories of consciousness, from dualism and abstract functionalism to the externalisms, do one way or another include presumptions about or verdicts on consciousness having to do with physicality – by which they always mean and usually say objective physicality. I ask again whether they are to be judged for their still passing by the subject. I hope so.

Anyway, having spent some time on that database, and flown over a lot of existing uniform theories of consciousness, and put together the criteria for an adequate theory or analysis of consciousness, let us now spend even less time on the objective physical world, on what it is for something to be objectively physical. If there are a few excellent books on the subject, notably those of Herbert Feigl[29] and Barbara

[29] Feigl, H. *The Mental and the Physical: The Essay and a Postscript* (University of Minnesota Press, 1967).

Ted Honderich

Montero,[30] it is indeed hardly considered at all by the known philosophers and scientists of consciousness. Or they take a bird's-eye view, far above a pedestrian one. I'm for walking around, going over the ground. Not that it will be done here and now.

Here let me just report convictions or attitudes of mine owed to a respect for both science and philosophy. I abbreviate what is a substantial inquiry in itself into the objectively physical, the objectively physical world. I boil it down into a fast checklist of characteristics. They are properties that can be divided into those that can be taken as having to do with physicality, the first nine, and those having to do with objectivity, the other seven.

Physicality

1. Objective physical properties are the properties that are accepted in science, or hard or harder science.
2. They are properties knowledge of which is owed or will be owed to the scientific method, which method is open to clarification.
3. They are properties that are spatial and temporal in extent, certainly not outside of space and time.
4. Particular physical properties stand in lawful connections, most notably causal connections, with other such properties. Two things are in lawful connection if, given all of a first one, a second would exist whatever else were happening. Think about that truth dear to me some other time.[31]
5. Categories of such properties are also lawfully connected.
6. The physical macroworld and the physical microworld are in relations to perception, diffent relations – the second including deduction.
7. Macroworld properties are open to different points of view.
8. They are different from different points of view.
9. They include, given a defensible view of primary and secondary properties, both kinds of properties.

---

[30] Montero, B. 'The Body Problem', *Nous* (1999); 'Post-Physicalism', *Journal of Consciousness Studies* (2001); 'What Is Physical?', in B. McLaughlin, A. Beckermann, S. Walter (eds), *The Oxford Handbook of Philosophy of Mind* (Oxford University Press, 2009).
[31] Honderich, T. *A Theory of Determinism: The Mind, Neuroscience, and Life-Hopes* (Oxford University Press, 1988).

Objectivity

And, to consider objectivity rather than physicality, the properties of the objective physical world have the following characteristics.

10. They are in a sense or senses separate from consciousness.
11. They are public – not in the consciousness of only one individual.
12. Access to them, whether or not by one individual, is not a matter of special or privileged access.
13. They are more subject to truth and logic than certain other properties.
14. To make use of the idea of scientific method for a second time, their objectivity, like their physicality, is a matter of that method.
15. They include no self or inner fact or indeed unity or other such fact of subjectivity that is inconsistent with the above properties of the objective physical world.
16. There is hesitation about whether objective physicality includes consciousness.

So very much more could be said about all that. You *will* be hearing about two counterparts to this checklist. It will guide us in two other locales.

Here and elsewhere it comes to mind to remark that philosophy is *as* alive and good and with as much future as science – since I do conjecture it *is* thinking more about facts as distinct from getting them. A good idea not get out of sight of facts, needless to say. We won't.

7. Perceptual Consciousness – What is and isn't Actual

On we go now from that database, the encapsulation of it, the pile of theories of consciousness, the criteria, and objective physicality. It seems to me and maybe others that if we learn from the existing pile of theories of consciousness and the resulting criteria, and to my mind the plain thinking about physicality, we need to make an escape from the customary in the science and philosophy of consciousness. There is a fair bit of agreement about that. McGinn is one who really declares the need for something new.[32]

---

[32]   McGinn, C. 'Can We Solve the Mind-Body Problem?', *Mind* (1989); *The Making of a Philosopher* (Harper Collins, 2002), *Consciousness and Its*

Ted Honderich

We need to pay our very own attention to consciousness, some untutored attention. We do not need to turn ourselves into what psychologists used to call naive subjects or to demote ourselves to membership of *the folk* – of whom I am inclined to believe that they are distinguished by knowing quite a few large truths about consciousness. We do need to concentrate, for a good start, on those two general and main questions at which we have arrived and respond to them directly out of our holds on being perceptually conscious. Here is an anticipation, in awful brevity, of what seems to me the right response.

What is actual for me now with respect to my perceptual consciousness, my perceptual consciousness as distinct from my cognitive and affective consciousness, is only the room, what it will indeed turn out to be sensible to call *a* room, but a room out there in space, a room as definitely out there in space as anything at all is out there in space. God knows it's not a room in my head. Anyway I know.

Yes, *what* is actual with you and me now, so far as perceptual consciousness is concerned, is a room, most certainly not a representation of a room or any such thing whatever, called content or whatever else – no matter what part representations play in unconscious mentality. We can all very well indeed tell the difference between a sign of any sort and a thing that isn't one. Perceptual consciousness is not just or even at all *about* that room, but in short *is* that room.

No metaphysical self is actual either, or direction or aboutness, or any other philosophical or funny stuff. What is actual is a *subjective physical world* in the usual sense of a part of the thing. Saying so is comparable to familiar talk of being in touch with the world as ordinarily thought of, or the objective physical world, in virtue of being in touch with a part of it. There is reason for the rhetoric, perfectly literal sense to be given to it.

Is a subjective physical world, since not a world inside your head, just a *phantom* world? Is it insubstantial, imaginary, imagined, dreamed up? If you are caught in a good tradition of philosophical scepticism, maybe scepticism gone off the deep end, and feel like saying yes, making me feel sorry for you, hang on for a while. Hold your horses. This is philosophy in English, not deep, not literary, not evocative, not deep.

Objects (Oxford University Press, 2004); 'All Machine and No Ghost?', *New Statesman* (2012).

8. Perceptual Consciousness – Something's Being Actual is it's Being Subjectively Physical in A Way

What about question 2? What is a room's *being actual*?

It is indeed its existing in a way not at all metaphorical or otherwise figurative, but a way to be *very* literally specified – ways guided by what was said of the objective physical world. This existence of a room is partly but not only a matter of a room's occupying that space out there and lasting through some time, and of its being in lawful connections including causal ones within itself, and of two great lawful dependencies that mainly distinguish this way of existing in particular.

The first dependency is the lawful categorial dependency of what is actual on what we have just inquired into or anyway glanced at, *the objective physical world*, or rather on parts or pieces or stages of the objective physical world we ordinary speak of perceiving, whatever that perceiving really comes to. The second dependency with my world is a dependency on my objective properties as a perceiver, neural properties and location for a start. Note in passing that this clarifies something mentioned before, the both epistemic and ontic character of our database.

So my being perceptually conscious now is the existence of a part or piece or stage of a sequence that is one *subjective physical world*, one among very many, as many as there are sets of perceivings of single perceivers. These myriad worlds are no less real for there being myriads of them and for their parts being more transitory than parts of *the objective physical world*. Myriad and momentary things in the objective physical world do not fail to exist on account of being myriad and momentary. I speak of *a* room, of course, not at all to diminish it or to allow that it is flaky, but mainly just to distinguish it from that other thing.

Subjective physical worlds and their parts or whatever are plain enough states of affairs or circumstances, ways things or objects are, sets of things and properties. These subjective worlds are a vast subset, the objective physical world being a one-member subset, of course of many parts, of the single all-inclusive world that there is, *the physical world*, that totality of the things that there are. Here is a summary table of these and other facts. It also covers what we will be coming to, cognitive and affective consciousness.

Just attend, first, to the left hand column of the table. You will not need telling again that it summarizes what was said earlier of *objective physicality*. Subjective physical worlds, our present concern,

A TABLE OF PHYSICALITIES

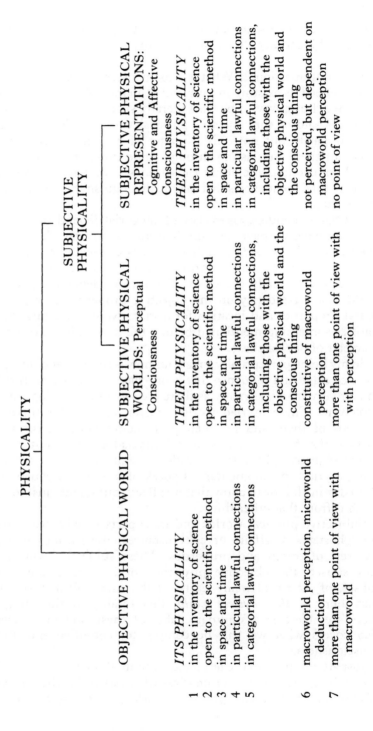

PHYSICALITY

OBJECTIVE PHYSICAL WORLD

SUBJECTIVE PHYSICALITY

SUBJECTIVE PHYSICAL WORLDS: Perceptual Consciousness

SUBJECTIVE PHYSICAL REPRESENTATIONS: Cognitive and Affective Consciousness

ITS PHYSICALITY
1 in the inventory of science
2 open to the scientific method
3 in space and time
4 in particular lawful connections
5 in categorial lawful connections

6 macroworld perception, microworld deduction
7 more than one point of view with macroworld

THEIR PHYSICALITY
in the inventory of science
open to the scientific method
in space and time
in particular lawful connections
in categorial lawful connections, including those with the objective physical world and the conscious thing
constitutive of macroworld perception
more than one point of view with with perception

THEIR PHYSICALITY
in the inventory of science
open to the scientific method
in space and time
in particular lawful connections
in categorial lawful connections, including those with the objective physical world and the conscious thing
not perceived, but dependent on macroworld perception
no point of view

8	different from different points of view	different from different points of view	no differences from points of view
9	primary and secondary properties	primary and secondary properties	no primary and secondary properties
	ITS OBJECTIVITY	THEIR SUBJECTIVITY	THEIR SUBJECTIVITY
10	separate from consciousness	not separate from consciousness	not separate from consciousness
11	public	private	private
12	common access	privileged access	privileged access
13	truth and logic, more subject to	truth and logic, less subject to?	truth and logic, less subject to
14	open to the scientific method	open to the scientific method despite doubt	open to the scientific method despite doubt
15	includes no self or unity or other such inner fact of subjectivity inconsistent with the above properties of the objective physical world	each subjective physical world is an element in an individuality that is a unique and large unity of lawful and conceptual dependencies including much else	each representation is an element in an individuality that is a unique and large unity of lawful and meaningful dependencies including much else
16	hesitation about whether objective physicality includes consciousness	no significant hesitation about taking the above subjective physicality as being that of actual perceptual consciousness	no significant hesitation about taking this subjective physicality as being the nature of actual cognitive and affective consciousness

characterized in the middle column, are one of two subsets of *subject-ive physicality*. All of that subjective physicality, like objective phys-icality, as already remarked, is a subset of physicality in general. You will know that I pass by an awful lot of stuff in the table and in all of what I have to say here in my hour. Very broad brush.

Subjective physical worlds are about as *real*, if differently real, I repeat, in pretty much the sum of decent senses of that wandering word, as the objective physical world, that other sequence. In one sense, subjective physical worlds are more real – as in effect is often enough remarked, but pass that by. All this is so however and to what limited extent the objective physical world is related to subject-ive physical worlds. It is because of the dependencies on the objective physical world and also on perceivers, and for another specific and large reason to which we will come, about subjectivity or rather indi-viduality, that these perceived worlds rightly have the name of being subjective.

You can say, then, that my being perceptually conscious now just *is* and *is only* a particular existence of something like what most of the leading ideas of consciousness and the existing theories of conscious-ness half-seem to take or may take perceptual consciousness merely to be *of* or *about*, say a room. They also take perceptual consciousness to be a lot more than just the existence of a room. Evidently the characteristics of subjective physical worlds clarify and contribute content to what was said earlier of the epistemic and ontic character of our data as to ordinary consciousness.

If you fancy aphorisms, you can also say about perceptual con-sciousness that the philosopher Bishop Berkeley wasn't near to right in saying *esse est percipi*, that *to be is to be perceived*. The better aphorism is *to be perceptually conscious is for something in a way to be*.

In talking of subjective physical worlds, we're not discovering a new thing, a new category. We're just noting and not being distracted from and using an old thing, putting it into a theory of perceptual con-sciousness, making a theory of perceptual consciousness from it and necessarily leaving other stuff out. There has certainly been talk and theory of some or other physical world *being there* for us, in the ordin-ary sense of a part of it being there. There's been talk of *the world as experienced*. There's one for you right now, isn't there? You're imme-diately in touch with one of those right now, aren't you? If this familiar fact doesn't give you a proof of Actualism with respect to perceptual consciousness, it's a very helpful pull in the right direction.

So much for an anticipation of the main body of the theory of Actualism with respect to just perceptual consciousness, whatever is to be said about cognitive consciousness and affective consciousness – including whatever is to be said of the beliefs and also the desires in which perceptual consciousness does not consist at all, but by which it is often accompanied or to which it commonly gives rise.

9. Cognitive and Affective Consciousness – Theories & *What* is and isn't Actual

To turn yet more cursorily to these second and third parts or sides of consciousness, what is actual with your cognitive consciousness, say your just thinking of your mother or the proposition of there being different physicalities, or your *attending* to this room or to something in it?

My answer is that *what* is actual, we need to say, and absolutely all that is actual, *is* a representation or a sequence of representations. And what it is for it to be actual is for it to be subjectively physical, *differently subjectively physical* than with a room. Cognitive consciousness, further, is related to truth. With respect to affective consciousness as against cognitive, say your now wanting a glass of wine, what is actual is also representation, subjectively physical, but related to valuing rather than truth. To come to these propositions, of course, is to come away entirely from the figurative to the literal.

For both cognitive and affective consciousness, as already anticipated, see the the right hand columns of that table. Note in passing, not that the point is simple and without qualification, that given the differences between (1) perceptual consciousness and (2) cognitive and affective consciousness, we certainly do not have the whole nature of consciousness as uniform or principally or essentially or primarily uniform. That in itself is a recommendation of Actualism, a theory's truth to your hold of your consciousness. You know, for a start, how different consciousness in seeing is from thinking and wanting.

If there is a lot of existing philosophical and scientific theory with respect to perceptual consciousness, maybe there is still more with respect to cognitive and affective consciousness. Since I am getting near the end of this lecturing hour, and discussion is better, here is no more than just a list of good subjects in another pile that you might want to bring up, a list of ten good subjects having to do with representation – a list with just a comment or two added:

Universal, Pure, and Other Representationism. My representationism, as you know from what has been said of actual perceptual consciousness, where there is *no* representation at all, is not

Ted Honderich

universal representationism. As you will be hearing in a minute or two, it definitely is not pure. The representation in cognitive and affective consciousness necessarily is *with* something else, one element of the fact.

Our Knowledge of Thinking and Wanting, Our Holds – and the essential comparison with Linguistic Representations.

Linguistic Representations – a Simple Classification from the excellent work of Austin, Searle and others. A large and worthy subject on which we depend .

Languages of Thought. A lot more than Jerry Fodor's single one, mentalese,[33] intriguing though it is – a lot more starting with English.

Evolutionary Causalism, also known by other names, for example as Biosemantics and Teoleological Semantics.[34] Hopeless in my perhaps insufficiently humble view.

Relationism or Computerism, with some *physical* rather than abstract functionalism in it. Also hopeless with actual consciousness. Hard to believe, by the way, that it has ever been a clear-headed answer to a clear question about anything like actual consciousness.

Lingualism as I call it – philosophy of language applied to philosophy of mind. Must be part of the truth.

The Durable Truth of *Some* Representationism or Other in the philosophy of mind. As already said, it has to be there somehow.

Dependency, Convention, Unicorns, how conventions come about and so on – Searle again.[35]

His perfect Chinese Room Thought Experiment[36] – and whether it's in fact also an argument for precisely Actualism. I myself will be saying so in a couple of minutes.

So much for the list of subjects having to do with representation that you might want to bring up. I again say one negative thing in

---

[33]   Fodor, J. The Language of Thought. Thomas Crowell, (1975); *LOT 2: The Language of Thought Revisited* (Oxford University Press, 2008).

[34]   Millikan, R. *White queen Psychology and Other Essays for Alice* (MIT Press, 1993); Papineau, D. *Reality and Representation* (Blackwell, 1987).

[35]   Searle, J. *Speech Acts: An Essay in the Philosophy of Mind* (Cambridge University Press, 1969); *Expression and Meaning* (Cambridge University Press, 1979); *Intentionality: An Essay in the Philosophy of Mind* (Cambridge University Press, 1983); *Consciousness and Language* (Cambridge University Press, 2002); *Making the Social World: The Structure of Human Civilization* (Oxford University Press, 2010).

[36]   E.g. Searle, J. 'Minds, Brains and Programs', *Behavioral and Brain Sciences* (1980); *Minds, Brains and Science* (Reith Lectures, BBC, 1984).

passing. As with functionalism, dualism and the raft of other theories we glanced at, all of these important subjects make or at least tend to make consciousness uniform, flatten it. It isn't flat.

10. Cognitive and Affective Consciousness – *Being Actual* is Being Subjectively Physical in A Way

Put up with just a few words more on some of that pile of subjects, the representational theories of and related to cognitive and affective consciousness. They admittedly do begin from reflection on our spoken and written language, English and the rest, linguistic representations, and in effect move on from that reflection to an account of *conscious* representation.

I report that it seems to me that none of this by itself can work. Searle, admire him as I do, can't succeed in reducing any consciousness to only this. Representation is as true of a line of type as of your thought or want. That is just as true when nobody is thinking it. Absolutely plainly, there is a fundamental and large difference between (1) a line of print on a page or a sequence of sounds and (2) a conscious representation or a sequence of such things. The relation of a conscious representation to language is only part of the truth..

Actualism saves the day. The greatest of philosophers in our tradition, Hume, began or more likely continued a certain habit of inquiry when he was in a way frustrated in coming to an understanding of something, in his case cause and effect. 'We must...', he said, 'proceed like those, who being in search of any thing, that lies concealed from them, and not finding it in the place they expected, beat about all the neighbouring fields, without any certain view or design, in hopes their good fortune will at last guide them to what they search for.[37] Pity he didn't get to the right answer about cause and effect. But let me be hopeful in my own different endeavour. In fact I take it there is more than good reason for hope.

Our maybe reassuring circumstance right now is that if we need to look in another field than the two-term relation of representation, we can in fact do that without going to a wholly new field. If we have to leave the field of thoughts and wants and of representation when it is understood as being somehow only a relation between the representation and what is represented, only a parallel to language, we can in fact do that, by way of another field that is not a new field.

[37] Hume, D. *A Treatise of Human Nature,* (ed.) L.A. Selby-Bigge (Oxford University Press, (1888)), 77–8.

Ted Honderich

I mean we can stay right in and attend to the larger field that we've never been out of, always been in since before getting to cognitive and affective consciousness. In fact never been out of it since we began by settling our whole subject-matter of consciousness in general, since we settled on an initial clarification of consciousness in the primary ordinary sense – consciousness as actual, actual consciousness. The smaller field is in the larger.

Cognitive and affective consciousness, thoughts and wants, are not only representations as first conceived in relation to spoken and written language. They are not only such representations, most saliently propositional attitudes, attitudes to propositional contents, the latter being satisfied by certain states of affairs. Rather, thoughts and wants are *such representations as have the further property of being actual*. That is the burden of what I put to you. That is the fundamental difference between a line of print and conscious representations. Representational consciousness consists in *more* than a dyadic relation. It is not purely representational, not to be clarified by pure representationism.

For the contents of that contention, you will rightly expect me to refer you again to that table – to its list of the characteristics of subjective physical representations. The right-hand columns.

Yes, questions and objections are raised by Actualism. One is prompted by the recent history of the philosophy of consciousness and some of the science of it. Supposedly sufficient conditions having to do with consciousness, it is claimed, fail to be such. Zombies could satisfy them, as Robert Kirk explained.[38] Do you simply say about Actualism that exactly the conditions for consciousness now set out in Actualism – say perceptual consciousness – could be satisfied by something but the thing still wouldn't be conscious at all?

There *is* a temptation to say a kind of replica of me or you that it could satisfy exactly the conditions specified and the replica wouldn't be conscious in the way we know about? That it would indeed be, in this different setting of reflection, just one of those things we've heard about in other contexts, a zombie? Put aside the stuff in zombie theory about metaphysical possibility and all that, which I myself can do without pretty easily. Do you really say there could be something without consciousness despite it and the rest of the situation being exactly what actualism says is what being conscious consists in?

---

[38]   Kirk, R. *Zombies and Consciousness* (Oxford University Press, 2005); 'Zombies', *Stanford Encyclopedia of Philosophy* (2011).

Well, sometimes the best form of defence is counter-assertion because it is true.

In the heatwave of the English summer of 2013, at a lunch table in a club, a medical man gave me a free opinion about diabetes. It led me, after reading up on the internet that the symptoms are thirst, tiredness, seeing less clearly and so on, to the seemingly true proposition about me that I had a lot of the symptoms. I fell into the illusion that I had diabetes – the diabetes illusion.

Think of my diabetes propositions about myself in relation to the 16 propositions on the checklist on the physicality of representations and hence on cognitive and affective consciousness, and the previous 16 counterparts with perceptual consciousness. Is it an illusion that our 16 propositions do *not* capture the nature of consciousness in its three sides? Is it an illusion that there *is* something else or more to consciousness?

If you fortidudinously do a lot of reading of what this lecture comes from, that labouring book with all the typos, will you share with me at least on most days the idea that a persisting elusiveness of perceptual consciousness really *is* itself an illusion? That it really is an illusion that there is *more* to consciousness than we have supposed, more that we have got hold of? I hope so. Keep in mind that there are more kinds of illusion than personal ones. There are illusions of peoples, cultures, politics, philosophy, and science. Hierarchic democracy for a start.

Is it possible to say something more useful quickly about and against the more-to-consciousness illusion? Well, let me gesture at another piece of persuading. You need to keep in mind *all* of the characteristics of perceptual consciousness and the other two kinds of consciousness. But think right now just of our large fact of subjectivity. In Actualism, it is a unity that is *individuality*, akin to the living of a life. A long way from a ruddy homunculus. Think in particular of the large fact itself that your individuality includes and partly consists in nothing less than the reality now of a subjective physical world, certainly out there.

Now add something pre-theoretical. It is pretty certain, and I'd say ordinary reflection proves it, if you need what you bravely and too hopefully call a proof, that there is at least *strangeness* about consciousness. Consciousness is more than just different. It is different in a particular and peculiar way. It is *unique*. When you really try to think of it, it pushes rather than just tempts you to a kind of rhetoric, in line with but beyond our database. Maybe you want to say consciousness somehow is a mesmerizing fact.

Ted Honderich

Actualism explains this, doesn't it? Consciousness for Actualism *is* those things, is on the way to mesmerizing, because in its fundamental part it *is* no less than the existence of a world. Actualism has this special and I'd say great recommendation that goes against the temptation of the zombie objection. As noted in the table, you get a suitably whopping individuality with Actualism, which I have not slowed down to talk about. You get an individuality that brings in an individual world – a real individual world not of rhetoric or poetry or Eastern mysticism but of plain propositions. It can be said, although the words aren't exact, that with Actualism you are a unity that includes the size of a world. That definitely isn't to leave something out.

So Actualism rings true to me. It gets me somewhere with consciousness. I don't think that's because I'm too perceptually conscious, not cognitive enough.

Do you now maybe entirely change your tune? I've known it to happen in seminars. Do you say that this externalism with perceptual consciousness *isn't* crazy, in need of exclamation marks, too rhetorical, circular, against good sense, strange, or in one of the other ways unsatisfactory? Those were more of Colin's McGinn's ideas[39] about a premature predecessor of the present Actualism.[40] Do you say more or less the opposite – that Actualism is old hat, or at least half or somehow old hat? That despite leaving uniformity behind what it comes to is philosophically some familiar idea – the idea that perceptual consciousness has *content*, with the addition, no doubt already made by somebody else, maybe the acute Burge, that the content is external?

Well, Actualism doesn't come to that, even with just perceptual consciousness before we get to the great difference of reflective and affective consciousness. What it comes to, in terms of a headline, is that the consciousness *is* the fact of an existence of the content – a content properly and differently conceived and described. In place of perceptual consciousness as something internal in some relation to something external, no doubt *some* kind of representing relation, we have consciousness as something external in lawful connection with something else external as well as something internal.

And there's no more to the fact of being perceptually conscious than dependent external content. There's no vehicle or any other damned thing in a variety put up or glanced at by various

---

[39] McGinn, C. 'review of Honderich', *Philosophical Review* (2007).
[40] http://www.ucl.ac.uk/~uctytho/HonderichMcGinnStrohminger. htm.

philosophers, including a brain-connection, sense-data, aspects, funny self, direction or aboutness, a higher or second order of stuff, and so on and so forth. And none of that stuff except the existence of representation and attitude in cognitive or affective consciousness either.

Do I have to try harder here? Will some tough philosophical character, maybe some lowlife psychologist, maybe even Ned Block or Dave Chalmers, say in their New York seminar that there is no news in all this verbiage? That Actualism is blunder from Bloomsbury? Will they say that it is a truism that we all accept already that the world, something close to the objective physical world as defined, is part of, maybe the main thing with, perceptual consciousness as somehow ordinarily understood – with another main thing in the story of it being some kind of representation of it?

Well, I don't mind at all being in accord with some or other truism of this sort. But it would be strange to try to *identify* Actualism with it, try to reduce Actualism to it. Even crazy. Actualism is the contention that being perceptually conscious is itself precisely a defined existence of an external world, not the objective physical world. Actualism is absolutely not the proposition, say, that what the story of perceptual consciousness comes to is representation and also the objective physical world. It is not some proposition somehow to the effect that what perceptual consciousness comes to is some kind of *represented* world – what by the way *does* indeed seem to be and deserves to be called exactly a kind of phantom world.

Actualism sure isn't Naive Realism either, which mainly has been just resistance to sense-data and all that, and to the effect that in perception we're in some *unexplained* relation to the objective physical world. Actualism isn't any other externalism either – Putnam or after. And of course we haven't just engaged in what is often called *semantics* – just made a change to the standard use of a word for some purpose. We haven't just more or less arbitrarily transferred the noun 'consciousness' from a state in a perceiver or from a relation of that state to an outer thing – arbitrarily transferred it to a kind of outer thing on the end of an explained relation. We began from a database, ploughed on with the logic of philosophy, and we have a different view of what is out there, its subjective physicality, and it has no unexplained relation or anything else unexplained to it.

And to repeat once more just a word about cognitive and affective consciousness, not only is Actualism not a universal or monolithic representationism about consciousness generally, it isn't a pure representationism either where it is a representationism. As you've heard, cognitive and affective consciousness are not a matter just of

Ted Honderich

representations. They are, to revert to the metaphor, a matter of *actual* representations.

11. Conclusions so Far and More

So we have seen something of the satisfying of two criteria for a decent theory or analysis of consciousness in the primary ordinary sense, which is to say that consciousness clarified as actual consciousness. That is, we have seen something of answers to the two questions of what is actual and what actuality is. There remain other criteria. I pass by or say no more about all that. I just put it to you that Actualism does very well with the criteria of reality and causation, difference in kind, subjectivity, the three sides of consciousness, naturalism, and the relations of consciousness.

There is also the greater hope, as you know, that Actualism, despite not being Naive Realism, does make sense of Naive Realism – which always seemed to have some sense in it despite uncertainty and the condescending labours on sense data of the Logical Positivist Freddie Ayer and those American allies. There is also the hope that Actualism liberates consciousness-science from a common hesitancy or tentativeness about consciousness. It does so partly by offering, in the brave way of philosophers and scientists who would be little Copernicuses, a whole different way of looking at things with perceptual consciousness. It does so, as much, by making all consciousness a matter of science's standard lawful connections.[41] There is no wisp of a ghost in this different machine, no *fin de siecle* lingering over what now needs to go into the past.[42]

It is my own attitude, then, that Actualism is a defeat of pessimism about understanding consciousness. More needs to be said about Chomsky in particular here, what he draws from the history of science – but that is for another day.

There is no general mind-body problem at all, which is to say no unique general consciousness-brain problem. No unique hard problem in Chalmers's well-known sense.[43] No mystery, no ground

---

[41] Honderich, T. *A Theory of Determinism: The Mind, Neuroscience, and Life-Hopes* (Oxford University Press, 1988).

[42] Cf. Nagel and Honderich in Honderich, T. (ed.) *Philosophers of Our Times: Royal Institute of Philosophy Annual Lectures* (Oxford University Press, 2015).

[43] Chalmers, D. 'Facing Up To the Problem of Consciousness', *Journal of Consciousness Studies*, (1995); 'The Puzzle of Conscious Experience',

Actual Consciousness

for McGinn's mysterianism.[44] Of course no reason at all for supposing that science can only deal with the 'neural correlates' of consciousness.

All the connection with consciousness in question, and within consciousness, is the ordinary connection of natural law fundamental to all science. Whatever the lovely research challenges of the connections in actual consciousness, there is no more a general consciousness-brain problem than there is a mass-acceleration problem, or a general heater-etc-and-room-temperature problem, or a general problem of whether if everything goes OK from Muswell Hill onward a 24 bus ends up at London Bridge.

Of course Actualism is a fertile theory, indeed a workplace. It is a workplace for both science and philosophy – it eschews both scientism and philosophism, the latter carried to an extreme by Wittgenstein, who should be better known than he is for the inane remark that 'no supposition seems more natural than that there is no process in the brain correlated with associating or thinking'.[45] Neither science nor philosophy is merely John Locke's handmaiden of the other. Also, by the way, does Actualism make more than a contribution to an old chestnut, the subject that is determinism's consequences for our freedoms and responsibilities? Actualism gives us a *standing*, doesn't it, one that can save us from propounding uncausal free will or origination, gives us a standing first having to do with my being and your being a necessary condition of a subjective physical world?

There remains a last matter for us now. Was ordinary consciousness in the primary ordinary sense, the core sense, the right consciousness to consider? My short answer can't be yes, since there is no possibility of showing that any consciousness is *the* right one.

In the free world of philosophy, anyone can follow that crowd that considers the consciousness that in our terms consists in both (i) ordinary-consciousness mentality plus (ii) mentality that is not ordinary-consciousness mentality. People can be still freer and consider consciousness where it also includes such facts of perception as those having to do with retinas. They can, differently, just consider

---

Scientific American (1995); *The Conscious Mind: In Search of a Fundamental Theory*, (Oxford University Press, 1996).
[44] McGinn various cited works; Flanagan, O. *The Science of the Mind* (MIT Press, 1991); Honderich, T. *Actual Consciousness* (Oxford University Press, 2014).
[45] Wittgenstein, L. *Zettel* (University of California Press, 1967), 608.

Ted Honderich

consciousness that consists in our perceptual consciousness *plus* the cognitive and affective consciousness that consists in the large fact of attention. They can consider, as many do, in my view fatally, consciousness in general without distinguishing our perceptual consciousness from our cognitive and affective consciousness.

But one thing that can be said for our choice of ordinary consciousness is that no inquirer can leave out ordinary consciousness, of which we can have an adequate initial clarification. This consciousness must surely be, in fact it *is*, what serves to identify the other additions, most obviously the addition of the mentality that is not ordinary consciousness. This combined subject, and in particular the addition, needs to be distinguished from other explanations of behaviour, say gravity or mere musculature, and it cannot be distinguished without reliance on exactly ordinary consciousness. If Actualism is a defensible theory of ordinary consciousness, no general theory can leave it out. It is essential. I don't think that is true of any other initial idea of consciousness.

All these conclusions are the result not of proof, for which philosophy as against science is too hard,[46] but of a weight of argument and judgement. Actualism, I propose, is a case of satisfying Hume's hope for pieces of philosophy – an inescapability of conclusions given prior acceptance of at least reasonable premises.

University College, London
t.honderich@ucl.ac.uk

---

[46] Cf. Chalmers, in Honderich (ed.) *Philosophers of Our Times: Royal Institute of Philosophy Annual Lectures* (Oxford University Press, 2015).

Training, Transformation and Education

DAVID BAKHURST

Abstract

In *Mind and World*, John McDowell concludes that human beings 'are born mere animals' and 'are transformed into thinkers and intentional agents', principally by their initiation into language. Such 'transformational views' of human development typically represent first-language learning as a movement from a non-rationally secured conformity with correct practice, through increasing understanding, to a state of rational mastery of correct practice. Accordingly, they tend to invoke something like Wittgenstein's concept of training to explain the first stage of this process. This essay considers the cogency of this view of learning and development. I agree with Sebastian Rödl that the idea of training (as developed, say, by Meredith Williams) is inadequate to the nature of infancy and child-parent interaction, and I draw on the work of Lev Vygotsky and Michael Tomasello to offer McDowell a richer picture, which acknowledges the child's active role in fostering the second-personal relations that underlie the possibility of language learning. Such considerations force us to revise the transformational view, but do not refute it outright as Rödl believes. I conclude by considering the relevance of McDowell's view of second nature to two striking ideas: Ian Hacking's suggestion that the development of autistic children is 'non-Vygotskian' and Derek Parfit's claim that persons are not human beings.

1. Introduction

At the conclusion of *Mind and World*, John McDowell writes:

> Now it is not even clearly intelligible to suppose that a creature might be born at home in the space of reasons. Human beings are not: they are born mere animals, and they are transformed into thinkers and intentional agents in the course of coming to maturity.[1]

According to McDowell, during their upbringing, or *Bildung*, human beings acquire 'a second nature'.[2] This occurs principally through the acquisition of language, which equips us with conceptual capacities that enable a form of life in which reason is manifest. To be

---

[1] J. McDowell, *Mind and World*, 2nd edition (1st edition, 1994) (Cambridge, MA: Harvard University Press, 1996), 125.
[2] Ibid., 84.

doi:10.1017/S135824611500003X

David Bakhurst

initiated into this form of life, McDowell attests, 'is the same thing as acquiring a mind, the capacity to think and act intentionally'.[3]

In a recent paper, Sebastian Rödl rejects this 'transformational view' of human development, and criticises my sympathetic treatment of it in *The Formation of Reason*.[4] I am drawn to the transformational view by my admiration for McDowell's philosophy and because similar conceptions figure prominently in the work of Russian thinkers on whom I have written in the past, such as Vygotsky and Ilyenkov.[5] Ilyenkov, for example, maintains that at birth the human child has a merely animal mode of existence and her mind is a merely animal mind. Only through enculturation does 'the individual for the first time become a person, a representative of the "human race", while before this she was merely a representative of a biological species'.[6] Rödl thinks such talk incoherent. For him, the concepts *animal* and *person* signify an individual's 'principle of being'; these are not statuses that can be acquired or lost in the course of a creature's existence so that a living individual could start out animal and become person. Moreover, Rödl argues it is intolerably paradoxical to portray the power of autonomy – which both McDowell and I think definitive of rational being – as a product of initiation or *Bildung*. Autonomy must be always-already present in the child, an aspect of her first nature, if she is to become a truly self-determining being.

In this essay, I want to explore whether McDowell's version of the transformational view might be developed and defended. I shall conclude by briefly considering the light McDowell's view casts on two striking claims advanced recently by distinguished philosophers: Ian

---

[3]   Ibid., 126.
[4]   S. Rödl, 'Education and Autonomy', paper presented at the launch of the Centre for Philosophy of Education at the Institute of Education, London, May 2012, and to appear in D. Bakhurst and P. Fairfield, *Education and Conversation* (London: Bloomsbury Academic, forthcoming); D. Bakhurst, *The Formation of Reason* (Oxford: Wiley-Blackwell, 2011).
[5]   See, e.g., D. Bakhurst, *Consciousness and Revolution in Soviet Philosophy* (Cambridge: Cambridge University Press, 1991) and 'Meaning, Normativity and the Life of the Mind', *Language and Communication* **17** (1997), 33–51.
[6]   E.V. Ilyenkov, 'Dialektika ideal'nogo' ('The Dialectic of the Ideal'), in his *Isskustvo i kommunisticheckii ideal (Art and the Communist Ideal)* (Moscow: Isskustvo, 1984), 68. An extract from this paper appears in English translation as 'The Concept of the Ideal', in E.V. Ilyenkov, *The Ideal in Human Activity* (Pacifica, CA: Marxist Internet Archive, 2009).

Hacking's suggestion that the development of autistic children is 'non-Vygotskian', and Derek Parfit's contention that persons are not human beings.

2. The Status of McDowell's Position

McDowell himself resists the idea that his position stands in any need of development. He tells us his notion of second nature is to serve as what Wittgenstein called a reminder for a particular purpose;[7] namely, that we need not gift the concept of nature to natural science, so that anything that eludes natural-scientific modes of explanation is cast as supernatural or occult. If we heed that reminder, we can say that human responsiveness to reasons is a perfectly natural phenomenon even though it requires a form of understanding – 'space of reasons intelligibility' – distinct from and irreducible to natural-scientific styles of explanation. The reminder, however, is designed to bring to mind plain facts about the natural course of a normal human upbringing. It is not an invitation to build a philosophical theory of second nature.[8]

McDowell suggests, then, that his talk of transformation is meant as a statement of the obvious, designed merely to draw attention to the undeniable difference in capacity between a newborn and a normal mature human being. But if this is all he intends, why does

---

[7]   J. McDowell, 'Comment on Hans-Peter Krüger's Paper', *Philosophical Explorations*, **1** (1998), 122, citing L. Wittgenstein, *Philosophical Investigations*, trans. G.E.M. Anscombe (Oxford: Basil Blackwell), § 127. See also the conclusion of Lecture 4 of *Mind and World*.

[8]   McDowell explains: 'What we are reminded of should be something that we knew all along, but were intelligibly induced to forget under the peculiar stress of philosophical reflection. What we are reminded of should be in itself – that is, considered in abstraction from the feeling of being confronted by deep and difficult intellectual problems that it is supposed to liberate us from – thin and obvious. I would be quite happy if someone responded to my diagnosis of some characteristic ailments of modern epistemology by saying, "Of course! How can we have been enticed into forgetting how obviously right it is to say that a repertoire of conceptual capacities belongs to the acquired nature of a mature human being?" And it is another way of making the same point to say that I feel misunderstood if someone responds rather as follows: "Second nature, that's an interesting idea; but don't we now need a philosophical theory of second nature?" This would be a refusal to take the reminder as I intend it.' ('Comment on Hans-Peter Krüger's Paper', 123).

David Bakhurst

he formulate his position so provocatively, saying that human beings are 'born mere animals' and later 'acquire' minds? That makes the transformation sound metaphysically significant. And there are times when McDowell affirms just that. In a sympathetic discussion of Hegel, he writes:

> We should not be frightened away from holding that initiation into the right sort of communal practice makes a *metaphysical* difference... Responsiveness to reasons, the very idea of which is inseparable from the idea of communal practices, marks out a fully-fledged human individual as no longer a merely biological particular, but a being of a metaphysically new kind.[9]

Such remarks help explain why McDowell questions the intelligibility of a creature's being born into the space of reasons, but they make it hard to renounce philosophising about second nature.

What, then, does McDowell mean to preclude when he disavows theorising second nature? His usual target is constructive philosophical theories that aspire to answer traditional 'How is x possible?' questions.[10] For McDowell, the proper response to such questions is to interrogate the frame of mind that makes the possibility of x seem problematic, so that the question becomes no longer urgent. This is McDowell's way with 'How is meaning possible?' The question looks unavoidable only because we work with a scientistic conception of objective reality that makes it hard to accommodate meaning in the world. But if we reject scientism and operate with a richer conception of nature, the place of meaning in the world is no longer a puzzle to be solved by theory. McDowell's reluctance to theorise second nature is of a piece with this. The question of how something that starts a mere animal gets to enter the space of reasons is to be exorcised, not answered.

However, it is one thing to deny we need a constructive account of how the space of reasons and its inhabitants are possible, quite another to say that invoking 'the bare idea of *Bildung*' will lay all puzzlement to rest.[11] After all, the idea of second nature is bound up with substantive claims in McDowell's thought – such as the view that its acquisition is a precondition of experience proper,

---

[9]   McDowell, 'Towards a Reading of Hegel on Action', in his *Having the World in View: Essays on Kant, Hegel, and Sellars* (Cambridge, MA: Harvard University Press), 172.
[10]   McDowell, *Mind and World*, xxiv and 'Postscript to Lecture V', and 'Wittgensteinian "Quietism"', *Common Knowledge* **15**, 365–372.
[11]   McDowell, *Mind and World*, 95.

rather than mere sentience. Moreover, McDowell represents the concept of second nature as philosophically fertile; for example, he claims Kant was unable to make sense of the self as 'a bodily presence in the world' because he lacked 'a seriously exploitable notion of second nature'.[12] But it is hard to see how such a notion could be seriously exploited unless we can say more about second nature's acquisition. And surely much could be said that would be less ambitious than the constructive project McDowell disavows, but nonetheless philosophically interesting.[13] It therefore seems worth trying to say more about the transformational view than McDowell is willing to.

3. Training

McDowell does tell us *something* about the acquisition of second nature. In *Mind and World*, he recommends generalising Aristotle's account of the formation of moral character to 'arrive at the notion of having one's eyes opened to reasons at large by acquiring a second nature',[14] and he invokes Gadamerian themes about the transformative effect of initiation into language, conceived as 'a repository of tradition, a store of historically accumulated wisdom about what is a reason for what'.[15] Both discussions are brief, but suggestive. More recently, in response to commentators clamouring for more detail,

---

[12] Ibid., 104.

[13] One might, for example, explore how in the course of their maturation and enculturation, and their acquisition of language, human children come by a conception of the world; that is, concepts, beliefs, forms of thought and reasoning, modes of self-understanding, and so on. To this end, we might emphasise the skills of narrative understanding that Alasdair MacIntyre in ch. 15 of *After Virtue* (London: Duckworth, 1981) deems central to the idea the unity of a human life, or the rich conception of folk psychology that Jerome Bruner in *Acts of Meaning* (Cambridge, MA: Harvard University Press, 1990) portrays as enabling our understanding of self and others. MacIntyre and Bruner, in Vygotskian fashion, describe cognitive tools that are part of the cultural inheritance that makes us what we are. And the significance of such tools is not only cognitive, since they influence many aspects of our mental lives, including the character of our emotions, feelings, and desires. Their acquisition is therefore genuinely transformative, since they enable distinctively human awareness and understanding. But neither MacIntyre nor Bruner are doing 'constructive philosophy' in McDowell's pejorative sense.

[14] McDowell, *Mind and World*, 84.

[15] Ibid., 126.

David Bakhurst

McDowell appeals to the notion of *training*. Second nature, he tells us, is 'no more than the idea of a way of being...that has been acquired by something on the lines of training'.[16] I propose to consider what might be made of this notion. McDowell's appeal to training is Wittgensteinian in two ways. First, it is deflationary and quietistic; it is supposed to be consistent with his aversion to theorising second nature. Second, training is a notion that figures prominently in Wittgenstein's own remarks on learning language and mathematics, so we might suppose McDowell means us to think of the child's entering the space of reasons along lines suggested by Wittgenstein.

In the *Brown Book*, Wittgenstein writes, 'I am using the word "trained" in a way strictly analogous to that in which we talk of an animal being trained to do certain things. It is done by means of example, reward, punishment, and suchlike'.[17] This resonates with McDowell's claim that human children are born 'mere animals'. But equally, it opens McDowell to the kind of criticisms provoked by Wittgenstein's remark. It has been noted that the term Wittgenstein uses, 'Abrichtung', is reserved for the training of animals and is not used of children.[18] Critics are quick to seize on this and lament the 'brutal' character of Wittgenstein's view of teaching.[19] Is this really what McDowell has in mind by training?

We should not be too quick, however, to jump on the critics' bandwagon. 'Abrichtung' is not the only expression Wittgenstein uses that is translated as 'training'. There is also 'Unterricht' – meaning 'teaching', 'tuition' or 'instruction' – which has no such unfortunate connotations.[20] Moreover, Wittgenstein sometimes uses 'abrichten' in tandem with terms for teaching such as 'lehren' or 'beibringen'.[21]

---

[16] McDowell, 'Responses', in M. Willaschek (ed.), *John McDowell: Reason and Nature. Lecture and Colloquium in Münster 1999* (Münster, Hamburg, Loon: LIT Verlag), 98. See also McDowell, 'Responses', in J. Lingaard (ed.), *John McDowell: Experience, Norm and Nature* (Oxford: Blackwell), 220, where he offers a more expansive view, referring to 'education, habituation, or training'.

[17] L. Wittgenstein, *The Blue and Brown Books* (Oxford: Basil Blackwell), 77.

[18] W. Huemer, 'The Transition from Causes to Norms: Wittgenstein on Training', *Grazer Philosophische Studien* **71** (2006), 205–225.

[19] See, e.g., M. Luntley, 'Training and Learning', *Educational Philosophy and Theory* **40** (2008), 697.

[20] Wittgenstein, *Philosophical Investigations,* §§ 6, 9.

[21] L. Wittgenstein, *Last Writings on the Philosophy of Psychology, Volume 1.* Edited by G.H. von Wright and H. Nyman, translated by

Training, Transformation and Education

The basic idea in Wittgenstein, and in Aristotle too, is that the teaching of fundamental concepts cannot presuppose the competence it is designed to instill. So when it comes to the child's acquiring rational capacities as such, learning must take the form of a movement from non-rationally secured conformity with correct practice, through a growing awareness of correct practice, to rational mastery of the grounds of correct practice.[22] It is training that is supposed to bring the child's behaviour into line with correct practice so that it becomes, as Jose Medina puts it, second nature to her.[23] Nothing suggests this process has to be 'brutal'.[24]

It remains to be seen, however, whether the concept of training can really be of use to McDowell. Meredith Williams develops the notion in the following way. The child learning her first language is normatively inept: 'the novice is precisely one who cannot engage in first-order normative practices'. But she has 'certain behavioural and perceptual capacities and abilities' that permit her to be trained to act in ways that conform to the norms governing basic language games.[25] At first, the novice 'is not able to see the meaning or significance of the words and actions of the master', but adults nonetheless treat her words as meaningful, and her utterances as judgements and requests, before they are such.[26] There is thus a division of labour in which

---

G. Luckhardt and M. Aue (Oxford: Basil Blackwell, 1982), §§ 203 (see note), 206.

[22] In *The Formation of Reason* (136–141), I call this 'learning by initiation'. Meredith Williams notes the parallel between Wittgenstein and Aristotle in 'The Significance of Learning in Wittgenstein's Later Philosophy', *Canadian Journal of Philosophy* **24** (1994), 173. I have more to say about McDowell's use of Aristotle and Wittgenstein in 'Freedom and Second Nature in *The Formation of Reason*', *Mind, Culture, and Activity* **19** (2012), 172–189.

[23] J. Medina, *The Unity of Wittgenstein's Philosophy: Necessity, Intelligibility, and Normativity* (Albany NY: SUNY, 2002), 167.

[24] Though tales of Wittgenstein's own practice as a schoolteacher do give one pause. As is well known, after completing the *Tractatus*, Wittgenstein worked for several years in an elementary school. He eventually gave up the profession after he struck a boy so hard as to cause him to collapse. Later that day, one parent told Wittgenstein 'he wasn't a teacher, he was an animal-trainer!' (reported in R. Monk, *Wittgenstein: The Duty of Genius* (London: Vintage, 1990), 233).

[25] M. Williams, *Blind Obedience* (London: Routledge, 2010), 105.

[26] Ibid., 238. See also 106: 'The status of the naïve learner's utterances (that, for example, they are taken as judgments or requests) is a function of the status extended to those utterances by masters of that practice. The

David Bakhurst

adults lend meaning to the child's words. To speak meaningfully is to participate in a practice or custom, and that requires an appropriate setting, which can be in place before the child is in command of the meaning of her utterances. This makes it possible for the child to find herself operating in a domain of meaning, and gradually to adhere to its norms so that she can deploy meanings to influence others' behaviour. Thus she steadily comes to act, not just in conformity with correct practice, but out of an appreciation of what is required, and with this she enters the space of reasons.[27]

In this way, training grounds the acquisition of basic linguistic concepts and the bedrock practices and judgements constitutive of the background to our lives. It secures the common ground – the fundamental agreement – that is the precondition of our normative practices. As Williams puts it, 'What we find natural is not a matter of our being attuned to certain metaphysical properties of the objects we are confronting, but rather is a matter of how we have been trained into the social practice of certain language-games'.[28] In this, the social dimension is essential – 'our acquisition of language is our enculturation into a society':

> Failure to grasp this essential point makes it mysterious how human beings can ever change from being creatures subject to conditioning to adults displaying their mastery of language through [e.g.] engagement in the world as scientists using the epistemic and logical apparatus of hypothesis formation and testing.[29]

For Quine, it's conditioning all the way up; for Fodor, it's hypothesis-testing all the way down. The truth is that it is conditioning up to a point at which, through enculturation, the child's behaviour acquires normative standing and, to invoke a famous phrase from *On Certainty*, light gradually dawns across the whole.[30]

The predictable objection is that no appeal to training could possibly account for the child's emerging facility with meaning. As

---

initiate learner speaks, makes judgments, requests, and the like only by virtue of a courtesy extended to the learner by those who have already mastered the practice.'
[27]   Williams, like McDowell, uses this expression, which of course originates with Wilfrid Sellars.
[28]   Williams, *Blind Obedience*, 100.
[29]   Ibid., 97.
[30]   L. Wittgenstein, *On Certainty*, edited by G.E.M. Anscome and G.H. von Wright, translated by Denis Paul and G.E.M. Anscombe (Oxford: Blackwell), §141.

Michael Luntley sees it, the lesson of Wittgenstein's reflections on rule-following and family resemblances is that what the novice must learn is radically underdetermined by anything her teacher can say. There is a gap that needs to be bridged. But conditioning could not do this, for it is one thing to be caused to conform to a pattern, quite another to grasp what a norm requires and act in light of that understanding.[31] Luntley concludes that we have to credit initiate learners with rational capacities from the get-go. He argues that there are empirical grounds for this attribution. But it also stands to philosophical reason, for '[w]ithout a responsiveness to reasons, an acknowledgement of correctness and incorrectness of application... there are no first moves with words'.[32] Indeed, only if the child is already equipped with reasoning skills is training even possible.[33] This Wittgenstein himself recognises when he represents teachers as saying things like 'This *and similar things* are called "games"'.[34] Such injunctions make no sense unless the learner has the capacity to work out the relevant notion of similarity. But if she has that capacity, then conditioning is unnecessary. Williams's (Vygotskian) idea of adults 'lending' capacity to the child is a fantasy. No amount of behaving as if a child has some competence is going to magic the competence into existence. So, Luntley concludes, we are better off reading Wittgenstein as friendly to a rationalist approach to learning.

4. A Plague on Both Houses

There is something unsatisfying about both sides of this controversy. Luntley complains that the kind of explanation Williams offers derives something out of nothing.[35] But his conception of

---

[31]   Some Wittgensteinians recognise that training must be distinguished from conditioning. For example, although in 'The Significance of Learning in Wittgenstein's Later Philosophy', Williams admits that '[o]stensive training or teaching, for Wittgenstein, has affinities with the behaviorist notion of conditioning' (178), she later claims that training is 'importantly different' because it aims to instill conformity with a normative practice rather than mere dispositions to respond (Medina takes a similar position, *The Unity of Wittgenstein's Philosophy*, 158–159). But this merely recognises the problem to which Luntley is drawing attention without solving it.

[32]   Luntley, 'Training and Learning', 709–10 n9.

[33]   Ibid., 703.

[34]   Wittgenstein, *Philosophical Investigations,* §69 (Wittgenstein's emphasis).

[35]   Luntley, 'Training and Learning', 698.

David Bakhurst

explanation stacks the deck in favour of his rationalist alternative. The fact is that where there is learning and development, you *do* get – not something out of nothing – but more out of less. So you must embrace modes of explanation that capture *becoming*. Otherwise you will find no alternative but to build into the child the very capacities you are trying to explain. Luntley cannot appreciate the developmental significance of the proleptic attribution to the child of abilities she does not yet possess because he favours a highly individualistic conception of competence. For him, there is a huge contrast between the child (a) making a movement or sound as a response to a stimulus and (b) intentionally making a meaningful gesture or utterance; (a) cannot become (b) merely because others treat it as such – either the child acts with understanding or she does not. If the lights are off, no initiation is going to turn them on; if the lights are already on, initiation is mere setting. (I parody, but only a little.[36]) Here Luntley ignores the constitutive role of context. The child's actions take on meaning because of the role they are accorded in the language game. This scaffolds the child's gradual mastery of those actions *as* acts of meaning, so that her moves in the game can become self-conscious acts (though as such they remain dependent on context). The development of the child's activity, of her mode of engagement with the world and with other people, is quite properly portrayed as the gradual mastery of techniques of language that enable the giving and taking of reasons (and much else besides). But this cannot be appreciated if, like Luntley, we focus on how it looks from the first-personal perspective of the child, which is after all in the process of taking shape.

Yet Luntley's scepticism about training is naturally provoked by Williams's talk of understanding how a creature subject only to conditioning changes into a fully-fledged inhabitant of the space of reasons. It is hard not to hear Williams as trying to answer the kind of 'How is x possible?' question McDowell would prefer to exorcise. [37] And if that

[36] Luntley ('Training and Learning', 710 n16) quotes Fodor and Lepore with approval: 'Wittgenstein suggests that first language learning is somehow a matter of "training"; but he says nothing intelligible about how training could lead to learning in a creature that doesn't already have a mind.' (J. Fodor and E. Lepore, 'Brandom Beleaguered', *Philosophy and Phenomenological Research* **LXXIV** (2007), 677–691).

[37] Someone might protest that Williams poses this question as one a Quinean must confront. It is not obvious that she thinks the same question is a live issue for the Wittgensteinian. Nevertheless, her text gives the impression that the appeal to training into social practices is a way to answer the question rather than to exorcise it.

310

Training, Transformation and Education

is her aspiration, critics will feel entitled to complain that she lacks resources to discharge the explanatory burden she has taken on.
Moreover, a Wittgensteinian should aspire to bring the natural
history of human beings into view by means of 'observations which
no one has doubted, but which have escaped remark only because
they are always before our eyes'.[38] But much that Williams says
strikes me as insensitive to the reality of infancy and the interaction
of child and parent (or other primary caregivers). The condition of
the initiate learner is underdescribed in a way reminiscent of the
behaviourist framework that predominated in Wittgenstein's time.
We are told little specific about the child's capacities. She has 'perceptual abilities' and 'natural reactions' that training must modify and
supplement with acquired responses. In this, the child is represented
as a passive recipient, blindly obeying the adults who 'calibrate' her
behaviour with the community's. The assumption seems to be that
parents actively train their children into the normative structures of
daily life, drill them in language norms by modifying their behaviour
by reward and punishment. But, as Rödl's aforementioned paper
nicely brings out, parents do no such thing. They care for their children in environments that are normatively structured, full of significant objects, and where there is a lot of language about. In time,
children start to understand some of that language and later they
start speaking themselves. But it is not clear that their parents *do* anything to make this happen.[39] So parents are much less active, and pre-
linguistic children much less passive, than the position implies.

Philosophical accounts of early childhood can be rather artificial.
Williams writes that the assertion 'This is a hand' is something
'one can readily recognize' as the sort of thing 'that adults say to
young children'.[40] But this strikes me as false. It is very unlikely
that a child, even G.E. Moore's child, would be told any such
thing. Of course, children are, for example, taught word-games and
songs that introduce them to language (such as 'Head and
Shoulders, Knees and Toes'), but it is one-dimensional to see this
as training, and contentious to assert that such practices are essential
preconditions of learning language. The fact is that children are, from
day one, included in activities expressive of our shared form of life,
activities that constitute the common ground from which the rule-

[38] Wittgenstein, *Philosophical Investigations*, §415.
[39] Of course it is important that they *not* do things that might inhibit
their child's development, such as radically isolating or otherwise abusing
them.
[40] Williams, *Blind Obedience*, 255.

311

following paradox appears an empty intellectual game. From within this activity, the meaning of 'cat' is not an open question to be closed by training, except in the mundane sense that, if the child's use of the word is eccentric, she can be shown how to use it properly.

5. Vygotsky

If we are to say something on McDowell's behalf about the acquisition of second nature, we must look beyond Wittgensteinian conceptions of training, and aspire to a richer appreciation of the psychological capacities of the pre-linguistic child and a more nuanced view of child-adult interaction. This Vygotsky anticipated, and that is why I recommend his approach to McDowell in *The Formation of Reason*.[41] Vygotsky represents the human infant as endowed with what he calls 'elementary mental functions', which include non-linguistic thought (basic problem-solving activity), pre-intellectual speech, sensory awareness, involuntary or associative memory, and basic forms of attention, volition, desire, and emotion. These capacities are portrayed as independent modules and their development is a function of the child's biological maturation. The nature of the elementary functions – their deliverances, development and interrelations – can be explained in causal or biological terms. They represent a unity, the principle of which is to sustain an animal life – to fulfil needs for food, comfort, warmth and safety, and to cope with the dictates of the immediate environment.

The mature human mind, in contrast, forms a system of 'higher mental functions' that includes linguistic thought and reasoning, intelligent speech, voluntary memory and attention, rational perception, desire, and emotion, and intentional volition. These higher functions are unified in a number of ways. First, they are 'interfunctionally related', in that the functioning of any one informs the functioning of the others and the development of any one makes possible changes in the others. Second, their common currency is *meaning*; they deal in content-bearing states, which can be expressed in propositional form, so that what can be remembered can be thought of,

---

[41] Bakhurst, *Formation of Reason*, 152–157. For more detail, see my *Consciousness and Revolution in Soviet Philosophy*, ch.3; 'Social Memory in Soviet Thought', in D. Middleton and D. Edwards, *Collective Remembering* (London: Sage, 1990), 203–226, and 'Vygotsky's Demons', in M. Cole, H. Daniels and J. Wertsch (eds), *The Cambridge Companion to Vygotsky* (Cambridge: Cambridge University Press, 2007), 50–76.

spoken of, reasoned about, regretted, and so on. Third, the principle of their unity is their role in sustaining the perspective of a rational animal life, self-conscious and self-determining.

Vygotsky argues that the key point in the transition from elementary to higher mental functions lies in the convergence of the developmental trajectory of two hitherto independent functions – pre-linguistic thought and pre-intellectual speech. This occurs when the child begins to deploy articulate sounds or gestures in problem-solving activity. With this, intellectual speech and verbal thought become possible, as do logical memory and forms of attention, perception, emotion and volition mediated by meaning, and as the child learns language so those possibilities are made real. As a result, the child's mind is restructured by her emerging facility with meaning.

It is central to Vygotsky's position that the higher mental functions are social in nature and origin. Meaning's home is communication, and communication originates in collaborative activities between individuals. Vygotsky illustrates this with his famous account of pointing.[42] He argues that the origins of pointing lie in the child's grasping for desired objects that are out of reach. Her grasping is interpreted by adults as indicating her desires and they respond accordingly. At first, then, the meaning of the child's act is established by others. Gradually she becomes attuned to how others respond to her grasping and she starts to deploy the movement to direct others' attention to objects she wants. In this way, the child's movement comes to have meaning for her, not just for others, and taking a physically simplified form, becomes a general means to direct another's attention.

So here is a pattern similar to the one Williams celebrates. The child's activity is first given meaning by surrounding adults, meaning that is only later 'internalised' by the child as she begins to point so that others should understand what she is indicating. With this, a movement that began in the space of stimulus-and-response becomes a true gesture, a performance in the space of reasons.[43] Although the case of pointing illustrates only one aspect of the child's entrance into meaning, Vygotsky takes it to be indicative of deep facts about the social nature of mind:

[42]   L.S. Vygotsky, *History of the Development of the Higher Mental Functions. The Collected Works of L.S. Vygotsky, Volume 4.* Translated by M. Hall. (New York: Plenum Press, 1997), 104–5.

[43]   Note that although Vygotsky here discusses an isolated gesture, he would be happy with the holistic view that, when it comes to the child's emerging facility with meaning, 'light dawns gradually over the whole'.

David Bakhurst

The pointing gesture most likely begins to indicate by movement what is understood by others and only later becomes a direction for the child himself.

Thus we might say that through others we become ourselves, and this rule refers not only to the individual (*lichnost'*) as a whole, but also to the history of each separate function. This also comprises the essence of the process of cultural development expressed in a purely logical form. The individual becomes for himself what he is in himself through what he manifests for others. This is also the process of the forming of the individual.[44]

This idea Vygotsky later expressed in his 'general genetic law of psychological development': each higher mental function originates in the interrelation of child and adult engaged in joint activity, and is only later mastered by the child.

Vygotsky clearly subscribes to something like the transformational view. Human elementary mental functioning is analogous to the psychology of apes, but the transition to the higher functions represents a qualitative change in the nature and structure of the mind. The higher mental functions are not simply more developed forms of their elementary counterparts, and there is no chance of a reductive reconstruction of the emergence of the higher functions out of the elementary. Instead, we must trace their emergence by attention to facilitating processes of biological maturation and enculturation. Vygotsky's position is consistent with the idea that a human individual acquires a second nature, one that is essentially cultural and historical in form. He might even have agreed that a human being 'acquires a mind', if by 'mind' we mean the higher psychological functions characteristic of rational thought, experience and action. But at the same time Vygotsky was no crass environmentalist. His view is compatible with a sophisticated nativism about the elementary psychological functions.

Interestingly, Vygotsky explicitly denies that training, in the sense of habit formation, plays a significant role in the child's entrance into meaning, while at the same time rejecting the rationalist alternative that grasping meanings should be understood as a kind of intellectual discovery on the child's part.[45] Neither training nor discovery will do. What is at issue is the transition from one mode of life, informed by a

[44] Vygotsky, *History of the Development of the Higher Mental Functions*, 105.
[45] L.S. Vygotsky and A. Luria, 'Tool and Symbol in Child Development', in R. van der Veer and J. Valsiner, *The Vygotsky Reader* (Oxford: Blackwell, 1994), 113.

certain developing style of psychological activity, to another differently-organised mode of being. There is a sense in which this transition brings into being the child's capacity to think for herself; so we cannot represent her as exercising that capacity from the outset. The motor of development is the child's entering certain kinds of social relation with caregivers, but this process is complex and multifaceted and cannot be subsumed under a single concept like *training*. Consider again the pointing example. On Vygotsky's account, the child's development could not happen without the contribution of adults tending to the child. But nothing like training is going on.

6. Tomasello

Vygotsky was writing more than 80 years ago – that's ancient history from the perspective of contemporary psychology. I recommend Vygotsky's position to McDowell not on grounds of empirical accuracy, but for its general shape. Vygotsky shows us how we might think the emergence of second nature without resorting to conceptions of training that have their home in the kind of behaviourist paradigm Vygotsky was keen to transcend. But of course it would be nice to offer McDowell some compelling contemporary empirical work, broadly consistent with Vygotsky's vision. In this regard, the obvious resource is Michael Tomasello's path-breaking reflections on language acquisition and the natural history of human thinking.

Tomasello's view is that human communication is fundamentally cooperative. Cooperative communication first emerged in evolution, as it emerges in human individuals, with natural gestures of pointing and pantomiming. He argues that such communicative acts presuppose intentionality on the part of the communicators: not just individual, but *shared* intentionality. That is, human communication requires that speakers have an understanding of a plural subject, a 'we', with joint goals and shared knowledge. Tomasello speaks of a 'shared intentionality infrastructure' that (i) establishes common conceptual ground among human communicators (making possible joint attention and the formation of joint intentions), and (ii) involves pro-social motivations to request help from and offer help to other people, and to share information, attitudes, and emotions with them.[46]

[46] M. Tomasello, *Origins of Human Communication* (Cambridge, MA: MIT Press, 2008), 11–12.

David Bakhurst

Tomasello argues that 'language acquisition is possible only when young children have available to them something resembling the full shared intentionality infrastructure'.[47] This emerges around 12 months of age, when children start to engage in joint attentional activities and to point communicatively.[48] Tomasello and his collaborators represent its origins in a way reminiscent of Vygotsky: it issues from the convergence of two lines of development. The first is 'a general primate (or perhaps great ape) line of development for understanding intentional action and perception, which evolved in the context of primates' crucially important competitive interactions with one another for food, mates, and other resources'. The second is 'a uniquely human line of development for sharing psychological states with others'.[49] Shortly after the convergence of these trajectories, children begin to construct shared goals and intentions, and to volunteer help when they discern that another's goals have been frustrated. They also begin to produce iconic gestures to indicate activities or absent objects. As the child develops language, these gestures are gradually displaced, taking up refuge in pretend play. This developing facility with shared intentionality, Tomasello argues, provides the foundation for the internalisation of social norms, shared beliefs, and cultural institutions.

Tomasello does much to establish this position experimentally and to defend its compatibility with evolutionary theory. For present purposes, however, the crucial point is his view of shared intentionality. Tomasello takes the shared intentionality infrastructure to have been forged by evolution. Though a facility for shared intentionality is 'not simply innate, or maturational', requiring for its emergence 'constant interaction with the environment, especially the social environment',[50] it does not issue from training, and once it is in place, it makes possible modes of teaching and learning that differ dramatically from training (at least if training is understood as akin to conditioning).

Shared intentionality has been a hot topic in philosophy for a quarter century or so. Where there is shared intentionality, you and I share the intention to φ, not just when you intend to φ and I intend to φ, but when you and I intend jointly to φ: I intend that

47 Ibid., 104.
48 Ibid., 139 ff.
49 M. Tomasello and M. Carpenter, 'Shared Intentionality', *Developmental Science* **10** (2007), 124.
50 M. Tomasello, *A Natural History of Human Thinking* (Cambridge, MA: Harvard University Press, 2014), 145–147.

you and I φ together, and vice-versa. That is, *we* intend that *we* φ together. Much of the philosophical discussion of the nature and possibility of such 'we-intentionality' considers the attitudes of mature subjects that have self-conscious understanding of their own mental states. It is important that Tomasello is also concerned with something more primitive. This is the basic intersubjectivity at the heart of joint attention and joint activity: where the focus of child and adult on a shared object of activity involves an element of mutual recognition of a common endeavour. This, Tomasello suggests, 'seems to be present in nascent form very early in human ontogeny as infants share emotional states with others in turn-taking sequences'.[51]

[51] Tomasello and Carpenter, 'Shared Intentionality', 124. In his recent book, *A Natural History of Human Thinking*, Tomasello distinguishes two kinds of shared intentionality. First, there is *joint intentionality*, which is essentially second-personal, involving collaboration and communication between ad hoc individuals in the moment. This presupposes 'personal' common ground between the participants, but need not rest on any conventional modes of communication or socially-established norms. Second, there is *collective intentionality*, which involves a relation between an individual and a transpersonal 'we', mediated by cultural common ground, group norms, and conventionalised modes of communication. Tomasello thinks that both forms of shared intentionality are distinctively human. Joint intentionality is a developmental prerequisite of collective intentionality, both phylogenetically and ontogenetically (children's facility with joint intentionality emerges around their first birthday, but they are not at home with collective intentionality until age 3), and collective intentionality is a precondition of many of the characteristic forms of human mindedness. This picture further undermines the usefulness of the concept of training. It now looks very implausible to think of training, as Wittgensteinians do, as the initiation of a normatively inept creature into forms of collective intentionality. Once we countenance the significance of joint intentionality (the hallmark of which is negotiation rather than training), we see that training is only one among many avenues of the cultivation of collective intentionality. To all this, I would add one cautionary note. It can be misleading to portray joint intentionality as essentially second-personal, for what is at issue is not just I-Thou relations, but primitive *first-person plural* conceptions of ourselves as 'we' (as Rödl's reflections (below) bring out). Lurking here are vexed questions of whether there is a fundamentally irreducible 'we-mode' of intentionality, an issue informatively addressed in M. Gallotti, 'A Naturalistic Argument for the Irreducibility of Collective Intentionality', *Philosophy of the Social Sciences* **42** (2012), 3–30, and M. Gallotti and C. Frith, 'Social Cognition in the We-Mode', *Trends in Cognitive Sciences* **17** (2013), 160–165.

David Bakhurst

A facility for shared intentionality is not merely cognitive. It rests upon a fundamental desire to 'join in'. Sebastian Rödl (with Tomasello in mind) brings this out nicely. He writes that, at around nine-months, the child's activity displays a significant motivational tendency *to be like others*. She not just imitates the behaviour of others, she imitates in order that they should recognise her as like them and that she should recognise this in herself. This she does for no other end. Knowing oneself as one of a kind, and sharing in this knowledge with others, is its own reward. Thus children engage in games the sole point of which is to establish mutual recognition. Rödl gives a lovely example, no doubt from life, where a father suddenly and for no apparent reason puts his forehead on the table in front of him, and then his child follows suit and they both roar with laughter. The game continues in the same vein. This, as he notes, is characteristically human behaviour. It is all about the first person plural – about *us* – and perhaps that's all it's about.

For Rödl, children's desire to establish their identity as one of kind is not mere instinct or the result of conditioning. Nor is it in the space of reasons, as this is usually understood. But it does manifest 'an incipient consciousness of the general', as Rödl puts it, and its deliverances are self-conscious acts, in that the child acts in light of an end, knows when she has achieved it, and in achieving it recognises herself through the recognition of others.

Rödl takes these ideas to undermine, not just the notion of training, but the whole framework of the transformational view. For him, from very early on – certainly before she begins to speak – the human child manifests her rational being. She does not start a 'mere animal', since the she is born with an orientation towards conspecifics that no other animal seems to possess, and she does not *become* a rational being. The *Bildungsprozess* is therefore better conceived as awakening and cultivating 'habits of reason'. This is education's role. But it is the formation of something always-already there, not its creation. Hence education is best seen as facilitating the child's 'growing into itself'. Now we can without paradox acknowledge autonomy as the end of education, but the price is to forsake the transformational view. Rödl writes:

> If children were born animals, the first act of education would have to be abrichten. Indeed, the metaphysical conviction that the child is an animal that becomes a person through education seems to be the only possible source of the notion that abrichten plays an essential role in the development of children. Observation surely does not suggest it... Education begins with the shared

consciousness of doing the same, which arises around nine months of age and in incipient consciousness of the general. From then on, abrichten is no longer possible; the form of the child's conscious-ness excludes it. Before that time, there is a logical possibility of abrichten of a human child. In point of empirical fact, it seems very difficult, if not impossible. In any case, such abrichten has no inner relation to the education that comes later.

This is a powerful passage. I don't think, however, that Rödl's in-sights wholly undermine the transformational view. Admittedly, what we have learnt from Vygotsky and Tomasello suggests it can be misleading speak of a transition from the 'merely animal' to the rational, or in terms of children 'acquiring a mind'. But what Tomasello and Carpenter describe as 'the big Vygotskian idea' can remain up front and centre: 'what makes human cognition different is not more individual brainpower, but rather the ability of humans to learn through other persons and their artifacts, and to collaborate with others in collective activities'.[52] In this sense, culture transforms the mode of life of the human animal. This is true of the species, but also of the individual: the child's entrance into culture, which is one with its learning language, transforms its life into that of an animal who is not just in the world, but who *has* a world, who can 'hold the world in view', as McDowell likes to put it. She becomes an animal responsive to reasons in the full sense: an animal that can, not just engage in 'the game of giving and asking for reasons', but can entertain the infinite and contemplate its own finitude. This is rational life, which finds expression in creatures who seek to make sense of themselves and who can take responsibility for their lives. We do not start out that way – except in the sense that we are thrown into culture from the outset. We become such through educa-tion, in the broadest sense of the word. In my view, this is the spirit of the position that emerges in *Mind and World*. So whatever one thinks of McDowell's formulations at the end of that work, we should con-tinue to insist on the transformative role of culture, an idea that, when seen for what it is, ought to be uncontentious, even if it also possesses a certain metaphysical gravitas.

7. Hacking on Autism, Parfit on Persons and Human Beings

My reader may wonder why I am keen to preserve McDowell's view of the acquisition of second nature, casting Vygotsky and Tomasello

---

[52]   Tomasello and Carpenter, 'Shared Intentionality', 121.

David Bakhurst

as means of developing and defending McDowell, rather than simply setting McDowell aside and concentrating on them. The reasons are two. First, I think elements of McDowell's view of second nature illuminate psychological development. And second, I think McDowell's overall project, of which his view of second nature is part, is profound. To illustrate this, I will consider the relevance of McDowell's position to the two claims I mentioned earlier: Hacking's on autism and Parfit's on persons and human beings.[53]

[53] I recognise, of course, that the idea of an alliance between McDowell, Vygotsky, and Tomasello (let alone Rödl) raises many questions about the compatibility of their respective views. In *The Formation of Reason* I take this up with respect to Vygotsky and McDowell, though there I largely overlook the following issue. McDowell's notion of second nature draws on a distinction between two modes of intelligibility – natural-scientific and space-of-reasons intelligibility – which he sometimes glosses in terms of the distinction between explanation and understanding ('Comment on Hans-Peter Krüger's Paper', 121). But Vygotsky explicitly rejects the dichotomy between psychological theories that aspire to causal explanations and those that maintain that psychological phenomena demand a different order of explanation – hermeneutical understanding (see *History of the Development of the Higher Mental Functions*, 7–8). Where does this leave the supposed union of Vygotsky and McDowell? I do not think Vygotsky would have denied that there is an important difference between explaining particular instances of belief, action, and other intentional phenomena, and explaining natural goings-on in which reason does not figure. Moreover, Vygotsky is clear that psychology cannot explain the higher mental functions by principles of biological or physical science. We need to employ explanatory principles appropriate to the subject matter under study, at each stage of its development, and this involves understanding the mind as a cultural-historical phenomenon. However, Vygotsky aspired to a systematic and comprehensive account of psychological development worthy of the name 'scientific'. It all depends, of course, on what counts as scientific, and he would likely have agreed with those who complain that *Mind and World* operates with too narrow a conception of science (such as G. Macdonald, 'The Two Natures: Another Dogma', in C. Macdonald and G. Macdonald (eds), *McDowell and his Critics* (Oxford: Blackwell, 2006), 224–225). McDowell subsequently broadened his view, but he continues to hold that responsiveness to reasons lies outside the reach of natural-scientific explanation. Vygotsky would have agreed that 'human beings are unique among living things – outside the reach of the sort of understanding achievable by a scientific biology – in virtue of the freedom that belongs with our responsiveness to reasons as such' (McDowell, 'Response to Graham Macdonald, in *McDowell and his Critics*, 237), but recommended that McDowell broaden his conception of science still further (rather as he proposes to do with the concept of nature). I'm inclined to think that Tomasello

Training, Transformation and Education

Hacking on Autism

Autism is a developmental disorder characterised by difficulties with social interaction and communication, narrow interests and repetitive actions. It is considered a spectrum condition, with 'low-functioning' individuals at one end, who have usually experienced significant delay or impairment in language development and have a low IQ, and 'high-functioning' individuals at the other, who have an average or better IQ and who have experienced no substantial language problems, save perhaps difficulty with figurative language. There are many theories of autism on the contemporary scene. One prominent view is that autistic individuals have problems with the concept of mind. They have difficulties 'reading' other people's mental states and hence problems predicting their behaviour, and this accounts for their social ineptitude, problems making friends, seeming lack of empathy, difficulties understanding jokes, and for the loneliness, anxiety and misery that can issue from the resulting social isolation. This is sometimes known as the 'mindblindness' theory of autism, and it is usually understood in terms of the paradigm 'theory of mind'.[54] This paradigm represents our vocabulary for psychological description and explanation (our 'folk psychology')

---

would concur – his work is clearly scientific, but hardly displays the kind of narrow naturalism that is McDowell's target.

Discussion of the compatibility of McDowell's position and Tomasello's, which would need to take proper account of the latter's recent *Natural History of Human Thinking*, must await another occasion, but I must address one obvious issue. McDowell asserts that children acquire the ability to think and act intentionally as they enter the space of reasons, while Tomasello attributes individual intentionality to infants and apes. This looks like an irreconcilable difference, but it need not be. McDowell sets the bar for intentionality very high: it requires the ability to form propositional thoughts presupposing a network of concepts and a repertoire of conceptual capacities, including self-consciousness. For Tomasello, in contrast, individual intentionality presupposes only the ability to solve problems about how to act by representing situations and actions 'off line', operating on such representations, and monitoring the plausibility and desirability of possible outcomes. There is no reason why McDowell cannot credit infants and non-human animals with such abilities.

[54] S. Baron-Cohen, *Mindblindness: An Essay on Autism and Theory of Mind* (Cambridge, MA: MIT, 1995). Baron-Cohen recognises that the mindblindness theory needs significant supplementation by other approaches. For a helpful review see his *Autism and Asperger Syndrome* (Oxford: Oxford University Press, 2008).

as, or as akin to, a theoretical vocabulary. Mental states and phenomena are unobservables; they are 'internal states' we posit to explain and predict behaviour. Autistic individuals, it is argued, lack a theory of mind, or are delayed in developing such a theory and poor at deploying it.

In a series of recent articles, Hacking offers an interesting variant on mindblindness.[55] He cites Wittgenstein's remark that 'The human body is the best picture of the human soul',[56] together with reflections from the psychologist Wolfgang Köhler (1887–1967) on human beings' ability to judge what others are thinking and feeling from their demeanour – i.e. their facial expressions and comportment (their 'body-language', as we might now say). In conversation, I can discern that one of my interlocutors doubts what I have just said and is impatient to speak, another is credulous, another bored, another uncomfortable with the topic. Köhler represents this ability as ubiquitous, as *the common property and practice of mankind*.[57] Psychology's failure to acknowledge the phenomenon is, he claims, a case of being blinded by the obvious.

Hacking contends that although 'Köhler's phenomenon' accurately describes the way in which neurotypical individuals can be aware of others' states of mind, this is not true of the autistic. They precisely lack this ability immediately to discern the mindedness of others. In contrast to theory of mind, Hacking denies that this is a deficit in theoretical knowledge. It is rather an inability to *see* (or perhaps better 'intuit') what others are thinking or feeling. It is not a matter of inference but of direct awareness akin to perception (hence 'mindblindness' is less of a metaphor than may first appear). The autistic can learn to work out what others are thinking and feeling by theorising. They can develop a *theory* of mind, but theoretical knowledge of other minds is knowledge of a different order from immediate awareness. To respond 'naturally' to a loving look, or a grief-stricken expression, one cannot be working out what is going on with the other person. One has to 'see' it.

Hacking describes the development of the autistic child as 'non-Vygotskian'. Because autistic children lack Köhler's phenomenon

---

[55] I. Hacking, 'Kinds of People: Moving Targets', *Proceedings of the British Academy* **151** (2007), 285–318; 'Humans, Aliens, and Autism', *Daedalus* **138** (July 2009), 44–59; 'How We Have Been Learning to Talk About Autism: A Role for Stories', *Metaphilosophy* **40** (2009), 499–516.

[56] Wittgenstein, *Philosophical Investigations,* II.iv, 178.

[57] W. Köhler, *Gestalt Psychology* (New York: Horace Liveright, 1929), 250–251.

they are not 'in society' in the full sense and are unable to 'internalize social relationships to form concepts of the mental'.[58] I think this is insightful, but it gets things backwards. McDowell's concept of second nature can help us see this.

The notion of second nature contains an ambiguity. There is the idea, central to the above discussion, of *a way of being*. Thus McDowell speaks of acquiring *a* second nature. But there is also the rather different idea of forms of activity (habits) that, though acquired, are internalised to the degree that they are exercised as fluently and spontaneously as innate or instinctual responses. This idea of second nature turns up in everyday discourse, when, e.g., a music teacher tells her student to keep practising so that the finger movements become 'second nature'. McDowell is sometimes criticised for conflating these notions,[59] and it is true that he does not distinguish them. But they come together in his thinking in the following way. In acquiring *a* second nature, the individual acquires conceptual capacities that become second nature to her in that they are exercised spontaneously (we deploy concepts without having to work out how) *and* in that the responsiveness to reasons they enable is, in at least some cases, immediate and non-inferential in character. For example, when we possess the relevant concepts we are able to acquire non-inferential knowledge of the world through perception and testimony; of morally and aesthetically relevant properties of situations and of how to act; of what others mean by what they say, and thereby *of their mental lives*. On the latter issue, McDowell writes:

[S]hared membership in a linguistic community is not just a matter of matching in aspects of an exterior that we present to anyone whatever, but equips us to make our minds available to one another, by confronting one another with a different exterior from that which we present to outsiders... [S]hared command of a language equips us to know one another's meaning without needing to arrive at that knowledge by interpretation, because it equips us to hear someone else's meaning in his words... [A] linguistic community is ... bound together, not by a match in mere externals (facts accessible to just anyone), but by a capacity for a meeting of minds.[60]

---

[58] Hacking, 'How We Have Been Learning to Talk About Autism', 504.
[59] See D. Forman, 'Autonomy as Second Nature: On McDowell's Aristotelian Naturalism', *Inquiry* **51** (2008), 571.
[60] J. McDowell, 'Wittgenstein on Following a Rule', in his *Mind, Value, and Reality* (Cambridge, MA: Harvard University Press, 1998), 253.

David Bakhurst

It is a natural complement to this view to hold, not just that we can know what someone is thinking by hearing meaning in her words, but that we can sometimes see what she is thinking or feeling by observing her actions or demeanour.[61] And these two dimensions to perceiving mind are interrelated, for to understand another's words is to see her as the subject of a mental life, which can find expression in ways other than speech. So we can say that it is a feature of psychological concepts that, in the normal case, their acquisition makes it second nature to us to discern the disposition of a person's mindedness in her demeanour, expression and actions, as well as in her words. This is a specific form of responsiveness to reasons, responsiveness to reasons for the ascription of mental states to others.

This McDowellian view equips us to say, with Hacking, that autistic people have trouble with this: they do not find it second nature to perceive the mental lives of others with such immediacy. But I think Köhler's phenomenon is not best seen as a mode of pre-conceptual awareness, the absence of which inhibits the internalisation of psychological concepts. It is an ability enabled by the internalisation of psychological concepts. If the development of the autistic child does not fit Vygotsky's model, this is not explained by impairment in Köhler's phenomenon. On the contrary, that impairment is precisely what needs explaining and its roots may lie in the autistic child's difficulties with shared intentionality, which may go back to autistic infants' problems with joint attention.[62]

All this is speculative. My point is that Hacking is on to something, but McDowell offers a better way to understand the predicament of the autistic person. Better not to describe autistic children's development as 'non-Vygotskian'. Most do internalise psychological concepts, but not in a way that enables lived experience of the minds of

[61] As McDowell maintains in 'Criteria, Defeasibility, and Knowledge' (in his *Meaning, Knowledge, and Reality* (Cambridge, MA: Harvard University Press, 1998)). Here he suggests an important qualification. In a case where, say, we discern someone is angry from their demeanour, we do not need to insist that their emotional state is itself an object of direct perception. We need only say that their anger is *expressed* in their demeanour in such a way that awareness of their demeanour constitutes non-inferential knowledge of their emotional state (see in 'Criteria, Defeasibility, and Knowledge', 387).
[62] See S. Leekam, 'Why Do Children With Autism Have a Joint Attention Impairment?', in N. Eilen, C. Hoerl, T. McCormack, and J. Roessler (eds.), *Joint Attention: Communication and Other Minds: Issues in Philosophy and Psychology* (Oxford: Oxford University Press, 2005), 205–229.

neurotypicals. (Of course, the reverse impairment also exists: resonating with autistic minds is not second nature to neurotypicals.) The McDowellian view suggests that there may be more than one way in which to compensate for this deficiency. The autistic can acquire theoretical knowledge of other minds – sometimes they are explicitly taught how to infer what others are thinking or feeling from their expression. But it might also be possible to cultivate a more immediate responsiveness to psychological reasons, rather in the way that someone who finds musical relations difficult to perceive may, by hard work, develop relevant perceptual competence (here the notion of training does get a grip). Perhaps the aurally-challenged musician may never hear intervals or harmonies as someone with perfect pitch does, and she will always sight-read with difficulty, but her developing capacities will, when exercised successfully, yield her genuine musical knowledge and not merely a theoretical surrogate. Where people have difficulties understanding other minds, we can hope for improvement along similar lines.

Parfit on Persons and Human Beings

An important aspiration of McDowell's philosophy is to foster 'a firm and integrated conception of ourselves as rational animals'.[63] There are many elements to this: understanding the continuity of consciousness, so crucial to our conception of ourselves as enduring persons, as an aspect of the life of a living animal, and not as some kind of self-sufficient domain only contingently attached to a particular body; understanding action as bodily movement imbued with intelligence, so that our doings appear, not merely as causal consequences of mental goings-on, or as bodily signs of the mental, but as mind-in-movement; and, picking up the theme just discussed, understanding thought and emotion as there to be discerned in the deportment of a living human body.

There are many tendencies in philosophy, and in the culture at large, that make such a 'firm and integrated conception' hard to attain. McDowell's remark just quoted appears in the conclusion of an article on Parfit, who has recently published a paper no more friendly to McDowell's aspirations than the work with which

---

[63] J. McDowell, 'Reductionism and the First Person', in his *Mind, Value, and Reality*, 382; see also his 'Criteria, Defeasibility, and Knowledge', 470.

David Bakhurst

McDowell originally took issue.[64] In this paper, Parfit denies that persons are animals: we are not human beings. A person is rather a part of an animal, the thinking part. Parfit argues his case principally by thought experiments of the kind for which he is famous. Suppose Parfit's head were transplanted onto Williams's body (presumably Parfit has Bernard in mind, rather than Meredith), the resulting person would be Parfit, but not the same animal as Parfit was once a part of. The same is true if we transplant, not the whole head, but just enough of Parfit's cerebrum to secure continuity of consciousness. So long as that is functioning, the resulting person will be Parfit, whether the brain-matter is housed in a human body or maintained by an artificial support system. But if this is true, then Parfit cannot be an animal; at best he's an 'embodied part' of one.

The argument is alluring, but (if you will forgive the pun) wrongheaded. I am uncertain that we know what we are imagining when we discuss such cases, and whether, so far as we do, our intuitions about them are sound. That we can enjoy the movie *Freaky Friday* does not show that its plot is metaphysically possible. Confronting Parfit's gruesome scenario, we might conclude that the resulting creature is a kind of chimera, a Parfit/Williams hybrid. But even if we grant the surviving person is Parfit, I am inclined to say that what his essay describes are events in the life of an animal, Parfit, who undergoes a dramatic 'body transplant' or is sustained by life-support system. This is a way for a human being to survive, admittedly a strange and no doubt vastly impoverished way, but it is still a kind of animal life. And if we want to say that only part of the animal survives, then why not say that only part of the person survives? This is surely no more counter-intuitive than the move to which Parfit must resort, namely, to portray the first-person pronoun as ambiguous, referring to the Inner-I (the true person) and the Outer-I (the body of which the person is strictly speaking only part). I, in contrast, believe that when we speak of educating 'the whole person', we mean it.

In my view, persons are animals of a kind that possess certain characteristic rational powers. Human beings are such animals. That conviction is firmer, I think, than any intuition prompted by Parfit's imaginary cases. I do not believe, however, that this matter will ever be settled by philosophical arguments that address them head-on. To overcome Parfit's view, we have to learn to stop thinking along lines that make the position attractive. In *The Formation of Reason*, I suggest that reflecting on the acquisition of second nature

---

[64]   D. Parfit, 'We Are Not Human Beings', *Philosophy* **87** (2012), 5–28.

can help us develop a sense of the unity of our rationality and our animality, so that we do not cut loose the thinking side of our nature from the animal being that is its cause and unity. The developing mindedness of young children is not a history that we can separate from the character of their bodily being. It cannot be cast principally as a series of events in inner space. And the interrelations with adults that are essential to its development are not plausibly seen as a relation between two 'inner selves', but as an engagement in which mindedness is on the surface, present in the character of their joint activity. Where are we to find the emerging mindedness of our children if not in the manner of their bodily engagement with the world? This, I believe, is an antidote to a certain kind of philosophical confusion about the kind of beings that we are. It is not a powerful antidote, one guaranteed to be efficacious. But I recommend it notwithstanding. The transformational view may celebrate our rationality, but it does not forget that we remain what we always were – animals – even though our rational powers make it possible for us to lose sight of this in spectacular fashion. This is a lesson of McDowell's philosophy really worth heeding, and it motivates my enduring interest in the landscape his ideas place before us.[65]

Queen's University
bakhurst@queensu.ca

[65]   An earlier version of this paper was presented at the 36th Annual Wittgenstein Conference on *Mind, Language, Action*, held in Kirchberg, Austria, in August 2013, and appears in the conference proceedings. I am grateful to the Oesterreichische Ludwig Wittgenstein Gesellschaft for the invitation to speak at that meeting and for permission to reproduce parts of my presentation in this longer essay, and to the audience for helpful comments and criticisms, which led me to revise my views into the form they take here.

Index of Names

Index of Names

For EU product safety concerns, contact us at Calle de José Abascal, 56–1°,
28003 Madrid, Spain or eugpsr@cambridge.org.

www.ingramcontent.com/pod-product-compliance
Ingram Content Group UK Ltd.
Pitfield, Milton Keynes, MK11 3LW, UK
UKHW020806190625
459647UK00032B/2241

* 9 7 8 1 1 0 7 5 4 5 6 6 3 *